LIFE

AND

WISDOM

THE LIVING OF LIFE
AND THE WISDOM
GENERATED THEREBY

GERALD PAUL KOOYERS

First Edition September 2016

ISBN-13 978-0615907482

Published by: MORIA CORPORATION
                RIGGINS, IDAHO
                UNITED STATES OF AMERICA

DEDICATION

This book is dedicated to my wife, Geneva Helene Westra Kooyers without whose complete faithful lifelong devotion, I surely would have been lost in the abyss. Without her I would have accomplished almost nothing. Her high moral character, her love of her children, grandchildren, great grandchildren and others, and of God through the Lord Jesus, are most exquisite characteristics of her beauty and most beautiful character.

The Holy Scriptures say lands and houses come from parents, but a good wife is the gift of God. I praise God for the astounding wonderful wife God Himself through his Son, the Lord Jesus Christ, gave to me.

Thank you, Geneva, for a life of patience and acceptance of my sundry wanderings and expeditions. Thank you for all your input and contributions for a wonderful life together.

Gerald Paul Kooyers

November 2015

Table of Contents

NOTE TO THE READER

This work is intended to give an account of the life of Gerald Paul (Jerry) Kooyers. The intent is to pass on wisdom accumulated by living the life. Some parts of this book may be offensive to some posterity. The intent is not to offend but to pass on truthfully the events of life and the motivations of life so that you can understand why things were done in the manner in which they were done. I hope this contributes to your understanding of your God given life and why you are here on Earth.

I present the theological parts as truthful and accurate, and have made the observations on experience and conclusions thereupon reached as close to the meaning of the never changing Holy Scriptures as I know how. You may so depend on it, and use it as a basis of understanding.

Acknowledgements:

Thanks go to my niece, Pamela Manthei, for the use of her photograph for the book cover. Geneva and I are holding the Mulder family Dutch Bible printed sometime in the 1600s. My great grandfather, Klaas Mulder, brought it over from the Netherlands by sailing ship about 1850.

FOREWARD

This is a book about a little of my life, that of me, Gerald Paul Kooyers. The goal is to pass on to you readers and hopefully some of my prodigy, accumulated wisdom gained from the experience of life. A very fine lady of an exquisite gentle and quiet spirit, my wife, Geneva Helene Westra, shared this life with me

I often wished that one of my ancestors had left me a book on accumulated wisdom. My maternal grandfather had what seemed to me an interesting life. I heard in family discussions just a tiny bit of gossip or watched the shaking of heads about some of the things he did. He was accused by my mother of fighting with every preacher in every church which he attended. Information indicated he once was a traveling salesman selling stock in a national Christian Daily newspaper for the United States which then failed. That made him lots of disappointed ex-friends all over the country of the United States.

None of his experiences were passed on to me. He once stayed at our home on 12th Street in San Jose, California for a month or so when I was about 19 years old, and I engaged him in conversation and learned a little. Unfortunately his Dutch brogue was so bad I had lots of trouble understanding him. He was not patient with my repeated questions. So I learned very little of what must have been a very, very interesting life.

I think he managed to deeply offend my mother so she did not give a good report of him. He was a bit impetuous and sometimes made quick decisions which disrupted the life of his family which included my mother as the oldest surviving sibling. So she passed on to me very little of any of my grandfather's accomplishments. He must have been a man of skill and intelligence, and a risk taker. The yen to take risks he passed on to me. He brought his family to the United States from the Netherlands in 1912 and in the process lost his youngest child. He worked at sundry things, bought a

11

farm and then about 10 years later lost it to the Depression in the 1930's. Then in the depth of the Depression, worked again at his specialty, that of the care and growing of plants, and then his employer gave him the opportunity with his sons to move to California from Grand Rapids, Michigan, to run a fruit ranch in the Santa Clara Valley (Now the heart of what is called Silicon Valley). As my own father said many, many times, "California is the land of opportunity." The move to California became a great benefit to his family, and of course, in the long run, to me and my family as well.

My grandfather's younger brother wrote more than 40 books in the Dutch language, two of which have been translated into English. He used the pen name of Rudolf VanReest. Many Dutch people from the Netherlands whom I have encountered know the name.

That younger brother was also a very influential part of a Dutch church movement during the 1940s in the Netherlands during German occupation leading a large group of Dutchmen out of the Greeformed Kirk (The Re-reformed Church) in the Netherlands to form a church group called in English, "The Liberated Church", in Dutch the Frihamacktins. Perhaps about half of the old church denomination left to join the new group. The dividing issue was whether the Synod of the Greeforme d Kirk could bind a man's conscience by its edicts. To me that is a very, very, important, interesting question, yet my grandfather never even attempted to tell me about it or explain it to me. Sad indeed.

So I am attempting to not make that same mistake by not telling you the things I did and learned. Yet I expect few of my prodigy will ever be interested in this account. I write it for the few of you that might be interested, and those of you looking for wisdom. I write it to you who would want to be wise and want to learn from the experiences of others, and of me their ancestor.

I have tried to correct the spelling and erroneous use of certain words, bad English, bad punctuation, etc. but a good editing job of this thing would cost me money which I do not have or want to spend. So please forgive and ignore the bad spelling, bad grammar, and all the errors. Remember, I am a product of the California Public School System. It stinks.

Therefore, this thing is not a piece of literature. I do not expect very many people to read it.

I want to give a truthful account. Therefore, some of what I write may be offensive to some of you. It might give what some might construe to be bad reports of some of you children's ancestors. I am sorry if I offend some of you. Truth sometimes is quite ugly, but I am trying to give to you wisdom.

However, my own terrible sins are not written about. A few not so bad ones are recounted herein to pass on the wisdom derived from the experience, but to give an account of my real terrible sins is impossible for my soul to do, except in private prayer of confession to my Lord Jesus. I think you will understand that. Nevertheless, understand that I have been washed clean of all my ugly sins, and maybe not so ugly sins, errors and omissions by the precious cleansing blood of my Lord Jesus Christ. Praise you Jesus! Understand I love the Lord Jesus deeply, and am committed to serving Him no matter what.

Jesus provided me with a most marvelous wife. The scriptures say lands and houses come from parents, but a good wife is from the Lord. Very, very true. Geneva has been a most marvelous wife, and my life most likely would have been a complete mess without her continuing stabilizing presence all the years of our marriage. She like her own mother has a marvelous capacity to love, especially to love her children, grandchildren, and great grandchildren, and yes, even me, her husband. And, of course, she loves the Lord Jesus. She also had the good fortune to have been brought up in a Christian home, educated in Christian schools, and learned the great very powerful biblical truths of the Reformed Faith from her parents, church, and school.

You do not need to read this whole thing. You can read any chapter in this thing by itself. Chapter one gives some of my ancestry. Two is about growing up. Three describes life during my college days. Four, some of the more interesting things we did as a family. That chapter seems quite inadequate as we did lots of very interesting fun things as a family, and I have not written about most of them. Five recounts the fun side of my life with a description of some of the more interesting, hunts, backpacks, and horse-packs. Six is about working for Litton Industries and doing research on Crossed Field Amplifiers. Seven is an account of being self-employed. Eight reviews my career and business as a commodity trader. Nine is probably the most interesting chapter in that the life changing events which occurred peaked in the summer of 1981 with the beginning of the end of the commodity business, the mine accident, my daughter Cindy and her eventual husband Guy doing a spectacular attempt at eloping, and the start of the construction of the Bighouse.

Chapter ten is all about the Bighouse and the criminal nature of American Savings and Loan Association, at that time the largest Savings and Loan Bank in the United States, and how its loan fraud scheme financially ruined me, the result of which, of course, changed my life

Chapter eleven develops my Eigen Theory of life. During my lifetime I did basic research on microwave tubes, made some original discoveries, and obtained a USA, Canadian, and Japanese Patent, and built with government money some marvelous microwave tubes, some of which were used by the United States Military in winning the Cold War against the Soviet Union.

I created a rather involved software monstrosity which was used to study aggregated military force structures for the United States Navy and the joint command of CINCPAC. (Commander in Chief Pacific) That software was developed on Stanford University computers, was funded by the Office of Naval Research through Stanford Research Institute, and then was installed on Military computers in Hawaii, Washington, and Taiwan.

I was the first to prove the feasibility of ion propulsion for space craft. I did a study and wrote a computer modeling program that proved that space propulsion with ion thrusters was feasible. My consultant at Litton, Oscar Buniman, a very, very interesting person, who was instrumental in helping to win the Battle of Briton against the Germans with the invention of the Magnetron in WWII, and a professor at Stanford University, suggested it, and thus his name is first on the published paper.

I created a commodity trading system that made me and some of my clients a lot of money.

All these accomplishments resulted in things to be seen in the real world, that of observation, testing and proof. Eigen Theory presented in this thing is stuff out into the intellectual ether realm where the results of theory cannot be tested in the real world before they are put into practice.

Yet my belief is that the Eigen Theory is my most significant contribution to humankind from all of my life, in that it resulted from revelation from God, through the Holy Scriptures, which came about as a result of asking God, my Lord Jesus Christ, a man like me, yet very God of very God, for the revelation, and thus the understanding. Therefore, of course, I hope you read that chapter very carefully, and try to deeply understand it.

I apologize for not conceiving of the Eigen Theory when I was young and in my prime. Then my powers of reasoning and memory were ten times better than now as I approach 80 years of age. Therefore, I have not provided solid logical proof of many of my assertions and conclusions as I normally would have been able to do in the past, since I do not have the productivity and mental strength as I had a few years ago. Nevertheless, the assertions and conclusions are verily true. You will be blessed if you work hard to understand them.

Chapter twelve is about living life, and the most important spiritual things I learned from a lifetime of learning things about God and about life.

Chapter thirteen recounts my interaction with a mysterious kind of very devastating evil, and attempts to pass on to you who read this thing some deep wisdom about enemies, friends, and evil.

Chapter fourteen sums up some reflections on and about life

There should be another chapter in this thing about lawsuits. Perhaps that might happen in another edition. I collected lawsuits like a dog collects fleas. It seems that if you have some visibility like one has when one is in business and are presumed to have some money, the vultures will descend on you like vampires to get some blood out of you. The legal system in the United States of America is a complete mess, and there is no real justice. It is nothing but a crock of male bovine scat that provides a very stinking fat living for attorneys, judges, and clerks; the party with the most money always wins. The only exception to this rule in my lifetime was when the judge was looking for a bribe out of me.

15

You can probably read any of these chapters on a standalone basis. No chapter is dependent on another and none is a prerequisite to any other.

Good reading. May the Lord Jesus bless you, yes, exceedingly.

This is me, Gerald Paul Kooyers, in 1952 at sixteen years of age.

ONE

ANCESTRY

This is an account of the ancestry of Gerald Paul Kooyers.

KOOYERS

My father, Jacob Mulder Kooyers, was born on August 30, 1896 in Fremont, Michigan. He died about February 21, 1983 in San Jose, California and is buried in the San Jose Cemetery, second row near top of the hill.

My father started working as an office boy at the Hastings Piston Ring Company at about 14 year of age. Hastings became part of General Motors. My father became a bookkeeper and accountant. At about 21 years of age the Lord called him to the ministry through the Elders of the Christian Reformed Church where he was teaching, I believe, Sunday School. The Elders promised him some support for his training. Thus at 21 years of age he went to prep school for four years, then four years at Calvin College in Grand Rapids, Michigan, and then three years of Calvin Seminary, graduating in 1928. He then became available for a preaching ministry and received one call only, and that was to the Indian Field in New Mexico. In 1929 he went to Westminster Theological Seminary in Philadelphia, Pennsylvania for a year and received a Masters Degree in Theology. He then became a Minister in the Presbyterian Church USA and served small congregations in Wisconsin where I was born.

We moved to California in the summer of 1946. My father then became the Pastor of the Mendocino Presbyterian Church in Mendocino, California in June of 1947. We moved to San Jose, California in June/August 1952 where he became the Principal of the San Jose Christian School. That soon failed and he became a cemetery lot salesman for the San Jose Cemetery Association. He was also a trade carpenter as well as was his father, and he worked at carpentry sundry times on vacations and such or when he was not employed as a clergyman.

My mother, Alice Margaret VanSpronsen, (aka Aaltje Margaretha Van Spronsen) was born in Rotterdam, South Holland, The Netherlands, on February 2, 1902. She died about August 15, 1987 in Ripon, CA and is buried alongside my father in the San Jose Cemetery.

My parents were married on July 11, 1922 in Grand Rapids, Michigan.

The story of my parents meeting each other is that a friend of my father had committed himself to seeing my mother home from some Christian meeting or lecture. It seems he had a conflict and convinced my father to walk my mother home from the meeting. That was the beginning of their courtship. They planned to marry sometime in the fall of 1922 but my grandfather came home one day and announced in his impetuous way that he had bought a farm and they were moving immediately. My parents decided that they would be married immediately and so the ceremony was performed before their parents and a few friends in the home of my mother's parents on July 11, 1922.

My family consisted of the five children following:
Howard John Kooyers September 21, 1923   Grand Rapids, MI
      Died June 1995 in Alaska while Halibut fishing, cremated.
Orneal Spronsen Kooyers   December 4, 1926   Allendale, MI
Gordon Jack Kooyers   April 3, 1930   Philadelphia, PN
      Died August 30, 2013, Oroville, California
Gerald Paul Kooyers   September 27, 1935   Athens, WI
Marcia Jane Kooyers Davis   December 14, 1936 Oxford, WI

My father's parents are

John A. Kooyers aka Jon Albert Kooijers b January14, 1852 Holland, Michigan
Jane Mulder aka Jantje Mulder b July 30, 1854 Ottawa Co, Michigan

18

They grew up together attending the Pillar Reformed Church in Holland, Michigan. They were married in about 1874 in Holland, MI. Eleven children were born to them of which 10 were raised to adulthood. These children were:

Henry Kooyers	m Mary Dunning
Klaas Willem (Bill) Kooyers	m Katie Tanis
Garrett (Gary) Kooyers	m Leatha Miller
Sarah (Gesina)	m Thomas D. Schutter
Lyda	died young
Lyda	m Theo. (Ted) Price
Benjamin Kooyers	
Minnie (Wilhemena)	m George Amiotte
Fred (Frederick) Kooyers	m Blanche Bouchard
Jacob Mulder (Jack)	m Alice Van Spronsen (my parents)
Anna (Johanna)	m George Scholtens

My grandfather John A. Kooyers parents are:

Hendrik Jon Kooijers   Born 1826   Winterswijk, Gelderlant, Netherlands
            Died February 16, 1852 Ottawa Co. MI

Harriet Damkot, aka Gerritje Damkot   b Oct 15, 1824   Winterswijk, Gelderland, Netherlands Died 1900, buried in the Southern Cemetery in Holland, Michigan.

These people participated in the Afgescheiden Movement (In English it is usually translated Secession Movement) from the State Established Church in the Netherlands. Harriet Damkot Kooyers, after the death of my great grandfather, Hendrik Jon Kooijers, married Hendrik Jan Esselinkpas aka Hank Pas, on October 30, 1853 in Holland MI. Pas was also from Winterswijk, Gelderland, Netherlands. They lived together to old age on a farm near Holland Michigan. He and Harriet are both buried in the southside cemetery, Holland Michigan. Pas died in1901. He was born in Winterswjik on December 22, 1813 the son of Solomon Esselinkpas and

19

Janna Geertruid Lammers. He worked as a wheel maker and farmer. He also joined the Afgescheiden movement in The Netherlands. When his brother Jan Berend decided to immigrate to the United States, Hendrik decided to join them. They left the Netherlands in 1847. All of this family perished in the Phoenix Disaster (Ship sinking in Lake Michigan) with Hendrik alone surviving.

Harriet aka Gerritje Damkot father's name was Jan Hendrik Damkot, born April 10, 1766 and died December 19, 1834. Her mother was Jan's second wife, Johanna Geertruid Rotmans, born May 30, 1779 and died January 17, 1835. Harriet was about 10 years old when her father and mother died. She emigrated to the United Sates when she was 22 years old in 1846 from Veenermans, Ratum55, Winterswijk, Gelderland, Netherlands. There is extensive Damkot genealogical information available on the internet as of 2010.

Children from these marriages are:

From Hendrik Jon Kooyers:

Gesiena Kooijers aka Sena Nies, married Nies Nies on Jan 16, 1867
John A. Kooyers aka Jon Albert Kooyers (my grandfather)

From Hank Pas

Janna Gertu
Johanna
Samuel
Jacob

Gesiena had five children with Nies Nies. Nies was from Groningan, Netherlands. After Gesiena died he married Beija Looyengoed and had nine more children. They lived in Holland, Michigan.

My grandmother, Jane Mulder aka Jantje Mulder parents' are:

Klaas Willems Mulder, Born 1818 or June 11, 1816 Rottum, Groningen, Netherlands

Charlotta Goslinga, aka Tjaltje Goslinga Boersma Mulder, was born June 10, 1823 in Wonseradeel, Friesland, Netherlands. Her mother's name was Trijntje Elles Goslinga. Name of the father on the birth form is blank. Trijntje died on April 2, 1841 at 53 years of age making her 35 years old when she gave birth to Tjaltje Goslinga. Trijntje is listed as a widow at her death in the archive in Tresoar, Wonseradeel, Friesland, Netherlands.

Klaas Mulders first wife was Jantje Korlelis Kuiper, they were married on October 3, 1842. Jantje was 23 years old, the daughter of Kornelis Jans Kuiper and Martje Freerks of Usquert (North of Kantens), Groningen, Netherlands. Records indicate Klaas Mulder immigrated to the USA in 1850. He did not have wife or children with him according to the ship manifest. The marriage record says Klaas was 24 years old at the time of this marriage, which would have indicated he was born in 1816. Emigration records show Klaas Willems Mulder, age 34, emigrated in 1850 from the province of Groningen, municipality of Middelstum; no women or children came with him. That would put his birth date in 1816. My cousins Bob Scholtens and Sandy Scholtens McDaniels, children of my aunt Anne Scholtens, conclude from their research that he was born February 27, 1817 in Kantens, Groningen, Netherlands.

My Great Grandfather, Klaas Willems Mulder, married Tjaltje Goslenga, aka Tryntje, aka Charlotta, widow of J. Boeresma on October 30, 1853 near what became Holland, Michigan. The marriage service was performed by Rev. Van Raaltje the leader of the Dutch immigration group (People involved in the Secession Movement) to Holland, Michigan. Children of this marriage are:

Jantje (aka Jane) born July 30, 1854 (my grandmother)
Klaas born February 10, 1857
Willemina born October 18, 1859
Petrus (aka Peter) born April 18, 1862

Peter (Petrus) died June 2, 1934 and is buried in the State Park Cemetery, Columbia, California.

According to the records of the Pillar Reformed Church in Holland Michigan, Charlotta (Tjaltje) Gorslinga (Gosselinga), from Bolswerd, Friesland, Netherlands was first married to Jetse J. (Siemon?) Broersma. I believe his first name might have been Siemon as his birthdate and death date match with the rest of the data. According to the records in the Netherlands, Tjaltje Goslinga and Jetze Jans Broersma were married October 2, 1844 in Tresoar, Wonseradeel, Friesland, Netherlands. Emigration records indicate Jetse Broersma, 49 immigrated to USA in 1846, and in his party were a wife and two children. According to the Pillar Church records, children from this first marriage are:

> Antje Broersma born December 9, 1846
> Tryntje Broersma born August 3, 1849
> Jan (John) Broersma born August 8, 1851

According to the records of the new Vriesland, Michigan cemetery, John Broersma died by drowning after living 36Y-10M-22D on 6/17/1888, (that would put his birth date in 1851), and was married to a lady with the first name of Maartje.

There apparently were no children of Klaas Mulder's first marriage to Jantje Korlelis Kuiper.

Klaas Willems Mulder's father name was Klaas Klassen Mulder.

The Pilgrim and Home Graafschaap Cemeteries index lists the death of Mrs. Klaas Mulder on June 15, 1863. This in all likelihood is Tjaltje Goslenga, aka Tryntje, aka Charlotta, widow of J. Boeresma, since Klaas Mulder, (my great grandfather) when he died in 1882 was buried next to her. This means that Charlotta's youngest, Peter, was about a year old when his mother died, and perhaps that explains why he wandered off to California to lead a mining and hell raising life, this is according to my brother, Howard, who had lived in Senora, California during the later years of his life. Peter is buried in the cemetery of the Columbia State Park in Columbia near Senora. The 1880 census does not list Peter so he was already out of the house when he was 18. Verbal family memories imply he left home when he was about 14 years old and was never heard from again, until my brother Howard heard stories about him when he was living near Columbia in the 1970s.

The Pillar Reformed Church records indicate that the Mulder family including Jane, my grandmother, and the Pas family with John Kooyers, my grandfather, were in that same Pillar Church, meeting in a rude log building in Holland Michigan. Thus my grandparents, John Kooyers and Jane Mulder, grew up together in that Church, and then married in about 1874, and raised a large family of eleven children, ten surviving to adulthood, my father the next to the youngest, born in 1896.

The 1870 census lists the father Klaas Mulder and four children with no mother. Charlotta had died 1863. The 1880 census lists Klaas Mulder, gardener, and a wife, Janna, keeping house. Thus Klaas Mulder must have married again, his third wife, in his old age. The Ottawa County, Michigan records indicate that Klaas Mulder died of dropsy on May 18, 1882. (Cemetery records indicate maybe May 20, 1881)

My father's recollection to me (many times repeated) was that, Charlotta, his grandmother was very well thought of and remembered as a very fine lady. This information he must have received from his mother who thought very highly of her mother and passed on fond memories. Of course, her mother had died when she was just nine years old. My fathers' grandfather, in all likelihood also passed on very fine memories of his wife and the mother of his children. My father had little recollection of verbal family stories since his grandfather, Klaas, died before my father was born. Charlotta's death must have been traumatic, dying fairly young, but maybe accepted as part of trying to live in the Michigan wilderness. Being the oldest then in the family, my grandmother Jane must have raised her little sister and brothers with help from her half-sisters, the Broersmas. The youngest, Peter, being only a year old, as her father did not remarry until a decade or so later. Life must have been tough in the Michigan pioneer wilderness.

According to the Pillar church records, Harriet Damkot Kooijers, aka Gerritje Damkot, my great grandmother, after the death of my great grandfather, Hendrik Jon Kooijers, married Hendrik Jan Esselinkpas aka Hank Pas, on October 30, 1853 in Holland Michigan. Klaas Mulder married Tjaltje Goslenga, aka Tryntje, aka Charlotta, widow of J. Boeresma, on October 30, 1853. The marriage service was performed by Rev. Van Raaltje, the leader of the Dutch immigration group to Holland, Michigan. Thus the marriages of my great grandmother, Harriet to her second husband, and my great grandparents, the Mulders, second marriages for both, were performed by Rev Van Raaltje on the same day. He must have been a very busy colony leader.

Let us try to understand a little of this Kooyers family heritage, that of Jacob and Alice Kooyers, myself being the fourth born, a fourth boy.

My father was a clergyman and took Christian faith very seriously. Around the dinner table in my families' discussions, it was established that we were Reformed. We were not Liberals. We were not Fundamentalists. We are Reformed!

My father was a pastor in a somewhat liberal denomination, these days called The Presbyterian Church in the USA. Liberals where disdained as essentially unbelievers. They did not accept Jesus Christ as risen Lord and Savior. My father tells the story of being at Presbytery, the meeting of the elders and pastors of a group of Presbyterian Churches. In that denomination pastors were not church members of a particular church but were members of Presbytery. He was then a member of the Presbytery, as I recall, the San Jose Presbytery in California.

The matter came up before the body to transfer the membership of the Pastor of The First Presbyterian Church in Palo Alto, California to another Presbytery. My father moved that the Pastor not be transferred in good standing because he had heard with his own ears that pastor preach that Christ was mistaken when He said He would rise from the dead. Normally any motion like this made by my father would die from a lack of a second to the motion. But lo and behold on this day, on this motion to his surprise, he heard a second of his motion from the back of the assembly. Now the matter had to be dealt with by the whole of the assembled delegates.

I do not remember who he told me made the second, but as I recall it was an elder who also knew the one that wanted to be transferred. Well, now comes a parade of pastors rising to defend the subject transferee essentially saying, "We all know him and he is a fine fellow". This is what my father called a mutual admiration society. Well, of course, the transferee was transferred in good standing by the majority liberals, but there was a vote and my father was surprised by the number of no votes. He did not know that there were that many pastors and elders that believed as he did.

Where did my father get this courage to go against the established order and defend the true faith of the Lord Jesus Christ? My father called it Reformed.

My father said many times he was the youngest boy in a family of five boys and four girls that lived to older adulthood, and for some reason I do not understand, my father's brother Henry was never mentioned. He apparently died young but was married and left a widow. The father of this family, my grandfather, was born in Michigan of immigrant parents. These immigrants suffered persecution because of their reformed faith in the Old Country, that of the Netherlands. You must not forget that! They suffered in the Michigan wilderness so that you can live in a free country and worship God free from persecution. The King, Queen, or Parliament, and in this our own country, the Congress, or the President, cannot tell you what you must believe. And you do not have to face persecution if you not believe what they tell you to believe. This is a tremendous heritage, one that you must not throw away or discard. Do not forget it.

My great grandfather, Hendrik Jon Kooijers, paid the price of his life for his emigration, an emigration so that he could worship God in freedom in the Reformed Faith. He died young at 26 years of age due to the hardships of immigrant life in the wilderness of Michigan. He died when my grandfather was but a month old. So he never lived to enjoy life with his wife and children. My great grandmother was then left alone with two small children.

The Lord Jesus provided a stepfather for my grandfather, a man of great quick thinking courage and common sense which enabled him to survive the Phoenix disaster, where maybe 300 to 400 Dutch emigrants died in Lake Michigan, when their ship, the Phoenix, one of the first propeller driven ships, the propeller shaft housing catching fire, the ship sank and the ship had not sufficient lifeboats.

Again the sturdy Reformed Faith gave these people courage, strength, wisdom, and faith to conquer the wilderness and then build farms and lives in this United States of America. Do not forget this heritage! The Reformed Faith has great value. Study it and understand it. It is really just very basic Christianity, true and accurate to the Bible. These people gave their lives for it. You, dear children, are descendants of this heritage!

Of course, a generation later your other ancestors, that of my mother and Geneva's, parents came over from the Netherlands, the Van Spronsens, the Westras, the Bumas, and the Posts. All of these came from similar racial stock and had the same Reformed roots. When they came to America they identified with the Christian Reformed Church, the denomination created by those early hardy Michigan pioneers in Michigan in 1857.

Now it has been said that in the long run all churches go liberal. So also is the drift of the Christian Reformed Church. One of my favorite authors, Whittaker Chambers, wrote, "In the west all intellectuals eventually become Communists." It seems it is the consequence of the dialectic for the solution of the problems of war and economic crises. Once one rejects God, then if there is to be a solution to the problems of war and economic crises, and the intellectual intends to do something about it, he eventually becomes a communist -- a communist is then defined as one who accepts terrorism and evil as instruments for social change.

Communism as a clearly identified ideological group is now dead, and in our time almost forgotten. But the ideas have survived. The dialectic is still there. Terror and evil and the silencing of the opposition to the progress of the dialectic of materialism are still very much alive in the political system of the United States. You dear children and grandchildren and great grandchildren must gird up your loins for the battle. The battle is for the Kingdom of the Lord Jesus Christ. Only belief in God and His son Jesus Christ as Lord and Savior will defeat the dialectic consequence of what is now days called liberalism or progressivism as some call it. Modern liberalism and progressivism is that which has metamorphosed out of the corpse of communism.

Liberalism is destructive of real alive Christian faith. You must do all you can to defeat it. In our time the Liberals have changed the name of the thing to Progressive. No matter what they call it, it is still the same godless evil ideology. Eventually, this ideology promotes evil, unlawfulness, and terrorism as instruments for social change.

VANSPRONSENS

I obtained a lot of the following information about my mother's ancestors from a document in my possession which was written by my great uncle, Karl C. VanSpronsen, the youngest brother of my grandfather, who wrote more than 40 books in the Dutch language under the pen name of Rudolf VanReest. He gave the document to my uncle Arthur VanSpronsen, my mother's youngest brother, in April of 1970 when my uncle and his wife Betty visited the Netherlands. The document was titled, "The Genealogy of the VAN SPRONSENS, July 14, 1544 to April 25, 1970."

My mother's parents were Cornelis Van Spronsen, (my grandfather), born April 26,1877, died in 1957 in Michigan and is buried in Ripon, California, and Alida Van Vliet, born 1878, died in 1948 in Ripon. They both are buried in the Ripon, Cemetery. They emigrated from Rotterdam, South Holland, The Netherlands, to the United States in 1912.

Children from this marriage were:

Johanna Wilhelmina, born 1900, died 1909. (My mother told me she died a few months after receiving a head injury when a heavy bowl she was trying to get fell on her head out of a cupboard)

Aaltje Margaretha, born February 4, 1902 (my mother)
Anna Gerarda, born November 12, 1906
Gerard Jan, born November 1908, died February 12, 1955 (auto accident)
Johanna Wilhelmina, born April 26, 1910
Jan, born November 20, 1913
Arthur, born August 23, 1915

My grandfather's parents were Gerard Jan Van Spronsen, born May 17, 1853 at Loosduinen, and Johanna Wilhelmina Westdijk, born February 27, 1854 at Mieuwveen, her parents were Cornelis Westdijk and Johanna Heijningen.

Gerard VanSpronsen moved with his family from Loosduinen to Ter Aar in 1857.

The children from this marriage were:

Cornelis, born July 30, 1875, died September 1, 1875
Cornelis, born April 26, 1877, died in Grand Rapids, Michigan, 1957 (my grandfather)
Jannetje Catharina, born May 11, 1878, died January 6, 1959
Arie, born January 2, 1880, died December 30, 1954
Johanna, born February 1, 1881, died February 10, 1881
Jozeph Marinus, born March 26, 1882, died 1918
Catharina Hendrika, born August 25, 1884, died January 10, 1885
Antonie Willem, born December 6, 1885, died December 27, 1885
Johanna Petronella, born April 24, 1887, died October 30,1964
Catharina Hendrika, born January 30, 1889, died May 31, 1962
Margaretha, born July 24, 1890, died February26, 1967
Pieter, born January3, 1893, died June 26, 1893
Pieter, born June 2, 1894, died October 8, 1894
Catherine Cornelia, born June 24, 1895 at Rotterdam, died September 15, 1895
Karl Cornelis, born April 12, 1897 at Rotterdam
Gerarda Johanna, born January 1, 1900 at Rotterdam, died January 15, 1915.

28

My grandfather's grandparents were Cornelis VanSpronsen, born September 16, 1801, at Loosduinen, and Jannetje Van Der Geer, born on May 13, 1813 at Rijnsaterwoude, married at Loosduinen in 1834. He was a gardener, or as my mother called them Truck Farmers, that is one who grew fruits and vegetables and hauled them to town to sell.

Children from this marriage were:

> Joseph Marinus, born March 7, 1842, died February 10, 1925.
> Pieter, born February 20, 1845
> Christina, born July 13, 1847
> Catharina, born September 11, 1849
> Gerard Jan, born May 17, 1853, died March 5, 1933 (my great grandfather)

My grandfather's great grandfather's parents were Joost VanSpronsen, born February 28, 1763 and Catharina Nuysin. They were married May 31, 1800.

Children from this marriage were:

> Cornelis, born September 16, 1801 (my great, great, grandfather)
> Gerard, born November 14, 1803

My great great grandfather's parents were Cornelis Van Spronsen, baptized October 13, 1727 and Jozina VanSanten. They were married on December 31, 1751 at Monster.

Children from this marriage were:

Everdina, born October 22, 1752
Neeltje, born July 28, 1754
Jacoba, born December 16, 1759
Adriana, born December 19, 1761
Joost, born December 28, 1763 (my great, great, great, grandfather)
Arie, born October 19, 1766
Johanna, born December 11, 1768

My great, great, great grandfathers parents were Ary Lourenszoon VanSpronsen and Evertje Van Der Veer, married on May 19, 1726 in the Kerk (Cathedral?). Evertje was Arie's second wife. It was also a second marriage for Evertje. Her first husband was Alewijn Van Dorp, November 29, 1716, from Culemborg. Evertje was born in 1689 and died October 16, 1772, she was from The Hague.

Ary Lourenszoon VanSpronsens first wife was Maria Daniels dochterAlkemade, from The Hague. They were married on January 28, 1714.

Children from this first marriage were:
Maria, baptized March 13, 1718 with witness Joris Cornelis Van deSnoeck
Maria, baptized November 17, 1723 with witnesses Lijsbeth VanSpronsen and Marijntje Van Alkemade.
Laurens, baptized May 3, 1726 with witnesses Jan VanSpronsen and Machtel VanSpronsen

Children from the second marriage of Ary Lourenszoon VanSpronsen were:

Cornelis, baptized October 13, 1727 (my great, great, great, great, grandfather)

Laurens, baptized November 6, 1729
Geertje, baptized May 20, 1731
Pieter, baptized January 27, 1734
Klaas, baptized December 5, 1736

Dutch custom is to baptize babies a week or two after they are born; sometimes even if the mother cannot be present.

My great, great, great, great grandfather's parents were Laurens Areyszoon VanSpronsen and Geertje Arendochter Vos, married on May 15, 1683, both residents of Monster. Their son Arie Laurenszoon VanSpronsen was born in 1692 and died June 4, 1762

As a side note understand that the emperor Napoleon Bonaparte conquered most of Europe in the early 1800 including The Netherlands. He decreed that everybody must have a full name including a surname. Before that in the Netherlands it seemed that people carried the name of their father such as Ariezoon, meaning Arie's son, or Ariedochter, meaning Arie's daughter.

The VanSpronsen name shows up in the records of the Netherlands during the so called Golden Age of the Netherlands (the 1600s). A peace treaty between the States of Holland and England on behalf of the Republic of the United Netherlands, was signed by J. J. VanSpronsen in 1654. In the archives of Gravenhagen appear many VanSpronsen names of persons who are buried there in the Cathedral.

In a book written by Dr. C. Wenger, "Glimpses of Mennonite History and Doctrine", there is a letter written on behalf of the States General of Holland, dated 1637, addressed to the City of Zurich in Switzerland where a severe persecution of the Anabaptists was taking place at that time, asking for the release of the property of those under persecution. This letter was signed by J. VanSpronsen.

In Reitstap's history, the coat of arms of the VanSpronsen family is described, (translated from the French): Blue background with silver lion, well clawed and tongue extended, with a gold crown, clutching a gold lily in his paws. Helmet symbol: the lion coming out of a fold plate.

My grandfather told me during the time he stayed at our family home for a month or so in San Jose (in about 1952 to 1954) that his family ancestors were very sound Calvinists and very good Christians going way back generations. From the paragraphs above the family does indeed go quite a ways back. Nevertheless, life at times was very tough. The number of children that died in infancy, and those that died at the time of the Spanish flu epidemic, and related causes in the 1918s of that and other causes, is quite striking to a 21st century person. My mother told me that in Holland she was always hungry. When she arrived in Michigan at about 10 years of age in 1912 she could not believe all the food there was to eat. Constant hunger was gone!

As I said before, I wish that I had been able to converse at great length with my grandfather Cornelis. That never happened. I since somehow received into my possession a writing of my great Uncle Karl VanSpronsen, my grandfather's youngest brother. I am going to include a portion of it here so that you dear reader will receive a little history and background of my grandfather and his ancestors.

Very fortunately for us Uncle Karl was a writer and very proficient in English although all his books were written in the Dutch language. Thus what follows is in English but understand that Uncle Karl translated the letters from my grandfather as my grandfather wrote only Dutch. Doleantie means to, "Feel Sorrow" and is the name of a reformation movement eventually lead by the theologian and politician, Abraham Kuyper. Uncle Karl's writing is as follows:

ITEMS OF INTEREST IN THE HISTORY OF THE VANSPRONSENS FAMILY AND THEIR ECCLESIASTICAL EXPERIENCES

Cornelis VanSpronsen (in the village circles he was known as the ("Goeie Kees") was born in 1801 in Loosduinen, a village near Gravenhage near the coast. Many gardeners lived there. In 1830 he was in the service and was involved in the "Ten Day Campaign", to Belgium to suppress the revolt there. Upon his return he married Jannetje Vander Geer, who was born in Rijnsaterwoude in 1813. She too was a girl of pious parentage. One of the nieces, a daughter of Arie VanSpronsen, still has the catechism book of Jannetje. The title translated is, "Brief Questions from Church History for the Use of Catechumens in Christian Families." It was published in 1824. In a simple manner this booklet describes the history of the church in a question and answer format.

Four children were born from the marriage of Cornelis VanSpronsen and Jannetje Vander Geer. The youngest son, Gerard Jan, was born May 17, 1853. When he was four years old (1857) the family moved from Loosduinen to Ter Aar, a village on the canal de Aar situated 10 kilometers above (north?) Alphen. Their father, Cornelis VanSpronsen, owned a mixed business, that is, he was gardener and cattle feeder. He must have prospered quite well here because he was able to get his four children, three sons and one daughter, started close to one another with house and land. Cornelis VanSpronsen died in 1883, his wife in 1893. At that time the economic conditions were very bad. Under pressure of these circumstances Gerard Jan first moved to Rotterdam, thereafter the oldest son Joseph Marinus moved to Gravenhage and finally the daughter Catharina Hendrika who was married to Hein VanVeen, moved to Rotterdam.

From an examination of the church archives (minutes from 1820-1930) at Ter Aar, I found the following: On March 20, 1872, profession of faith was made by 17 people before the minister and the consistory. Among those making profession of faith is found the name Gerard Jan VanSpronsen; he was therefore 19 years of age.

At the time of the Doleantie (1887), Pieter VanSpronsen was the leader of the Doleantie at Ter Aar. He was the brother of Gerard.

In the acts of liberation of the Doleantie one finds subscribed the names of P. VanSpronsen and G. J. VanSpronsen.

When the Gereformeerde Kerk was established at Ter Aar, P. VanSpronsen assumed a place of leadership. In the minutes of January 12, 1903, we find: "At his retirement (periodic) as Elder, appreciation was expressed to P. VanSpronsen by the senior member on behalf of the assembly for his zeal and perseverance in comforting the sorrowful and participating in the joy of the joyful. The wish was expressed that the brother might have many years so that he might reflect on these things."

From the history of the VanSpronsen family it appears from earliest times, already in the 1500's, that they participated in the Reformation of the Christian religion. From the historical records it may be noted that during the time of persecution when many believers (Protestants?) had to flee from France and Belgium to Northern Netherlands, a distinguished member of that group married a daughter of the VanSpronsen family.

When in the Golden Age (i.e. the seventeenth century) various VanSpronsens held important positions in the Government, this was possible only because they were members of the contemporary Reformed Church. In those days the Reformed (Gereformeerde?) Church was the state church, and whoever was not a member of this church could not be given governmental office. From the ancient baptismal registries it appears that several of the VanSpronsens were witnesses at the baptisms. This clearly indicates that throughout they were very active members in the church.

The golden thread of the covenant of grace as it runs through this family is clearly a sign of the grace of God, who is faithful to those who are true to Him.

We see this thread continuing, by God's grace, through the family of Cornelis VanSpronsen, (Author note – this is my grandfather) the oldest son of Gerard Jan VanSpronsen, born April 26, 1877 at Ter Aar. In his youth he was of much concern to his parents. He was an adventuresome soul, with a lot of energy and initiative. But he was also one who gave it all up quickly and wanted to try something else. Thus he pursued different trades. When father and mother VanSpronsen moved from Ter Aar to Rotterdam he quickly met a girl from an unbelieving family. Her name was Alide VanVliet. Her father worked at a brewery in Rotterdam. Her parents did not attend church.

Naturally this did not meet the approval of father VanSpronsen. But the Lord's ways are wonderful. This marriage was the means by which Kees' wife found the Lord, and became a believer. Together they experienced much sorrow in the Netherlands. Cornelis began with a vegetable store, which produced only a deficit. Thereafter he went to work at the boats of the Holland-American line, and therein he became involved in the rail and dock strike of 1903. He, however, did not participate in the strike, and remained day and night aboard the ship where his wife Anna brought him food. Later he became coachman for rented coaches. After that he became inspector for a life insurance company and went to live in the city of Zwolle.

That was not to be for long either. He moved to Amsterdam where he began a laundry. His wife Anna washed while he picked up clothes and returned then again. Here they experienced the blow of their life. Their oldest daughter Johanna Wilhelmina, a sweet girl, died suddenly during a Saturday-Sunday night in 1909, while she was only 10 years old. Kees, the father, was lying on bed playing with their youngest, when the mother screamed as she discovered that her oldest daughter lay dead in bed. I still have the telegram that Kees sent to father: "Suddenly our child Johanna died." Father VanSpronsen was on his way to church when the telegram came. Immediately he went to Amsterdam to be with his children in their time of need.

In 1910 Kees bought a piece of land in Rodkanje, near Oostvoorne, on the island Voorne and Putten. It was poor ground (sandy) and the summer of 1911 was very dry and nothing grew. When early in 1912 his house there burned down he decided to migrate to America. (Author note: My mother told me he used the insurance money from the house to buy the ticket to America.) He left for England by boat and there took a ship to New York. Originally his plan had been to take passage on the, "Titanic", but when his land could be sold earlier he was able to leave a few months earlier. In this way the Lord spared his life. The Titanic crashed into an iceberg and all third class passengers were drowned.

His wife Anna remained in the Netherlands with the children because of insufficient funds. However, after working in a factory for six months, he had saved enough to let her and the children come to America. It was a hard voyage for Anna for her youngest child died while at sea. Therefore, she had to remain several weeks in quarantine and could not immediately go to meet her husband. At his departure father VanSpronsen had said to him, "Go with the blessing of the Lord".

This blessing was for Kees to experience in America. He remained faithful in the service of the Lord; he nurtured his children in the fear of the Lord, and had the joy of seeing that in this new land his children continued to walk in the way of the VanSpronsens. In their marriages they were faithful to the covenant and their children were taught the ways of the Lord.

In my files are many letters from my brother in America; they all testify to faith in the Savior.

When I married my wife, Marie Taal, on October 27, 1921, I received a letter from Kees from Grand Rapids dated November 1, 1921, which reads as follows:

Dear brother and sister:

Psalm 125 as we sing it in church:

1 Blest the man that fears Jehovah
Walking ever in His ways.
By thy toil thou shalt be prospered,
And be happy all thy days.

2 In thy wife thou shalt have gladness.
She shall fill thei home with good.
Happy in her loving service,
And the joys of motherhood.

3 Joyful children, sons and daughters,
Shall about thy table meet,
Olive plants, in strength and beauty,

Full of hope and promise sweet.

4 Lo, on him that fears Jehovah,
  Shall this blessedness attend.
  For Jehovah out of Zion,
  Shall to thee His blessing send.

5 Thou shall see God's Kingdom prosper,
  All thy days, till life shall cease.
  Thou shall see thy children's children;
  On Thy people, Lord, be peace.

He continued his letter as follows:

These lines came to my mind when I received notice of your marriage. Hearty congratulations, also on behalf of my wife. Mrs Marie VanSpronsen, nee Taal, is now the third in the family whom we know only by mail. We are increasingly possessed with a desire to take a trip to the Netherlands.

It seemed strange to us that in the last while no letters were coming from you, but this puzzle is now solved. When one is busy with plans for marriage then one's thoughts are concentrated on one matter. However, we hope that now your goal having been realized, we shall soon receive correspondence from both of you and that once again your thoughts may be directed to America.

My wife instructs me not to forget to ask for a picture of your wedding. We had one from sister Toos too and this has a prominent place at our house. So don't forget.

Brother and sister, may the Lord give the one thing needful for a happy married life, for this is pure and divine love. Both of us wish you this.

I also ask a favor. I would like to know how much Abraham Kuyper's Gemeene Gratie (Common Grace) would cost and whether or not this is still available. If the price is not too high I will send the money.

Fondest greetings from both of us.
                    Your brother and sister,
                         Cornelis and Anna

Write back quickly, "alstubelieft" (please)!

In 1929 Kees was able to realize his wish and he and his wife made a trip to the Netherlands. He was permitted to see his aged father alive. Unfortunately, not his mother. She passed away in 1919. Those were happy days.

The last night that he spent under his parental roof he composed a short poem-- he was adept at poetry. His sister Kate found it when she cleaned the room. It read:

We slept together
In the house of my father.
In down and in feathers.
O lord wilt thou spare him,
For yet a few years.
Maybe we'll see him again.

In 1949 he was permitted once more to come to the Netherlands. Then he saw his brothers and sisters again. During the visit in the Netherlands his brother Arie's wife passed away. She was the first of the several who died in succession. Kee's own wife had passed away in 1948. She too was permitted to enter eternal glory.

The last years of our oldest brother are best known to his children. He spent his last days in the "Holland Home" in Grand Rapids. He was buried next to his wife in Ripon, California.

His children walk in the way that was taught them.

SOLI DEO GLORIA

The words of Uncle Karl are here finished.

To give you dear reader a little understanding of the Christian commitment of these ancestors let me give you a brief history. The fundamental Reformed Christianity with roots in what is called Calvinism put down deep roots in the Netherlands in the 1500s. The King of Spain had acquired the lowland provinces north of France and south of Germany. The King, being a Catholic determined to stamp out Protestantism. Great cruelty was expended in this effort to stamp out reformed Christianity in the Netherlands. A long, very bloody war followed where the Dutch were helped by the English. After the defeat of the Spanish Armada, by the English and Dutch, the Dutch Republic prospered greatly and became the dominate commercial power in the world. Calvinist Christianity became the state religion of the northern Netherlands Dutch Republic, and was known in English as the Reformed Church.

As happens over the course of time, State Churches as well as most protestant denominations deteriorate and depart from deep Christian commitment and love of Jesus Christ. Stirred by the Holy Spirit ordinary people then read their Bibles and know something is wrong and seek pure and loving relationship with God and their fellow believers. Eventually people want their own church and not that of the government or some corrupt denominational hierarchy. This is viewed as a form of rebellion and treason by the State organized Church or the King as the case may be.

The secession movement (in Dutch called the Afscheiding) in the Netherlands in the 1830s captured the Kooyers and because of persecution they immigrated to America.

The Doleantie (to feel sorrow), was also a deep reformation and came about in the 1880s and captured and spiritually moved deeply many of the VanSpronsens. Many of the Doleantie movement people also immigrated to America, and most joined the Christian Reformed Church, the denomination started in Michigan in 1857.

The Liberation movement (in Dutch called the Vrijgemaakt) occurred in the 1940s and again captured and spiritually moved deeply many

VanSpronsens. Many of the Liberation Movement people after WW II and the German occupation also immigrated to America, again many joining the Christian Reformed Church.

My great uncle, Karl Van Spronsen, youngest brother of my grandfather, wrote a memorial volume (464 pages) on Klaas Schlider, Professor of Theology, and the spiritual leader of the Liberation Movement. (*Schilder's Struggle for the Unity of the Church*, Rudolf Van Reest, Translated by Theodore Plantinga, Inheritance Publications, Neerlandia, Alberta, Canada, 1990)

The people who become involved in these movements love the Lord Jesus deeply and are willing to suffer for their faith. Their faith is a very important part of their life.

Psalm 139 expresses this understanding rather well.

I have in my possession a collection of papers and photographs of the VanSpronsen family put together, I believe, by the wife of my cousin Bob VanSpronsen of Ripon, sometime in the 1970s. If one is interested in the family history and children of Cornelis VanSpronsen one should obtain a copy. I have a copy in my files; it is in a blue file/binder.

There is a family story that when coming over to the United States by ship in 1912, my grandfather's wife and children, which included my mother the oldest child at the age of about 10, were stuck and confined on Ellis Island where the recent immigrants were quartered, perhaps because of some sickness. After waiting for them for some time (weeks?) my grandfather crawled up on to a hitch bar underneath a wagon pulled by horses to smuggle himself into Ellis Island. Once inside he bribed the guards to let his family go. He then got back outside the same way he got in. Outside he then received his wife and family of four children, including my mother, (the baby had died on the trip over), and promptly took them to Michigan by train.

My grandfather once told me an interesting story. He was managing a fruit ranch at the time near Sunnyvale, California. How he got involved he did not tell me. In San Jose, California, occurred the last lynching recorded in the Western United States.

As I recall the story, the owner of a large downtown department store was the victim of a kidnapping of his young son, maybe twenty, or so. The kidnappers killed the young man and dumped him into a shallow grave on San Francisco Bay. One of the kidnappers got caught, as I recall, collecting the ransom money, and was placed in a cell in the City Hall Courthouse on James Street. A very large angry mob gathered in St. James Park across the street from the City Hall, which included my grandfather.

Eventually, the mob was able to overpower the police and the kidnapper was dragged into the Park where a rope was put around his neck and the other end of the rope thrown over a limb of one of the large trees in the park. A lot of the mob had a turn at pulling on the rope to cause the body of the kidnapper to go up and down in the air off the ground twenty feet or more again and again. i.e. quite a dance to great shouting and cheering of the mob.

My grandfather did not admit to having a hand in this, but it was obvious he was an eyewitness to all this given all the details he told me.

TWO

YOUTH AND GROWING UP

My earliest memory is waking up on Christmas morning and going down the stairs to look under the Christmas tree and see if I had received a present. My first present was a set of little wooden farm animals. I remember playing with them by the Christmas tree. We had a hand water pump in a porch off the kitchen. It was usually my brother's job to pump water for my mother. I remember walking through a cornfield; it seemed very big then but probably was quite small, to Sunday school. A big man led us in singing as I sat in the front row. I remember my father taking me on a walk down town where he would get me an ice-cream cone. This all occurred in Oxford, Wisconsin. My family moved from Oxford, probably in the summer of 1939 when I would have been about 3 years and nine months old.

One day our Uncle Garrett, my dads' brother, came to town and since he was a train Engineer, we all went down to the tracks to watch the, "400", come through town. It came through town unbelievably fast with a great cloud of dust and noise, and was pulled by a huge black engine with lots of black smoke going into the sky. The motto seemed to be 400 miles in 400 minutes including stops. It had to be doing 80 to 100 miles an hour. I was simply thunderstruck. Remember this was in about 1939 and I was almost four years old. Even my uncle was very impressed. I held my father's hand

and just shook as we were no more than 15 feet from the tracks and the noise was astounding just watching it approach. This was before the day of diesels so the engine was a huge steam engine and very, very big.

When I was almost four years old we moved to Hixton, Wisconsin. My father was a Pastor and he moved about every three years. Again the parsonage was next to the church with a big field behind both in which we raised a huge garden where my endless job seemed to be hoeing corn and beans under my brother's tyrant kind of supervision. Behind the garden was a row of old horse-parking places (sheds, not really stables) where people at one time parked their horse and carriage when going to church. I remember only a very few times anybody taking a horse and buggy to church. Eventually my father turned part of it into a pig pen. One day the pig escaped and ran away. After a time there came a report of a loose pig up in the hills behind town. My brothers were sent after it and after an adventure of some sort, the details I do not remember, the pig was captured and returned to its pen.

We had a three hole outhouse on the edge of the garden next to the woodshed behind the house. The garden seems huge since I remember many very, very boring and terrible times, as I hated hoeing beans and corn, sweating in the hot sun. There seemed to be no end of sweat jobs like that which I remember disliking a lot. Maybe it was because when there was a job of that sort, it turned my brothers into dictators, robbing me of my freedom.

In my memories Halloween seemed to be the big event in town. My brothers were always thinking of ways to keep our outhouse from being pushed over, even to the point of wiring it with an electrical coil from a model T automobile. This of course was supposed to give the hollow weeners an electric shock. No matter what, our outhouse got pushed over every Halloween. How the hollow weeners kept from falling into the hole I will never know.

I don't remember toilet paper unless it was maybe used on rare occasions, or maybe my mother must have had her own private supply. Old Sears and Robuck and Montgomery Ward catalogs served the wiping purpose. As you can imagine, catalog paper is rough so not much time was spent wiping.

The outhouse had three holes but I do not remember any company on any of my visits. Sundry vermin lived in the outhouse, such as spiders, beetles, and such, and maybe a wild cat when it got cold.

A sport for us kids, probably instigated by my brothers, was to go down by the railroad tracks and harass the hobos. The hobos, of course, were what we would call nowadays, homeless. They rode the freight trains and periodically would get off to beg for food. There was a hobo jungle between the tracks and the Trempolow River which was on the other side of the road from our house. We would sneak down there and throw rocks or old fruit at the hobos until we got a chase started. I don't remember ever getting caught but it was very exciting.

The hobos must have had the way clearly marked as invariably they made a path to my mother's house where she always feed them a bowl of soup. I read a story a few years ago that the hobos did indeed have a way of marking different ways and houses. They had different symbols placed here and there which told them what to expect down the road. My mother, most of the time, always had a pot of soup on the wood stove. She fed thousands of hobos.

I was rather an independent sort. I remember a time, the first day of trout season when I was about 5 or 6 years old. I got up out of bed at first light and went down to the river. I fished upstream until I got to a dam where my brothers would swim once in a while. One of my brothers asked me what I was doing there and told me to get. I got out of his way and kept on fishing. Once in a while out in the field along the river I would encounter some hogs, which were very big and ugly, so I had to be careful. I returned home about dark and my mother was fit to be tied. She was so glad to see me she forgot her anger of me being gone all day so did not give me a licking. I came home with two trout and two suckers.

Our swimming hole was just across the road in front of the house and church and down a slight slope to the river. A good part of the summer was spent in the swimming hole. Sixty years later when I visited Hixton, kids the age I was were still swimming in that same ole swimming hole.

School was, of course, always a big thing. I remember most of the time being quite bored. We had to walk about a mile through town to school. Wisconsin could get quite cold, even 30 degrees below zero. One time I was so exhausted I just lay down in a snow bank and just gave up. My brother, probably Gordon, kicked me out of the snow bank and dragged me home.

One day on a Sunday while we were eating lunch there was a big screech of tires and loud crash occurred about a block away downtown. We ran down there to see what happened and there was my very young and beautiful first grade teacher dying on the pavement in the middle of the street from an automobile accident. She would give a slight twitch once in a while, but nobody but me paid any attention to her. It seemed a puzzling rather shocking loss to a small boy.

One dark dreary day we moved to South Range, Wisconsin near the city of Superior. My father seemed to stay in a town only about three years or so. The grass must have seemed greener to him at the next place. He always seemed successful in his ministry as he often recruited new people to come to church, but the frustrations must have got to him and we would move on. He usually had several churches to serve. In South Range, he served three churches. He preached at one at 9am, another at 11am, and another in the evening. He did a lot of calling on people in the evenings during the week so he was often gone in the evenings.

My father was often at home during the day. My favorite activity when my mother and sister got too intrusive was to go up to my father's study and be very quiet in a corner and color a book or something. It was required that I be quiet in his study. I loved the smell there as he sometimes smoked a pipe while he was studying. In those days you should remember, a man was not a man unless he smoked. My father never seemed addicted to tobacco as he could quit and start with seemingly no effort. Part of the problem was he always received a can of tobacco at Christmas time from somebody. He usually received several cans of tobacco and boxes of cigars, which, of course, he thought should not go to waste.

In South Range we lived just across the street from the railroad tracks. It was just like the song, "The train came through the house". The railroad used big steam pusher engines to help the freight trains climb up out of the Lake Superior basin. The pusher engines would back down the tracks to Superior after it pushed the train up the hills. These pusher engines would come down very quietly so you could hardly hear them until they got opposite the house where they would blow the whistle for the road crossing in town. Usually that made one, who was not used to this, to jump straight up out of bed. Visitors would be quite bedeviled by this piercing whistle during the middle of the night.

Marcia, my sister, and I to make a few pennies would pick up coal from the tracks as the tracks made such a sharp bend across from the house that coal would fall out of the coal car and leave it along the tracks.

Summer evenings were spent playing, "kick the can". Almost every kid in town would participate. Somebody would be, "it", and everybody else would go and hide. The "it" person would go looking for the others, and if he or she found somebody, they both would run back to the can. If the "it" person got to the can first the "it" would jump over the can and say the name of the person he or she found and they would be "caught", and then would have to help the "it" person find the other kids. If the found person got to the can first that person would kick the can and then everybody who had been caught would go free. We would hide anywhere, in people's yards, sheds, and outhouses, anywhere. This game would go on until the 9 O'clock passenger train arrived in town, because then we were required to quit the game and go home to bed.

My sister Marcia and I would make money picking wild strawberries across the tracks in a swamp. They were very small and it took lots of work to make a quart. My mother was also really into blueberries. She would organize all of us into sundry blueberry picking expeditions. We drove our old car to the blueberry patches in the woods. I enjoyed blueberry picking a lot as I would wander off by myself and eat as many as I liked while I picked my bucket full. My mother canned 200 quarts of blueberries one year. Needless to say we ate blueberries a lot of the time. They were very, very, good.

One time my sister Marcia caused me a big problem. There was a fat lady who lived about halfway to school, Mrs. Peterson was her name, I still have not forgotten. Marcia called her a fat old lady as we ran by her house. Sure enough she came marching right up to my mother's house and laid out the whole scene to my mother. Marcia and I received quite a licking, which one does not readily forget. It cured us of ever insulting anybody again.

When the Walt Disney movie, "Snow White and the Seven Dwarfs", first came out, my mother took us on the train to Duluth, Minnesota to see it. We sat through it twice and yet I still refused to leave. My mother ended up dragging me out of the theater.

GOING TO CALIFORNIA

In those years we traveled to California just about every summer. In 1935 my Grandfather, Cornelius Van Spronsen, asked my father to come to California to perform the marriage ceremony of my mother's youngest brother, Art Van Spronsen. It seemed my grandfather was having another one of his feuds with the preacher. In later years I learned it was Nicholas DeVris, a really saintly man, a missionary to China who was chased out of China by a rebellion there in about 1928. (I believe it was the Boxer rebellion) and with whom my brother Gordon and I played golf in California when he was almost 90 years of age. (He lived to be 95; in those golf days he was an intern pastor at the Palo Alto Christian Reformed Church where I was an Elder) In the days of the 30's a clergyman could travel by train free or half fare so my father went off to California in December. He walked around in shirtsleeves enjoying warm California weather in Sunnyvale, California. When he returned to Wisconsin the story goes it did not get above 30 below for six weeks. Thus the California bug bit him.

One day he was looking out the frozen windows with my mother and said, "Let's go to California". Well it did not happen as a permanent move for another 11 years but we started to travel every summer to California. In 1939 my Dad acquired as I recall a Chandler car. My Dad proclaimed, "This car will go to California!" So off we went in 1939, 1940, 1941, 1945, and 1946. We camped along the way just about any place my Dad decided. Parks, churchyards, woods, anything worked as a campground. We kids very much enjoyed the adventure. We took along a lot of stuff. My mother made a level small bed for my sister and I and we lay on top of all the stuff between the front and back seats. My mother canned lots of California fruit so on the return trip the car was full of fruit jars. Many times we traveled all night, especially across Nevada, as it usually was hot and very dry. (No air conditioning in those days) My mother would freak out if my dad or brother Howard went above 50 miles per hour, so the trip was long and slow.

California was lots of fun. My grandparents were on a fruit ranch in Sunnyvale, California, farming cherries, apricots, and prunes, about 70 acres for Dr. Schermerhorn of Grand Rapids, Michigan. My mother was the oldest child in the family; she had three brothers and two sisters (another sister had died in childhood in the Netherlands). It was a ball of fun with all these relatives. There was lots of banter, jokes, and fun times with lots of hard work cutting apricots or processing prunes. My grandfather with his strong energetic sons dried the apricots in the sun after treating them with sulfur smoke, and operated a prune dryer, which had a huge oil fired burner processing theirs and their neighbor's prunes. There was lots of heavy work and my mother worked right along with the men. When my Uncle John was the manager in later years he paid her the same amount as a man. This was unusual in those days.

While cutting apricots, when one encountered a rotten one, he or she usually threw it at someone to take away the boredom. Lots of times this got out of hand and degenerated into a slop pan water fight. The slop was from washing out your apricot pit pan in a barrel of water that became concentrated fermented apricot juice. My uncles usually put a stop to it and my cousins and I would have to go back to work. Often my uncle John would get right into it, especially if my Aunt Joe was around. He loved to pester her. She had married a man older than she who was quite dignified. This seemed to provoke Uncle John even more as he would even dump his sister into the slop barrel up to her neck. Usually that was after she had plastered him when he did not expect it with a fine rotten apricot.

When we did not have to cut apricots we and my cousins would build rubber guns out of old tire inner tubes. We engaged in endless rubber gun fights. It was sort of like hide and seek game with one army searching for the other. Often we would ambush the other side in a great strategic attack.

My cousins had a goat. That goat would eat prunes and spit out the pits. One day we conceived a scheme to make some money. There was a trailer park down by the highway (El Camino, highway 101, ½ mile away) full of Okies. There was a great shortage of housing in those days and Okies lived in vast trailer parks where they just permanently camped out. My uncle for some reason had a cute wagon with a setup so the goat could pull the wagon with a harness. We hitched the goat to the wagon that held about a dozen or so kids and drove the goat and wagon down to the trailer park. As I remember we charged a nickel for a ride around the trailer part. I don't remember how much money we took in but we had a busy day. The goat gave out from exhaustion so we had to load the goat into the wagon and pull the wagon home ourselves. My Uncle John saw us coming home and went into convulsions of laughter. It seemed he had never seen anything so funny as a bunch of kids hauling home an exhausted goat standing up and loaded in the wagon with us kids pulling the whole thing from the wagon tongue where the goat was supposed to be.

My dad got a new Chevy in 1941 so the trip that year to California was made in style. The war interrupted these summer odysseys. Gasoline was rationed so we could not go. In 1945 with the war coming to an end my parents somehow got enough gas stamps to go to California. (Gasoline was rationed and ration stamps were required to buy gasoline.)

In California everything seemed the same only more fun. My Uncle John was now managing the ranch and the war had made fruit growing very profitable. My grandfather and my Uncle Art had made good money during the war working the ranch and left for Ripon, California where they purchased property. The war came to an end with the atomic bomb while we were in California in August. My parents were very, very glad the war was over as my two oldest brothers, Howard and Orneal, were army trained and ready to be with the invasion forces going into Japan. These were very great happy times, and time of great celebration.

The war had a great effect on everybody. My brother Howard (born September 21, 1923) signed up when he was 18 years old as soon as the war started. After his basic training he went into the signal corps and was stationed in Boise, Idaho. His girlfriend, Carol Brown, from Black River Falls, Wisconsin decided she was going to take the bus and go see him in

Boise. My mother talked with her and made sure that when she arrived in Idaho she was to get married. (This type of thing was always my mother's highest concern). I do not think Carol had her parent's permission to leave. Howard ended up spending most of the War on the Island of Biac on the north coast of New Guinea. We knew this soon as Howard had developed a code system with Carol for use in their letters to pass the censors. The Japs had built a very good airbase on the island. The USA invaded and took over the base but the Japs still had half of the Island and the US forces the other half where the huge bomber base was built. It was a dangerous place but Howard and his buddies learned to make alcohol out of local pineapple juice and spent the War in an almost complete state of drunken dissipation. The war did not do Howard any good.

Carol spent a lot of time in our house while Howard was oversees. She was there with Ronnie, their first child, and I played with him a lot. Carol was a very fine, very kind, very loving lady. As a child I enjoyed being around her, and enjoyed having her in our family very much.

My brother, Orneal, the second oldest (born December 4, 1926) went to the University of Wisconsin for a term and then was drafted into the army. He was trained as a soldier for the invasion of Japan itself. What a relief to my parents and my family and everybody else when the Atomic bombs were dropped, Japan surrendered, and the War was over. What joy enveloped my parents to know their sons were not to cross the beaches into Japan. Orneal was with the first troops into Japan and spent his time there decoding messages for General MacArthur's headquarters in Tokyo.

In June of 1945 I had a medical operation for a rupture (hernia) that I was born with. I spent 14 days in the hospital. The first four days I ate nothing and continually vomited green fluid from the effects of the ether used to put me out during the operation. Then I started eating thin soup and Jell-O. I never had a bowel movement the whole time I was in the hospital. The nurses tried several times to give me an enema, which never worked but caused great discomfort. I hated immensely this business; it was horrible. When I finally got home, I spent much of the next week in the outhouse, much to my great relief.

There was a little wild kitten that came to visit the outhouse. I tried to catch it one day and received an immense scratching all over my arm for my efforts. That taught me a good lesson.

Because of the recovery period from the operation, I was not supposed to do any pushing or running of any kind. The hospital scare caused me to follow the instructions explicitly. When we got to California my cousins took to teasing me unmercifully because I could not run to chase them. I planned my revenge carefully, and when I could run well with no ill effects, I worked them over quite properly taking them by surprise.

In 1946 my Dad made the decision to go to California permanently. Again we moved and since my Dad believed in taking as little along as possible, my toys were given to my cousins in Fond du Lac, near Duluth, Minnesota. Everything I cherished was gone again. The trip to California was as usual very exciting.

We camped at Yellowstone Lake in Yellowstone Park for a few days. The lake was full of large trout about 16 inches long. I would walk along the beach, and people would give me their fish, I suppose so they could catch some more. My mother would cook them and we feasted on fish for days. What a treat as we were poor and did not always eat the best of everything. On the trip to California in 1945, one day we stopped at a restaurant. They had steak on the menu. I did not know what steak was. Meat was rationed in Wisconsin so I had never seen steak for five years. When I saw what my parents had ordered, of course, I wanted it too. We used to take butter along to California, as in California they had no butter. California had lots of steak.

My brother, Gordon, when driving in Montana, sideswiped a truck. It smashed up the whole side of the car but otherwise no one was hurt. California that year was more of the same great fun, but the owner of the Ranch sold it in the fall of 1946. The story was that the 70 acres sold for $144,000, an unbelievable sum for those days. (Prune land like it sold for $200 per acre in the 30's or for seventy acres that would be $14,000) Land a few miles away from that ranch in the 1990's sold 100 acres for $60,000,000.00 (sixty million dollars)

My Uncle John and his family left for Michigan on January 1, 1947. It was very sad for us as we came to California and he was leaving for Michigan. Housing was very scarce in California at that time and we were living in a three-room shack on the Ranch. The new owners were not friendly and attempted to evict us. My Dad resisted and those were trying times. He received a call to be the pastor of the Mendocino Presbyterian Church in Northern California that spring. He delayed leaving the ranch until school was out for us children so in June we went to Mendocino.

MENDOCINO

The very little city of Mendocino was a wonderful, beautiful place. It was an old lumber town that was becoming somewhat of a ghost town. It was on a fairly level ridge that made a point that extended out into the Pacific Ocean. The ocean met the level land of the point with 100-foot high cliffs. In the old days lumber was loaded from the south side of the point into lumber schooners for shipment to San Francisco. The town was started about 1852 and supplied a lot of the lumber for construction of San Francisco in its very earliest days. When we arrived all the activity was over and the place was in ruins. The last mill on the flat along the river below the town, named Big River, burned in 1939 after being closed for some years. A lot of the homes were still owned by the Mill Company. They slowly burned down as every year a fire would consume one or more of them. The place seemed in retrospect perfect for growing up. A river to play and fish in, a vast ocean to fish in, lots of hills and valleys to hunt in, and interesting people, and we walked to school.

The first summer was a little lonely for my sister and me, as we did not know anybody. But once school started we had lots of friends. My friends taught me how to fish and hunt. Ocean fishing and working the rocks for abalone was the most productive in the beginning, but later on we learned to catch Salmon in the ocean and dig clams along the mud flats on the River.

Sometime in the winter and spring of 1948 Warner Brothers came to town to make the movie, "Johnny Belinda". My sister and I through the school principal were hired on as, "extras". Soon my parents and my brothers were also hired. Warner Brothers used the Church building where my father

53

served, in the movie so he was on the payroll but did little. My mother managed to get into quite a number of scenes and she can be seen today in that movie. It was my first taste of Capitalism. I seemed to be bathed in money. We were paid $15 per day, a huge sum of money to a 12-year-old boy for those days. With some of that money I bought my brother Orneal's 22 rifle and an old Winchester 25-35 deer rifle from some local old codger.

There was a movie star about our age in the movie. He started to play practical jokes on the rest of us kids to keep from getting too bored waiting for the next scenes to take place. Pretty soon we started to give him trouble in turn. We had lots of fun and it never really seemed to get out of hand. We were required to attend school in a school bus and when we were needed for a scene we would be called out to march, walk around, or move or cheer or whatever to make the movie. We would then return to the school bus to suffer some joke by the movie star kid. It seemed to be all of us "extra" kids vs. the movie star kid.

It was fun to watch the director tell the actors what he wanted and create what he wanted. The scenes were run over and over again. Sometimes each one was done a little different each time. One day I asked the director what kind of movie they were making. He was patient with me and he answered, "A very expensive one that was going to be very good". Jane Wyman won the academy award for best actress that year for her work in that movie, released in 1948.

In school I played basketball and baseball and the clarinet in the band. My dad would not let me play football as my brother Gordon got hurt playing football and he thought it was not worth it. He was probably right. When out of school during our junior high years we boys played football as much as we could. It was usually played in a wide ditch between a road and a fence. After each play we usually engaged in loud arguments and shouting. It was a rough game of tackle as only young boys can play without pads or helmets of any kind. The plays of my team were usually complicated as I usually thought them up. If my teammates were capable of executing them they usually worked, usually to the disgust of the other team and that caused another argument. I don't remember ever fighting over football but we usually argued more than we played. In high school these kids that I had played with became quite good in their league.

One of my not so good memories is of the great Halloween Caper. Halloween was always a very different holiday than anything else. The chums I had in those days thought about it for weeks in advance. It seemed our chance to really stir things up and do things, which were completely unacceptable otherwise. All kinds of outlandish schemes were thought up and reduced to action. Almost all of those kids never had the imagination or courage to put anything into practice like I did. So my first or second Halloween in Mendocino, I don't remember which, became a thing never erased from my memory. It started with a few pranks such as ringing doorbells and then hiding in any nearby bushes. This had been going on for weeks in preparation for Halloween. People would come to the door and look around and shut the door. Some kid would do it again while the rest hid. Some people would ignore the ringing and we would go away somewhere else, but some, who perhaps had an anger streak or else would wait by the door, jump out and we would have a chase. We would run down the street, through yards and alleys until the pursuer would get tired, and usually cursed us resoundingly. We thought this was great fun. We were always much faster than the pursuer and I never remember anybody ever getting caught.

Well on that Halloween we tricked and treated for a while and rang doorbells and then the serious pranks got started. First we found a huge lot of chicken cages behind Mendoza's store. There must have been a truckload. We piled them in the middle of the highway that came through town. We let the air out of lots of tires, and then somebody got the idea of painting the schoolhouse door. We must have, "borrowed", the paint from somewhere, I don't' remember what color the door was, but we painted it a weird green and slopped paint all over the place. We probably did other things, which I have forgotten, but the next school day a big investigation was started. The principal was determined to find the perpetrators and he gave the fifth degree to all of the known hooligans in town that were in his school. Well they must have fingered me as eventually I was interrogated. I never have had the perchance to lie so the principal soon had me admitting my part in it. The others lied rather well so I was pinned with the whole responsibility of the deed. The principal soon had my father involved. Everybody was shocked that the preacher's kid did this awful deed of painting the schoolhouse door green! Well, I ended up painting the whole school front doors with a color much to the principals liking and scraping off all the green paint scattered about. It was lots of work. It took me Saturdays and after school for weeks. My father said, "No more Halloween for you". He meant it. Every Halloween after that I stayed home contemplating my navel and thinking good thoughts. The next time I ever went out on Halloween was to escort my children trick or treating at the direction of my wife, Geneva. Needless to say, that experience taught me to be more discreet, and to pick better friends, and to get my kicks elsewhere then from abusing government property. That probably is a very important lesson for a kid like me growing up to learn early in life.

One of my best friends during my junior high years was Bobby Halter. Bobbie's mother was single and he was her only child. She would not let him play near the river or the ocean so a lot of the things we could have done together we were not permitted to do. Bobbie obeyed his mother and did not go near the ocean or the river. To me that was a tragedy. It seems Bobbie's father drowned in the River or Ocean, I don't remember which. We became friends after some encounter that resulted in a fight. I was never a very good fighter and normally avoided fights. How this one came about I do not remember, but we rolled around in the dirt for hours, and I would not give up and as I remember took quite a beating. This must have impressed Bobbie as somehow a truce was called and we started to talk, and talk some more, and became the very best of friends. He was the Altar Boy in the Catholic Church. My father usually was very anti-Catholic as in Wisconsin the Catholics gave him a very bad time. The Mendocino version of Catholic was a very mild Portuguese type. The Portuguese were forever having religious parades down the main streets and we were forbidden to go to them, to my disgust. Once when Bobbie's mother made a trip to the Bay Area Bobbie stayed at our house. On Sunday I went off to the Presbyterian Sunday School and Bobbie off to the Catholic Church. My family became very fond of Bobbie. His mother married and Bobbie departed out of my life. I heard later he became a football star in Walnut Creek, California.

Another unusual friend of mine was Lloyd Lowe. Lloyd was a grade or so lower than me and I don't remember how we became friends, probably through some conversation or other. I don't remember any of his family, now days we would call it dysfunctional. His family did not seem to exist or in any way control his activities. Consequently, we did lots of outlandish things. One day we decided we were going to live off the land. I had made a deal with my mother that she would let me do most anything as long as I would tell her where I was going to go. Our living off the land adventure started with a rowboat trip up the Big River about five miles to a campsite right on the river. The first day we hunted pigeons. We hunted all day. One of us would work the flat along the river while the other would be out in the river in the boat. The pigeons would be high in the Cascara trees eating the Cascara berries. The flat person would hunt with the 22 rifle and shoot them out of the trees and the river person with the shotgun shoot them as they flew near over the boat. The first day we hunted all day and got two pigeons. We cooked the birds over a fire on a stick and licked the bones clean. We repeated the exercise the next day and got two more pigeons. Again we licked the bones clean. The third day we gave up half way through the day, rowed home very tired, with splitting headaches from hunger. It was humiliating and we did not talk about it or tell anybody about it.

Another day again Lloyd said, "Let's go live off the land". Since I have a character flaw in that I find it very hard to quit any project no matter how difficult, we went to live off the land again. The result was the same with very few Pigeons and lots of hunger with a terrible headache. The one difference was that Lloyd brought along a bottle of Four Roses, which he said he found on top of a fence post. The second night we managed to consume this bottle and that was my one and only state of inebriation in my whole lifetime. That experience gave me the cure and I resolved that that was never to happen again. It was a real good lesson that kept with me throughout my life.

Again Lloyd said, "Let's go live off the land". Again we proceeded up the river. The first evening there we left the river and proceeded up along the edge of a swamp. A large deer jumped up from the brush across a waterway. We both shot almost simultaneously, me with my 25-35 rifle and him with a shotgun. The deer dropped in its tracks but we never found a hole in it. That night we feasted. The next day we feasted. Two boys and two dogs consumed the whole deer in three days. What a great feast. I still remember sitting by the campfire with a steak on a stick over the fire. After eating the steak and talking awhile, I would put another steak on the stick and eat again. We ate and talked for three days. We had done it. We never again went to live off the land, as we knew we could do it. Lloyd was a very special kind of friend. After we left Mendocino I never expected a letter from him or to hear from him again and I didn't. He was that kind of person.

We seemed to be the only non-Portuguese boys near our age living in town. Somehow we got to calling each other, "Portagee". Once we started that we never used each other's real names again, it was always Portagee this and Portagee that. We never socialized at school together or at any other social functions, it was almost as if we were in two different worlds, until there were fish to catch or animals to hunt, or clams to dig, or some far out escapade in which nobody else would get involved. Lloyd would say under his breath when he would pass me by at school, "Hey, Portagee let's get some abalone in the morning". That's all that was said. I knew we must be in for a low tide, would gather my stuff and sure enough there he would be down on the rocks ready to gather abalone before light the next morning.

The years went by and Lloyd and I decided to go out on the ocean. He had somehow had access to or obtained a 14-foot boat. We rowed out into the open sea (It was a good thing my mother did not know what I was really doing.) and fished the ocean bottom for rockfish. We caught some nice rockfish, red and yellow ones plus blue ones, the names of which I have forgotten. One day as Lloyd was rowing back to the cliff where the boat was beached; I decided to put on a Salmon lure just for fun. Would you believe a Salmon took it and I caught a large Salmon, maybe about 25 lb. The whole town heard about it and soon we had lots of company out on the ocean. Nobody had ever done this before. Commercial fisherman went out of Noyo harbor about 10 miles north. Never had anybody just launched a boat over the beach below the cliff on the point and gone Salmon fishing. Then everybody seemed to catch fish but us. Eventually we learned the right method of using a frozen anchovy behind a flasher. We would tie a black thread around the nose of the anchovy and tie it to a metal strip, which went through the anchovy. We could tell when we put the anchovy into the water whither it would catch a fish or not. We became quite good at catching salmon. I soon was bringing home 100 lb. of salmon a day. My mother was overjoyed. She fried it, she baked it, she canned it, and we smoked it, and she gave it away to sundry friends of hers. Our family feasted. One day Lloyd caught a 42 lb. fish. It was the biggest one we ever caught. I still remember putting the gaff through the fish as it lay on the surface of the water and putting both feet against the gunwales of the boat to pull the fish into the boat.

That summer was great fun. It was probably the best summer I ever had. We would go out on the ocean at dawn, catch our limit of salmon and return. Then we would meet our girlfriends on the beach for an afternoon of surf playing and swimming. It was also my last summer of fun. That fall we moved to San Jose and after that I worked on real jobs in the summers.

One day my Dad decided he wanted to Salmon fish. He had become good at river fishing for Silver Salmon in the fall season. As our little boat rounded the point away from the little beach by the cliff we encountered the ocean swell, that day maybe a little larger than normal about 30 feet. My dad took a few waves and said, "Go back". I said no, "We just got here and are going fishing". He said louder, "Turn back". Again I protested and insisted that we just got here and were going fishing. My Dad a third time said, "Turn back now" in a tone of voice that indicated he was real serious and meant business. I turned back. I guess I had not realized just how used to the open ocean I had become. Swells were not a problem in a little boat except if you got seasick as you just went up and down, sometimes as much as 50 feet from peak to bottom. The real danger out there was whitecaps. Our little open boat would take in water from whitecaps and it was difficult to bail fast enough. Another danger was fog. Sometimes it just moved in on the surface without warning. You could often see fog out to sea on the horizon but you could never tell when it was quickly about to move in. Our best defense against fog was the bell about a mile offshore in the middle of Big River Bay. You could hear this bell usually if there was a swell and could navigate to the beach below the cliff by sound triangulation off the bell. It took good directional hearing.

My best school friend at school in the junior high years was Wilson Locke. Wilson's family was also a little dysfunctional as he lived with his mother and grandparents. Wilson was the class leader and a very good student. I became his friend also through a fight. I had not been in school two weeks in the 7th grade when he started to ride me. A fight got started and then we became friends and remained good friends until the day I left five years later and then he even took over my girlfriend, whom he was just supposed to watch over.

When we started the 9th grade new kids came into the class from Comptche, a town about 15 miles back from the ocean out in the boonies, which had its own first to eighth grade school. Two boys, Neal Wells and Ronnie Washburn, were very, very good students and an intense competition between us got started. Our class at that time consisted of 10 boys and 3 girls. The girls were plain Jane quiet types who did not seem to influence anything or amount to anything. The principle had held 3 boys back to repeat the eighth grade. This left our 9th grade class with 10 very intelligent, very competitive boys. We did not know that at the time as we thought we were just normal. To show you dear reader how this worked out, nobody from that high school hardly ever went off to college. When anyone did, especially the valedictorian, they usually bounced back home after a semester or so. Almost nobody graduated from college who had gone to that high school. However, in our case, in our class, as in years later it turned out, five of the ten boys in the 11th grade junior class graduated from the University of California at Berkeley, and all of us completed at least four years of college, the class clown becoming a pastor. In those days only 4.0 students or near that got into the University of California. It was a very tough University and still is.

This class of very intelligent, aggressive, competitive boys made high school very interesting. We set out to conquer the world. When we became sophomores we attempted to take over the student government. We failed in the fall, but when spring came we set up a popular senior football player as president, created a party, and sweep the elections by working hard on the 7th and 8th graders. The class above us was mortified. We also started publishing a daily school newspaper, called the Soph News. It contained school gossip plus foreign and national news, which we got off the radio the night before or early in the morning. We were all politically inclined, disliked Truman very much, were very concerned about the communists taking over China, and opposed to socialized medicine. These were the major political issues during those days.

We had an excellent debate team that won lots of debates. The school principal let us set up special classes in algebra II and trigonometry. The competitive nature of the thing made us all very good students. I was very fortunate to have been in such a class.

The parsonage where we lived was a few hundred yards from the beach. The beach was below about a 60-foot high bluff. Big River flowed into the ocean across that beach. The beach was about ½ mile long and was terminated by cliffs on either end. During winter when the water was high the beach on the north end was washed out to sea and the river channel then moved to the north end of the beach. As the water dropped in the spring the ocean would fill up the river with sand and a pool would be formed where the channel had been and the river would make a new channel on the south end of the beach. Each year the river did this a little differently. However, the pool water was usually a little warmer than the ocean. The ocean was very cold maybe 60 degrees Fahrenheit or so. Nevertheless, we swam in the ocean. The breakers were usually nice and high about 6 feet or so and we played endlessly in these breakers. Nobody had ever heard of surfing or I am sure we would have done it. Someone got the idea of using large tire inner tubes, from 18-wheeler trucks on which to ride these breakers. With these only our legs and lower body turned blue from the cold. We played a sort of game of chicken in that the bravest was the one nearest the beach, since when a big wave came along, which was quite a regular occurrence, the wave would break farther out and catch the ones closest to the shore and dump them over and give a wild ride along the bottom of the ocean right up onto the beach. After a while one learned how to do this so as to not get too much sand in one's mouth and to protect one's head from banging on the bottom too hard. It was great fun and our main summer entertainment; remember there was no TV in those days. Summertime, we spent almost every day on the beach; usually we waited until after the fog went out to sea and the sun came out. We could not stand the cold water for more than a half hour or so. We would then lie on the hot beach sand until we got too hot and then again go out into the surf.

One day I got a bee in my bonnet to take the rowboat my brother Gordon had salvaged out into the ocean so I could fish in the ocean with the boat. I discovered an account of that event in the writings of my sister Marcia. Here is her version of that event.

"Another day, I can still remember seeing in the distance, my very dear godly worried mother, standing back from the edge of the cliffs, watching my brother and me down on the river. We were frightening her terribly, and she was watching and praying for us.

My brother had found an old boat up river and he was determined to take it out into the ocean, so he could deep sea fish. He couldn't find anyone to go with him, and I knew if he went alone the danger would be very great, as he needed someone to tell him, as he rowed which direction the waves were coming from, so he could head into them. As I sat in the bow of the boat, I saw the current take us much to close to the dangerous rocky cliffs, and I hung on tightly as the crashing waves rose higher and higher where the mouth of the river met the waves of the ocean. I felt the awesome power of the sea in those disquieting moments. God truly watched over us in a special way that day. We did not even have life jackets on; we didn't know anyone who had any. We never did it again. We found a cove and climbed the cliff. No one else ever took a boat out that river mouth in the five years we lived there."

That is my sister's recollection. I did not fear the task as both my sister and I had swam in that cold ocean most every day in the summer, so I thought if we capsized we would be able to swim out of it, given that we did it at high slack tide where there would be no current to sweep us out far into the ocean.

My father's church had a fairly active youth group. My sister and I and our Christian friends formed the core of the group, but sometimes all the kids in town except for the Catholics would show up. A favorite activity on a cool afternoon or evening of a youth group party on the beach was to build a bonfire. The beach back from the ocean in those days was covered with perhaps a 10-foot deep layer of driftwood, which extended ¼ of a mile or so back away from the beach. This driftwood is gone now but in those days logging and log rafting in the ocean was still going on and huge amounts of driftwood from the ocean would end up on the beach. Young teen-age boys are full of energy and seem to get carried away and in consequence; we would try to see how big a fire we could make. We would pile wood upon wood sometimes 10 feet high. Eventually the fire got so hot we could not get near enough to it to put any more wood on it. Then we would all stand around the fire slowly rotating so as to keep one's front and back at the same temperature at a distance from the fire that one liked and sing songs and tell stories. Sometimes we had a youth group leader who would even try to teach us something.

Another really great youth group party as we got older was to go up the river a half-mile or so from the beach, it was still nice and sandy there, and have a crab feast. Some of us boys would get some bait from the meat market, usually an old cow lung or so which we would convince the butcher to donate, put it in a crab net and drop the net with the help of a small rowboat in the middle of the river. We would do this on the incoming tide, as the crabs would come in from the ocean with the tide. We would do this an hour or so before the party was to begin. By the time everybody showed up we had a nice mess of crabs. We would take seawater, put it in a 50-gallon drum, and build a fire under the drum. The crabs were thrown into the boiling water in the barrel, and when the crabs floated to the top, and were nice and pink, they were ready to eat. You can still see this type of thing today in San Francisco near Fisherman's Wharf. These were really great, very memorable feasting beach parties. We would just stuff ourselves, again sing songs and tell stories and sometimes get a Bible lesson if we had an aggressive fairly new youth group leader who was still full of enthusiasm.

Canasta was our favorite card game. This seemed to be the one activity where I really mixed with the Portuguese Catholic girls, as they loved to play Canasta and so did I. Otherwise, except for school and my paper route we did not see or mix too much with the Portuguese Catholics. They were really nice pleasant girls and they and their mothers were very hospitable serving us cookies and milk during the Canasta games. The Portuguese boys did not seem to play Canasta. I don't remember why.

During my years in Junior High before after school sports began in the 9th grade, I usually played pool down at the pool hall every day after school. My mother was not aware of this as I think in all likelihood she would have objected if she knew. I also bought a 25-cent milkshake at the Remedy store almost every school day. My income even as a lad was such that I could afford this. When I was a kid in Mendocino I do not remember ever being poor even though my parents seemed and appeared to be very poor as they never had any money for anything besides necessities.

My high school baseball career went into high gear when I was a sophomore, playing about half the time and hitting good. In my junior year I could not hit a thing. About that time the school nurse tested my eyes and asked, "What happened to your eyes?" It turned out I was nearsighted and had myopia. From that time on I needed glasses to see the blackboards and that explained why I could not see the ball to hit it. I have worn glasses ever since.

I played basketball also. I played on the "B" team during my freshman and sophomore years first string usually as a center as I had grown quickly and was as tall as anybody. (I was and am still 6' 0") In my junior year I played on the varsity but mostly sat on the bench. We had a very good team that year that took the league championship. We had a very good coach those years. He had come from UCLA and was known as Bullet Bob Baker. One time the Harlem Globe Trotters came to town and played a town team. Of course, the Globe Trotters really put on a show of great skills. Towards the end of the game when the Globe Trotters tried to catch up on the score, Bullet Bob put on quite a show himself, never missing a jump shot from the key area, matching the globe Trotters basket for basket. It was a very memorable show. Bullet Bob's one handed jump shot was sort of unusual in that it had an almost flat trajectory; I guess that's why they called him Bullet Bob. The one handed jump shot was fairly new to the sport of basketball at that time, the two handed shot being what most players had been using.

In my junior high years I had a friend by the name of Teddy Station. He went on to be a great baseball pitcher with drop ball the like of which I have never seen since. Teddy had a sort of girlfriend that lived in a company house just below us next to the old cable drum building that was used in the old days to pull train loads of lumber cars up the slope from the beach flat to the flat on which the town was located. Teddy somehow had inherited a cow and he would sporadically milk the cow and give the milk to the girl's family. Teddy tired of this and somehow I got the job of milking the cow and keeping the milk. Well, one day the cow was sold much to my relief and I gladly lost my job. My dad promptly saw a great opportunity. Where he found a very old decrepit cow with a busted horn and the other horn half sawed off I do not know. She was really ugly, skinny, and ready for the glue factory. The pasture Teddy had been using was mill property. Today it is part of the State Park created around Mendocino. The pasture stretched from the bluff over the beach to the road that came from town and led to the town dump chute, and included the right-a-way of the old railroad that hauled lumber to the point. The building I used as a barn for the cow was the old drum works building.

The day we got the cow she moved into the pasture of 6 inches of clover and she mowed in a straight line making a path through the clover expending a very minimum amount of energy. In hindsight it is a wonder that she did not overeat, bloat, and die. She survived, grew fat, and started to produce huge amounts of milk. It was my job to milk her, feed her, and take her to visit the bull and everything else. She really tied me down but gave me very valuable experience in learning to be responsible. For example, I had to stay home by myself to milk the cow and did not go to my Brother Neal's wedding in 1948.

Interacting with an animal like a cow is a very valuable experience for a kid. I had no stanchion so the cow had to stand still while she was to be milked. I fed her a little grain so she would eat her grain while I washed her and started milking. After finishing the grain she wanted to leave and I wanted to finish milking. This was a contest I had to win. As you might expect battles occurred between her and me. I was armed with a stick and she defenseless except for the capacity to flee or maybe kick. I was faster than her so that did not work. As the months went by we came to understand each other's needs and I got the milk and she got the grain. Nevertheless once in a while she kicked over the bucket and I vented my anger and frustration. Those were good experiences for me. I learned patience and determination. No one ever told me anything about a cow and I learned everything on my own from my own experience.

Periodically she would go into heat for a bull. She would march up and down the pasture bellowing very loudly. It disturbed my mother's sleep at night. Sometimes you could hear her even when the Sunday church service was going on. It was a very unpredictable business to milk her during these periods.

She produced great amounts of milk. My mother made butter (which I often had to churn when my sister made up some excuse why she could not do it), my dad made cheese (some of the most rubbery stuff you ever ate). My favorite was what my mother called rice-do-pop. It must have been some

Dutch word. It was made by cooking rice in milk in a double boiler with a little sugar. It was very good and was served best when cold as a desert.

During my junior high years I learned my first capitalist lesions. A friend, Walter, suggested we peel cascara bark. Cascara is a laxative medicine. The cascara tree can grow to 50 to 80 feet tall. One climbs the tree or cuts down the tree and peels the bark off of it. This is done in the springtime when the sap first starts to run; usually April to June There was a buyer in Fort Bragg who would buy the bark. In April the price was high to give us kids an incentive to go out and peel the bark off of the trees. By July when we had it nicely dried, (We dried it in the sun, usually on top of a south facing roof.), the price would collapse and we would get little for it.

I conceived of the idea of drying mine real good and storing it away in a very dry place and keeping it over the winter. This had the advantage in that I could dry it well in the late summer sun. The problem was that in Mendocino the climate was cold and wet and quite foggy so that the bark could mold easy. The buyer would give one almost nothing for moldy bark. Every year the buyer would ask me, "Is this this year's bark?" I always answered quickly, "Yes sir". My bark was always in excellent condition so I got top prices once I had figured out the system.

My friend who taught me the bark peeling was older than me but he knew where the cascara trees grew since his father had taught him well. I perceived that if I always gave him a little advantage he would continue to take me with him and teach me all he knew. We often just climbed the tree and peeled the bark and let it fall on the ground climbing as high as we dared. We peeled it with a sharp pocketknife or hunting knife. After we had peeled a tree the rule was that one person would make two piles of the bark and the other person would pick which pile he wanted and then put his bark into his burlap sack. I perceived that it was important to give him the advantage so I always picked the smaller pile. When I made the piles, I always made one slightly bigger so that he could then pick the biggest pile. This whole process made for a very stable relationship and he taught me everything he knew about the bark peeling and drying business. Eventually, I had learned all he had to teach me and we went separate ways. In retrospect I wonder how as a kid I was able to intrinsically or instinctively understand that a long-term benefit could be generated by a short-term loss, in this case letting a pecking order be established to my short-term disadvantage. This friend was not a very likable person and he eventually did not amount to anything and became a drifter type like his father. One year I got 30 cents a pound for my bark and I had several hundred pounds. This was a lot of money for a kid.

Another project that generated weekly spending money was my paper route. Mendocino City had a weekly paper called the Mendocino Beacon. I delivered papers to about 15 people who had subscriptions and in exchange would receive additional papers to sell on my own. This paper had been around for years and years and the equipment was really out of the long past. Usually there were not enough papers for me and I would hand crank the press all by myself to get a few more. This was on Saturday morning and nobody was around and I had the whole paper plant building to myself. I do not know how I got this job but some kid must have given it to me. I did it for most all the years I was in Mendocino. The kid before me just threw the paper on people's porches, but I got in the mode of delivering each paper to each door, ringing the doorbell, or knocking on the door. This was usually about 9am Saturday morning. I soon learned that I would get a tip for good service. Soon I delivered the paper to everybody that way along with pleasant conversation with the lady or gentleman that answered the door. The paper cost 7 cents. With a little service like this I always got a dime and some people gave me a quarter. It was great and I earned my weekly spending money for a couple hours work. Slowly the number of subscriptions diminished and slowly the number of people who paid me for the paper increased. That route became a very lucrative thing.

One time I decided to expand and got the job of delivering the daily paper from Santa Rosa. That was a lot of work for very little money in comparison and I soon passed that job on to another kid.

In the spring about March the steady winds usually began to blow and we like most kids would fly kites. We usually made our own but sometimes somebody would have a store bought kite. Like everything else, I wanted to go big and do something few others did. Thus we started to fly kites farther and farther and make bigger kites. Eventually I started to fly them over the ocean from the point west of the town. I made a roller on an axel with a handle that was maybe 18 inches in diameter. On that thing I could wind kite string fast and in large quantity. I mounted it on to a set of crossed pieces of wood so it was stable and the string could be wound in from a flying kite. The record was a kite out over the ocean for a little over a mile. This record was set on a somewhat quiet day with a steady wind from the south so that the kite was out to the north just above the ocean. The weight of the string when the kite was out a mile kept the kite low just above the water. The point had 100 to 150 foot cliffs to the ocean so letting the kite out over the ocean worked. A mile out the kite could hardly be seen. It was only about six feet long with a fairly long tail. We used 18 balls of 300 feet of string each and as I remember got it out 5,300 feet. I was very proud of that record and no other kid came even close.

In September of 1952 we moved to San Jose, California. My father had been there several months, but my mother had continued to work at the Bank of America in Mendocino until September. The change was tough. I was going to a new school, had to make new friends and adjust to the city. We lived at 101 South 12th street near San Jose State College and walked about a mile to San Jose High School

SAN JOSE.

My father had accepted a job as principal of the San Jose Christian School. He worked there through the summer but soon after school started the school folded. He then sold cemetery lots for a while in San Jose.

High school in San Jose called for a lot of adjustment. It seemed tough. I had to make new friends and compete with a lot of new very smart kids. I had a class in solid geometry with the best students in the school. They were forever trying to get the teacher to take us to the auditorium and give us a concert on the piano. The teacher was very, very good on the piano. The students seemed to be able to manipulate him quite easily.

English class seemed to be headed for disaster when I was required to memorize Beowulf. Consequently, I dropped fourth year English since I did not need it to graduate. I switched to choir, which I have always enjoyed. One day the director wanted volunteers to sing for the School Play. Why I volunteered I do not remember. In the Play we were to sing all five verses of Bless Be the Tie That Binds. We sang it more than a hundred times in Play practice. I can still sing it today from memory. There is lots of dead time during play practice so I became friends with two other boys in the Play choir, Peter Del Grande and John Engebretsen. We did lots of things together like miniature golf, movies, and car tag. Car tag we played on the streets of San Jose. The game was played by trying to just bump the car ahead of you on the bumper. We played this on the streets of San Jose on the East side of town where we lived. I never remember the cops catching us even though tires are screeching and the sound must have been heard by a lot of people. My brother Gordon had bought a 50 Studebaker with an overdrive that would kick in at over 30 miles per hour. In 2nd gear overdrive I had an extra gear with enabled me to stay close to the guy ahead of me and touch him for a tag. My brother Gordon had gone off to make war on the Communist North Koreans and fortunately for me had left his car behind. Car tag taught me how to drive and handle an automobile well, especially on the streets of San Jose. For those of you who might think playing car tag unbelievable, remember those old cars had big bumpers and the bumpers were designed to take blows. People used to push around all kinds of things with the bumpers.

A few days after Gordon had returned from the Korean War we had left the house and were walking down 12th Street when a car half a block away backfired. When I looked around Gordon was gone. I found him flat in the gutter of the street. It had taken him a fraction of a second to go from walking down the street next to me to lying in the gutter. I never forgot that. War must be horrible.

One day I saw an ad in the paper for workers for the fall election. I had been quite an anti-Truman debater and desired immensely that Ike be elected President so I went to the meeting. There were only a handful of people at the meeting in a downtown hotel. They must have thought that somebody had to do the job so I was given the job of precinct chairman for the precinct where I lived on the east side of San Jose. I had just turned 17 and wasn't even old enough to vote. Voting age was 21 in those days. My job was to find out how everybody intended to vote in my precinct and to get every one of them to the polls on Election Day. I did just that. I went out almost every evening for the few weeks before the election and talked to every Republican and a lot of Democrats in my precinct.

On Election Day the election officials put up a list on the outside of the polling place which was updated every half hour or so as to who had voted. I called up my Republican voters that had not voted yet and who I knew intended to vote for Ike and I would go pick them up with a car (I believe it was my brother Gordon's which I borrowed that day) and bring them to the polls. At the end of the day every one of my Republican people and those Democrats in my precinct who intended to vote for Ike had voted. Of course, Ike won big and we finally had a new Republican President for the first time in 20 years. It was a time of great rejoicing.

San Jose High School was a large school with a good football team and lots of school activities. It was very good for me. I had to learn to study to compete with the good students in my math and science classes, something I did very little of in Mendocino.

I signed up for sports and played on the varsity basketball team. The coach needed to cut the team roster down to 15 players and I was the last one cut, but that was not before I got very late into a game with the High School from East San Jose, where I missed an easy layup on a neat pass from Mitts Fukamura, the quarterback on the football team. The ball hung on the rim for a full two seconds while I watched it before it fell off onto the floor. I can still see it all in my mind. My only chance for glory on the San Jose High basketball team and I blew it.

I joined the Junior Statesman of America Club and had lots and lots of fun debating other students and going to meetings. I was selected as a delegate to regional conferences where we debated and passed resolutions of a political nature. In the spring I got to go to the State Convention in Bakersfield as a delegate. I made lots of friends while being a Junior Statesman.

San Jose High was an excellent transition for me from Mendocino to college. I learned to study and make friends and adapt to a more cosmopolitan culture.

THREE

COLLEGE DAYS

SAN JOSE STATE

In the spring of 1953, the year I graduated from High School, my brother Neal showed up in San Jose at our home on Twelfth Street in early June. He was going to register for summer school at San Jose State College. Years later it subsequently became San Jose State University. He invited me along to go with him to the registrar's office so he could register for the classes he was going to take. He was intending to become an administrator in the public schools system. We walked west to the campus which in those days started about 7th street and went to 4th street. When the clerk at the registration desk handed him the forms, he says to her, "How about him", meaning me. She handed me the registration forms.

It seems there were no requirements to take college courses at San Jose State College during the summer session. I had applied for admission but I do not remember the status of that application at that time, in fact my High School had sent my record stuff to the San Jose Junior College. I had later to correct that so my application to San Jose State was in fact sent. Anyway, I just looked at the forms. Neal suggested I take algebra as that would give me a jump on mathematics even though I had taken lots of mathematics in High School. I scanned the college catalog for maybe another course and decided I might as well take Psychology as that seemed a basic requirement no matter what one's major was.

Well I enrolled in a 5 unit Algebra course and a 3 unit Psychology course. Since I had just graduated from High School and was used to studying a little bit those courses seemed very easy. Neal told me which professors to pick for the classes. This was a six weeks session that would be over near the end of July so the classes met every day. I soon got into the mode of doing the math homework every day and doing the psychology reading every day. I do not remember it as a lot of work, and as soon as the end of the session I had two A grades on my record. That was a really great beginning to my college education and I have Neal to thank for it.

My Dad was working on a carpenter job out in San Francisco Bay building catwalks between high voltage power poles out in the salt ponds. He asked his boss if an apprentice could work on this job. His boss said sure and I became an apprentice carpenter.

Soon another man on the job had his son working with him and we became a five man crew with the contractor boss watching over us. The other man and his son put the 4x4s posts down into the mud and two or three feet of water by jumping up and down on a frame driving the 4x4s down. (They both were big and heavy) My Dad and I nailed on the cross pieces and nailed on the planks that were to be walked on. The fifth man on the crew drilled holes and put bolts into the cross pieces and planks to make the walk strong and stable. Soon it became sort of a game as to how much footage we could do in a day. Soon we were very productive and the boss could hardly believe it. He was finally making money on this project. Soon the boss bought us beers, soda pop, and candy snacks, and I remember it as a rather fun job. Every once in a while somebody would sink into a deep hole and maybe get submerged and get all wet, usually with a lot of cursing, and laughter. Of course, my father never cursed, and I never did when he was around. We were working vast salt ponds in hip boots, very good American made ones, as the boss gave them to us after the job was finished, and I used them for duck hunting and fishing for many years.

Fall came and I started my college education in earnest. My major became Civil Engineering. I am not sure why I picked that except I have always liked building things and thought it might be a good profession. I took a very full load of course work as that is my style, but also because Engineering majors required more course work than other majors so often it took five years for a lot of students to complete Engineering. I was already used to college because of my summer school experience so I had a jump on the other new students. I did very well that first quarter getting all A's except for a two unit course in slide rule use.

I have always liked chemistry and usually did well in it. Freshman engineering chemistry was a large class of about 300 to 400 students and we met in a large auditorium. Lab classes were also scheduled and those classes were small, maybe 25 students. At the first class meeting, the professor said, "Look around, 2/3s of you will be gone before finals in the spring quarter". I did not believe it, but he was right. The San Jose State Engineering department used that chemistry course to weed out engineering students from the Engineering program.

After getting several high grades in the first quarter midterms, I was approached by a secretarial type lady from the athletics department that asked me if I would be willing to tutor other students in my class that were having trouble, these were football players. I said sure. That became a fun project for me. I would just drill those men over and over in chemistry questions that I thought might be asked on the exams. That professor had an interesting way of giving tests. The tests were all multiple choice where one filled in with a special dark pencil the answers to a multiple choice question on a test sheet form. The answers were then read and scored by some special kind of machine. His wrinkle was that more than one answer could be correct. He gave 2 points for a correct answer and a minus 1 point for every incorrect answer. There were five possible answers to each question. So if one thought that at least two answers were correct, if one filled in all five answers, one at least got 4 points for the correct answers and lost 3 points for the incorrect answers for a net gain of one. I taught those boys that if they had no idea what the answer to the test question was, to fill in all the answers, since then if they were lucky and the question had more than one answer they at least got 1 point, but if they were unlucky and the question had only one answer they received 2 points for the correct answer and lost 4 points for the incorrect answers for a net loss of 2 points. Of course if they filled in nothing they received no points either way.

Every quarter the same thing happened. Those players would flunk the first midterm and I would have another job teaching them chemistry. It got to be fun. They even invited me to their fraternity parties. That became a rather sad experience for me, however, as that was the first time I encountered girls so drunk they did not know what they were doing. I found it rather sad and repulsive.

I got my first A+ in that chemistry class. Teaching those players chemistry taught me even more chemistry, and I constantly got the highest grade on tests in the class, even though it was a rather large class.

The next summer, the summer of 1954, I again enrolled in the six week summer session with Neal. I had taken the full bore math load all during my freshman year and got all A's in math so I had completed all my calculus requirements. I was then able to take a class in Intermediate calculus, English, and American constitution to complete some of my liberal arts requirements. This gave me a big jump over all the other Engineering students as I was way ahead of most in math preparation. English classes always gave me a lot of trouble and I usually got a C for my efforts. Taking summer session class made a lot of sense as it was tough to get a cannery job before the fruit harvest started.

After the six week session ended I needed a job. I answered an ad for a dishwasher at a cannery cafeteria. I operated a dish washing machine. I lasted one night. The boss did not like my performance as I did not get the washed dishes to the new stack in the time that he thought it ought to take.

But I had learned the ropes on the cannery operation. At the change in shift about midnight, the straw bosses would go out to where the prospective types looking for jobs were standing just outside the cannery gate. After several nights, I soon perceived that he was hiring the biggest people. Since I was surrounded by a crowd of Mexicans, and they are a little shorter than most on the average, I stood on my tiptoes and got hired.

I soon regretted that as I was given a job of dumping 60 pound boxes of peaches on a conveyer belt. That was real work and I would go home exhausted. Then an automatic machine that could dump a whole stack of peach boxes showed up. I was then given the job of stacking empty boxes on a box pallet as they came down a roller shoot. I would stack 4 boxes at a time. That really developed muscles in my wrists. I still have them today.

When peach dumping and box stacking was taken over by machines I was given a job on a pear sorting machine. That was a lot easier job. There was a crew of about six that operated the machine. Soon the boys operating the machine understood that once we had sorted all the available pears that needed to be sorted, we were sent home. Of course, that resulted in less pay as we had then worked less than a full shift of 8 hours and no overtime. Soon the boys slowed down the machine so that no matter how many pears we had to sort it took almost a full 8 hours to do it.

Very fortunately, after a week or so of this activity, one night a straw boss came out and got me and took me to help him run the whole bank of conveyers and dumpers that provided peaches to the whole cannery. The next night all the boys on the pear machine got laid off. The conveyers fed about 100 women running about 100 peach machines. The straw boss said that he did not care how big a mess I made of peaches all over the plant floor, the object was to never let any woman run out of peaches. I loved that job. It was really complicated. I had control over maybe 30 electrical switches that turned on and off the conveyers and other machines that controlled the peaches coming into the plant and feeding all the peach machines. Timing was important, so anticipating when to shut things off just before the peaches dumped all over the floor of the plant was the key to the job. After a night or two I had it down pat and stood and watched the 100 women work like very speedy honey bees from my platform above the plant floor. The ladies would take peaches off each little conveyer belt to their machine and put each peach on a little spinning pivot so that it would go through the machine, without cutting the woman's hand off, removing the pit and cutting the peach in half and putting it on another conveyer belt so the peaches could be put into a can. I loved it.

They kept me on way into October when there was hardly anybody working in the plant. I was going to classes during the day and working the night shift from midnight to 8 am. After a few weeks of that, and what I thought was an important Friday night football game which I wanted to see, I called in and quit. That indeed was a fine, fun cannery job. I had to join the teamsters union. I still have my old union card.

The sophomore year at San Jose State was a downhill run academically. I started to play on two intermural basketball teams, so I was playing basketball four nights a week. I also took a stronger interest in skiing and went skiing in the Sierra Nevada Mountains almost every weekend after Thanksgiving Day. My grades went from an A average to a B average. I also got a job grading and correcting math papers for the math department. That seemed an easy job for the amount of work I had to do and the money I made. I have always enjoyed math.

Because I attended two years of six week summer school, I received upper division status during the winter quarter. I was invited to join the San Jose State Honor Society because of my high academic success. The society was called Tau Delta Phi as near as I can recall. It was limited to men and had possession of the Campus Tower. From the upper story of the main classroom building was a door to the tower. The Tower had three floors. As I recall the first floor was sort of a study and snack area, the next floor was a recreation area and the third floor was a meeting room. The campus bell type structure was above that. Women were not allowed above the first floor.

The society had an interesting and complicated initiation ceremony. The first part of the night was spent in psychological hazing with members asking the initiates questions and telling us how dumb and stupid we were. Then we were asked to walk the plank. We were told we did not have to walk the plank but that no initiate ever had ever refused to walk the plank.

About a week before the initiation ceremony a long plank was extended from the top of the Tower out into the area above the main plaza of the campus. Thus the plank hung at least five stories above the plaza and was a very imposing and intimidating sight. On the night of the ceremony we initiates were run around and confused so that when it became my turn to walk the plank and sit down in a chair on the end of the plank, I fully believed I was walking out over the main campus plaza. In fact the plank was rather put out over the back of the Tower so that if an initiate fell he would fall into a net about 10 feet above the roof of the main building below. It took a lot of courage to walk out into midair and feel the edges of the plank with my feet. I was tightly blindfolded so could not see anything. I heard in the distance the sounds of traffic on the streets of San Jose. I knew I was really walking the plank out above shear space. I took my time and made out to the end and sat down in the chair and returned to much congratulation from my handlers.

Then I was dumped somewhere in the Santa Cruz Mountains and told to walk home. I soon had my blindfolds off and discovered some other initiates wandering around in the woods. We soon discovered a barbeque type picnic feast in the woods where the other initiates were discovering each other and we enjoyed congratulations and being welcomed into Tau Delta Phi by the old members.

As I recall the ceremony I sometimes wonder what the purpose of it all was. In hindsight it created a bonding among the members. The psychological hazing and demonstration of courage had its own effect. The Society was intended to be one of service to the college, to the administration of the college, and sometimes we were given sundry projects to perform for the college. It turned out to be a very fine group of fine young men enjoying each other. I was put in touch with other outstanding students at the college and so established friendships among the best students.

I then had the pleasure of initiating some of my San Jose High School friends into the organization in the spring quarter as they had not obtained upper division status as quickly as I had. In the spring I was elected secretary of the organization. The established pattern was to write the meeting minutes as humorously as possible. One meeting when I was secretary a motion was made where someone included the words, "supposedly intelligent", members of the fraternity. An amendment motion was made to strike the word supposedly. It carried and I wrote the motion down quite humorously, and everybody enjoyed a great laugh at the next meeting when the minutes were read. That was the nature of the organization. We had lots of intellectual fun and enjoyed each other.

A fellow student from Westwood where my brother Neal taught, Carl Sunquist, lived across the street from my family on 12th Street. We became friends and then duck hunted together. He suggested a good summer job was to work for the State of California as an Engineering Aid for the Department of Highways. All one had to do to get a job was pass a test. I soon passed the test and went to work in June for the Division of Highways in District Two, located in Redding, California. I chose Redding because it was near Westwood where my brother Neal lived and near lots of good trout fishing places.

I drove my old car a 1939 Packard Coup to Redding went into the District Office there and went to work. They sent me up to what is now highway Interstate Five just above Shasta Lake formed by Shasta Dam. The project was to build a four lane road about 7 miles long from just above the Lake towards the town of Dunsmire. I drove up to the project and walked into the State Project Engineers office and he gave me the job of inspecting the concrete batch plant the Road Contractor had built to provide concrete for the bridges and culvert structures on the project. A State Engineer who was at the site where the cement mix was being poured would send me notes at the batch plant as to increase or decrease the amount of water in the batch of cement. Concrete is stronger if less water is used, but the stuff will not come out of the mixer truck if not enough water is used. So the water content is sort of a balance, and needs to be guessed at the plant as a little water is usually added at the pour site too.

The contractor guy running the plant went by the name of "Tiger". He called everybody Tiger and everybody called him Tiger. He was a very hard working contractor type who managed his men well. I was just a kid, of course, and stood around watching everybody work.

The State Highway Project Engineer was very unhappy with the Contractor as he figured the Contractor was constantly trying to rip off the State of California. That was probably true. The State Project Engineer especially despised the concrete batch plant where I was working as the contractor just could not get enough concrete mix out of it in order to pour the structures quick enough. After watching a while, a few weeks, or so, I took Tiger aside and told him not to tell anybody what I was going to tell him, but laid out for him a method where he could increase the output of the plant. He liked the idea and he soon implemented it. It worked. We more than doubled the output of the plant. The project Engineer did not really believe it that that plant could put out all that concrete, and Tiger was completely overjoyed. From then on I was his complete buddy and he supplied me with everything he thought I needed including beer and snacks and lunch at the local eatery.

I spent the whole summer watching that batch plant. I soon learned to guess how wet the sand was that was being used by just looking at it and increased or decreased the amount of water to be added to the truck based on my guess. Notes from the site Engineer soon trickled to a minimum.

I rented a room in a motel near the north end of the project. The motel owner just hated the State of California and was forever coming up with schemes which would involve me and rip off the State of California. He would suggest things like increasing the amount of the motel room rent and we split the difference. He must have had a new scheme a week.

One evening I was practicing my archery skills behind the motel as I intended to hunt deer with the bow and arrow. The sound of the arrows hitting the target must have stirred up one of the largest bucks I have ever seen as a form like a shadow emerged from the forest behind my target in the shape of a huge mule deer. The deer season was closed in that area so I just watched it. When I told the motel owner about it later he first did not believe my story as he had never seen a buck around there. He then thoroughly chewed me out for not putting an arrow into it. He said he could have used the meat and would have fed me lots of meals. That motel owner was constantly on my case with some new idea on how to rip off the State. The State must have really done him dirt.

Another young Junior Engineer like me was on the project and the boss Project Engineer allowed us to camp out with no electricity in one of the old houses the State had bought where the highway eventually was to go. We were on full expenses the first month of the project and had lived in the motel. After that we were on per diem so in order to save money for college we camped out.

I figured we needed some meat to eat so one evening I obtained some sidehill salmon behind the place by putting a hole in the heart of a young doe with my trusty 25-35. She was delicious. The other kid was appalled that I would do something illegal like that; he came from an upper class

79

family, but he ate the meat anyway. After all I needed to save my money for college, and he was a poor student also trying to stretch his pennies.

It was there I had the closest call of my life in an automobile. The State had provided me with a Ford pickup. I usually drove to Dunsmire for supplies. One evening I was driving to Dunsmire in the pickup, as why should I use my own gas when I can use the States? Maybe some of the attitude of the motel owner had rubbed off on me. Highway 99 was a very busy two lane highway. There seemed always to be people who drive much slower than everybody else on that highway.

I approached a long tangent with room to pass a string of cars. Ahead of me maybe ¼ mile or so another car moved out to pass. I assumed that driver could see ahead and had lots of clearance to pass. Just I was passing a long truck that car dives back into the right lane. There dead ahead of me is an oncoming truck. I and that truck are both going about 60 mph and there is no way to go except for a big crash. I had less than a second to react so I dove right into the brush on the left hand side of the road just missing that truck. Again the Lord Jesus was watching over me. I disappeared into this thick high brush and came to a stop just petrified. It took me 15 minutes to get control of my shaking. Very fortunately, after I had got out and looked around a bit I saw I could get that State truck backed down hill out of that brush. The pickup did not seem to be damaged much. It was rather beat up anyway, probably the oldest State truck on that job site, and so the new dents were not too obvious. That experience made me into a much more careful driver. The lesson to be learned is never make assumptions about other drivers. You never know what other people will do or what motivates them or maybe they are half asleep.

One evening as we were sitting on the deck of the house talking, we heard a big crash and a big splash and looked out on the highway just below us and saw where a tanker trailer of a gasoline truck had capsized and spilled 5000 gallons of gasoline all over the highway. We both ran down there, I went one way to stop traffic and he went the other. The truck driver just sat there in his truck white as a sheet, petrified, and speechless. I understand now that God intervened on my behalf to cause that gasoline not to explode. It seems incredible it did not catch fire. Gasoline was running down the highway ditches and all over the highway. The trailer had flipped over and must have scraped down the highway but did not cause any sparks to set the whole thing on fire. If it had caught fire we both would have been completely fried in a ball of fire for sure, the more so since we were above the highway.

The relating of this story of my life gets me to reflecting about God's sovereignty and free will. I have come to some conclusions after a lifetime of studying physics and reflecting on life. The basic laws that govern the universe are Einstein Relativity, Quantum Mechanics, and something probably close to what is called the Standard Model governing the four forces present in the universe. The nature of the particles and energy that make up the universe, as we little understand it, gives to us vast numbers of statistical fluctuations of energy particles. I have concluded that God integrates over this vast statistical soup of particles and energy, and makes observable things happen. God makes everything happen that does happen. Nothing is deterministic. God gets the sun up every morning. The sun rising is not the result of some deterministic law of physics, but God Himself integrating over the statistical random fluctuations of the grand canonical soup of the wave particles that make up the universe, and gets the sun up.

Thus there is a profound mystery of my complete free will, subject to the limits of time and space, and God's sovereignty, and the fact that God determines everything. So into my life God watches. Not one hair of my head will fall without the will of God. This is a profound mystery integrated into my freewill, but it is true. So God Himself delivered me from the fireball that in the normal course of events should have enveloped me and my housemate and sent us into eternity.

The cops showed up, and it took the highway maintenance people three hours to put the highway in condition for use again. Traffic was backed up for miles and miles as this was highway 99, eventually to be Interstate Five, and the main highway from California to Oregon and it carried lots of traffic.

I spent a lot of the evenings and most of the week ends that year fishing for trout. There were lots of high mountain lakes I could hike into in that area and catch trout. I fished the Sacramento River once in a while but did not have much success. One evening there I ran into an old Indian. He showed me his creel and I could hardly believe it. It was full of very large brown trout. Catching large brown trout is not easy and takes lots of skill. That just fired me up to work a lot harder at trying to catch trout.

One weekend I decided to go home to San Jose. In Redding I picked up a hitchhiker. My brother Howard had told me never to drive that old 39 Packard over 50 miles per hour as it would throw a rod. Well it is a long way from Redding to San Jose so soon the speedometer would go to 51 then 52, then 53 and so on. Just out of Red Bluff going over the top of a little hill, sure enough a rod blew. It made a lot of racket at five miles an hour but I very slowly idled my way into Red Bluff. I found an old repair shop and the owner agreed to fix it and have it ready by Monday.

Now both the hitchhiker and I were out on the highway hitchhiking. Nobody picked us up so we split, me walking down the road to out of town a little ways. After a while I was picked up and my hitchhiker had been also picked up by the same driver. The driver was suspicious of us as we knew each other but after we explained the situation he calmed down. He would not indicate where he was going but I said I was headed to San Jose. I fell asleep and the first thing I knew we were in Oakland. I walked to the bus depot and caught a bus for San Jose. Somehow I had caught the local bus as it made dozens of stops and I arrived in San Jose after dawn. I walked home to 12th Street much to the joy and greeting of my mother.

My brother Howard, always helpful, said he knew a guy with a two door 48 Chevy sedan for sale, so soon I had another car, I believe for $300. The Packard had cost me $50. Sunday afternoon he went with me to Red Bluff where Howard paid the repairman, I believe $37, and Howard drove the Packard back to San Jose. Eventually my dad ended up with that Packard. If you did not drive it over 30 miles per hour it was ok. I could hear that car coming two blocks away as the rods rattled and made lots of noise.

UNIVERSITY OF CALIFORNIA

The previous spring I had done some reflecting. My grades had dropped off do to my goofing off and I reflected on my education. San Jose State was changing to a semester system rather than a quarter system in the fall so this would be a good time to change colleges if I wanted to. I applied for transfer to both Stanford University and the University of California at Berkeley. I got accepted to both places and into the College of Engineering at Berkeley.

Thus come fall I worked right on into the beginning of the semester to make as much money as I could and showed up at Berkeley a week late. I registered for classes and walked down Bancroft Avenue looking for a place to live. I stopped at the first rooming house I came too and talked to Ma Furman. We made a deal for room and board.

Ma was Jewish and we received lots of very interesting Jewish food. I liked it. Another kid was there who also came from San Jose. We got to playing chess at dinnertime sitting across the dinner table from each other with his tiny little chess board between us. He beat me every time for the first month or so. He was an arrogant type and told me everything I did wrong and made fun of it. Soon he had taught me everything he knew and I started to beat him. Soon I won every time. After a month or so of that we quit playing chess.

At my exit interview with the State Highway department I was asked what I liked least about the job. After thinking for a moment my answer was I did like all the dirt. That got me to thinking about dirt and what I wanted to do the rest of my life. I concluded I really did not like dirt so when I got to Berkeley I changed my major. In typical fashion as I thought about it I thought that I might as well try the most difficult major there is and if I could not hack it I would scale down a bit. That major turned out to be Engineering Physics. Thus I embarked on deep studies of a theoretical nature as that major turned out to a major in Physics while I was enrolled in the College of Engineering. Therefore, I had to take all the tough Engineering courses plus take all the high powered theoretical Physics courses in the Physics Department in the College of Letters and Science, among some of the toughest, smartest, students around, as Physics at Berkeley was one of the highest ranked Physics Departments in the world.

Well I got down to work but it was tough and I had a hard time of it. Very fortunately, again by a provision of God, I changed living quarters. I had been going to the Alameda Christian Reformed Church on Sundays when I did not travel home to San Jose. My aunt and uncle lived there with their two daughters. My cousin Geraldine was a little younger than me and her sister Evelyn maybe about four years younger. Geraldine was a very cute little girl back in the days at the Sunnyvale Ranch and was known there as the Alameda Cream Puff. Evelyn was a beautiful girl with a lovely kind, friendly disposition. She, unfortunately, later died young, a victim of breast cancer, leaving a husband and two little girls. I was integrated into the Alameda young people's scene by this neat family.

The Alameda Church had a real nice ministry where service men serving on the Naval Base and elsewhere were invited to various homes on Sunday for a major meal and fellowship. College students were included in this ministry. Thus I became involved in this ministry and benefited from the beautiful hospitality. There I met Vern Ehlers. Vern was a first year graduate student in Physics. Vern was living at the International House in Berkeley. International House primarily served graduate students from all over the world but served a few American citizen students. Vern's roommate moved out and he suggested I move in. Even though I was an undergraduate, the I House accepted me and I moved in. That was one of the best things that ever happened to me in my academic career. Vern was a superb roommate. He is very friendly, studied hard, and did not goof around at all. I soon adapted his habits and my grades rapidly improved.

Vern is a very remarkable person. His father was a clergyman, and Vern had committed himself to a very righteous moral outlook on life. He was a sickly child so his mother home schooled him when nobody else knew that such a thing as home school existed. His mother worked him really hard; he was very intelligent so he became a rather unique person in my life as most highly intelligent people I have met in my life were very lazy. They become lazy because life is very easy for them and they do not need to work hard. Vern was different. He worked hard, was highly intelligent, and a very highly moral person. That combination made him an outstanding human, and a very outstanding student. He eventually became a United States Congressman from Grand Rapids, Michigan, at the time the only PhD Physicist in Congress. He was first elected to Congress in the spring of 1994 in a special election. The Republicans took over the House of Representatives in 1995 and Vern worked closely with Newt Gingrich, the Speaker, computerizing the business of the House of Representatives.

After a good junior year at Berkeley I was ready for another year working for the California Division of Highways. When I laid out my course requirements to graduate in the spring of 1957 I concluded I needed one more course than I would be allowed to take in any semester in the normal course of events. Thus I found a correspondence course I could take that would work and I could do it in the summer. It was an upper division course in Physical Chemistry. So I signed up for it hoping I could complete it during the summer while working for the State of California. Once I got to Redding I did the first lesson and got a D grade. Working even harder on the second lesson I got a C. This was not going to work, so I went back to trout fishing on the weekends, and then fishing all of the rest of my spare time too.

I had another great summer. I was placed on a surveying crew and we went all over northern California staying in motels on full expenses so I got to save all my earnings for going to school. The survey crew mainly ran what are called P lines, or preliminary routes for sections of proposed new highways. We were in places like Happy Camp on the Klamath River, the area around Bebier, the Trinity Mountains, and such. It was a very good summer as I fished lots and lots of fun creeks, lakes, and rivers, always by myself as none of my fellow crew members had much interest in fishing, and they would go home on weekends anyway, as I was the only summer intern employee on the crew.

Back in Berkeley for the fall semester, I still did not get back to that correspondence course. Come spring I was in panic mode as I needed that correspondence course to graduate. I was already carrying the maximum course load permitted by the University so I could not add another course. I resolved that I would do a lesson each Saturday morning. When I completed the lesson I would allow myself to go to the Cal rugby game in Memorial Stadium. This was sufficient motivation to get me to concentrated work. It worked. Soon I was cranking out a lesson every Saturday and getting an A on every lesson. When I got the lessons all done I signed up for the final exam, a three hour thing in the Chemistry Building. I got an A and then got an A for the course. That just goes to show what being really motivated will do.

I received a simply marvelous education from the University of California. I had taken all the tough theoretical inclined physics courses plus an engineering curriculum that included an astounding diversity of classes, from control systems, Betatron and Cyclotron design, heat transfer, structures engineering, materials science characteristics, ditches and pipe design, and what not else. It was simply a huge diversity of engineering plus the theoretical physics. That major required very, very few liberal arts courses. That was fine with me. The only liberal arts course I took at Berkeley was a year of German in which by working like a dog I only got a B. In that spring of 1957 I received my BS in Engineering Physics, but since I figured it was a waste of my time, I did not go to my graduation ceremony.

The college of Engineering had suggested I do graduate work. That got me to thinking. I eventually applied to the Physic department in the College of Letters and Science for graduate status. I figured graduate work might be a possibility and I wanted to keep my options open. I had received a really nice offer of a job at the Lawrence Radiation Laboratory in Livermore. The Livermore Lab had an extremely high reputation for applied physics so they interested me a lot so I accepted their offer of employment.

The work would be very, very secret. In hindsight it was hydrogen bomb design. My coursework in physics and nuclear reactor engineering must have really interested them. To work there I needed what was called a Q clearance. I filled out a huge form about everything I ever did plus every organization I had ever been a member of. The form was really huge. The FBI investigated everything I ever did. They even talked to my old High School teachers in Mendocino. Getting the clearance would take three months, so to keep me occupied I was given the task of building an alpha particle counter till I got my clearance.

I pretty much worked by myself with no supervision. I played penuche every lunch hour with the lab workers. I learned to braze brass to make my own vacuum type little counters. It kept me occupied. Sometime toward the end of July I got the Asian flu. It was going around, and there was an epidemic of it. I caught it and was very sick, one of the worst debilitating sicknesses of my life. I ran a very high fever for days and days. I just lie in bed with nothing to eat and water only to drink in the hot summer of Livermore. Vern Ehlers, who also had a job there, and I had rented a very simple apartment, and he checked on me once in a while to see if I was still alive.

I still remember very clearly that after I passed the crisis and the fever broke, I went into downtown Livermore to buy a meal. Man oh man was that meal good. I can still picture it in my mind today. It felt really great to be alive.

My life changed very radically that summer. Vern and I one day in the spring had discussed the possibility that maybe we ought to find a wife. I don't remember who suggested it but the idea came up that there are a lot of nice Christian Reformed girls in Ripon near Modesto. In 2008 I wrote a note to Vern to help him celebrate his 50th wedding anniversary. It is as follows:

> Vern, I still remember long conversations we had together at the I House in Berkeley about young ladies and where they could be found, and that Ripon, California was a good place to look. Well, the rest is history. As you remember we indeed traveled periodically to Ripon, and we both found very lovely young Christian ladies to be our wives. Wow! What a blessing. Indeed the Lord is good.

> And think of it, about a year later we both were married to lovely Ripon girls and now after 50 years, children, grandchildren, and yes, Geneva and I have 3 greats too.

> Vern, I take this opportunity to thank you for your most excellent example to me of very high personal integrity, and very hard working studious demeanor which very positively influenced me in my

academic pursuits. As a roommate you were quintessentially superb. Thanks Vern.

And yes, memories too, of a very out of character Vern, watering the crowd on Bancroft Avenue with the I House fifth floor fire hose on the day of that infamous Cal riot called, "The Great Panty Raid". My ears still titillate with the soft murmuring moan of that doused crowd yet engaged in that great water fight.

Ah, memories are such pleasant things.
May the Lord continue to bless you and Jo.
Jerry

Geneva too sends her greetings and congratulations to you and Jo.

So back to the narrative. About that time I had joined the Christian Reformed Church in Alameda. I also had an uncle, aunt, and cousins in Ripon. So off to Ripon we went to look around. My cousin Betty Lou VanSpronsen fixed me up with one of her friends who was a senior in High School. Vern found a dental assistant. So we would go to Ripon once in a while on weekends to date these young ladies.

My dating with the girl who was a friend of my cousin Betty Lou fell apart for some reason. My grandfather Cornelius VanSpronsen then passed away about the first week in June. So I went to Ripon for the weekend to attend the funeral which would be on Monday. I was also to be one of the pallbearers. Sunday night I attended the Immanuel Christian Reformed Church, the one I usually went to when I went to Ripon. The custom there was that the young men and young women would gather in respective large circles or maybe several circles and talk and visit after the evening service. After a while some boys would wander over to the girls' circles and talk to the girls. Many a date got started this way. Well I wandered over to a circle where a girl was that had turned me down before so it took a little courage to maybe try to ask her out again. While talking to the girls in that circle I noticed there a young lady by the name of Geneva who seemed much more interested in me than any of the other girls in the circle. I asked her out for a coke or such, I don't remember what. We drove to Modesto and dragged 10th street. That was something I normally thought very little of doing, but for that evening it seemed appropriate. Well that started a very, very lovely relationship, and Geneva became my wife, but that is told in another chapter.

It turned out I knew Geneva a little bit as she had once come with my cousin Bob Van Spronsen and his parents to visit my parents in San Jose when I worked for the cannery in 1954. Also I had been recruited a few times to go along with a group of young people to sing for the insane asylum inmates in Stockton by a lay preacher type who went to preach to the inmates at the asylum. We would stop at Geneva's parents' house in Stockton to pick her up as she was the group's piano player. She knew a lot about me as she and the other girl I had dated were friends and the other girl talked a lot about me to Geneva.

Come September with the start of College I reflected a bit and wondered if I would really like working at the Lawrence Radiation Laboratory on Hydrogen Bombs. I had not met any mentors I liked and I seemed to have been forgotten in the time I was waiting for my clearance. There is nothing very esoteric about making alpha particle counters. Perhaps the flu also had a negative impact. I decided to go to graduate school at Cal and seek a PhD in Physics.

My room was still available with Vern at the I House. I started classwork. Geneva and I married on November 23, 1957. In the spring there were what are called the preliminary exams for the PhD. The graduate school in Physics was a rather large graduate school as schools go with as I recall maybe 80 students taking the preliminary exam. The nature of the thing was that the upper 2/3 of the test takers passed the written exam, the rest usually tried to take it again. I ended up about in the middle of the test score distribution so I passed. Next was the oral preliminary exam. I faced three professors and they asked me technical questions. One is highly nervous in these situations. One of the questions they asked me was what is the power required to operate a conveyer belt carrying sand. That was easy. Then what was the energy of the sand coming off the conveyer belt. That was easy too, but the energy of the sand coming off the belt is half the energy put into the belt to carry the sand. They asked me, "What happened to the other half of the energy". You can understand that that is rather befuddling if you have not ever thought about conveyer belts before.

I stammered around and confessed I did not know. The answer was it went into friction heat. After a few more questions they advised me to either go for a masters degree or take the oral test again next semester.

Somehow I had misunderstood the course requirements for a masters degree so that one of the courses I had taken did not count toward the masters Degree requirements, so I would not get the degree after the first year in Graduate School. But then in the beginning I did not plan to finish with a Masters Degree so I was not careful about what courses I took.

Come June Geneva and I went to Stockton to be with her folks. I needed a job so I must have seen an ad or otherwise came to interview with an engineering company that made tomato paste machines. Tomatoes were dumped into one end of the plant and paste came out the other. I interviewed them and they hired me on the spot. They gave me the job of making engineering pipe drawings of paste plants. I sat at a drafting board most of the day and made drawings of pipes, heat exchangers, condensers, pumps, motors, and more sundry pipes for the manufacturing shop and sub-contractors to fabricate and integrate these parts into paste plants.

The key to making a tomato paste plant work is a feedback control system. They were using a radioactive source to measure the density of the paste, and fed that information back into the amount of heat and pressure to be applied to the tomato mixture as it flowed through the plant. I understood feedback control systems from some of the engineering course I had taken, so the operation of the plant interested me. Unfortunately, the owner of the company and his number one assistant who was not a graduate engineer and was not much older than I was, were very, very secretive about how the plants worked. That frustrated me and I received very little mentoring.

Come fall given these frustrations, we went back to Berkeley to get my masters degree with our little son Sheridan who was born on September 9, 1958. My folks encouraged me a lot in this and my mother promised me some money for it as now that I was a father and did not expect Geneva to work. Soon I was engaged in Physics classes. I was required to take another oral exam to receive my masters degree; again some tough questions before three professors. This time I was a lot more relaxed and sailed through all their questions flawlessly. They suggested I continue with the PhD program.

As usual, even though I only needed three units of coursework for the masters, I instead took 9 units, I suppose for the fun of it, so I was taking a class in Statistical Mechanics. Come final time when I sat down to do the three hour final, I realized I did not understand one question of the 10 questions on the exam. It was a tough course and I had had trouble with the work problems and midterms, but this was one of those defining moments in my life. My thinking at the time was that I had reached up into the academic pursuit ladder as far as I probably was capable of. Psychologically I was finished with college. I got a C in that course which is essentially a failure in a graduate course but I had enough A's in other courses so I signed up to receive my Masters degree in Physics. I received that in January of 1959 and went to gainful work where one is paid to work. Again I skipped the graduating ceremonies.

The Gerald Paul Kooyers and Geneva Helene Westra Kooyers family when they moved to Idaho in 1980.

Left to right: Lucinda Jane, Geneva, Kimberly Joy, Gerald, Brenda Sue, Sheridan Clark, Susanne Rachelle, Crystal Jean

FOUR

FAMILY

OUR HONEYMOON

Our honeymoon was a very memorable event, as all of you dear readers would expect. However, I will explain the nature of it so as to pass on some learned wisdom to you. Let me start with how I first met Geneva.

I was a very poor student at the University of California in Berkeley. I met and courted Geneva during the summer of 1957. The initial bonding meeting occurred on the day before my Grandfather Cornelius Van Spronsen's funeral. I was to be a pallbearer the next day so I was in Ripon, California.

At the evening service of the Immanuel Christian Reformed Church in Ripon, where the funeral of my grandfather was to take place the next day, the culture in those days was that young people stood around and talked on the church lawn after the service. After most of the people had left, the boys would wander over to the girls, engage in conversation, and many a date would start here. There was a young lady, her name has long been forgotten, and I thought I had enough courage to ask for a date one more time. You young ladies who are reading this should understand that young men have very fragile masculine egos, and to be turned down for a date is very humiliating. Therefore, it takes great courage to stir up enough juice to try again. I walked up to a group of girls and soon perceived that Geneva, who was also in the group, was much more interested in me than any of the other girls standing around. Soon everybody else left and I invited her out for a ride and a Coke.

In those days the THING TO DO was to drag 10th street in Modesto. (Later this got integrated into a movie, I think named, "American Graffiti".) Well after evening church service we proceeded to 10th street, dragged a while, and had a coke and that was the beginning. I had thought that dragging 10th street was extremely stupid, and normally did not do it, but in this case it started a very, very, beautiful marriage relationship which only God could have put together.

We started to date at least three times a week and our courtship went very, very, fast. We were ready for marriage, were very compatible, of the same roots, believed in the same God, and held the same values. I would see Geneva on Wednesday usually at Catechism, as she still seemed to be attending Catechism even though she had already joined the Christian Reformed Church, and then would see her Friday night for a date. I left after the date, drove to the Sierra Nevada Mountains, camped for the night sleeping on the ground in my wool blanket as I was too poor to even afford a sleeping bag, and fished a favorite or perhaps explored a new trout stream on Saturday. I would be back in time to take Geneva out to dinner and a date on Saturday night. Geneva's folks after a while would invite me to stay on Saturday night, and I would sleep in Geneva's younger brother Earl's bed with Earl! On Sunday, of course, I went to Church with Geneva and her Family, and was invited to dinner with her family. Several times I went with Geneva and a group of people from the Christian Reformed Church who went to the Insane Asylum in Stockton to conduct a church service for the insane. They needed Geneva to play the piano. We would sing and pray with the insane, and a lay preacher would preach to the insane. Believe it or not, I enjoyed this and saw it as a service to God. After a Sunday night date after Church with Geneva, I would return home to Livermore to an apartment I shared with my college roommate, Vern Ehlers. (Vern eventually became a Congressman from Grand Rapids Michigan, more about that somewhere else in these memoirs).

I had taken a job about the middle of June at the Lawrence Radiation Laboratory in Livermore. Until I got my "Q" security clearance, I worked on making an alpha particle counter for the Laboratory. Since I was destined to be a Hydrogen Bomb Engineering type if I continued in this job, the alpha particle counter did not excite me all that much, but I learned a lot about lab work and making and brazing brass together to make vacuum type alpha particle counters.

That summer I got the Asian flu. I was extremely sick, got very debilitated, a very high fever, but survived. I had no one to look after me so went through the whole process by myself. I remember after I finally passed the crisis, I went to town to get some food. After many days of sickness in bed with a high fever and with no food, this meal is still the most memorable meal of my lifetime. I still remember it. It seemed very great to be alive and to have survived the flu.

Geneva and I discussed marriage and she asked me to ask her father. This seemed like a superfluous thing to do, but I understood it and, of course, this was very appropriate and the right thing to do. Clarence Westra's comment was, "You are a very fast worker." He said yes and we were engaged. We went out to dinner with her folks and there announced our engagement. We had chosen a ring set together. I do not remember where I got the money, maybe from my first paycheck working at the Rad Lab.

At the end of the summer I decided that maybe I did not really want to become a Hydrogen Bomb Engineer, and decided to return to Cal for graduate studies. Both the Physics Department in the College of Letters and Science, and the College of Engineering had offered me graduate student status, so I returned to Berkeley in September, and took up graduate studies in physics. The program was designed for a Ph.D. in physics.

The time spent away from Geneva seemed tough. I could only see her on the week end and then not every week. We planned our marriage for the Saturday before Thanksgiving Day so we could spend our honeymoon somewhere during the Thanksgiving Day holiday when there was no school. I soon became immersed in my studies and Geneva in planning the wedding.

We were married on Saturday November 23, 1957. My brother Neal was the best man, my brother Gordon, the second, and my brother Howard the usher. Geneva's friend Theresa was the maid of honor and her sister Tracy the second. All went very well and we managed to avoid tragedy in our get-a-way from the reception. The culture in those days was to car chase the bride and groom around and follow them. Therefore, all these chasers had to be ditched. This is not as simple as it might seem. It involved high speed races down county roads, through orchards, along ditch banks, high speed sliding turns, etc. etc. (A lot like the TV show, "The Dukes of Hazard", but this was long before that show was even thought of) We all ought to be glad our culture doesn't do this anymore. It was all great fun, and necessary if we were to have a peaceful time together, yet in hindsight was very dangerous.

Anyway, Geneva's cousin Fred was our driver and he was very good. It was very exciting and involved a very good run through the country side. (It was sort of like you now see in the movies) The cops stopped some of those who were trying to follow us, and that helped us to get away. We made it, caught up with Geneva's Car which we had hid somewhere and made a clean getaway. I had rented an apartment in Berkeley for us to live in and had told nobody where it was so we went to our apartment and spent the weekend in our new home at peace and nobody found us.

I went to school the next three days and we left for our honeymoon about noon on Wednesday. It was difficult for me to plan something as I was without money so I had decided to show Geneva the place where I had spent my growing up years, Mendocino. This was before Mendocino had become a tourist trap. It was even more run down and dilapidated then when I lived there. We found a really old musty, terrible motel (it just collapsed into ruins a few years after we stayed there and disappeared) that was very cheap and stayed there Wednesday night. The next day, Thanksgiving Day, we rented a boat and rowed up Big River and went fishing! Yes fishing! It was cold, windy, although I remember Geneva laying out in the sun at the Old Boom for a while, about 3 1/2 miles up the river. Geneva remembers it as just plain miserable and cold. I don't remember if we caught any fish.

We then drove to Fort Bragg found a really nice motel and had a very, very nice Thanksgiving Feast at a nice restaurant overlooking the Noyo River. It still is very memorable. This seemed so nice in contrast to the misery on Big River that it made our honeymoon a very great success. Friday we continued our trip north through the Redwoods and eventually returned to Berkeley.

FAMILY HISTORY

After our honeymoon Geneva and I settled down in Berkeley, California where I was a graduate student at the University of California. The apartment I had rented before we were married cost $90 a month. Geneva had been working at an insurance company called National Life and Accident in Stockton, California. She had her job transferred to the Oakland office and went to work at $40 a week doing secretarial work and answering the phone.

$90 a month for the apartment was too high and Geneva disliked the electric stove anyway which seemed to burn a lot of food so she searched and found an apartment on Telegraph Avenue about a mile and a half from the campus for $65 a month. It had a small cozy kitchen that looked out into a sunlit airspace, had a nice bathroom with a shower, and one room with a bed which came down out of the wall so it could be put away during the day, and had a window that looked out over Telegraph Avenue. We moved in and I walked about a mile and a half to classes and Geneva drove her car to work in Oakland.

Life was pleasant with me studying away and Geneva working. She then discovered she was pregnant. That was a big surprise. Another couple we had met at the Christian Reformed Church in Walnut Creek where we were going on Sunday, we discovered had rented an apartment in a house a half block away on the nearest side street. Alex Draght was also a graduate student in Physics. Vonnie, his wife, was also working supporting her husband and she discovered she was pregnant about the same time as Geneva did and they commensurate together over this seemingly disruption to their working careers supporting their husband's education. So, it was a great joy to discover we were going to be parents, and this joy was mixed with the sweat of the financial complications thereof.

Alex and Vonnie became great friends of ours. We went to church together, discussed physics together, and anticipated being parents together. Alex somehow acquired a cat, and he trained it to do sundry tricks, after all, one cannot study physics all of the time. I had never seen a cat before that would do tricks so it was interesting and fascinating.

As a young woman just 21 years old Geneva was still tied a little to her family so we journeyed to Stockton every few weeks or so and stayed the week end with her family and usually took over her younger sister's bed, which used to be Geneva's. Her older brother Ralph was married and in the army in San Francisco, but her younger siblings, Earl, Tracy, and Clarence Jr. were still home. Geneva came from a fun loving family with lots of talk and banter, so these times were lots of fun and a relief from college coursework. Her parents had a 160 acre row crop farm with some pasture and her Dad milked a few cows to generate a little cash flow. Her father and I sometimes would fish for Striped Bass in the Delta sloughs and the ship canal from the bank. I do not remember catching anything, but we had very, very nice very long conversations about all the world and church problems and became lovely friends.

Our little son Sheridan showed up on the 9th day of September 1958 at the Stockton, California hospital. We had rented a little house in Stockton. Stockton has very hot summers For an air conditioner it had a huge swamp cooler driven by what seemed to be an airplane engine. The very loud sound it put out drowned out every other sound, but Stockton being the hot steamy place that it is, even all night long, this was indispensable. One night Geneva woke me up in the middle of the night and said the pains are coming. My sister, Marcia, had had lots of false labor for her first little one, Titus, born about a year before, and had told us stories of going to the hospital and then coming back home a few times, so we waited. Come morning the pains were the same so we waited some more and I went to work. I kept in contact by telephone, and Geneva got everything organized in anticipation, and midafternoon she called me and said she was ready. I went home to her and she looked flushed so I knew it was the real thing, and we went to the hospital. Sheridan Clark Kooyers showed up about 7PM. I heard the doctor shout it's a boy through the space above the door to the delivery room. I was overjoyed. Mother and baby were both fine. Sheridan was beautiful.

Sitting at a drawing board all day long making pipe diagrams for the manufacturing operations eventually became a little boring. I decided I had little future there as even though I knew and understood how to make tomato paste machines and understood feedback control systems, the boss did not confide in me or teach me anything of the engineering feedback secrets, so when fall came I decided to go back to Berkeley for more study. My mother had encouraged me by sending me $1000 for at least to get a masters degree. We found an apartment on the same street as Alex and Vonnie and moved in.

Every day after classwork and study, I played with little Sheridan. He was even able to stand up on a couch at four months of age. I only needed to complete one course and pass an oral exam to obtain the masters degree in physics. But as usual I did not want to waste my time so I took three, 3 unit courses. One of those was a physics course in Statistical Mechanics. That was either the most difficult course I had ever encountered or the professor so obscure I understood nothing. It was all about ensembles and grand canonical ensembles interwoven with complicated statistics and statistical distributions. When I sat down to do the final three hour exam there were 10 problems, and I did not understand even one of them. I concluded from that experience that I had studied enough and it was time to find a job.

During the spring of the previous year I had taken the written preliminary exam for the PhD in Physics. My score was in about the middle of my class, and they usually passed the upper 2/3s of the class, so I passed. I had failed the first oral exam for the PhD, so the next semester I elected to take the oral exam for the masters degree, again three professors asking me questions. I was a lot more relaxed and answered all their questions without even a pause as I understood them all. They suggested I continue on with the PhD program, but at that point I had had enough and had a family to support, so I got my masters degree in Physics and left the University of California. I had received a really superb education.

I went to work for Litton Industries in San Carlos, California. Geneva and I settled in at an apartment in Redwood City. Out of my salary of $625 a month we soon paid my mother back the funds she lent me. Come summer we also bought a 58 Ford two door sedan in Stockton for $1000. It had 20,000 miles on it, and the spare tire had never been on the ground.

In the fall Geneva and I started looking at houses as the amount of rent we paid was more than the monthly payment on a home. There is a gradation of the cost of homes as one went down the San Francisco Peninsula towards San Jose. We looked in San Carlos, Redwood City, and Palo Alto. Come

October we bought a brand new 3 bedroom 2 bath home in Santa Clara on Cooper Drive for about $17,500 with a 30 year 4 ¼ % Deed of Trust loan. The same home in Palo Alto was about $25,000. My mother again lent us the down payment of about $1000. We soon paid that back also. The experience of being poor students had made us very frugal so paying back my mother's loans and buying cars and houses were very easy.

On December 30, 1959 Brenda Sue Kooyers arrived. Geneva's calculations said Brenda should arrive about the end of November. She didn't. We had curtailed our traveling in anticipation of her arrival so we were a little frustrated when she did not show. Finally, we just traveled anyway and visited Geneva's parents over Christmas in Stockton. If Brenda showed up before the first of the year she would be a tax deduction for 1959. We did what little we could to encourage it by doing lots of walking and sure enough Brenda showed up on December 30th, 1959. She was born in the San Jose Hospital in east San Jose. I discovered the Doctors entrance so I used it to visit Geneva anytime in the day or night. Geneva's sister Tracy, a high school student at the time, had come back with us from Stockton, after we had been there for Christmas, so she watched over little Sheridan while I visited Geneva or went to work.

We settled in on Cooper Drive and planted lawns and a garden, and poured cement patios, and built a play sand box with the help of my Dad. My Dad loved berry patches as well as I did, so we soon had a real nice boysenberry patch, artichoke plants, corn, beans, and tomatoes. Sheridan loved to play with water, for as soon as he was able to walk around and play outside, he had water hoses watering everything. That frustrated Geneva a little bit so my Dad removed the handles from the water spigots. That frustrated me a little bit as invariably it seemed when I wanted to turn a water hose on, it had no handle on the spigot.

Litton's policy was to let its Engineers go to at least one technical meeting a year. Litton also shut down the plant the first two weeks of July for vacation time. Thus during the end of June of 1960 Geneva and I drove to Seattle to attend the Electron Tube Research Conference at the University of Washington. We then traveled to Victoria, British Columbia on the island hopping ferry and then visited Butchard Gardens with its beautiful flowers. We ferried back to Port Angeles in the USA and traveled back to California along the Pacific Coast. Geneva's mom took care of Sheridan and Brenda while we were gone.

In the 1961 vacation time we traveled with our 58 Ford two door. The first night we camped in Modoc County on a little lake up in the mountains, the second night on Lake Walowa in Oregon, and the third night in Dry Falls Park at Grand Coulee in Washington. We had ferried over the Snake River west of Clarkston, Washington. I recall the water being blue and very pretty, and I could see the bottom all across the river on a cable ferry. I may have fell in love with the Snake and its tributary the Salmon River at that time, as of course, at the time I write this, 49 years later we live on the Salmon River.

We then went into Canada, and the first night we slept in our car as we did not find a campground. That did not work well so from then on I found a good place to camp or rented a motel. That was a turning point in my life as I internally with mental reflection resolved to give up being frugal and to spend money whenever it was required to provide comfort or needs for me or my family.

We traveled the, "Big Bend", highway along the Columbia River, a 200 mile stretch of old gravel road which is now under a huge reservoir on the Columbia River. That was the last year it could be done so we did it, much to Geneva's disgust, and created in her a loathing of dirt dusty roads, especially in not well built old American cars which let the dust creep in through all the cracks.

We made it and wandered some more in Canada and then went to Glacier National park in Montana. We camped on the east side of the park, and one day I hiked back about six miles in to a lake the Glacier Fishing Guide said had some real nice rainbow trout. In Glacier one always thinks about the grizzly bears. Those bears have a very bad reputation of being very dangerous when encountered. I did all the things one is supposed to do to avoid bears and I did not see any. The lake was really beautiful and one could see these very large trout swimming around in the clear water. But they simply would not bite, not on anything I presented to them. Eventually

I hit on the idea of letting a fly sink to the bottom, maybe 15 feet deep, and when a very large trout would swim by, slowly raise the fly from the bottom. It worked. A very large trout took my fly and the fight was on. I landed it and was proud of my success. I hiked back to Geneva and the kids. The next day, as I remember, we drove home to California, driving all night. I loved those kinds of vacations and excursions. Eventually, Geneva did too and we have since enjoyed lots of camping vacations and holidays.

Crystal Jean Kooyers showed up the following April, the 9th of 1962. That summer we went camping with my folks. We camped several nights at Injun Jim Campground on the Feather River in the Feather river Canyon above Oroville. The campground is now under water of the Oroville Lake. Crystal was a baby and Sheridan and Brenda played on the beach by the river. Grandmother, Alice Kooyers, made dams in the river's edge sand beach with Sheridan and Brenda.

I noticed very faint slight flashes of light down in the main stream of water as it entered the very large backwater pool where the kids were playing. I studied the flashes, investigated, and surmised some large trout were feeding below the riffle as the water entered the very large pool. I rigged up my fly rod and made some casts into the riffle from a large rock above the riffle. Sure enough a very large rainbow trout took my fly and the fight was on. I then caught another one, and when I walked back into camp all eyes were on me as the other campers were astounded at the size of my rainbow trout. That was fun.

In May of the following year, 1963, Crystal, about a year old, managed to fall off of a stool she climbed up on while watching her mother cook. She loved to climb. She fell to the floor and encountered something on the way down and broke her little arm. Off to the hospital. Doctor gave her a shot of Demerol while we waited for him to set her arm. With pain gone she started to shake her arm. I had to hang on to the arm to immobilize it so the break would not get worse while Crystal just jumped around and rotated and gyrated. It took all of my concentration to keep the arm even a little immobilized. Eventually, with me holding on for dear life, the Doctor got a cast on the arm.

A few days later we heard a clunk and sure enough the cast had fallen off.

Back to the Doctor to get another cast. Crystal was a very active, very fun child. That summer we made a tent camping trip to the Utah Parks, Zion, Capital Reefs, and others, Crystal with her cast and all.

Lucinda Jane Kooyers arrived the next year on May 22, 1964. We went north to the Redwoods and Mendocino County for a camping trip after Geneva's sister's wedding in July. The stress of camping with all the little babies finally got to me. Normally, Geneva would watch one, I watched another, and Sheridan took care of himself, as he usually stayed out of trouble. With four we were pushed over the brink as seemingly, Geneva and I could not watch them all at the same time, and I concluded I must reluctantly give up tent camping in woods and on rivers and creeks in sundry beautiful places with lots of little babies. One reason for this Geneva thinks is because I then could not try to catch fish! I had to help take of children.

The summer of 1965 we did not take a vacation. I had been encouraged by my employer, Litton Industries, to participate in what was called the Honors Coop Program at Stanford University where one worked ¾ time and went to school ½ time and Litton paid double tuition to Stanford. I had been accepted into the program upon the recommendation of Oscar Buneman, a Stanford Professor, who also was a consultant for my work at Litton. We had written technical papers together. I was accepted into the program for a Doctorate in Electrical Engineering. This program required from me an immense amount of work in classroom courses so I had little time for any extra stuff and was expected to attend the summer session at Stanford as well.

Litton had liked my work doing research on Crossed Field Amplifiers. They had given me a stock option on Litton stock. Litton stock had done extremely well going up by a factor of 32 during the seven years I worked there. My stock became worth a lot more than anybody expected. We sold part of it and Geneva started looking for a larger home closer to work. She found a very nice five bedroom 2 ½ bath home on an acre in Los Altos Hills.

In February of 1966, after I had left Litton and its July vacations, we moved into our new home in Los Altos Hills on Todd Lane. We also acquired a new 1966 Chev station wagon which would hold all our kids and camping stuff too plus a carry all bag on top. Late that spring my brother Orneal, wife Martha, and their family came home for a furlough from New Guinea and stayed with us. Neal had a tent trailer, and Geneva and I rented a little house trailer, and off to Idaho we went for a camping trip to the Sawtooth Mountains. The highlight of the trip was when we camped at Redfish Lake, probably one of the most beautiful camping sites known to man, right on a sandy beach looking across the lake to the snowcapped Sawtooths. It was spectacular. We eventually got to Glacier National Park. There we parted company, with Neal and his family proceeding on to Michigan, and we returning to our place on Todd Lane.

When the Orneal Kooyers family came home on furlough from Papua New Guinea they usually lived with us for a while. They stayed with us for extensive periods of time in about 1961 at our home on Cooper Drive in Santa Clara, and again at our home in Los Altos Hills in 1966. These were really great times as Martha, Neal's wife, is very compatible and very cooperative. Geneva did a superb job accommodating this family and integrating them into our family. After years in New Guinea when each of their children came back to the States for college they usually stayed with us at various times. Our home was the Stateside home for Penny, Cory, Leah, and Pamela.

Our fourth daughter Susanne Rachelle Kooyers was born to us on December 12, 1967. This was about a year and a half after we moved to Todd Lane in Los Altos Hills. The years in Los Altos Hills were very pleasant ones with lots of children and babies and lots of fine Christian friends at the Palo Alto Christian Reformed Church, Jerry inviting many new Church families and visitors over for dinner, often informing Geneva in the car on the way home from Church. Our five bedroom 2 ½ bedroom house was on an acre of ground that was fairly level on top of a ridge, with a spectacular view of the Santa Clara Valley, and had lots of room for gardens, trees, and a swimming pool. I had made a deal with an adjacent neighbor to use a very old well on his property. It was over 300 feet deep and as soon as any water was pumped out of it the water table dropped down to almost the bottom of the well. After some experimentation and working with a water well guy, I could get about 20 gallons of water a minute out of it. I used it to irrigate my whole yard with rain bird sprinklers.

We built a swimming pool on the acre which the whole family enjoyed very much. We installed showers, landscaped it, and built a nice large exposed aggregate cantilevered deck around the pool. Many times friends and relatives, especially those from Ripon and Modesto, would visit us for very enjoyable times with picnics, barbeques, and sundry get-to-gathers. Many birthday celebrations were held in our back yard around the pool.

We raised rabbits. Geneva many times has said she enjoyed eating the rabbits more than chicken. Geneva has a recipe that includes a sweet sour type of glaze that really added to the rabbit flavor.

We had a large raspberry patch, and a large boysenberry patch. We enjoyed many raspberries and boysenberries summer and winter as we froze lots of them for later eating. The acre had a few old apricot trees as the acre was at one time an old apricot orchard. So in season we had lots of apricots also. From the roots of some of the apricot trees would volunteer up wild plums, as the apricot trees were grafted on to wild plum rootstock. With the huge amounts of wild plums Jerry experimented making wild plum wine. One time Geneva and Jerry visited a wild plum winery near the California/Oregon border near Alturas. That wine tasted just like Jerry's wine, none of which was what one might call good or excellent.

Our last daughter, Kimberly Joy Kooyers, was born to us on December 21, 1973. She is what Geneva calls a tag-a-long meaning the little one came to us later in life when we thought we were not going to have any more children.

A very, very eventful thing happened when Kim was two and a half years old on May 22, 1976. We were concerned about a small child being near our swimming pool and Geneva had just started Kim on swimming lessons. Kim told me latter that a yellow ball had gone into the pool and she was reaching out to get it when she fell into the pool. She sank to the bottom eight feet down and lying on the bottom looked up to the surface and wondered where her daddy was.

Sheridan was 17 at the time, Cindy 12 and Susanne 7. Brenda and Crystal were most likely working at part time jobs in Los Altos. It was the Saturday of Cindy's birthday and preparations were being made for a party. I was at work at my Palo Alto office and Geneva was at a Peninsula Bible Church women's retreat with niece Leah Kooyers. Kim was missed and Sheridan directed Cindy to look for Kim. Cindy says she went through and around the house, looked in the garden, and eventually the pool. She saw Kim at the bottom of a very cold pool, dove in and pulled Kim out while yelling for Sheridan. Sheridan took Kim, told Cindy to get the neighbors, the Vetterleins, and call an ambulance. Sheridan gave Kim mouth to mouth breathing and Kim started to breath. The neighbor Ralph Vetterlein told me Kim was breathing when he arrived. Cindy called me at my office, and I started home, and as I was about to turn on to La Paloma Road, I saw the ambulance make a right turn in front of me so I followed it to the El Camino Hospital. Barbara Vetterlein was in the ambulance with Kim and she gave me the high sign that Kim was alive. At the hospital our Pediatrician, Dr. Austin showed up. He and the hospital gave Kim oxygen and slowly warmed Kim up as Dr. Austin told me her temperature was in the low 80's when he arrived.

Geneva or I stayed with Kim the whole time. My sister Marcia Davis had invited Geneva and Leah to the retreat. They went just for the morning sessions, and in the afternoon Marcia asked the women to pray for Kim. Soon the Church and all of Geneva's friends and family were praying for Kim. It was 24 hours before Kim regained consciousness. As Geneva was carrying Kim around waiting for the Doctors to release her from the hospital she was singing the hymn, "Jesus Loves Me." The nurse said, "Yes, He surely does love you." The evening before this accident, Geneva's parents were visiting. Kimberly stood on a stool and sang, "Jesus Loves Me", for them.

Dr. Austin said, "It usually does not turn out this way." To us it was a miracle and the Lord's gift to us and an answer to prayer. She may have been under water for 20 minutes or so. The water was cold and the human body has an automatic reaction that when cold water is encountered the auto breathing mechanism stops. Dr. Austin said there was no water in her lungs. She recovered quickly and soon she was her old self. It was very tough on her, however, to get her to learn to swim. She would also often wake up from a nap saying she would dream that she drowned.

At the time I am writing this in 2011, Geneva was cleaning out one of her cedar chests and discovered a letter to us from Vilma Bussi, one of our close neighbors. Vilma commented what a beautiful bunch of children we have and was very impressed with the way our children responded to the emergency; Sheridan knowing what he was doing and getting Kim to breathing quickly, Cindy diving in the deep water and getting Kim out of the pool quickly and doing what Sheridan told her to do quickly, Susanne comforting Cindy who was blaming herself for not finding Kim quicker. She was very impressed with these marvelous children and their interaction with each other.

In about 1963 we went camping with another family, the Vyfinkels, on the Middle Fork of the Tuolumne in the Sierra Nevada Mountains. Their family had children slightly older than our children. That river was my favorite trout fishing stream. It was early spring, maybe early June or perhaps Memorial Day weekend as that was a holiday when one did not need to go to work. Snow melt kept the streams of the Sierra in good volume at that time of the year and one needed to time his trip so that the water temperature was rising above 50 degrees Fahrenheit. Rainbow trout do not bite much in water below 50 degrees. We camped in a rather remote spot that was accessed only by logging roads. Today one cannot get to that spot without a very long hike as the logging roads are now in great disrepair and the bridges are washed out. It was a very lovely place to camp right on the river. The weather was great and the water was just warming up and I was catching lots of rainbow trout. The limit at that time, I believe, was fifteen fish and we were feasting on them, sometimes even two or three meals a day. There were lots of mouths to feed, and fried in bacon grease they are very delicious, and they disappeared quickly. Once the inventory of fish went below fifteen I often went fishing again.

I usually fished up river from camp, there being some nice holes nearby, and the fish were lying on the bottom of the river because of the cold water. That morning on my second time out I decided to fish below the camp which I seldom did. In hindsight it was the Lord's Spirit directing me. I was fishing about 100 yards below camp. As I was watching my line I see a small human hand come out above the water. Without even thinking about anything, I immediately went out into the middle of the stream and grabbed the hand and drifted with my hip boots and all down to the bottom of the pool riffle where I could wade out of the river. The hand belonged to my dear five year old son Sheridan. He was coughing and sputtering and very cold but alive. I took him back to camp where his mother, wife Geneva, warmed him up.

The kids with their father, Tony VyFinkel's, help had built a bridge of limbs and small logs so that they could cross the river. Sheridan apparently had somehow fallen off the bridge when he had followed the Vyfinkel kids across the river. The bridge was rickety and it took more than a little care to use it.

As I reflect on the event I understand the hand of the Lord Jesus was on me. Why did I fish downriver that day? That is something I seldom did. Why was I in that pool at that particular time and not somewhere else? The timing was perfect. The Lord Jesus works in marvelous unfathomable ways. My son's life was spared. Thank you Jesus!

Another year we camped again with the Vyfinkels and all of our and their kids in the Mendocino National Forrest above Lake Pillsbury. We perhaps were deer hunting during the bow season as it was in the summer, perhaps July, though the rifle season there usually opened the first Saturday in August. We took my four wheel drive Toyota Land Cruiser back on a non-existing jeep trail which we made ourselves to a lovely camping spot on a very tiny stream. We left the Vyfinkels car back on the main dirt access road. Now days one would not be able to legally do this as the area has been classified as road less wilderness. But we loved to do such a thing.

Tony would go down to the stream and hold his hand in the water a little ways above the bottom of the stream, and with his other hand chase the small trout around the pool. The trout would hide under his first hand and then Tony would grab them. He caught enough this way to supply us with fish for breakfast each day. Tony, at that time a fairly green Dutchman from The Netherlands, had lots of fun interesting skills like that.

In the early mornings and late evenings we would ride around on sundry jeep trails in the Toyota looking for deer. Mrs. Vyfinkel, (Alice) spotted 10 times as many deer as any of the rest of us did. It turned out she was colorblind and seemingly could make out deer in the brush and trees much easier than any of the rest of us. I would stop the Toyota and use my field glasses to find the same deer. I was amazed at her uncanny ability to initially see deer where none of the rest of us could.

I do not remember the year of the first time we did it, but in about 1967, I suggested to Geneva's brothers and sister a camping trip to Lake Almanor. The first year we camped near Chester on the lake and the next year somebody found the spot on the lake at a place called Kokanee Lodge, where one could park an RV, primitive tent camp, rent a primitive cabin, or stay in the lodge. That started a tradition, and all of us camped there for years, coming back year after year. We all had acquired water skiing boats so the time was spent swimming, water skiing, driving around looking at deer, playing games, sometimes fishing, and going to restaurants. We had lots and lots of fun with Geneva's family, playing cards, and games, especially monopoly, lots of banter, stories, and political discussions. Geneva's parents came too. The children enjoyed their cousins very, very much. We all learned to water ski. We did it every year until about 1978. Lake Almanor is such a gorgeous spot to view Mt Lassen over the water, hopefully very smooth, as one water skis. We usually had lots of nice smooth water early in the morning. We took our down jackets along, however, as the water was warm but the air often cold.

In about 1965 Geneva and I and another couple, Gene Koenig and Pat Vartanian, Gene's future wife, and two high school boys, Jim Scholten and Dave VanderWeide from our CRC Church went back packing in the high Sierra Nevada Mountains. We went after golden trout. These are high altitude trout and are found only at high altitude. We went into the area between Yosemite National Park and Kings Canyon National Park. We parked the Toyota Land Cruiser at about 7,500 feet near old mine diggings and the first day hiked up to the 10,000 foot level to camp near a lake. I spent most of the day trying to keep people moving as everybody got tired and lagged behind, except for Jim Scholten. He was tough.

We spent the night near the first lake and our bodies acclimated to the high altitude. The next day the climbing was not so steep and we discovered a small lake that held lots of beautiful golden trout and we caught a nice bunch. It turned out only Jim and I could catch trout. The rest never figured it out. Consequently, we really never had a food surplus as it is a lot of work and takes a lot of time to catch enough trout for six of us. We had brought along freeze dried stuff and the calculated amount of sugar, flour, dried fruit, and other food stipulated by conventional wisdom, but all of us slowly got hungrier and hungrier as the days went by. Actually, that was good as we toughened up and got leaner and stronger.

We camped by some extremely beautiful lakes in very beautiful clear weather such as one comes to expect in the Sierra Nevada. Jim and I climbed a peak one day just to see the top of the Sierra Nevada for many, many miles.

We were about a week in a huge somewhat of a basin at about 11,500 feet that held lots of lakes. This was in about the third week of August and the nights were cold, below freezing. I chose that time to go so as to not have too many snowfields to cross as snow lingers at high altitude. As the time came to think about going home we went up to what were called the Royce Lakes at about 12,500 feet. They were huge very deep lakes but did not seem to hold any trout. From there we crossed a divide and went cross country with no trail down through a large basin that was full of huge well rounded boulders as big as automobiles. It took a little skill and nerve but soon I had even Geneva leaping from bolder to bolder, backpack and all, to descend through this basin. We camped that night by a lower altitude lake at about 10,500 feet where we caught some nice rainbow trout.

Before we left to go home I decided to consume all of our reserves of food and get rid of the weight so we ate three meals instead of one which consumed everything we had except for a light breakfast of maybe tea and sugar for the morning. We even disputed over how many little red hot candies each one of us was entitled to put on our pudding desert.

After very refreshing sleep, which one really enjoys when physically tired, we had a light tea breakfast and descended down to our Land Cruiser, very rapidly it now seemed to me as everybody was now in great physical shape, especially, Geneva.

As the Toyota descended down to civilization a discussion developed as to where we would obtain a milkshake and hamburger. That it seemed, was all our minds thought about. What a marvelous and very memorable back packing trip!

PETER PAN LAKE

I made many really great back packing trips into Peter Pan Lake. In my mind it is the most beautiful lake in all of the Sierra Nevada Mountains. A friend at the Palo Alto CRC had told me about the area; it's called the Silver Divide. One can drive to the Edison Lake trailhead from Fresno and from there proceed up into the high Sierra.

The first time into Peter Pan, sometime in the early 1960's, I had recruited a CRC friend who was a young, I thought tough, but green Dutchman. He later in life went back to The Netherlands, after working a few years in San Francisco, moving up in business opportunity from auto mechanic, to auto salesman, to management, then back to The Netherlands where he became a big gun businessman in the automotive industry.

We hiked along Edison Lake and then up to what are called the Graveyard Lakes. On the way we started seeing all kinds of stuff along the trail, apparently thrown away. We then came up on a group of boy scouts sitting by the trail. They looked exhausted with their big heavy packs. That explained all the stuff scattered everywhere. I had learned that if I kept my load down to less than 40 pounds and that of girls and kids to less than 30 pounds one did not need to rest so often. Those scouts were probably carrying 50 pounds or more.

We continued on and camped at the middle Graveyard Lake, fished a day or so, and then decided to go over a pass to the west into the basin where Peter Pan Lake was located. I always carried topographic maps with me so I could plan a route that did not seem too terribly difficult. This was a steep but fun climb, but with no trail along a sort of a sloping granite ledge up to a pass. We then descended a steep talus and grass slope down into a beautiful flowered basin, and then made a drift to the South where we came to the outlet stream from Peter Pan Lake, which has an elevation of about 10,000 feet. We could see it was full of trout. What a marvelously beautiful lake. The water was slightly green near the outlet with a beautiful clear sandy bottom, a deeper blue out into the middle and then a spectacular glistening white snowfield descending to the lake with probably a glacier at the far end of the lake to the south. The first evening we camped near the outlet and caught a limit of fish, 15 each, about 12 to 15 inches long. We feasted. I carry a slab of bacon in my backpack; the bacon we eat for breakfast and save the bacon grease. Trout fried in bacon grease with a good amount of salt and pepper is simply delicious. It is such a lovely thing to feast on rainbow trout fried in bacon grease in the glorious beauty of the Sierra Nevada. We were already several days on the trail and had worked hard so we had very good appetites. It is important to eat lots of salt too when expending lots of energy while sweating, climbing mountains.

The next day we moved our camp around the lake a little bit to the south west to a flat point above a very lovely beach with a nice large flat rock that would serve as a nice table about 30 inches high and to hold the camp stuff. The point also intercepted a slight breeze so the mosquitoes were slightly less bothersome. The beach was a great place to swim and take a bath in the not too cold water. We hiked up to another lake above Peter Pan called Ann Lake. It held fewer but larger trout. The outlet of it flowed down into Peter Pan near the table rock campsite. After a few days of exquisite fishing we descended down along the outlet stream of Peter Pan. That, it soon turned out, was a cliff and a waterfall. We carefully worked our way to the south and descended to Olive Lake. There was a Forest Service trail into Olive from the north and we met some horse packers. We were running out of sugar. I like sugar with tea for breakfast. So I negotiated a deal where we traded fish for sugar. We ended up with lots of sugar. Now we could catch more fish too and not exceed our limit.

From there we went down the Olive Lake Trail to where we found a main trail, called the John Muir Trail, and spent maybe three days or so making a circuit back to Edison Lake covering maybe 15 to 20 miles a day. At altitude like that I adopt the Arab style and put a large handkerchief into the back of my cowboy hat so that my neck is protected from the sun. My friend either thought that was below his dignity or did not have a cowboy handkerchief so he ended up with a badly sunburned neck.

We returned to civilization had a great meal at a restaurant and returned home. It was a most lovely, beautiful, very memorable trip. I learned a few years later that my friend told other people I had almost killed him by all the hiking we did. He never complained no matter how tired and sunburned he got. That is a very desirable characteristic in a man.

One trip into Peter Pan as I recall was with my nephew Cory Kooyers. Cory was young and really tough. He grew up in New Guinea. I thought I would find a shorter way into Peter Pan as the Graveyard Lake route takes two days. Thus I left Los Altos early in the morning and drove my Toyota as far as I could toward the Devils Bathtub Lake making my own jeep trail cross country in the scattered forest and started up from there. In those days cross country travel by vehicle was not regulated except in areas defined as wilderness. Not knowing the way and not reading the topographic maps correctly we ended up climbing an 11,000 peak before the high of the ridge of the Silver Divide. We discovered my mistake on top of the peak but now had to descend about 1000 feet to a saddle and climb back up to the Silver Divide Ridge. It was exhausting. Near the top we would take three steps and sit down and rest. Rest a bit and repeat the process. We came to the top and had to descend a 70 foot cliff. Carefully done, we descended to Ann Lake above Peter Pan and being quite exhausted just crawled into our sleeping bags and camped as best we could right on the ground.

In the morning we fished Ann Lake and caught lots and lots of real nice Rainbow trout. We moved our camp down to the old rock campsite at Peter Pan and enjoyed the marvelous fishing and spectacular views of Peter Pan. The thought of having to go back over that mountain ridge just intimidated me something fierce. Memories of the exhaustion just haunted me. Well, the return was a piece of cake. That taught me a very important lesson. One must get acclimated to altitude. Spend a few days at least at high altitude if you can before doing something strenuous, nevertheless, always at least sleep the first night at altitude and then take it easy the first day. Our time was limited so after a few days we returned to Devils Bathtub, but now I had worked out a good route from Bathtub to Peter Pan.

I made another trip into Peter Pan with Cory sometime later but this time the lake was still frozen over. We came in from the east and descended a huge snowfield from the ridge that was a bit dangerous since it descended right down to the frozen lake, but when you are young you think you are going to live forever. We were disappointed at not being able to fish so we went over a ridge to the west and descended down to Olive Lake. We had some fishing at Olive but the water was just warming up and we mainly fished near the inlet streams where the fish were coming to spawn.

That trip also taught me valuable lessons. If one is to go into the High Sierra to fish mountain lakes one must study the weather pattern and determine how much snow has fallen and when it is expected to melt. I had planned my trips into Peter Pan to arrive about the third week in July. Then the ice could be expected to be off the lake and the fish have spawned and are hungry. One should really go a week or two or so earlier or a week or so later depending on snow accumulation that happened during the past winter.

From Olive, since we did not have really good fishing, we decided to climb back up to Ann and do a side slope traverse over a huge snowfield to the pass to the south where we could descend down into Margaret Lake. That traverse was a bit hairy. We did not have ice axes so we had to very carefully use our fishing poles like an ice ax and move very, very carefully, kicking steps in the now melting afternoon snow crust to make a reasonably safe trail. If one fell, however, it was all over as the snow field was somewhat steep all the way down a 2000 foot drop in elevation.

Reaching the pass and after descending a very steep but not long slope from the top of the pass, we descended a long sloping marvelously beautiful valley to Margaret Lake. At the Lake we moved a little to the northwest and found a very nice flat rock upon which to make camp, located just a little above the lake. What marvelous fishing for Brook Trout. Every cast produced a 10 inch or so Brookie. If the fish got off the hook, one always caught another before the lure got back to the pole.

We fished, as I recall a day and then went around the lake to the outlet where there was a very nice huge table placed by the CCC (Civilian conservation Corp) many years before. We camped there a night. The fishing was not as good at the outlet, probably because it was on a major Forest Service trail. We then followed the Forest Service Trail from Margaret to Edison where we had left our vehicle. Thus I now had another way into Peter Pan Lake.

Another trip into Peter Pan I seemed to have mostly forgotten, but it included my daughter Brenda, Cindy Rooks, a friend of Brenda's from the PACRC, perhaps her brother, David Rooks, and others. We went in and out by the way of Margaret Lake and the traverse, but this time there was no snow so it was reasonably safe going across a talus and low brush slope. I clearly remember on the return trip being very hot and tired and drinking very cool water from a melting snow bank on the way back to Edison with Brenda and Cindy. Brenda remembers a long steep switchback trail. That would have been the trip where Brenda said she forgot and left a blouse shirt on a rock at Peter Pan. Brenda remembers swimming and bathing in Peter Pan. I always want a bath too, but usually memories of swimming in cold mountain lakes are quickly forgotten as one jumps in and out real quick. Brenda seams a little different and feminine tough as she actually went for a swim in the cold water for the fun of it

In the summer of 1978 we made another trip into Peter Pan, my last, with my daughter Brenda and her future husband Mark, son Sheridan, my niece Pamela, and my niece Penny's husband Erik Schering, my little 10 year old daughter Susanne, and my nephews Titus and Dwight Davis. Having the benefit of experience I planned to spend the first night at Devils Bathtub. Sheridan twisted his knee about 2 miles up the trail. He has an old football injury. He could not continue. I told the rest to proceed up to Bathtub while I went back with Sheridan to the Toyota and brought him to the Oldsmobile Station Wagon. We had enough stuff with backpacks and other stuff that we had taken two cars. Sheridan said he could drive home so I left him with the Olds and went back to catch up with the rest. As I recall they had not made much progress. We proceeded to Bathtub and camped at about 9,000 feet.

The next day we hiked up to the upper end of Bathtub and scaled a series of benches by the route to the top of the 11,000 foot ridge I had pioneered with Cory. At the top I was presented with a dangerous snow cornice which I had not expected. I had taken my climbing rope along as I expected to belay down the troops from the cliff at the top. So I then very carefully with my climbing rope around me and the other end held on to by Mark and Erick, chopped a way through the cornice with my ice ax. We then let everybody down the cliff through the snow/ice channel I had created, I descending last with the use of my ice ax.

We descended down to Peter Pan along an easy route to the old camp with the flat rock. There was a lot more snow and snowfields and Peter Pan was surrounded with snow, the lake ice, however, was almost gone.

Mark and Brenda made a spectacular picture swimming in the creek going into the lake with snow all around them. Very brave they were. It was a little premature for fishing as the water was too cold. We had a very delightful time. Neat bonding occurs among a group like that when you are out in the wilderness, preparing food together, and having great discussions about sundry subjects gathered around a real nice big fire. There was lots and lots of nice firewood near that camp at Peter Pan.

Some of these trips into Peter Pan merge into one another in my memory. I had worked out another route to Peter Pan and I remember twice going from Peter Pan to the Margaret Lakes and once from Margaret Lakes to Peter Pan. The route goes cross country with no trail up from Margaret through a beautiful glacier formed valley and couvar with a steep climb near the top to a pass, and then requires a traverse across a snow field that is a little dangerous, because if one slips one will slide down two thousand feet. The traverse ends at the trail from the top of the Silver Divide to Ann Lake. The upper Margaret Lake has fantastic Brook Trout fishing as fish hit a lure on almost every cast, sometimes as many as three hits on one cast of a lure. From Margaret is a fairly easy seven mile or so trail back to the Lake Edison trailhead.

On one of my trips through Margaret I encountered a very zealous forest service employee who was proceeding through the wilderness sifting camp fire ashes for evidence of tinfoil, writing tickets to careless campers, and burning every table and any other symbols of civilization he found. The CCC (Civilian Conservation Corps) had built these tables in the 30s, were very stout, made of logs, and greatly appreciated by backpackers, because one then does not have to sit on the ground when one eats. I could hardly believe it. Some self-righteous theologian of the Forest Service hierarchy decreed that all tables in the wilderness must go. What folly. What stupidity. Still even now 40 years later, that arrogance of the all controlling communist left intellectuals, still makes me angry.

I made many trips into Peter Pan. On one trip Brenda discovered a blouse shirt she had left forgotten behind on a rock five years before. It was still there but quite rotten. I once left a nice cooking grate behind that I did not want to carry out underneath a log near the camp. It was always in the same place where I left it, and I got to use it again and again without carrying it in. Apparently nobody but us used that rock camp over the period of about

20 years. The Sierra's were like that, spectacular, extremely beautiful wilderness that very, very few people ever used.

On that last trip into the area in 1978 I took along friends and nephews and little daughter Susanne who was 10 years old. Susanne has a neat way with her Dad. I ended up carrying her back pack on top of mine most of the time no matter how much I protested. She slept right alongside of me in her own sleeping bag every night. I had taken a parachute and soaked it in waterproof chemical several times for many hours. I rigged up a way to make a tent out of it and as many as nine backpackers could get under it when it rained. That way I did not have to take a lot of tents along. Susanne remembers descending down through that ice channel I made. She remembers returning by the Graveyard route as I apparently did not want to attempt to let everybody climb up that ice channel.

The trips into Peter Pan with the marvelous beauty and the stupendous trout fishing to be had there are much cherished memories.

TRIP TO THE FAR EAST

In 1973 Geneva and I traveled to New Guinea. It was in the spring of 1973 and Geneva had just become pregnant for Kimberly. Geneva usually had rather unpleasant morning sickness with her pregnancies, but she took some pills which helped greatly. So Kim went to New Guinea with us.

The trip came about because I had a work project in Taiwan as a sub-contractor to Stanford Research Institute. I was a civilian but sent under Navy military orders with the rank of colonel (must have been a Marine) to install a computer program on the Taiwan Chinese military computer. I made several trips there but on the last one when the project was completed, Geneva flew over by way of Japan and I met her at the Taipei airport. After a few days showing her around Taiwan we flew to Hong Kong for a few days doing all the tourist things, and then we flew to Port Moresby in New Guinea by way of Manila in the Philippines, landing at the Manila airport in the middle of the night.

Changing planes we then arrived at Port Moresby in the morning. We changed planes again, and we flew to Lae on the north coast of New Guinea, where we met my brother Neal, a missionary at that time with Wycliffe Bible Translators. We spent the night in Lae and drove by car the next morning up through the countryside to the highlands of New Guinea. Wycliffe has a home base in the highlands at a place called Ukarumpa. We met Neal's wife Martha there and spent a few days touring the area. One day we walked a ways and met with a primitive tribe were we were the guests of honor. Very strange food was presented to us on banana leaves. I looked to Neal for advice and he suggested I eat a little of each and leave the rest. I ate a little of each of the very strange food and left the rest which was soon eaten by my host. I purchased some nicely hand carved arrows from my host. He eagerly accepted my money.

We then flew by Wycliffe bush airplane to Wewak on the north coast of New Guinea. Neal then had us rounding up supplies in the few stores in Wewak. We spent a few nights there in a hotel type building or some missionary facilities, I do not remember which. We visited some very nice spectacular beaches. One beach had huge trees right up to the beach so we could actually play in the surf in the shade of the trees. What fun as it is always very hot and muggy in New Guinea. The tropical fish were many different colors! What a sight.

We then traveled by light truck from Wewak to Pagway on the Sepik River. On the way we stopped and visited with another Wycliffe missionary by the name of Phil Stalson, a friend of Neal's located in an out of the way bush place. We visited and had lunch there and continued on to the Sepik. We arrived before the double canoe coming down from Ambunti arrived that was going to pick us up. During the wait I wandered around a bit until the double canoe showed up. We loaded up the canoe with the supplies we had bought with us and then boated up the Sepik. The Sepik is a huge deep river. The flow can vary quite a bit from wet season to dry season and the level, therefore, has a huge variation. Tribal people's homes along the river are built on stilts. Occasionally, the river gets so high it flows into the homes on stilts even though the homes are ten feet above the high water level river bank. These river people can actually tie up their canoes right to their houses.

We arrived at Ambunti a little before dark. Neal's facilities of a house and shop are right adjacent to both the Sepik River and the Ambunti airstrip. Geneva and I slept in a double bed in the guest spare room. We got as far away from each other as possible as the temperature is about 93 degrees day and night and one sweats all the time, and one avoids being anywhere near a heat source such as Geneva. When the rain came through the screen onto us, we just welcomed it on our bodies to cool us off.

Martha prepared her usual very nice meals and we enjoyed the hospitality. There was a local market in Ambunti where fresh food could be purchased. Neal believes maintaining health is very important so he imported his meat and necessary protein.

One day we travelled by canoe up to Madiwai, the village where Neal and Martha and family spent the first five years (from 1961 to 1966) in New Guinea. We had to travel through a huge grass filled lagoon. The water was high so we encountered little trouble. We arrived at Madiwai and met with their village friends and looked around the house they had built there. Crocodiles are a serious problem when they are not hunted. So there are lots of bad croc tales banished about. We never saw any. Their hides are a good source of revenue for the people.

At night Geneva and I sometimes in bed would listen to a, "sing sing", the soft sound coming from a distance. This went on for hours and hours. I once read where whales sing to each other with the song varying slightly each time it is repeated. That is what the Sepik singers did. One person would develop a song with a very melodious sequence with the background of a quiet drum sound. Then after a while another person would pick it up and repeat the song with a slight variation. Others joined in as the spirit moved them. The music would come and go, with louder and softer variations as the night continued. This Neal said, sometimes goes on all night.

The mosquitoes were so thick one seldom opened one's mouth when outside. Anytime one of the almost naked people came into the house there was an attempt to kill the accompanying mosquitoes as quickly as possible.

One evening we went for a walk out of town through the jungle to the home of Neal's informant, the person who spent a lot of time with Neal teaching

Neal the Waskuk language. As we walked along we heard the sound of hollow logs being hit in sundry interesting sequences. Neal said information was being communicated from log to log to all who could hear that we white people were approaching. It was not Morse Code but some such thing that sent information by the sound of a Nimbutu, (a solid round nicely carved stick about three feet long and two inches in diameter out of iron wood where the communicator causes the end of it to descend onto the log by the control of his hand to make the sound) hitting a hollow log. We arrived at the residence of Buria and his wife Mucachua where we were given refreshments.

Well, all good things come to an end; so one day we again boarded a Wycliffe airplane and flew directly to Port Moresby over the Owen Stanley Range of mountains. The mountains are quite high and our pilot did not seem to clear them by very much as we even saw mountains above us in the scattered clouds we were flying around. We then flew to Sydney Australia by commercial airline.

We stayed in a hotel there and looked at all the sites of Sidney and then rented a car, and traveled out into the Australian countryside. We found an exquisite hotel out in the middle of nowhere that seemingly was a destination resort for honeymoon couples. What a nice place to stay. The service was exquisitely high class British. The utensil service was all sterling silver with very many forks, spoons and knives, the napkins linen, and very beautiful marvelous hotel accommodations.

The landscape and fauna of Australia was miles and miles of eucalyptus trees - very, very boring. In California eucalyptus trees are considered an obnoxious weed. In Australia they are not any better but the locals don't know any better.

After a couple days of this we returned to Sydney and flew to Fiji. I would have much rather flown home through Tahiti but the French and Australians were having a standoff because the French were testing nuclear weapons in the South Pacific. So there was no way to get from Australia to Tahiti without going back to the United States.

We spent a day in Fiji, rented a car, and drove halfway around the island. It was mainly farms and sugar cane, green and pretty, and fairly level. We made the mistake of eating in a local restaurant before we boarded our flight home so on the flight home we got sick. That was the first time we got sick on the whole trip so we were very fortunate. But then we never otherwise ate the local food or drank the water. In Taiwan and all other places we even brushed our teeth with bottled water.

CHURCH AFFILIATION

When we arrived in Redwood City in February of 1959, since we had been attending the Christian Reformed Church in Walnut Creek where we were members, we started going to the mission operation of the Christian Reformed Church in Palo Alto. We became the sixth family to join that new church group. Soon after we arrived Rev Frank DeJong became the pastor. Rev DeJong was a very likable person and had started a number of new Christian Reformed Churches. About a year and a half after we arrived Rev. DeJong encouraged the group to become an organized church. I was elected a deacon and served that church as Deacon or Elder for the next 15 years or so. Brenda was the first baby to be baptized at the Palo Alto Christian Reformed Church.

The church kept on growing with lots of new young couples with families and new immigrants from Canada and the Netherlands so we made a large number of very close friends which have been dear to us for many years. We have camped out, fished, hunted, and hiked many places with these friends over the years.

Susanne went to Los Altos Christian School for the 3rd and 4th grade. When Crystal started the 8th grade we put her in a Christian School. There was a kindergarten to 3rd grade school adjacent to our home property on Todd Lane. It was very conveniently located adjacent to our home over the back fence by a path and an excellent public school so our children usually went to that school, Bullas School, until they had completed the 3th grade. Then they went through the 4th to the 6th grade at Purissima School in Los Altos Hills a few miles away. Crystal attended Covington Junior High School in Los Altos in the 7th grade and we were not impressed with the sex education given to the students. Crystal made friends at her new Christian

School and she asked me several times if she could go to Sunday school at Peninsula Bible Church. Her real good friend Jan McCuistion went to PBC as her dad Walt was a pastor there. I finally said ok, so I would take her to Sunday school there. Eventually, I would go to the early 8AM church service there, as the Pastor, Ray Stedman, was a most excellent preacher, and then Sunday school, and then Crystal and I would go to the 11 AM service at the Palo Alto CRC. Soon the whole family was doing this together.

The Christian Reformed Church has Calvinist roots and has the sovereignty of God as one of its main tenants. At the CRC I seldom heard sermons on the sovereignty of God, but at PBC the pastor, Ray Stedman, preached the sovereignty of God. We all enjoyed PBC very much and soon we were not attending the PACRC at all. PBC does not have church membership so the migration was easily done.

This shift in church attendance was extremely good for my family. The leadership of the Sunday school and the youth programs at PBC were very, very, good and my children grew in the Lord.

Changing churches like that is not easy. We had lots of very good friends at the Palo Alto CRC. I had been in the church leadership. The CRC practiced church discipline so we had to go through the process of visiting with the Elders to explain what we were doing.

Perhaps another factor in us leaving the CRC was a previous event when the PACRC was vacant with no pastor. I was on the Elder Board at the time and the method for finding a new pastor is to do a search of pastors who might be interested in coming to Palo Alto and make a list of three men and submit it to the congregation for a vote. One would be selected to Call with a letter of Call asking him to come and be our pastor. I had suggested the name of Peter DeJong, a man I had encountered in Seattle when my brother Neal and his wife were there teaching for a time in the Christian school, and who we also visited in Smithers, British Columbia once while passing through on one of our vacations traveling with Neal and his family. Peter DeJong had served several large CRC Churches, was about 60 years old and seemingly was interested in a smaller Church with less work as a final place before his retirement. DeJong had written lots of articles for publication and was thought of as quite an articulate conservative. I knew him as a most excellent solid, gifted, preacher. The Elder Board at my suggestion placed his name on a "trio" of names to be voted on to Call. At the election for a new pastor he got three votes, mine, Geneva's, and the local right wing extremist. I guess, I thought to myself at the time, "These people here are not my kind of people", I do not belong here.

We left the CRC in good standing. Nevertheless, it was a bit traumatic especially explaining it to relatives and others who have remained in the CRC. Most people just never do understand how significant the concept is, that is well preached at PBC, that of,

"Christ in you the hope of Glory." (Colossians 1:27)

This concept is that through the Holy Spirit, God Himself lives within the believer, the believer is a home for God. Jack Crabtree, a PBC pastor at the time, first taught me well this concept and has put it very well, I quote him,

"Are you acting out your life? Are you acting out what you conceive of as a life of righteousness with other people as an audience, or even with yourself as an audience? Or are you, in fact, striving to live a righteous life utterly dependent upon God, utterly dependent upon God's Spirit working in your behalf? Are you utterly dependent on God's work, expecting, as God has promised, that he is going to come into your life and transform you from the inside out? Are you counting on that? Is your life based on that? The difference is extremely subtle. No one can tell you if you are a hypocrite. You can't be absolutely sure you can know if you are a hypocrite. But you have to know that the difference exists, because that difference is the difference between life and death, heaven and hell, condemnation and eternal well-being."

That is the concept. It is very important. In the CRC I never ever heard it taught.

MOVING TO IDAHO

In 1980 we moved to Idaho. Some of the more significant events that happened in Idaho are told about in other chapters. At the time of Brenda's wedding to Mark Lawler we started thinking about moving to Idaho. The real estate market was hot, and I thought about selling our Todd Lane home. Our friends the Carmichaels were at the wedding and Phyllis was a Real Estate Agent, and I discussed it with her. We listed it at what I thought was an outlandish high price of $495,000 and Phyllis sold it in about a week.

I recruited the sons of our friends, rented and borrowed several trucks and just loaded everything we had into the trucks and just left and took everything to Idaho. I had already moved my dogs. I had rented a truck the summer before and loaded it up with stuff for the ranch and towed the 66 Chev Station wagon behind the truck. I piled the dogs into the Station Wagon. Zena, my prime Plotthound bitch sat on her haunches by the steering wheel most of the trip, and that entertained lots of people passing me by as Zena looked like she was driving the Station Wagon.

I had gotten a bee in my bonnet to be a bear hunter with a pack of bear hounds. My first hound, the bitch, Zena, came from North Carolina with a long pedigree of bear hound ancestors. (More than seven generations). My second hound was Tobin, a dog from the Pacific Northwest again from a long line of bear hunting dogs, a very long pedigree. Well, high hopes generate inspiration so soon I had twelve pups of very long pedigrees. I kept eight and soon had very high hopes of a very successful hound pack. I farmed Tobin out to a guy in Susanville, California to be trained. After three months or so the guy called me and said Tobin was not going to make it. Tobin just did not have the killer instinct.

I picked up Tobin and I could hardly believe the muscles on that dog. He could run miles and miles and never tire. Unfortunately, he had no interest in bears or for that matter any other game or trash critter. He just loved to run and run.

The bear hound project was a disaster. I did not have time to hunt in the fall, and spring bear hunting was difficult as the bears also loved to run in the spring when they are thin and with no fat on them, and the high water in Elkhorn Creek made so much noise I could not hear the hound music. I never got any bears with hounds.

My hounds, however, consumed lots of dog food and produced lots of dog feces. I built a kennel with a water supply near it so cleaning the kennel was a fairly easy job except in the winter time when everything froze. After a few years I culled out most of the hounds that did not hunt, and sold the ones that at least hunted a little bit to some guys from Kooskie.

End of dog project, a little wiser and poorer. I just did not have the time to be a serious hound hunter with the mine, the rafting business, and my commodity business.

I figured out while living at the ranch that I needed some horses if I was going to hunt elk. A passerby offered me his horse by the name of Hondo. The horse had been up Wind River and he needed to get rid of it cheap. A Church friend, Bill Potenger, offered me his hunting horses, two mares, Doll and Easy, with two little fillies. They turned out to be very, very nice horses. The fillies, we named Ginger and Nutmeg. When they became two years old, I had Potenger train them. He did an absolute marvelous job and I soon had two more very, very fine mountain horses. I also acquired two old geldings ready for retirement from a sheep rancher in Riggins. I had befriended him when I rescued his vehicle from falling into the Salmon River. It seems he got too close to the edge of the road with a cliff down to the river and his tires had gone off the edge but the vehicle tittered on the edge. I hooked my land Cruiser wench to it and pulled it back on the road. Adventures like that seemed to be common as every once in a while people would get into trouble and come knocking at my door. Ours was the last telephone up the river from Riggins. Those horses also were very fine, very gentle horses, but of course after a few years they died. Bad things like that always happened when I am gone and not at the ranch. Lucky fell upside down into a trench by the big house and he became bear bait. Neg developed an abscessed tooth, and my son-in-law John Cook with the help of a little lead turned Neg into another bear bait.

Hondo turned out to be a terrible horse causing severe horse pack string wrecks, fortunately with no injuries to the people involved. After a discussion one day with Pottenger, probably at church, he suggested he find me some good horses in exchange for him to have Hondo. I agreed, and Potenger proceeded down to Boise where he found for me four really nice horses. I don't remember how much I paid for them but it did not seem like very much, maybe a couple of grand. The horses I named "CJ", a real tough fast appaloosa gelding maybe five or six years old, a tall but skinny boned appaloosa grey mare I named, "Dingbat", again maybe five or six years old, a smaller grey Arab mare I named, "Silver", and a bay mare I just called, "Bay Mare." So I ended up with eight really nice horses to hunt and pack with. I could pack or ride any and all of these horses. This made for some really great elk hunting pack trips. The ranch was a place that was an almost perfect place from which to hunt elk. My friends and sometimes my brokers, and I enjoyed some superbly wonderful elk hunting trips from this ranch for a period of fifteen years.

I figured out a few years later why Pottenger wanted Hondo. It seems people always wanted to borrow horses from him. Well, when he lent them Hondo, they never wanted to borrow his horses again. Hondo was a small appaloosa who would do all kind of strange unexpected things and had a complete mind of his own, so any trip with Hondo was sure to be miserable and sure to have a horse wreck.

The wisdom to be gained from this experience is to really be careful about having to do business or have adventures with a passerby. Yet people in trouble need help. The Christian calling is to help people in need. One needs to be very wise, use prayer, and use a lot of discernment when helping such. All the people I found in trouble out in the boonies in the end, however, were never a risk to me or my friends.

As I write this I recall several such adventures. To give you dear reader a feel of life on the ranch on Salmon River, and to pass on a little wisdom, I relate here the story of Terry the Tishbite. That was the name we gave to a drifter which came and passed through our lives.

My old hunting buddy, Dale is a chimney sweep. He is a solid lovely Christian man with a unique sense of humor and he has had at times a prison ministry. He is prone to empathize with people down and out as really fine Christians are wont to do. Somehow a drifter wandered into his life and Dale must have employed him to help with sundry things and maybe help with chimney sweeping. Well elk hunting season came along and Dale brought him elk hunting.

It seems Terry had walked all the way from central Oregon to Idaho and lived on dandelions and cottontail pods. Dandelions are yellow flowers and cottontails are a plant with a bushy sort of thing on the end of the stem that is eatable and seems to grow by the side of the road.

Terry wanted nothing to do with horses so on the horse ride into our wilderness hunting camp he walked all the way, about five hours to camp. I do not recall him falling far behind the horses, but then the trail is steep and the horses are heavily loaded so I rest the horses a lot, and we take our time. After we set up camp, Terry wanders through the woods finding editable things to eat and demonstrates to Dale and me how to eat them. This includes mushrooms and insects and sundry other stuff I do not remember.

As I recall we had a fine hunting trip and Terry was fine quiet company but did not talk much. Understand that Dale talks a lot and is always trying to tell me some joke with a play on words. I have to concentrate on Dale's story or I lose the punch line of his play on words. This keeps hunting trips with Dale lots of fun and interesting. Dale always gets up very early in the morning and hunts hard so we usually are very successful if the game is there to be harvested.

Returning to the ranch after the hunt, Terry stayed at the ranch. Dale and I had talked a lot about Terry and somehow it seemed that Dale was very happy to pass Terry on to me.

I had a very huge pile of sawed log rounds of fir that needed to be split into firewood. I made a deal with Terry for him to split wood with an axe in trade for three square meals of Geneva's cooking. He seemed quite frail and I expected little. What resulted was amazing. It started very small but every day Terry split more wood than the day before. As time went on his muscles grew and grew, and he returned to full manhood eating three squares of Geneva's with lots of exercise. Now in case you do not know it, Geneva is a very good cook, and her meals are simply wonderful, so Terry returned to full health. After a month or two or three, I ran out of things for him to do.

Mick Carlson wandered by one day in need of a sheep herder. He must have heard from daughter Cindy or someone else that Terry might need a new place to hang out. Sheep herding is a very unique job. One lives with the sheep out in the wilderness, just you and the sheep, and maybe a few coyotes and/or wolves, and some bears and cougars, all of which follow the sheep too, and pick off one now and then. Mick sends a pack string out once in a while with some food; otherwise, you are completely on your own with nobody to talk too. Usually Mick got for sheep herders, Peruvians, Navahos, Basques, and such as they seemingly have the temperament to stay with the sheep all by themselves for long periods of time and survive.

After a couple of years or so of this Terry departs, perhaps going back to Oregon. At least he was spotted walking on the road headed for Lewiston, I think by my daughter Cindy. My daughter Crystal going to Lewiston the next day spots him on the road, turns around and goes back and picks him up, and gives him a ride. She takes him to the Goodwill in Lewiston and helps him buy some Goodwill clothes. That is the last any of us have seen of Terry.

One has to read between the lines and think about this to try to figure this story out. One concludes that Terry was addicted to something and needed to dry out. Maybe he also was in a bad situation he did not want to tell us about it no matter how many questions we asked him. He had traded his bible, a Revised Standard New Testament, to me for a complete NIV (New International Version) bible that was a lot smaller and compact so it was easy to carry around. I wrote a note in the bible I received from him saying I obtained it from Terry the Tishbite, so every time I now pick that bible up I am reminded of Terry.

The name Tishbite stuck because, like Elijah the Old Testament prophet from Tish, Terry ate locus and wild honey with dandelions, cottontails, and mushrooms and other insects, and bird eggs, in fact anything that can be picked up alongside the road, thrown in too.

Living at the ranch was interesting in that you never knew when somebody in need might show up, and being Christians we did what we could to help everybody.

Another interesting encounter was started one very black dark night when Geneva and I were returning to the ranch from town in a very severe rainstorm. I mean really pouring down sheets of rain. As we crossed the

Manning Crevice Suspension Bridge and got to the other side in the headlights by the side of the road is a man carrying a small gasoline can. Of course, in the semi wilderness like we were in, we always stopped and asked if someone needed help. In this case it seemed to be insane to be walking in the complete black of night with no light in a downpour carrying a can. That seemed quite incorrigible.

He said he was going to town to get some white gas for his stove. Town was still 15 miles away, and so at least a five hour walk in the rain, and that seemed to me to be quite stupid, so I offered him a ride to our place where He could spend the night. He agreed and got in the car.

The next morning Geneva invites him for breakfast and we get the story that he has a photography project and needs to go into Burgdorff Hot Springs and get some winter pictures for a magazine. Normally, most people go into Burgdorff by snowmobile in the winter time from McCall.

It seems like a perhaps reasonable story, even though to get to Burgdorff the way he was going would require a 30 mile trek over deep snow with snowshoes. We take him to town to get some gasoline. He tells us he is from Michigan and has been hired for a project to get a story and pictures of Burgdorff. It is now the dead of winter so that seems to me a sort of nasty ordeal, but then who am I to judge the complete miseries of the project just to get some winter pictures. He says he has made it partway and has been taking animal pictures. He says he has a small tent in which he does not make a fire so as to not scare the animals and just spends all of his time watching for animals and taking pictures.

In Riggins he not only gets gasoline but also additional supplies and I offer to take him up to the snow line with my pickup for his return trip. I do not remember where he had left his two pack frames, but I transported him and two pack frames up the French Creek switchback grade to where the road crosses the ridge before the Fall Creek watershed. Even though the road has very little snow on it, he says this is far enough as he intends to go cross country across fall Creek and go up a draw to where his camp is on the next ridge. We say our goodbye and he is on his own.

129

Maybe three months or more later in the spring he shows up at our door skinny as a rail. He has been living on Top Ramen soup mix for three months and he is starving.

Well Geneva feeds him her wonderful meals, but he takes it easy knowing if he eats to much too quick it would be bad.

He says he needs to talk to his wife in Michigan and get some money so he can go home. He used our phone (we are the first phone on the river as one descends the river from the wilderness) to call his wife. Eventually, after a few days and several phone calls, he says his wife is going to send him money. He goes to town and that is the last we ever see or hear of him.

This is a strange story and my thinking is he was running from something, maybe his wife, or a past conflict with his wife, his creditors, or maybe the cops. Understand he was in a complete wilderness for maybe four months with not any contact with anybody but us. I presume he must have rebuilt a relationship with his wife on the phone so that she eventually found some money for him to use to come home.

He never made it to Burgdorff. He said the snow was too deep. I could have told him that before he started.

That is not the end of the story. About 20 years later I was talking to a friend of mine, Ron Smith, and told him this story. Ron said that that guy must have been the person that broke into his cabin on Fall Creek. Yes, somebody broke into Ron's cabin and made a real mess of it that same winter. Ron's cabin was not more than a ½ mile from where I left the pilgrim.

Well things are not always as they seem. Since I grew up in a marvelous Christian home, I think the best of people. I never thought that would be picture taking pilgrim was telling me lies, and I believed him, even though his story had seemed a little preposterous. You dear reader may learn a little from this. We who grow up in wonderful Christian homes think the best of most people and think most people are nice people; consequently, we have very little street smarts. In fact the Westminster Catechism (I grew up learning it) says all men are depraved and come short of the glory of God. So even though you know intellectually that all men are depraved, and therefore, evil, you do not really believe it because you grew up in a nice Christian culture where you encountered very few seemingly evil people.

In fact, as an old acquaintance I had at Litton Industries (actually he was more than an acquaintance as at times he, two friends, and I had rented a seasonal duck blind near Los Banos, California where we could hunt ducks and geese on Wednesdays, Saturdays, and Sundays) used to utter under his breath, as he periodically wandered by my desk, and disturbed my concentration on deep thinking physics of electrodynamics, "People are no damm good". Yes, unfortunately, that is true.

I never asked him why he was again thinking such and repeating it in my ears at that time once again, but he repeated it enough that it became a law of nature in his brain. I wish I had thought about his reflections a bit and presented the Westminster Catechism to him. It might have been a time for a great Christian witness.

Another time I was driving my pickup home to the ranch from Riggins. A little before the Partridge Creek bridge I encounter a car upside down in the in the middle of the road, completely blocking the road. Traffic had gathered, even though normal traffic on the river road is very light, with about a half dozen cars waiting up river and maybe three of us down river from the upside down car.

Here was my neighbor from French Creek, Jungert, drunk as a skunk walking from his upside down car to me and very quietly asked for help to get him out of there now, quick. Normally, his wife drove him to town every day so he could spend a little time at the bar and down a few. That day wife was gone somewhere and he attempted to drive his car back home in his inebriated condition.

Well a neighbor is a neighbor and he needed help, and the sheriff would show up after a while, and he would most assuredly get a DUI with lots of bad consequences for him. He had a little time as it would take 25 minutes for someone to get to town and call the Sheriff of Idaho County and if the sheriff deputy came from Grangeville that would be another hour or so.

The Salmon River Road proceeds up the river canyon with steep banks on the canyon wall side and the rather very cold, very large, fast flowing river on the other side, maybe 50 vertical feet below the road. This road is narrow and then was just a gravel graded dirt track. If ones car somehow climbed the bank because of an incautious driver, in attempting to correct the trajectory one either flipped upside down onto the road or went back across the road into the river like Geneva did when she hit a rock, broke the kingpin on her front right wheel, and sailed through the air for the river. Very fortunately, she hit the only pine tree in half a mile, flipped upside down, and slid down to the river, but stopped just short of the water when the river was very low. Daughter Kim got her mother and little niece, Katie (2 ½), quickly out of the car as she said it might catch on fire. They then climbed back up to the road and walked to daughter Cindy's house about a mile away. They were a little banged up and bruised but otherwise sound with no serious injuries.

Jungert was lucky as he was just upside down, and not in the river where for sure he would have gone to his eternal reward, probably; because he must have been going real slow. So, quietly without any fanfare, I took my winch cable from the wench built on my pickup front bumper, and proceeded to his car and wrapped the cable around his car, and attached it to the frame, and proceeded to wench his car back right side up. He had told me he did not care how much I damaged his car as he wanted it out of there quick. It almost takes more time to tell it than to do it. He quickly got in his car and drove off up river, seemingly sober.

Yes, one will do most anything for a neighbor. Everybody else just stood around and watched. I did not like any possible publicity, so I quickly put my cable away, got into my truck and drive off up river after him.

Here is another Jungert story. For some reason I decided to get into the cow business. I had a little talk with my friend at church who had found some excellent horses for me. He said sure, he would sell me his cattle. I bought 10 or so cows. They were of the Herford type with some Holstein blood in them. The Holstein blood he said gave the calves more milk and they grew faster and bigger than pure Herford.

Well now I was in the cow business. I needed a bull so I bought a nice gentle Herford bull from another friend on the Little Salmon River. Well my cows get bred and come next spring I start having calves. It seems my cows have BVD (bovine viral diarrhea). With BVD the calves are born rather weak but if you find them quickly after they are just born and get them to a warm barn and doctor them a bit they will survive. This of course keeps me busy as every day I search for new calves. Some cows think it is a nasty thing for somebody like me to carry off their new calf, so it is a very tricky business.

Well, I lose a calf or two but I have a nice expanded herd. As cows are wont to do they wander off now and then. Once in a while they wander up river to French Creek where Jungert lives. So periodically when I get a call from Jungert, I saddle up my appaloosa, CJ, and chase cows. CJ must have done it before as he just loves getting behind the cows, and bites them on the butt to make them move faster. Once in a while a cow aims a hind foot at CJ and me so one has to be quick and careful. Understand that CJ is a quick, agile, horse with lots of stamina so he is impatience following cows. In fact one time when I was chasing cows from French Creek in the dark on CJ going after some cows who had run up a draw he ran just below a big limb and I was suspended like Absalom in the air in the dark for a few seconds before descending to the earth with a crash, losing my glasses in the process. That occasion developed some nasty bruises. Obviously, one had to be careful around CJ.

Eventually, CJ did one too many stunts, and I resolved to sell him. A problem was he always moved too fast. This is great when one is riding around the countryside. But when one is leading the pack string and CJ goes too fast, the string protests with one nasty thing, or another. And this causes lots of trouble. I loved ridding CJ as he walked really smooth, had lots of personality, lots of get up and go, and unbelievable stamina.

Well one time we were heading back from elk hunting camp to the Ranch with a full pack string with elk and camp and what not, so I packed CJ and rode another one of my young mares. CJ's pack must have had a raddle in it as about ½ mile away from camp he just bucked and bucked until he was rid of the whole thing and scattered the pack contents all over the countryside. I caught CJ, took everything else off him and loaded another young horse I had available with everything that had been on CJ and let CJ loose to get home by himself. That was enough. I resolved he had to go.

Well, one day ole Jungert is driving past my place going home from the bars and says my cows are in his raspberry patch. I say, really? Well I can't remember how the conversation flowed from there but it was cordial with a little banter. I must have muttered something about them cows as by this time I was not really thrilled by the cow business. Do you want to sell those cows? I did some mental calculation trying not to lose any money from the experience and six grand entered into my head. I said I would sell them for $6,000. Without any hesitation he said, "I will go home and get my check book". Thirty minutes later he hands me a check for six grand.

Wow! I am rid of those cows. I do not have to track down CJ from off the mountainside somewhere and ride him up to French Creek to chase cows again. What a relief!

The end of the story is that Jungert bragged in the bars in the town of Riggins that he had really put one over on Kooyers. That fall after the grass was gone he had them cows trucked to the sale yard and got nine grand for them. Yes, he made a really nice profit, but we were both very happy with the deal.

The really funny part of the story is that Jungert did not have and never had a raspberry patch! Maybe he did put one over on me! No, I was very glad to be rid of those cows.

Tracking down CJ from somewhere on the mountainside was not as difficult as it might seem. I had an SR 250 1980 Honda dirt bike. It was a fantastic piece of machinery. By trial and error I had learned to run the thing without getting killed.

I had watched my eventual son in law, Guy, ascend the mountainside opposite the ranch White House where we lived, across the Salmon River, on a very loud dirt bike, very early (maybe 5 AM) one summer morning. I mean the mountainside is almost vertical with a 2000 foot climb. I think he was trying to impress my daughter Cindy with his prowess. Let's face it, he was very good, and I was very impressed, even though I had decided I did not want him for a son in law.

I had acquired a new SR 500 Honda in California through a friend of mine that came to work for the mine. He loved dirt biking and thought I needed one too. That 500 bike would have killed me. If one opened the throttle too quickly it could jump from one side of the road to another. Prudence told me to sell it. A kid came to look at it and gave it a trial run. He came back from his run and said this bike can climb telephone poles! Yes indeed. He bought it, and I went to McCall and bought the 250.

My friend, Dan Fodge, taught me a lot about dirt bikes. I soon was navigating the Salmon River Canyon slopes. I used to climb up the Elkhorn Creek slopes where my horses were wont to graze. If I was able to get above the horses and chase them for a while they would go down to the barn. I put out hay or grain and soon had those horses trained so that if I got near them and revved the motorcycle real good they would get the message and head for the barn. Horses are very intelligent and learn quick.

One day we got a call from the Riggins EMT (Emergency Medical Technicians) that a woman was injured up Partridge Creek, and that they may need help. It turned out that the woman injured was Margaret Tatro. Her story is very interesting. She was the daughter of Dead Shot Read, who was known as the last of the western gun fighters in the United States. The history of Dead Shot is recounted in a little book, "Rewards of Rage", by Art Colson. Dead Shot eloped from the Lewiston, Idaho area with a 14 year old lady who had nursed him back to health from gunshots wounds. They went out into the wilderness and lived on the South Fork of the Salmon River where they raised a large family. In later years the State of Idaho harassed them for truancy about their children so they spent winters in the Sweet, Idaho area. There Mrs. Tatro as a young girl attended a little Pentecostal Church. She eventually then went on to bible school in Alaska and met John Tatro. They then became Baptist missionaries and spent near 40 years in Japan. When the Tatros retired they returned to Riggins. All of the Dead Shot Read children, of course, grew up in the wilderness and were very competent at hunting and trapping. Billy Read, Dead Shot's son, and Margaret's brother, was employed for years as a government trapper in the Riggins Area. He had taken his dear sister deer hunting and that is where our story begins.

They had driven up the road along Partridge Creek toward the Carlson owned Basin fields. Three quarters of the way up to the Basin fields they spotted a very nice mule tail buck. They shot it and proceeded to where it

135

went down. They encountered a very steep deep draw between from where they shot to where the deer was. In descending into this draw Margaret fell and broke her hand and leg and got bruised up plenty bad.

So when I am about to leave the ranch to go to Partridge Creek, not knowing what we might be in for, along comes a passerby whom I engaged in conversation. I explained the EMTs might need help and he agreed to accompany me and see what the situation was.

It turned out that that tough young cowpoke, as that is what he looked like, was indispensable for the project. The EMTs were three rather weak looking, very pleasant, otherwise very competent ladies, who must have some time or other volunteered, and then got trained for the Riggins EMT corps.

We met the EMT truck at the Partridge Creek Bridge over the Salmon River and followed them up the road to where the road crossed the same draw that Mrs. Tatro had fallen into. We volunteers then received instruction from the EMT ladies and all of us ascended the draw to where Margaret was with her brother, Billy Read. This was not easy. As we ascended the terrain became very steep with periodic cliffs as high as seven feet or so.

We got to Mrs. Tatro and the EMTs bandaged her up and put blow up splints on her injured limbs, and gave her a few shots to make her sleepy and take away the pain. We tied her down to a stretcher and then the ordeal began. She was a rather heavy woman and the six of us were really inadequate for the project. But we carefully carried her down the draw taking plenty of time, especially down the cliffs. The cowpoke was indispensable. He was very strong and sort of directed each of us as to where to carry the weight. We made it to the EMT truck in good shape and they left for the hospital, and the cowpoke and I continued on with our normal activities.

Again, this is what people do for neighbors and passersby and other fellow humans on Salmon River.

Another time after a nice snowfall a young couple knocked at our door and said they needed help. They were from McCall and had gone up river for a fun ride. They said they had been driving in deep snow and their vehicle had got too close to the edge of the road and needed a tow.

I loaded them up in my Toyota Land Cruiser and we drove up river for about 10 miles to their vehicle. Their vehicle was in a very precarious situation. It had stopped on the very edge of the road on the edge of a cliff and hung up maybe 100 feet above the Salmon River. They were very lucky to be alive. If they had fallen into that cold river there is little chance of getting out, especially after such a fall.

I looked it over for a while. I had a real good transfer case driven wench on my Toyota, and good 4 wheel drive, and good tires. But with my wench cable attached to that vehicle if it slipped over the cliff chances are my Toyota would go into the river too. I am normally brave but usually not too stupid. The spirit told me to forget it. I said I was sorry but I could not help them. We returned to the ranch and Geneva fed them one of her great meals, and we put them up in the Red Barn cabin for the night as it was rather late and dark by this time.

In the morning they called a tow truck service and the tow truck came by and picked them up and they went upriver. The tow truck guy charged them about $750. Wow. I was appalled. What a waste of hard earned money. What a way to end a recreational drive on Salmon River.

Another day a kayaker knocked on our door and asked to use the telephone to call the sheriff for help. He had lost his kayaker friend.

The river was running at spring flood near 70,000 to 100,000 cubic feet per second. Just to let you get a picture of that imagine in your mind Niagara Falls. When Niagara Falls is at max flow in the daytime it is about 200,000 cubic feet per second or about twice the flow of the Salmon River at that time. The river water is very cold, maybe 39 degrees Fahrenheit. This guy was one of those extreme adventurers where running the river at that flow is a fun exciting challenge. He is extremely well prepared and has all of the latest high Tec stuff.

Well it seemed the last time he had seen his river partner was about 20 miles or so up river when they both were trapped in a violent eddy and were going past each other in opposite directions going around in a violent circle around a suck hole. He said he finally make it out of the eddy without being sucked under and continued down river. He waited in the next convenient quiet eddy for his partner. After a while his partner's kayak shows up but no partner. The kayak is passenger less.

Well he waits for a while and then decides to climb up the bank and walk back to the powerful circular eddy with the suck hole. He has to climb up a very steep mountainside; maybe 1000 feet or so in elevation and then climb back down to that big bad eddy. Still he can find no partner. He climbs back up and hikes back down to his kayak. After searching around for quite some time and more, he tows his partner's kayak down to our place to use the telephone.

The sheriff agrees to send a helicopter in the morning. Well about the time the helicopter shows up, partner is found walking down the road. It seems that somehow they missed each other in the climb over the mountain from one eddy to another. Eventually partner decided to swim down the river and forget the kayak. After spending the night in some bushes he walks down the road towards town where he is found.

What really impressed me was the high Tech capability and the shear ability of these men. They were very good athletes, in very good physical condition, knew what they were doing, and capable of facing anything the river might present to them. What they lacked was a clear plan in case they got separated.

One day for some reason I have long forgotten, I was traveling alone out in the boonies with my 88 Ford diesel pickup up the multiple switch back very long French Creek grade. Very few people travel this road. I encountered a man walking down the road. He was a man I slightly knew. He told me his truck was stuck. I offered to help him. We drove up the grade about five miles towards Burdorf and turned off on a jeep trail to an old homestead. It is a very pretty place with a nice large spring that flowed into a hanging valley over the French Creek Canyon. There his pickup was mired in heavy muck up to above both axels. He had left his wife Anita with the truck and she was cold and miserable. Well it was not easy but I travel in the boonies with lots of equipment and with the wench and deadmans (A steel post driven into the ground) I managed to pull the truck out of the muck and he went on his way with his wife.

Over the years as I run into Anita, as she occasionally works at sundry very low wage store jobs; this memory comes back to me. Here seems a tragedy of life. She had an outstanding supreme talent as a piano and organ player. She and her husband had five children and were very active in the Assembly of God Church leading the youth and she playing for the services. The story is somebody discovered him drinking a beer and he was canned from his ministry. Then later they divorced.

This memory brings sadness to me. They were Christian people with lots of talent having a fine family, and now in later middle age and early old age, her countenance shows a very, very sad person. I do not know the details and those would be immaterial anyway. People need the Lord Jesus. People need to forgive each other. Husbands and wives need to forgive each other and go on. Old age in poverty, as I well know, is a miserable way to live. Divorce leads to poverty. Absolutely avoid it no matter what the cost and pain may seem.

I am reminded of an old quote attributed to Ben Franklin. "There are only three true friends in life – a faithful dog, ready money, and an old wife." Yes, as I well know, and through which I have experienced great joy, an old wife in old age is the best true friend you will ever have.

When we first came to Riggins Geneva and I joined the Riggins Community Church. It is an independent Church, originally started by some women in the 1950's. There were some really nice Christian people there and it became our Church home.

We had come to Riggins permanently in June of 1980. Our ranch about fifteen miles upriver from Riggins was called the old Howard Ranch which was one of the earliest white man permanent habitations in Idaho. People by the name of Shearer settled there in about 1861 or so just after the huge Gold Strike in Florence about 5 miles north of the Ranch by the way the crow flies. The Shearers son was a confederate army officer. He was captured by the Union. He escaped but was captured again and then escaped again. He then went west and came to Idaho and worked for his parents running the river ferry at the ranch. The ranch and ferry were on the main trail from the north Idaho gold strikes to the southern ones. This Shearer's son led the volunteers at the battle of Whitebird against the Nez Pierce. He again led the volunteers in the Sheepeater War against the Sheepeater Indians. There he took an arrow in his knee, and he eventually died from the lingering effects of that wound. The Howards bought the ranch in about 1893, after that it was called the Howard Ranch. We were the fourth owners of that Ranch.

The Howard Ranch was especially enjoyable for Geneva and the children. In the summer Susanne and Kimberly and mom went to the lovely beaches just up river a quarter of a mile or so. They thoroughly enjoyed swimming in the river on hot days to cool off. The climate at the Ranch is unique as it is in the bottom of the Salmon River Canyon with the canyon walls making the wind currents very quiet at the Ranch. The wind only blows when a local thunder storm moves through. Cool air descends down the Elkhorn Creek drainage making the Ranch area near the Creek about ten degrees cooler than the flat areas. It is an extremely beautiful place.

In the first few years we were at the ranch many friends and relatives came and visited and enjoyed the beach and the river. Kim grew up on the ranch from six years old until she graduated from Salmon River High school in 1992. Kim loved riding her horse on the beaches and into the river. She usually rode Silver as that Arab mare would go most anywhere it was encouraged. Kim for a while was the mascot for the Salmon River High Savages. She was really cute with her plastic spear doing a Savage War Dance at the basketball games while the band played an appropriate war dirge for the opposition team. She attended Pepperdine University and graduated in 1996. Kim and her husband Derrick were married in 2003. To this day when their family vacations (Kim, Derrick, Ryan, and Jack) she loves to spend time on the Salmon River beaches.

Susanne went to the Salmon River schools for five years from the 7th to 10th grades. We sent her back to Los Altos to attend Los Altos High school for her 11th and 12th years. She lived with our good friends Nat and Del Hansen and did well there. In the summers she worked for her dad in the office at the Ranch and her mom doing sundry things. She worked for our rafting company, Salmon River Challenge (SRC), once in a while rowing a supply raft as she was too young to be a licensed boatman to carry passengers.

140

(Boatlady?) She did well and never flipped over her raft because of a wave or rock. After High School graduation she went to Cal Poly University in San Louis Obispo, California, and graduated from there in 1991. She went back to the Bay area after college and worked for a marketing company in San Francisco for a while. She met her husband Brian Schlador at Peninsula Bible Church (PBC) in Palo Alto and was married there in 1992. After she and Brian started their family she then worked for her uncle, Gordon Kooyers, in his insurance agency business. They then moved to Idaho and have three children, Jacob, Kayla, and Tyler.

Cindy went to Salmon River High School her junior and senior years. She fell in love with Guy Carlson and they were married in February 1982 while Cindy yet 17 and she was still in high school. They have four children, Christy, Niki, Cassie, and Cody.

Crystal went off to the University of Idaho as she had just graduated from Los Altos High School in 1980 when we moved to Idaho. She married John Cook in June of 1982 with an outdoor yard ceremony at the Ranch with boatman of SRC serving the celebration meal. They have four children, Katie, Warren, Dustin, and Annaliese. Crystal, who was the music teacher at the time, at a Salmon River High school basketball game, once sang the National Anthem. My hair stood on end and my eyes filled with tears. She sang a cappella with no accompaniment. She started at a high pitch and with her extremely high clear voice just sang out strongly, her voice never cracking on the very high pitched notes. I watched the crowd and fully half of them turned their eyes from the flag to see who was singing. I have never heard the National Anthem sang better than that in all my years of listening to Television and being at other public events. It made me a very proud father to have such a talented daughter.

Brenda graduated from Los Altos High in 1978, was a student at Cal Poly University, and married Mark Lawler at PBC a few weeks before we left for Idaho in 1980. They have three children, Matthew, Joshua, and Megan. Brenda graduated in 1982 with a major in business. Mark's comment when spending time at the Ranch was, "This is so great. It is as close to heaven as one can get."

Sheridan graduated from Los Altos High School in 1977 and went to the

141

University of California at Davis and graduated in Electrical Engineering in 1981. After graduating he came to the Ranch where he worked as a computer programmer on his dad's VAX 750 and developed the electrical control system for the hydro and the very unique electrical switching system at the Bighouse at the Ranch. He left to work at General Electric in San Jose in 1985. In 1989 he married Phebe Mintz. They have four children, Rebecca, Sarah, Jeremiah, and Elizabeth. They moved to Idaho in the year 2001.

In 1991 I must have come into some funds. I owed Sheridan for work that he had done and had been unable to pay him. Here is a letter I wrote to him when I was able to pay him some.

Dear Sheridan,   September 9, 1991

Happy Birthday!! When I looked at the calendar to find out what day it is I saw it was your birthday.

Enclosed you will find a check for $10,000. For tax purposes consider it a gift.

Sheridan you have been a very fine son, one a father can be very proud of. I thank you very much for your pleasant spirit, patience, and your endurance through some of the strange things I have lead you. I remember the times you spent here on the ranch with very pleasant memories. I remember the productive times you spent on the hydro system, the computer programing, and all the work you did. Again thank you very much. I also appreciate very much your patience in waiting for this $10,000.

Looking back it seems all the financial ventures I encouraged you to inter turned out to be mistakes. I apologize. In hindsight I should have been much more careful and not so presumptuous. I am thinking about the Voss place purchase, the Moria money put into Salmon River Challenge, and all the work we put into Salmon River Challenge. Of course, most financial ventures that one inters into will probably not work out. That's something to remember when you prepare to inter into sundry financial ventures. Yet the right venture at the right time can be very, very rewarding as you no doubt observed in the managed futures business in the late 1970's. I went into that at just the right time. The industry had just been started and had been proven successful by others. I entered at just the right time and road the crest of expansion and excitement to a lot of success. The time for that business has now passed. It's quite over regulated and enough people have been burned badly enough so that it is an extremely hard sell. I believe it is just plain over. Only the very large extremely well capitalized and managed firms will now succeed and even then very bad things can happen as you no doubt have read about the Jones and Solomon Brothers troubles.

We are still trying to sell our place. Whether we will be successful or not I do not know. We have stopped making payments so the place will probably be foreclosed unless we sell it by January 1st. Your mother said you might be willing to lend this money back again. If I need it I will let you know, but this time I will pay you interest and make it a new deal.

The shingles has been very hard on me. It started when I was at your house and I did not know what it was. It's a great deal of pain. In fact so much so I can't stand it without drugs. It has been a time of great trial for me with the Lord. I have come to believe that in all likelihood old Job had the shingles. The doctor says the shingles are touched off by stress. Old Job had lots of that. In my case I have just gone through more stress than any time of my life.

You talked like you might come hunting this year. I would certainly love to have you come. This year the seasons have been changed a little so that we are going up the mountain on Monday October 14th. So far only my cousin John Van Spronsen is going for sure on the hunt, so there would be only the three of us. This may very well be the last year for a hunt up behind the ranch. Your mother drew a cow elk tag so she may well go with us also.

Cindy wants to use the printer so I think I will stop this letter.

Again I thank you very much for being a kind, patient son. May the Lord Jesus continue to bless you very, very, much.

Your father,
Gerald

As of 2013 we have twenty grandchildren and eleven great grandchildren. We try to spend time enjoying everyone. Life on the Salmon River is delightful even though we have lived through our trials here. We grow in the grace and knowledge of the Lord Jesus. We love Him. We now fellowship at the Little Salmon Bible Church in Pollock, Idaho. We are not members of that Church as I find assenting to their statement of membership unacceptable.

FIVE

MEMORABLE HUNTS HORSEBACKS BACKPACKS

My interest in fishing, guns, hunting, and such started at an early age. In a previous chapter I recounted getting up early in the morning and fishing all day when I was about 5 or 6 years old in Hixton, Wisconsin. My Mother was very concerned about me, and was so glad to see me when I got home, she did not give a spanking. I caught two trout and two suckers.

Occasionally my brother Howard would recruit me to go squirrel hunting with him. This was about the only thing I remember he every really did with me when I was still a child. He would recruit me or order me along, I do not remember which. We would go to a squirrel patch, must have been an oak forest or somewhere where there was lots of squirrel food. Howard had some kind of old Model T or otherwise decrepit old car. Arriving at the site he would sneak into the woods with me with the dog following. The first squirrel found, I was ordered to watch and not lose sight of it. This was no easy task as the squirrels usually soon went high in a very large tree. The dog watched the next squirrel. The third squirrel Howard found he would shoot. After the sound of the shot all the squirrels would hide. Howard would then come back to the dog and shoot the squirrel the dog was watching and then come and shoot the squirrel I was watching. If I had lost sight of that squirrel, I would receive a cuff and a chewing out. The dog never seemed to lose sight of his squirrel. Usually we got two or three squirrels out of this try. We then would get back in the car and proceed to the next squirrel forest and repeat the process. I learned to enjoy this a lot especially when I eventually learned not to lose sight of the squirrel and occasionally receive a good job grumble from my brother Howard. Those were depression years and even though food was plentiful in rural Wisconsin, there was no money to buy it so squirrel meat was enjoyed by the whole family. It may have been a real necessity, but I did not know it.

My sister Marcia was a real tomboy and scrapper and just a year younger than me. Howard recruited her also. When she lost her squirrel Howard was kind to her and did not give her a cuff or chew her out like he did me. It seemed in the end Marcia got better at keeping track of her squirrel than I did mine. These experiences taught us to be comfortable in the woods and not get lost at a very early age. I had just turned seven in the fall of the last year we were in Hixton so my sister Marcia had to be six. At the time that I write this that seems a very young age to be left alone in the woods watching a squirrel, but my mother must have somehow trusted my brother Howard and his ability to find us. Howard was twelve years older than me so he was about 18 or so at that time.

After moving to South Range, Wisconsin, and brother Howard went off to the war, I acquired my own BB gun. I was about eight or nine years old then. I used to love to wander in the woods by myself One day I found a red squirrel in a relatively small tree. Red squirrels are smaller than the bigger gray squirrels Howard hunted. There were no other trees close by so I had that squirrel sort of trapped. I shot him again and again with seemingly no effect. He got mad at me and made lots of noise and actually got closer to me. Eventually I must have got a lucky shot and stunned him and he fell out of the tree. I jumped and stomped on him quick and I had my first squirrel!

Taking the life of an animal seemed very normal in my growing up. We had chickens and pigs and ducks which we killed and ate as required for life. Nevertheless, when I shot my first bird it was rather traumatic. My

146

first BB gun was an old cast off of somebody's and was very weak. I sneaked up to a little bird in a lilac bush, got about a foot away and shot him. Blood squirted out from a neck wound. The sight made me a little sick. Hunting animals seems to be encoded in our genes; however, and even though we are taking the life of an animal I eventually become comfortable with doing it. Nevertheless, to me it was never a pleasure or something enjoyed. What is fun and enjoyable is the challenge of the forest and woods, rivers and streams, and skill at handling rifles, pistols, and shotguns, and becoming quite good at being successful at stalking and pursuing game. Of all the things I ever hunted we usually ate what we shot. The exception to that would be varmints or pests.

MENDOCINO

Sometimes there were even exceptions to that. One was shooting ocean ducks from a top of a 100-foot cliff on the point at Mendocino with a 22 rifle. It took considerable skill and it seldom happened that I hit one. These ducks would fly just above the water about a foot or so and traveled very fast, maybe 40 miles or so per hour. We would shoot down on them from the top of a cliff above them. You could see where the bullet would hit the water and adjust your next shot to get closer to the duck. It taught me how much to lead a duck with a 22 rifle and gave me valuable skills, which I used in later hunting. At that time I had a 22 semi-auto and I used up lots of ammunition.

Varmint hunting along the ocean cliffs near the Mendocino town dump was also similar. There was a chute built on the edge of the cliff above the ocean where people would go to dump their garbage and trash. It was about 300 yards or so from our house. There was a series of indented cliffs in the area so one could go out on the point of one and see the opposite bank. Ground squirrels would detect our presence and run for their burrows along the side of the cliff. With my 22 semi-auto I would shoot at them as they ran. Usually I got in four or five shots in before they reached their hole. This also was good practice.

How I acquired my 22-rifle came about this way. We got to California in 1946 and were living in a shack on the Fruit Ranch run my Uncle John

VanSpronsen. My brothers had just returned from the war. My brother Orneal acquired a 22 semi-auto rifle. He would target shoot in the orchard. He also taught me to shoot the 22. After we moved to Mendocino in 1947 I bought the rifle from him. The funds used were part of the great sums I earned as an, "extra" in the movie Johnie Belinda which was made in Mendocino in the spring of 1948. So when I was 12 and going on 13, I acquired my first rifle. Not long after that I acquired an old long hexagon barreled Winchester 25-35 from some old timer in the area for $15. (That was about a day's pay as an extra and extremely good pay for a kid.) It had a peep sight which I did not like having never used one before. I added a buckhorn rear sight to the rifle. This could easily be done as the peep sight folded down on to the stock. The old geezer from whom I acquired the rifle represented he had taken many, many deer with the rifle. That old 25-35 was for me a frustration. It was really too heavy and long to carry through the thick brush common to the hunting areas of Mendocino. I did not like the peep sight, and I never could find a running deer in the buckhorn sight.

My first encounter with a legal buck occurred soon after I had acquired the rifle. My dog, Stumpy, (He was half dachshund and had a tail about two inches long, consequently, the name Stumpy) went into the woods as I was proceeding along the edge of a clearing south of the Compche road. He jumped a nice big 4-point (western count, 4 points to a side) buck and the deer ran right across the clearing in front of me. I don't even remember getting the gun up. I just looked at it astounded.

My buddy Wilson Locke invited me hunting with him and some of his friends. They had an old Model T type of pickup and we jumped in the back. We went hunting near where Wilson lived. We spotted a deer in a clearing above us and ran after him. These friends of Wilson were track stars and they just chased the deer like a pack of hounds. This astounded me as my Dad hunted deer by going along very, very, slowly and very, very quietly. When I was small my Dad used to let me follow him. I was always making too much noise and constantly told to be quiet and not step on sticks. So to run after a deer like a bunch of track stars was something completely beyond my experience. We followed the deer trail down into a gulch. It forked so some took the left gulch, some followed up the ridge between the gulches where the deer went, and I took the right hand gulch. I slowed down and walked and moved up the left side of the gulch about 50 yards above the bottom. I had not gone very far when I heard a shot and a shout. Soon here came the deer down the gulch. He crossed from my side to the other side angling up and across from me. I opened up. I shot at him at about 100 yards as he ran opposite me on the hillside. Eventually he must have thought something was fishy so he turned around and ran back to the bottom of the gulch. I shot some more. I even reloaded my gun. Then the deer came on my side of the gulch right toward me. He crossed about 6 feet from me going flat out. My last shot was taken from the hip as he sailed by. I had fired a total of thirteen shots and never touched him. I could not believe it. My friends did not believe it. They said they thought there was a war on with all that shooting. Needless to say they never invited me to go hunting with them again. I was embarrassed and completely mortified. After that I hunted when I could by myself.

In any organized hunt which seemed to happen quite often, since I was usually the youngest and known to be the worst shot, I was assigned the role of running the dogs. California permitted deer hunting with dogs in those days. Generally we used dogs that had Australian Shepard blood in them. They functioned as jump dogs. Jump dogs ran the deer for 10 minutes or so and then came back to the dog runner. This is in contrast to hound dogs, which run the game for hours on end, and sometime for days or until the dog is exhausted. Using jump dogs in the thick brush where we hunted moved the deer around, hopefully past the standers who waited at clearings or ridges for the deer to pass by after they were disturbed and jumped by the dogs. I don't remember these hunts being very successful, but I enjoyed them very much as I usually had lots of action. A lot of the time I was crawling or just barely pushing through the thick brush. That experience taught me in later life to try to avoid the brush, but brush has always since then drawn me like a magnet, and it seems no matter where I have hunted I usually end up in a brush patch.

Once this other kid and I were assigned the job of running the dogs in what was called the pigmy forest south of Big River about 5 miles inland from the ocean. This pigmy forest as you can tell by the name is a rather thick stand of small pines and other trees not very tall. Where we hunted it was quite flat and so the other kid who was older than I got lost and lost his sense of direction. Since he was older than me, I had to defer to his judgment. We wandered around for hours completely lost. I wasn't lost but he sure was. I knew we should not separate so I stayed with him. Eventually, I convinced him that we should proceed north where I knew the river to be. At dark we hit the river canyon edge so he finally believed me completely. We descended the steep Redwood covered canyon wall to the river and walked toward the ocean. We eventually got out to the highway about midnight near the ocean but by that time no small part of the town was looking for us, including as I recall my brother Howard who must have come to Mendocino and had organized the hunt. That experience taught me to rely on my own judgment in such case, as I concluded that I was better at most things than others, especially in the sense of direction. I still have not lost that ability today. In a thick forest I always know where I am going and how to get back where I want to go. The key is to look back once in a while so you can recognize the landscape when you return.

In another place in this account I tell of trying to live off the land with Lloyd, "Portagee" Lowe. I spent lots of time on the river. It had the name of Big River. I guess because it was the biggest river around. My Dad somehow acquired a model 12 Winchester shotgun. Of course, usually anything my Dad acquired was considered family property, so I got to borrow it most any time. I hunted ducks with it on Big River in the late fall after salmon season. We had an old rowboat my brother Gordon had salvaged out of the ocean near the breakers. It wasn't much, but we fixed it up and it worked. We would row up the river and pass shoot at ducks as they flew by or worked the ponds on the tidal flats along the river for puddle ducks such as Mallards. Tidewater extended about 5 miles up the river so there was a nice stretch of river to row around. Above tidewater the forest came down to the river and the river was difficult to navigate because of the rocks and current. The flats were great places to hunt.

One day as I was rowing up the river with a buddy, I saw large numbers of dead mud hens floating by. Mud hens are a sort of trash duck like bird, also called a coot, which tasted badly so we seldom ate them. That year the area was full of an astounding number of mud hens. After a while I heard shooting and then came upon Joe Gots and another kid making war on the mud hen population. It seems he had started a one-kid war to eliminate mud hens from the river. That day he must have shot hundreds of them just to get rid of them. That was not my style.

I had had a bad experience with Joe Gots. When I first got to Mendocino when I was about 12, the friends I had decided to form a gang. This was before gang became such a bad word. We built a clubhouse on one side of a small gulch behind Gary Hater's house. On the other side of the gulch some, "enemies", built their clubhouse, behind Glen Walbridge's house that also became a fort. Ours was much more elaborate than theirs. I was an engineer even in those days, so I designed a three-story job between some trees out of old lumber we procured somewhere. Joe belonged to the enemies and lived up in Furrytown Hill east of town and walked a little way through the forest to get to the fort area. Of course, we challenged our, "enemies", to a fight. Dirt clods and apples were the weapons. We just threw them at one another. We also made elaborate decorated shields to defend ourselves from the clod and apple missiles. We waged war on one another periodically. We all were friends at school but once we got to our clubhouse we were, "enemies".

Well one day we decided to have a serious war. As I remember it was on a Saturday and lasted most of the day. There were about 3 or 4 of us on each side and we made charges and counter charges across the gulch to capture each other. We were getting tired and two of my side had retired to the clubhouse. I sometimes was quite aggressive and managed to capture one of the enemies. I then organized a great charging sweep and we captured all of them. We decided they must suffer for their defeat, so we forced them into the bottom of our clubhouse and locked them in with some old burning inner tubes. In other words we gassed them. That was not my idea but it must have made sense. Well after their screams, shouts, and coughing became serious we let them out. They were really wiped out. That was the end of our dirt and apple wars.

Since the gang thing then became a little boring, I decided to join the other side which included Glen and Joe Gots. Joe Gots and I decided to build a really spectacular clubhouse. Back in the redwood forest halfway to his house a redwood tree had half fallen against some other redwood trees and was on about a 45-degree angle. We could climb up the slanting redwood tree and get into the top of the other redwood trees. Wow, what an opportunity. There were three redwood trees with their tops about 20 feet apart. I soon conceived that we could bring lumber up there from the ground and build a platform for a real tree house using the three trees to

151

support cross members. The spot chosen was about 100 feet off the ground so it was also real scary. We "found" the lumber and got started. I soon discovered it was no easy task to get the lumber up into the trees and I remembered a block and tackle that I had. I went to get it but when I returned Joe recognized it as his. I had procured it on one of our raids on the enemy's clubhouse and forgotten where I had got it. Joe took great offence at this and accused me of stealing his block and tackle. That ended my great tree house building project. Many times I have looked back and much regretted not building that tree house. It would have been spectacular. Imagine a tree house 100 feet up from the ground in a redwood tree! 99 out of 100 kids would have been too scared to even climb up there.

That 12-gage shotgun that my dad had acquired was very dangerous. For some reason once in a while when I operated the pump action to inject a new shell the gun would fire without the trigger being pulled. Once it almost shot my foot off and another time after I had shot at a duck and was lowering the gun it went off and the load just missed Portegee Lloyd's head. That taught me a very important lesson that must be remembered. "Never trust any gun". Always point the gun at some innate object and treat it at all times with respect as if it were loaded. This is a very important lesson for everyone to learn early in life. It has stood by me well. I have never had a gun accident since and no one in any of my camps has had a gun accident. A rule of thumb is never hunt with or be around or camp with people who are careless with guns or even inadvertently point guns at anybody they do not intend to shoot.

My brother, Orneal, had graduated from college, got married, and moved to Westwood, California in the Sierra Nevada near Lake Almanor. He asked my dad if he would send him the 12 gage to hunt ducks there. My dad made a box for it in the shape of a shotgun, boxed it up and mailed it to Westwood. It never made it. Somebody stole it from the mail. My dad had it insured and got more money from the post office than what he had paid for it. In hindsight it was probably God's providence getting that thing out of our lives before somebody got killed or seriously injured by it. The lesson from that is, get rid of anything dangerous before it disrupts or destroys your life.

I had a friend from Sunday school named Fred Johnson. Not many kids came to Sunday school and his mother was involved in the church so she brought him every Sunday. His father was a retired naval petty officer. That in itself could make anybody a little weird. Fred detested his dad and the feeling was mutual. The feelings between them must have come from the military environment and the fact Fred probably almost never saw his dad when he was growing up, and so once retired his dad did not seem to work and was always there bossing him around. I would often spend Sunday afternoons with him at his parent's ranch. His mother would bring me back in the evening for youth group or other Sunday evening activities. Fred was a gun nut and completely fascinated by guns and explosives.

He sometimes would shoot up a whole case of 22 ammo in a week. That amounts to 500 rounds in a week. I never could have afforded that. I sometimes maybe shot up a box a week. (About 50 rounds) His father called him a stump hunter. His father hated guns so Fred just shot up everything he saw. No bird, snake, or anything that moved was safe around that ranch. One time the creek below his ranch, a tributary to Little River, (i.e. in contrast to Big River) you can see the early pioneers there must have had lots of imagination in naming rivers, was just full of salamanders. I mean hundreds of thousands of them. I have never seen anything like that before or since. They crawled all over the place and got into everything. Fred decided that this was too much and started a one-kid war on salamanders. He shot thousands of them. And I helped.

Once, Fred and I happened on to a case of dynamite. We could not believe our good fortune. Try as we might we could not make the stuff go off. It was probably just as well. That however started my interest in gunpowder. I was reading a Scientific American magazine in the High School library one-day when somehow I got detention for something I did and discovered the formula for black powder. 15% charcoal, 10 % sulfur, and 75 % saltpeter. Wow! The charcoal I made. The Sulfur was easy to get as it was used on grape leaves and for drying apricots, and I found a ready supply. The saltpeter was bought down at Mendosa's store. Sometimes the clerk or a Mendosa would ask me what I was going to do with the saltpeter, but vague answers always worked and they always sold it to me. After all, my dad was the preacher. I never knew what real buyers of the stuff used it for. I never thought of making a pipe bomb and that was just as well. Fred might have if he had been involved in this project, but I never really told anybody about what I was doing. My sister watched, however, but probably did not really know what I was up to either.

My best success was shooting rockets out over the ocean. They were beautiful. I used paper towel type of cardboard tubes stuffed full of black power as propellant. They did not have much control surface so were rather erratic in flight, but they worked spectacularly. Once when I was messing around a spark somehow flew into a can of black powder. It went off and the blast just went by my face in a big red ball of fire. After that I became spooky around the stuff and lost interest in making any more rockets.

Fred's parents place was covered with huge redwood stumps left over from pioneer logging days. Fred's dad and Fred were forever trying to burn them out to increase their pasture and open fields. Redwood just does not burn very well, especially underground and wet. Well black powder with a large excess of saltpeter will burn right down into the stump and get it started burning. We discovered this one day trying to blow up a stump. I had used a little there in an experiment to help Fred with his stumps. It is difficult to get gunpowder to blow up unless it is confined. In our experiments the powder never blew up; it just burned hot and got the stump burning. Adding a bunch of saltpeter helped it burn real good.

WESTWOOD AND MT BALDY

I spent many very enjoyable days hunting deer in the California forests. My brother Orneal moved to Westwood, California near Lake Almanor. He always invited my dad and me to hunt with him. My brother Gordon was gone to the Korean War.

I believe it was the summer of 1952 that my brother Howard invited me to hunt with him and his friends up on Mount Baldy in the Mendocino National Forrest. Howard's trips always approached being an ordeal, but that just made them more fun and exciting for me. Howard worked at his job till the last minute and we left San Jose about 8PM headed for Ukiah and then Mt Baldy. It was an all-night drive with dust so thick breathing was near impossible. Numerous stops were made in the middle of a very dark night where discussions were held as to which way to go. It was difficult to pass up a bar that was still open, as usually somebody needed a drink. This always caused another discussion. I was a high school kid then and had enough sense to just keep quiet. Usually Howard won all the discussions or arguments you might call them with his friends and we kept on going. Just before daybreak we could not make a steep hill with whoever's car we had, and then Howard remembered that there was a spring here below the road, so that is where we stopped and made what was supposed to be a camp. Dawn was seen beginning with a sliver of light to the east so we started to hunt. I shall never forget the shear amount of gunfire I heard that morning. This was the opening day of deer season in the days when California had a $50 bounty on mountain lions and, consequently, there were lots and lots of deer. I heard shooting almost continually. I do not remember that many deer strung up, but there must have been plenty harvested even if only one out of a hundred shots connected to a deer.

On the way home I convinced Howard to drop me off in Cloverdale, and I would hitch hike to Mendocino where my mother and sister were. That was the summer we moved to San Jose and Mother was still working at the bank and staying at Dr. Preston's house. I had not stood by the road very long when two guys picked me up. They were headed for Fort Bragg, which was beyond Mendocino so I looked forward to a full one shot ride to Mendocino. They had just bought a gallon of cheap red wine, which they soon opened up and started to consume. I was seated, in the front seat between them. The driver could hardly keep to the road. I started to worry a little bit so I used all the persuasive powers I possessed to convince them that I should drive. I had been on the high school debate team so even though I was only 16 years old I could present a convincing argument. This best argument I had was that if I drove they could consume the gallon of wine in peace. Eventually, after a harrowing miss of an oncoming car, they decided to let me try a little and they would see how I did. At that point I was prepared to abandon ship if I had too. I started to drive. The road is still the same today after 50 years. It is steep up and down and very curvy. They forbid me to shift gears as this car had lots of power. My dad had always taught me to not lug the engine so I had always shifted gears on hills. That day I lugged that car something fierce; it did have lots of power. I did not in no way want to offend them so as to lose my driving position. They approved of my driving. I drove all the way to Mendocino about a 3-hour drive in those days. At Mendocino I got out and bid them goodbye. That was a mistake I still regret to this day. I should have driven them to Fort Bragg. They did not make it. They had a serious accident between Mendocino and Fort Bragg, the details of which I do not know; except that serious injury was involved.

I went with Howard again to Mt Baldy in subsequent years. It became one of my favorite places to hunt. The first day out hunting and the year I had started college, Howard threw me a pack of cigarettes and said smoke these; they will keep the mosquitoes away. Well I smoked the pack and then another pack. The next Monday morning as I was walking across the campus of San Jose State College where I was going to school, I had this cigarette crave. Right there I stopped, sat down, and thought about it. I resolved never to get hooked on cigarettes and told myself never smoke another pack of cigarettes. It was one of the best decisions I ever made. I was always able to enjoy a cigarette or cigar when the occasion called for it but never got addicted. Remember, my grandfather, Cornelius Van Spronsen, used to say a man was not a man unless he smoked. His sons, my Uncles, were terribly addicted to cigarettes.

In the summer of 1955 I was working for the California Division of Highways based in Redding California. Some friends, who worked on the same project, building a four-lane highway through the Sacramento River Canyon north of Shasta Dam, were bow hunters, and since we talked bow hunting a lot, I became interested in bow hunting. I acquired an 80 lb. pull glass recurved bow and started to practice. Like most everything I did this was too much. 80 lb. pull is too much for anybody but an archer in the English Medieval Army. Archeologists are digging up the bones of these archers and they were deformed resulting, the archeologist's say, from too much bow practice. Well I could practice awhile but soon tired and did not have the time to practice all day long. It was probably just as well.

I enjoyed archery hunting very much. The open season on deer was earlier than gun season and I saw lots and lots more deer. It fact the old time archery hunting was fundamentally different. Hunting with guns the search was most important factor for if you saw a legal deer you usually got it. In archery, the stalk is the most important, as I saw lots of deer but the trick was the skill to get close for a shot. Consequently, I crawled a lot, hid behind bushes, used trees and bushes to screen myself and sneak up on the bucks. However, in the end I found this to be a lost cause. Many times after a long careful stalk, and I got into position for a shot, the deer would bolt at the sound of the bowstring, and the arrow would go where the deer had been and not where he was located when the arrow got there. Remember dear reader; archery today (in the year 2000) is fundamentally different than in 1955. Technology change has made archery a completely different sport. I have a compound recurve bow now that with a 35 lb. full draw pull that puts the arrow out at 3 or 4 times the velocity speed as the old 80 lb. bow.

Once when I was behind the motel above the Sacramento River where I was staying for the job I was on, practicing my bow shooting at a target. The sound of the kerplunk, kerplunk of my arrows must of stirred up the curiosity of a very, very large mule tail buck. At first I just sensed a shadow, and then I could not believe it. Here was moving the largest buck I had ever seen, and perhaps even to this day was one of the finest heads I had ever seen. He was seemingly just floating along behind my target! In hindsight, I often wish I had shot him. The motel owner was somewhat of a thief and poacher, at first did not believe my story, as he had never seen it, and then thoroughly chewed me out for not shooting it when I told him about it. That motel owner was forever coming up with schemes to defraud the State of California offering to split the take with me if I would cooperate in submitted false vouchers and such. I was determined not to do such a thing but I always gave him vague answers so as not to disturb my cheap motel rent. That guy really hated the State of California. I never did determine why.

DUCK HUNTING

We had some really great duck hunting in Westwood, California where my brother Orneal lived. He would invite me up during my college years. Opening day was the best. We would hide behind a stump or some other minimal concealment on a shallow point between two arms of Mountain Meadows Reservoir. This was a Pacific Gas & Electric company lake near Westwood on a creek called the Hamilton Branch. On opening day the ducks would fly back and forth between the two arms of the lake and we would pass shoot at the ducks. We usually got our limits after a few hours and went home. The primary ducks we got were Redheads and Canvasbacks. Orneal was always really nice at inviting us to go hunting. There was a student at San Jose State from Westwood that I came to know - - Carl Lindquist was his name. He invited me to go with him when he would go home to Westwood for the weekend. We would hunt geese later in the season on the mud flats northeast of that same lake. We would lie down in the mud and camouflage ourselves and wait for a flock of geese to fly over in range. When I would jump to shoot, the geese would flair off, it took a little skill to hit them. It is always quite exciting trying to lie down in the mud and not move at all hoping the flock would fly right over you.

In the fall of 1957 when I was a student at the University of California in Berkeley and Orneal had left Westwood and moved with his family to Mt. Shasta, California, I talked a couple of friends from the Alameda Christian Reformed Church to go duck hunting at Westwood. I believe we drove most of the night and camped out or slept a little on the ground at the lake. The limit that year was 10 ducks. We went to that same place on the shallow point that Orneal hunted. They were not the best shots. These ducks are moving fast and dodge quickly when they think somebody is going to shoot at them. We shot up all our shells and had to go back into Westwood for more. I ended up shooting 27 of the 30 ducks that constituted our limit. I estimated I got one duck for every 3 shots, so I shot up almost 5 boxes of shells. My friends also shot up 5 boxes of shells each. My shoulder ached for a week. I never remember shooting anywhere near that number of shells before or since or to have had such great duck hunting.

Geneva and I married in November of 1957. My ducks were stored in one of my friend's freezers. One of the first trials of our marriage was when I retrieved my ducks from my friend's freezer and expected Geneva to make a meal of them, and of course, I had lots of them. Ducks are not that easy to make into a delectable feast. My expectations were too high. Geneva became a very marvelous cook as the years went by. These ducks were her first real tough cooking challenge.

I went to work at Litton Industries in San Carlos, California in February of 1959. Of course, with a new job one makes new friends at work. We also started to attend the Palo Alto Christian Reformed Church. There also I made new friends.

Wendell Wilke was the Forman of the night machine shop when I first came to Litton. He had a silver plate in his skull as a result of injuries during World War II as a member of a bomber crew over Europe. He, I, Jim Ross, and another friend of Wendell's decided to lease a duck blind near Los Banos for as I remember about $900 a year. We had some nice hunts there. Only two of us could hunt at the same time and I usually hunted with Jim Ross, also an Engineer at Litton. There I got acquainted with Bob Craig who was a professor at Stanford and who later started Physical Electronics Laboratories, which made microwave devices, where I worked for about six months after I left Litton. One day during a lull in the shooting I wandered over to Craig's blind. There he had lined up one duck less than his limit of cock Sprigs. He only shot cock Sprigs. I was very impressed. He soon shot one more and went home. I usually shot what came along hoping to get a few Sprigs. I usually limited out on Spoonies and Teal when it came time to go home.

DEER HUNTING

I always loved deer hunting and always looked for new places to hunt, especially in the Sierra Nevada Mountains. Dave Sailor was an electronics technician in our group at Litton, and we became friends by swapping hunting stories. That is usually how one acquires a new hunting buddy. We would hunt my old favorite place, Mt Baldy, in Mendocino County. I returned to the old place my brother Howard had showed me. By that time there were a lot more roads into the area, fewer deer, and fewer hunters. I never remember getting a deer there with Dave in all those years, but we had lots of fun and worked hard. We usually went there opening day, usually the first Saturday in August, and also on Labor Day weekend.

Geneva was usually bugged by my going off hunting so one year I decided to take her along. She brought me great luck. We went to the Middle Fork of the Moqualame where I had trout fished the summer of 1957 when I was courting Geneva. The year before I had driven around on the logging roads in the area exploring for a place to hunt. I stopped by a camp where I saw a nice buck hanging in a tree and talked to the hunter. He suggested I walk up the ridge above his camp, as he believed there were more bucks up there. I pussy footed up that ridge and sure enough a real nice buck got up from behind a log and ran crosswise from me and I got in a couple of fast running shots and missed.

I returned to that spot the following year, and Geneva and I camped where two forks of the Middle Fork of the Moqualame come together. There the Middle Fork really begins as a fishable stream. At daybreak Geneva and I walked up that ridge. There is lots of shooting going on so I was sure there were deer around. In California deer hunters can be really thick with very large numbers of them. We came to a huge down Cedar log where two hunters, a father and son, had just shot two deer and were preparing to drag them out to their camp. We climbed up onto the log. It was about 10 feet in diameter so on top of the log one had a view of a bowl with about 300 yards of visibility to the north up the bowl. The area had been logged several years before so there was lots of brush for deer to feed on. We had not been there five minutes when three bucks came down the opposite side of the bowl. I lay down on the log and took careful aim with my 270 Husqevarna Fapinfabrinks I had bought from my brother Orneal. I shot and missed three times before the deer started to run. On the fourth shot I was lucky and hit him in the head as he ran, and he flipped over. Since Geneva was on the log along side of me and since I had had her buy a license and tag also, and me being greedy as usual, I took careful aim at the second buck that had now stopped and was looking at me. As I shot I saw dust fly just above his back and then both bucks reversed direction and ran back up the bowl. We went over to where I had shot the deer and there was my first legal California Buck! We butchered him out and dragged him to the pickup and them went home.

I thought about the hunt and slowly realized my gun was not shooting where I thought it was. Sure enough when I went to the rifle range the sights were off. I had hunted 13 years in California for deer and had not got a buck. In

160

all those years I never seriously sighted in my guns. In hindsight how stupid I had been. Needless to say, from that day on I always sighted in my guns before the season at the rifle range. It became almost a fetish.

My brother Orneal had felt the call of God to be a Missionary. One day in 1961 he showed up at our home in Santa Clara and announced he was joining Wycliffe Bible Translators. He sold me his guns. I acquired his 270 rifle and two shotguns, a modified 12 gage Higgins, and a Winchester 3 ½ inch mag 12-gage pump. The 270 was a Husquevarna Fapinfabrinks. It was beautiful and once sighted in never missed. It would shoot a ½ inch group at 100 yards using the Jack O'Connor's load of 59 grains of Hodkins #1031 powder and a 130-grain bullet. 1031 is a slow burning powder that really does the job. The powder has to be stuffed into the shell, however. Dave Sailor loaded them for me in the early days before I got my own hand loading equipment. I sighted it in to be 3 ½ inches high at 100 yards. That put the bullet within 4 inches of point of aim all the way out to 375 yards. From then on I got my deer or several of them almost every year.

The next year Geneva and I returned to the same place on the opening day for the Sierra Nevada area. The log was occupied so we sat down on the slope of a gully about 300 yards from the log. We had not sat there long when some shots rang out way up the bowl. Soon more shots, then more shots, then more shots getting closer. I said to Geneva, "He's coming this way". Sure enough this large buck with a beautiful rack one could see from any distance came just a smoking down the bowl at rate of speed hard to believe. I shot at him once as he turned and came down and crossed the bottom of the gully. As he came up out of the gully he turned to my left, broadside to me and leaped over a large thorny buck brush about 50 yards away. I lead him a little bit and caught him in the chest cavity as he leaped over the bush. He fell and continued down the gully. I left Geneva on the slope and went down to where I shot him. He left a very clear blood trail and I found him about 80 yards further down the gully slope. He was beautiful.

I yelled at Geneva to come on down but she promptly got lost. From this I learned that Geneva will get lost in five minutes in the woods if left alone. I never have left her alone in the woods by herself since. After tracking her down, we butchered the deer and dragged it back to the road where we loaded it into our 61 Ford Station Wagon. He was one of the larger bucks I had seen up to that time with a high 4x3 rack. My first nice buck! I had him mounted as I thought I would never get another one like him again. He still hangs on my wall. His hide showed at least four near misses from the other hunters. He had fur off his head, stomach, and legs from bullets that just grazed him. That was California hunting - hunters all over the place. At least 20 shots had been fired at him before he ran by me.

That spot was an unusual hunting place. These are the kinds of places one has to find to be a successful California deer hunter. It turned out that the bowls formed by the headwaters of the Middle Fork of the Mokualame were below a forest road that ran off of State highway 4 which ran over the Sierra Nevada. On opening day hunters would pour off of highway 4 onto the forest roads and hunt. They would move the deer down into a series of bowls into several large brush patches near the stream. It was one of those really great places to hunt on opening day, as lots of hunters are around to move the deer. Years later my nephew, Dwight Davis, shot a really huge trophy deer in the same area.

BOB WIRE HUNTING BUDDY

When I went to work the next Monday morning I asked the night machine shop foreman, Bob Wire, how his hunting had gone. He told me about a large 4-point buck he had got up in Siskiyou County. He asked me how I did and I told him my story. He must have been impressed as that conversation started a very long and very successful hunting buddy relationship. Bob was a very good shot and any game within his range was always taken. He almost never missed a shot and if he did he was very embarrassed about it and would not talk about it. Good hunting buddies are very hard to find. It is even harder to find one who is a good shot and is congenial and whose personality does not clash with your own.

Bob had a brother who worked as a banker in the Walnut Creek area. Bob, his brother, "Neut", a fellow who worked at Philco Ford, and I started to make the Sierra opening day trek to Dorris, California where Bob grew up. Bob's dad had been a logger and had been killed when Bob was young so Bob being the oldest helped his mother raise the family. Bob's sister lived in Dorris also with her husband and family. We all hunted an area called The Burn. It was a large area where the Forrest Service tried to have a controlled burn. It got away from then and turned into a huge very hot firestorm. The burn was an area that sloped to the west and had patches of very thick brush with open grassy areas. All the trees were completely gone except for an occasional patch of trees in some ravine. It was the finest black tail deer habitat that has probably ever existed in the Siskiyou Mountains.

We would leave work on Friday afternoon, drive six hours to Dorris, stop at Bob's mothers for a while, and drive up forest roads to camp at a place called Poison Spring. There would be 30 or so camps at the spring. We would put out our sleeping bags on the ground for a few hours sleep and wake up early for a leisurely breakfast of bacon and eggs. Before first light we would proceed to The Burn by a road that followed a contour through the burn. We would separate about ¼ mile from each other and walk downhill through the burn in roughly parallel paths. We always got deer. There were four of us and usually four more or so including Bob's brother-in-law, his sons and their friends. We always got lots of shooting and several deer. In 1964 I had acquired a Toyota Land Cruiser. It would go most anywhere. One year I shot a buck about a mile down the slope and while I was walking uphill to the Toyota I concluded I could get the Toyota in there down a steep logging skid trail. Well, when Bob saw me coming he could hardly believe it. I drove to my buck, picked up Bob's, Billy's, and Neut's, plus other hunter's bucks! I had a rack on top so we loaded seven bucks in the rack and put seven hunters in the Toyota and just moved up the hill as pretty as you please. It was great. That Toyota was extremely well built. My son Sheridan and I had modified it when he was sixteen, but that is another story.

I started hunting with Bob about 1962. We would hunt Dorris opening day for the Sierra and usually make a hunt or two in the Sierra later in the season. Bob was a lucky hunter and a very good shot. We enjoyed lots of very fine hunts together and took lots of deer. The trip to Dorris became a tradition which we did every year until I moved to Idaho. Bob's mother always served us an outstanding dinner on Sunday afternoon with Bob's favorite food before we left on our way home. Eventually it was just Bob and I - sometimes on our way to Idaho to hunt Elk.

The most memorable hunt in the Dorris area occurred after we had started to camp separately from the crowd at Poison Spring, and while using a dry camp with the Toyota in an area to the east of the main burn. Bob and I had been working this ridge, as was our usual method. One of us would slowly proceed along the top of the ridge with the other about 100 to 300 yards below. We would work in parallel paths to each other hoping to jump deer past each other. Large trophy Mule and Blacktail bucks often bed near ridge tops so as to have a quick escape route and often cross over the ridge to escape a hunter. We were working a long tree covered brushy ridge when it changed general direction to the left. We stopped to talk on a large rock that overlooked a bowl. Bob did not believe in being real quiet like most other hunters. We would stop somewhere and talk in a normal voice and sometimes shout and talk across from ridge top to ridge top or across a bowl. After we had talked for a while, from this rock Bob said in a normal voice, "A buck just crawled across that clearing on his stomach." as he pointed down into the bowl to our right. It seemed our talking often did disturb the game about and get them to start to move. It often would just get the deer to run so as to make noise and attract our attention to them. I moved over to an adjacent rock, which gave me a view about, and started to glass the brush and trees below me in the bowl. After glassing a while, low and behold I got eye contact with a deer. I could look right into his eye and saw part of his horn and knew he was big. I was hunting that day with my 378 Weatherby Magnum. Rather a cannon for this job but we were on our way to hunt Elk in Idaho so I was hunting deer with it. I loved that rifle although it kicked like a mule. But that is another story. It shot a 270 grain bullet at 3100 feet per second and would shoot through most anything. Well I moved my scope sight over to where I thought his shoulder should be and shot right through several screening fir trees. The buck disappeared. I left Bob on the rock to watch and walked over to where the buck should be. There he was dropped in his tracks but still alive. I had hit him above the shoulder a little high but enough to stop him. That bullet had over 6000 ft-lbs of energy at the muzzle and always did the job. I did not want to damage the head as it had one of the nicest racks I had ever seen. I finished him off with several shots from my 22-mag pistol. Bob was wondering what was going on and shouted at me. The 22 mag makes a lot of noise. I yelled for him to come over and when he got there he was very impressed. It certainly was a beautiful buck. I had it mounted and it still hangs on my wall. He was a Blacktail, certainly the largest I have ever saw or ever taken.

Ten years or more later Bob shot a very large Blacktail buck not 300 yards from the same spot. He took it on a hunt on the way to hunt elk in Idaho with me. He said it was third in the record books for Blacktail bucks.

On another hunt I had dropped below on a long sloping ridge downhill. There was another brush-covered ridge about 600 yards to the West of the ridge I was on. I heard a shot or two in the distance and sure enough here came a nice buck running down that ridge just below the ridge top. He was really moving jumping over small bushes. Again I was hunting with my 378. It takes time and practice to hit running deer. In California if one expects to take any deer at all one has to become good at running shots. The range was about 500 yards. The 378 Weatherby is very potent at that range; the problem is to hit the deer. Bob had a rule of thumb to aim for the deer's nose. Since I was a Physicist/Engineer, I was more scientific then that. At 500 yards, if the deer is moving at about 40 feet per second and my bullet is moving at 3100 feet per second, the time to travel 1500 feet to the deer is about ½ second. In that time the deer will travel 20 feet; thus one needs a lead of about two deer lengths or so. My first shot was slightly high and a little in front of his nose. The second caught him through the chest cavity as he cleared a small bush. It was the finest shot I ever made. He tumbled downhill for 50 yards or so and came to rest just above the bottom of the gulch. There was a large bush maybe eight feet high just above where he lay. I butchered him out and used the top of the bush bunched together to hold my block and tackle. By that time in my hunting career I had concluded I would not drag deer out of the woods but butcher them out right on the spot where I got them. I now carry a small seven-strand block and tackle and a lightweight deer bag in my rucksack at all times when hunting deer or elk. I left the fully skinned out and butchered deer hanging on the bush and came back later with Bob with our backpacks. We cut the deer in half and carried him out as easy as pie even though we were two miles or so from camp uphill.

That is the absolute best way to handle a deer carcass. When I think of all the deer I dragged out of the woods all I can think of is how stupid I was. First, why pack out hide and feet that one has to find a place to throw away anyway? Second, dragging all that weight puts a strain on the arms and back. Third, sometimes the hide gets worn off dragging it along and the meat gets bruised. Fourth, if the hide is left on, the body heat of the deer does not get out of the meat quickly. Fifth, carrying half a deer on the back is far easier than any other method. I learned this lesson to never forget it on a memorable pig hunt, but that is another story, which I will soon get back too.

In that same general area a few years later I was hunting with my brother in law, Don Davis, and his sons. Titus took his first buck on that hunt. Another year just Bob, I, and my son Sheridan were hunting there. I believe it was Sheridan's first hunt. Sheridan and I had advanced to a lava rim overlooking an open area backed by trees. Bob was off to our left approaching the same lava rim. It was foggy early on opening morning. We were sitting on the ridge for a few minutes when the fog lifted slightly and there was a nice large buck about 200 yards away. I said to Sheridan, "Quick shoot him". I was watching him through my field glasses and as the fog lifted I could see his antlers and as the fog drifted down he would go out of sight. I saw him clearly several times and whispered each time, "Sheridan, quick shoot him". Sheridan never found him in his scope. It was very frustrating for him, and eventually the deer moved off out of sight. It was a disappointing way to start a deer-hunting career although certainly much better than the way I had started mine. That was a memorable day as an hour or so later Sheridan and I moved a nice 4 pointer past Bob and he got it. We butchered it out and went back to camp with it. We had a snack and then started to drive out to another area. I spotted a set of antlers behind a bush about 100 yards off the road. I put the glasses on him and was convinced it was a deer. Again I moved the scope over to where his shoulder should be and fired. The buck jumped up and ran off in a streak. We walked over to where I had shot and here was a bush no more than 8 inches high. I could hardly believe it. This buck had lain down with his nose on the ground and had stretched out like a cocker spaniel in a straight line, with his whole body stretched out in a straight lying flat on the ground behind that little bush. The only thing from my view he could not hide was his horns. I was dumfounded. I did not think it was possible for a whole deer to hide behind an eight-inch bush. On the way back to camp in about the same area I shot a forked horn buck on a hillside where he was watching me. I should have let Sheridan shoot it, but it looked like it was about to run away and I panicked. It was a very nice fun hunt for Sheridan's first hunt.

PIG HUNTING

Pig hunting I did down in the Big Sur area of the Los Padres National Forest. I was introduced to it by a friend from work at Litton. His father in law was the Mayor of Carmel, a city just north of the Los Padres National forest near Monterey, California. He was a thorough going poacher and big talker with lots of stories of hunting pigs and deer in that area. He even told stories of arrowing deer in the Carmel City Park. I don't remember his name so I will for the purpose of this narrative call him John.

Several of us from Litton would go hunting with him. It was usually an ordeal. We would leave the Bay Area in the evening, drive to Carmel where he stopped to visit his relatives; that took about four hours, and then proceed to Bouchers Gap where there was a very primitive Forest Service camping spot. Depending on what time we got there we would sleep an hour or two or start up the hill with no sleep. John's theory was to get to the top of the Mountain where he said the pigs were by first daylight. It was about a 4000-foot climb from Bouchers Gap to the top of the mountain to an altitude of about 6000 feet. As you can understand this was an arduous climb. And what made it even more fun was it was done in the dark, of course, with no flashlights, as they might scare the pigs, and usually in a pouring down rain as we did this during January through March when there was nothing else to hunt. Some young men are constantly trying to prove themselves, I guess to prove they are really men. So this exercise became a contest as to see who was the toughest. I did not understand this at the time, as I would climb mountains just for fun. I usually dropped back as I had little ego problem so I was comfortable to be last. I had great long-term stamina, however, and after a few hours I would be near the lead and in the best shape.

John always carried a bottle of whiskey in his rear pocket. It was shaped so that it would fit there. Every half hour or so we would take a brief stop and take a swig of his whiskey which he offered us. After a swig or two to be polite, I figured I did not need that and would decline the subsequent swigs. I do not remember ever shooting any pigs on these expeditions but several times we would encounter them in the complete darkness and could hear them grunting but never see them. John said we could see them in the

167

moonlight and that was always his dream, but it never happened as usually it was very black in a pouring down rain and vision was limited to maybe the trail. Once I remember not even to be able to see the trail and had to feel it with my feet. Light came with a great relief to me and we would scale the mountain as fast as John would lead us. It was great exercise and I would come home Saturday night tired and worn out, a great physiological healing from the concrete walls of employment at Litton Industries.

Sometimes we would hunt up a trail along the Little Sur River and climb Pico Blanco. This was a limestone peak about 4000 feet above sea level. The climb started from about sea level so again we climbed about 4000 feet if we got all the way to the top. This area became one of my favorite places to hunt as spring came early here and the flowers and blossoms on the chaparral were very beautiful. We had to cross the Little Sur River several times and had to take off our boots to cross. There was even an old homestead along the trail with its own set of domestic flowers and bushes – somebody's wonderful dream place that came to an end. I eventually even hunted deer and pigs there with my friends long after I had forgot about John.

The trip in and out of the Little Sur area was usually over a very muddy road. John had a little Volkswagen Bug. When the thing slide off the road into the ditch from the slimy mud, the four of us would just pick it up or maybe bounce it back into the road. That impressed me with Volkswagens.

Eventually on one trip up Pico Blanco John forgot his whiskey. What an eye opener. John had no stamina without the whiskey. He was as good as finished. He became the weakest among the party and asked to turn back. He became very embarrassed at his lack of prowess and the betrayal of his own perceived perception of manhood. That was the last of John. He left Litton a year or so later and I lost track of him.

Apparently, and I have no scientific basis for this, alcohol from whiskey will proceed directly into the bloodstream. Therefore, if one has no reserves of blood sugar stored in one's liver, alcohol can serve as an emergency source of food. Perhaps that is what our old primitive ancestors used whiskey for. I have never read anything about that.

I really loved the Little Sur Trail as a neat way to spend a day in the forest. The trail followed the river for a few miles through a redwood forest and then climbed up through scattered chaparral, then Oak forests with Madrone and California Bay, grass clearings, and then up into dense chaparral. It was a beautiful sequence of different foliage with a wide variety of plants and animals.

Once I was on a hike there with Wendell Rooks and his son and my son, Sheridan. The trail passed over a notch in a ridge and before us was a large open bowel about 500 yards across. A coyote jumped out of a bush 30 yards in front of us and ran across the bowl at his maximum speed. I had my 270 Husquevarna with me and took aim at him. As I remember, the first shot was behind him, the second above him, the third in front of his nose, the fourth made no dust and the last just below his nose. All of this occurred, as he was going flat out and dodging right and left. Wendell was very impressed as the shots each time missed him only by inches. However, I never touched him.

One day I decided to go pig hunting there by myself. Usually I always hunted with somebody as it is much more fun to share the hunt with somebody. I was proceeding up through an oak forest with scattered Madrone and Bay and here and there a Redwood, and heard rustling of old leaves and sure enough there came a herd of wild pigs. California had no closed season on wild pigs. Sometime in the past people had introduced European wild boars to the Los Padres National Forrest. They are big and black with tusks and often aggressive. They have interbred with domestic pigs gone wild. Most of these wild pigs were black with a white spot or so and some red mixed in. I picked out the biggest and shot her, then not wanting a good thing to get away shot the next biggest also, both sows. I removed the innards and dragged them down to near the river. They were both rather large maybe 200 pounds each. What to do, as I was about 4 miles from my Toyota I decided that the best thing was to go get some horses so I left the pigs on a log and walked out. After a few phone calls I perceived horses were a lost cause. I went home and called a few friends but none were interested until I called my new hunting buddy Bob Wire. Sure he would go. My neighbor next door in Santa Clara suggested I use his "deer carrier". This thing was an aluminum frame with handles at both ends with a large motorcycle wheel with a brake operated by a hand lever. He swore by it.

I had got the pigs on a Saturday. My old college roommate, Vern Ehlers was coming for a visit on Sunday. My wife was aghast that I was considering going back after the pigs and not seeing Vern. Vern years later became a United States Congressman from Grand Rapids, Michigan, so going back after those pigs was probably not a good decision. My hunting code moral standard, however, was not to waste game, so Bob and I took the deer carrier and went back to the Little Sur River for those pigs. We left about 4 AM and got to the trail at daybreak about 7AM. We soon got to the pigs about 9:30. We loaded the pigs on the deer carrier and tied my rifle on top. Then began the greatest physical ordeal of my whole life.

We had near 400 pounds of pork on the carrier. We pushed hard to make it go uphill until we discovered that the thing wanted to go downhill all the time so we had no rest. We then turned the thing sideways and lifted it up inch by inch up each side hill. We had to cross numerous gullies and ridges following a deer trail to get up to the Forest Service trail. I have forgotten the number of times we decided that this was impossible and sat down to rest. After 10 minutes rest and a discussion as to how stupid this was, we would try some more. It was exhausting work. Once while descending a ridge, I lost control of the brake and the whole thing careened down into the gully and even flipped upside down just missing Bob. Bob was young and quick in those days. How my rifle escaped serious damage I will never know. We reloaded and rested some more and kept going.

Eventually, we got to the Forest Service trail and started downhill. The brake got hot and did not work as well as I came to expect. Then we had to cross the Little Sur River over large rocks in the bottom of the creek. I don't remember dumping the load into the creek but I would not have been surprised if we had. We had spent all day at this whole business and it got dark. We were now in a Redwood Forest and the fog moved in from the ocean. I could not see even my hand in front of my face. Fortunately, we had made it to the point where the trail became mixed with an old logging road, which run up the Little Sur River a mile or so. I concluded it was impossible to proceed when I had walked into a large Redwood Tree, which I did not see.

I left Bob and walked out to find the Toyota. By this time I was determined to succeed no matter what and was prepared to shoot the lock off the gate on the logging road. I lost the trail and had to crawl on my hands and knees through thick brush and Redwood forest in the pitch black up to the road where the Toyota was. I actually discovered the road with my hands. You dear reader may find this hard to believe but that is exactly what happened. I took little mini steps and walked down the road. I searched for the Toyota by sonar. I would whistle and listen for the echo. With my hands in front of me I felt for the Toyota. I found the Toyota, started it, and to my great joy had light! I drove to the logging road gate. There I discovered the chain and lock was made to look locked but wasn't. So I opened the gate and drove the Toyota right up to the pigs. It was a terrible trail but the Toyota would go anywhere. Bob was real happy to see me. We loaded the pigs and went home. When I climbed into bed with Geneva and lay there, my heart was racing and would not slow down. I was that exhausted. I have never experienced that effect on my heart ever again.

Several lessons were learned from that whole experience. One is to forget the deer carrier idea. It might work on a smooth road, but how many deer or pigs does one need to move along a road? Another was why take the head, hide, and legs home? You can't eat them and just have to find a place to throw them away anyway, and the garbage collector will wonder what you have been up to. I resolved once and for all never to do that again. From that day forward I butchered my game in the woods and packed out only the meat. As a comparison, a year or so later, Bob, Sheridan, and I were in the same area, shot a pig, hung him up with a rope, butchered him, put half of him in each one of our pack frames, and carried him out at a normal walking pace. What a comparison. Never again would I drag or otherwise try to bring out large game whole.

Since I had so much pork I decided to make some wild boar ham. I acquired some sugar cure and a salt injection needle and cured the hams. Somehow I decided to wrap the hams in tinfoil as a final cover. Big mistake. After letting the hams sit in a box covered with the sugar cure, I took them out and let them hang with the tinfoil wrapped around the hams as a final cover. After a few months curing time it became time to try them out and eat them. On a regular hanging ham a black mold will form on the outside of the ham. This is very normal. In my case however the black mold formed inside the tinfoil and the juices instead of drying out penetrated the whole ham. Wow, a bite of that was like a bite of Limburger cheese! It cleared out my sinuses. At first I thought it might poison me so tried it little bit by little bit. I do not like to waste food so we started to eat it. You should have seen my children's reaction. But we ate it. Geneva would put it into a scalloped potato dish. One time we even fed it to the Christian Reformed Church Pastor, Henry Bouma, as I recall. He liked it! I got to really enjoy it, and was disappointed to have it all eaten up. My kids however did not share my enthusiasm.

ELK HUNTIING ON THE CLEARWATER

In February of 1966 I started my own business. This gave me the absolute right to take my vacation anytime I wanted. Bob Wire also started his own business at about the same time. Thus when fall came we started discussions about big game hunting in someplace else besides California. We did some research about where to hunt and decided on Idaho.

Our first Idaho hunt was in the fall of 1966. Bob had a friend and wanted to take him along. We loaded up our rig; maybe my Toyota or Bob's pickup, and proceeded to Boise where we visited the Fish and Game Department to get ideas on where to hunt. We decided on the Selway area so we drove to Darby, Montana and then drove into Idaho on the Darby Road which travels across the State west to Grangeville. Today that vast area is classified as wilderness.

We hunted various places with no success and eventually came to an area around Elk City. It was very cold and we had no tent stove, being very inexperienced. We sat around the fire until we just had to go to bed and shivered all night even in a very good sleeping bag. Bob's friend in the morning just would not get out of bed and go hunting. I started to jump small herds of elk off of south facing ridges and slowly started to learn a little about elk hunting. The cold got to us so we started home stopping in Riggins, Idaho. Wow, a nice warm place. We enjoyed hot showers in the Bruce Motel, now called the Big Iron Motel. A friendly fellow, (Riggins has always been a very friendly place) at a Shell Station in town told us about a place up the Race Creek Road. We went up there and set up camp.

We hunted downhill from camp and soon had a couple of does so we would not go home skunked. This was a two deer area so we filled our second deer tag here. Bob's friend gave me a hard time about shooting does.

We started for home thinking we would hunt what is called the Owyhee Country out of Jordon Valley, Oregon to fill our first deer tag. We again spent a warm night with a hot shower in a Motel in Jordan Valley. Next morning we started out towards a place called South Mountain. We ran into a rancher in a pickup. We are always friendly and so was the rancher, and he asked if we knew where we were and where we were going. We said no. After a while he told about a place he thought nobody had yet hunted this year. He gave us very detailed instructions as to where to find the place. That is a bit unusual as most people give very vague directions to anyplace. That gave him a lot of credibility in his words of instruction, so we followed them to a tee into a very wild place that eventually became a wilderness.

It turned out that I now believe that that rancher was a man by the name of McKensey as his daughter Robin became a close friend of my daughter Kim about 20 years later, since he lives in the same house on the same ranch near where we met him on the road. Kim and Robin had become great friends at a Christian Camp they attended every summer, Shiloh Bible Camp, near McCall, Idaho.

We parked the pickup at the bottom of a draw. Bob's friend declared there were no deer around here and decided to stay at the pickup, I guess he was tired of fruitless deer hunting. The area was open scattered juniper and grass and a few sagebrush and really did not look like most deer habitat.

Bob and I started up a ridge as is our usual procedure about 150 yards or so apart. Bob jumped a nice buck from under a juniper and it ran up the ridge about 100 yards off from me. My 270 promptly put a hole in his lungs and heart, and Bob and I dressed him out. We dragged him under a large juniper bush and continued hunting.

A few minutes later I hear Bob shooting and I wandered over to where Bob is looking at the ground. Bob is an excellent tracker. He said he shot a very huge buck at about 300 yards or so with his 308. (He usually hunted later with a 300 Winchester Mag.) He must have not aimed high enough as he shot him in the front leg. This could be determined from the deer track that showed only three legs, the impression of the one front hoof deeper that the hind leg track marks. There was very, very little blood. Our code of hunting ethics is that that deer must be found and used.

Thus began a rather long hunting odyssey. Tracking was very difficult on the very dry soil of the scattered juniper lava rim type of stuff. We would lose the trail, circle until we picked it up again and then continue on and on. When we got close to the deer it would jump and run off. It eventually started a descent into a rather deep valley. Finally I told Bob I would get on a ridge point where I could see down into the canyon and suggested he continue to follow the deer track. After hours of this stuff I saw the deer run into a thick patch of juniper and aspens. I yelled down to Bob where the deer was hiding. He carefully approached the patch from the side and when the deer saw him it jumped and Bob got a shot. As I have said Bob is a very good shot.

I went down to where Bob was and walked up on what I thought was a mule. I asked bob why he had shot a mule. Before he answered, I saw the antler rack of a very, very large mule deer. This was the biggest deer I have ever seen, probably way over 300 pounds. Bob has the head mounted on his office wall. I am still amazed at the sheer size of that mounted head every time I see it. We dressed him out and went back up the canyon to the Toyota for the pack frames.

We found Bobs friend who at first really did not believe our stories. We dragged my deer down a little ways to the Toyota. We found a juniper tree, hung the deer up and skinned out my deer and loaded him into the Toyota and drove up the road to where Bob's deer had crossed the road on his way into the canyon. By now it was completely dark so we took a lantern and flash lights and went down into the canyon where Bob's deer was. When we got there, the gut pile had already been buried by a mountain lion. We built a rather large fire. Bob's friend by this time was rather spooky. We skinned out the deer and divided it up into three pack frame loads. It took us a while to climb out of that canyon in the dark with heavy loads, and, of course, Bob wanted the head. We got back to the Toyota about midnight. We loaded everything up and drove all night home to California crossing the Serra Nevada about sunup. This was a very memorable first Idaho hunt, and it started our yearly, year after year, trip for Bob and me to go to Idaho to hunt every following year but the next year. I never saw Bob's friend again.

The next year I had a work commitment to deliver a computer program to General Electric. Bob went to Idaho by himself or with his friend, I do not remember. Bob ended up on the Clearwater watershed out of Weeipe, Idaho at a place called Foot Rot Corrals. He had made arrangements with an outfitter called Cline. Bob told me all kinds of stories of hunting with Cline around Foot Rot Corrals. As I remember, Bob got a cow elk that year. Cline was upset that the Forest Service was going to build a road right through his prime hunting territory, so he was going to give it up, retire and not outfit any more.

The next year, 1968, Bob and I got ourselves outfitted with lots of good camp gear, used my Toyota or his pickup or his Toyota, and we hunted there at Foot Rot every year (except the year we backpacked to Bear Point) until 1978. Foot Rot was on top of a ridge and we could hunt down either side. If one descended down to the creek on either side of the ridge it used up most of the day for a hunt. The Forest Service did build that road, so after a couple of years we did not hunt to the east where that road was.

We made friends with the other people who camped there also to hunt elk. It depended on the year but usually perhaps six to ten hunters camped at Foot Rot Corrals. Some had horses so we usually had help getting our elk back to camp. Over the eleven years we hunted there we averaged about one elk a year, usually a bull, but in the early years sometimes a cow when it was still legal to take cows. Some years we got skunked, and some years we got two elk. It was a lot of work walking down into the bottom of the creek every day. I usually tried to get in shape at home before I went hunting, nevertheless, I unusually showed up quite out of shape, but a week to ten days of hard hiking, and packing elk put me into great shape.

There is where I met Al Osborn, the man who got me into the mining venture. Al's son Russ, and a mining engineer out of north Idaho whose name I have forgotten, and a farmer from around the Moscow area camped there and hunted there every year also. We had lots of fun hunts with those three men. They also had horses. The grain farmer loved to build fires.

175

The whole area had been burnt over at one time and there were lots and lots of dead snags about. Quentin, the farmer, forever got cold from being out in the rain and snow and fired a new huge standing snag almost every day. He built the fire at the bottom of the snag and after a day or so it would fall over. It would continue to burn so all of us would stop at a burning snag fire and warm up periodically while we were out hunting. One could go from snag fire to snag fire and dry himself out. One year some Forest Service zealot got all excited about all the fires and asked everybody a lot of questions, but none of us knew anything about all those fires. Maybe space aliens did it. She made lots of threats not believing any of our stories.

BEAR CREEK AND MARSHALL MOUNTAIN

In 1978 Al Osborn showed up and told lots of mining stories and offered Bob and me a chance to go to the Marshall Mountain area and stay in the Cabin of Shirley and Arty Johnson near Bear Creek on a small lake and hunt elk. Bob and I went there and hunted a bit, but it is very steep country that is very difficult to hunt. Al gave me the big pitch about gold mining and that is how I got involved in the mine, but that is another story.

After a week to ten days at Foot Rot we were normally ready to move on, usually after a foot of snow or so, which tended to make hunting miserable. If we had any we would take our elk meat down to Riggins and have Bill Potenger cut up and freeze our meat. After a good hot shower, a comfortable bed in the Bruce Motel, and getting warmed up in hot ole Riggins, a steak meal at Somervilles Cafe, we would head into Hells Canyon and camp at Low Saddle. We had found that place in our wanderings. Bob and I would do our usual thing of Bob on top of the ridge and work our way out to Stormy Point with me a couple of hundred yards below him. After a day or so we had our two deer, nice muley bucks, and we would then go home to California.

We did that for a number of years until one year we heard lots of chain saw noise. Turned out about six hunters from Oregon were camped not far away and they were going down into Hells Canyon from there and trophy hunting for really big Mulley bucks. I saw six magnificent heads in their camp. They were using a chain saw wench to drag their bucks up out of the canyon. Hunting there at Low Saddle was never the same after that. The word had got out and the place had been discovered.

One year after getting skunked at Foot Rot and still wanting an elk, we asked around Riggins, and the area up around Marshall Mountain was suggested. Bob and I attended the Pentecostal Church on that Sunday night, something Bob usually never did. I still remember the syncopated beat on the hymns we sung. Pentecostal Churches sometimes have a real knack for that. Monday morning we got up, and from the Bruce Motel where we usually stayed, ate breakfast at Somervilles and drove up the Main Salmon River Road. We crossed the Manning Crevice Bridge, a mile above which Geneva and I later lived for 15 years, and went up the switchback road up French Creek and then the road toward Burgdorff. We turned off to go toward Marshall Mountain. We stopped and glassed the area around Marshall Lake from high up on a road. We could see elk tracks down in the meadow above the lake in the snow quite a way below the road. I suggested I drop down the road a bit and then descend down to below Marshall Lake and work up past the Lake, while having Bob descend directly to the meadow area where we saw the tracks and take a stand.

Bob liked the idea so I got my stuff together and went down. I found an elk trail and started to move up toward the lake. I had not slowed down as much as I should have as I was closer to the lake than what I thought and, consequently, jumped the herd of elk before I expected to jump them. I heard them run out but did not see them. A few minutes later I hear two shots. I moved up above the lake, and there in the snowy meadow is Bob with a magnificent six points to a side herd bull. The herd had run right past Bob. Bob had also shot a cow, but it had not dropped, so Bob went to try to find the cow while I get the guts out of the bull. I had already had the bull mostly skinned when Bob returned a couple of hours later. It seems he had shot the cow high and it was bleeding plenty of dark blood, but not a super huge amount of it, and he had followed it to the top of the ridge to the east but thought continuing on the track was hopeless.

It was near getting dark, so we climbed up to the road and drove to Burgdorff and rented a cabin. The caretaker said Burgdorff was closed, but would open it for us and rent us a cabin. This became a very memorable time as it got quite cold and we would soak in the giant hot springs pool at

Burgdorff and float around for hours. It took us three days to back pack that elk out of there as we were in no hurry and did one trip a day. I can still remember clearly floating in the nice hot water and staring out into the very cold starry sky with the temperature about zero degrees - absolutely wonderful. In that situation the back packing aches and pains are not felt.

Bob wanted to mount the head so we packed the whole thing out head, hide, and antlers. It was not easy to get that bull out of there. Going back the next day we found an old jeep trail (now closed to 4 wheelers) that started to go up Marshall Creek to the Lake. The jeep trail crossed the Creek. It looked like I could make it across on the ice. Well that is when the fun started as the Toyota fell through the ice into about three feet or more of water. The water was about half way up the engine. We unhooked the fan belt so the water would not splash and short the spark plugs; I somehow got my hand under the water to unloose the wench under the freezing water. The Toyota had a power take off wench from the transfer case. So with the motor running at idle in the lowest gear range (my son Sheridan and I had installed a Chev 396 Camaro motor with a four forward speed truck transmission with a granny low, so with the low range Toyota transfer case we had huge amounts of low speed power), the wench running and pulling at the same time we eased out of the sink hole as pretty as you please. Subsequently, I found a better way to cross that Creek. Our hunting trips were full of fun challenges like this. Bob was an excellent hunter and never missed what he shot at so we got lots of game.

After packing that elk out, we stopped at South Mountain out of Jordon Valley on the way home to do a little deer hunting. This was several years after our first hunt there and there was a lot less game. Bob and I did our usual thing and worked a long up sloping ridge toward South Mountain. After a mile or two or so the ridge petered out in a bluff overlooking a deep draw about 300 yards wide at the top. I pussyfooted up there and jumped three bucks out of the brush on top of this bluff. The first buck up the other side was magnificent. Shooting down at him at that distance while he was rapidly moving disturbed my aim and my 270 shot hit the ground just in front of his nose. I worked the bolt for a second shot, and a new shell would not enter the chamber. I frantically worked the bolt but nothing happened. I watched the buck run over the ridge. I then heard Bob shoot. Then out of the draw walked this buck the likes of which one never expects even in his dreams. His rack was more than three times the width of his body. He was huge, probable bigger that the one Bob shot a few years earlier in this same general area. Bob's buck had an ordinary rack. This buck was a magnificent trophy with a rack to match. But it was not to be. My gun was jammed and I watched with my field glasses the trophy of a lifetime gently walk over the ridge about 300 yards away. It turned out I had a case separation from reloading the shell case too many times. That was the greatest hunting disappointment of my whole life.

We dressed out Bob's buck, a nice three pointer, and went home.

THE MOST MEMORABLE HUNT

A hunt in Idaho in the early 70's was the most memorable experience of my life. If I were to look back over my life and ask, "What was the highlight of my life", this hunt provided the greatest esthetic event of hunting.

It all came about early in the year sometime in the 1970's when Bob Wire and I decided to hunt again in Idaho in the coming fall. We obtained our licenses and somehow received an application for special hunts. Special hunts required a drawing randomly from the applicants to see who is the lucky one. Well we put in for a Rocky Mountain sheep hunt. Expectations for this are rather low as very few permits are given out. We studied the maps and picked a first and second choice area. We knew little about that part of Idaho where the sheep hunts are done. But we studied the maps awhile and picked an area along the Salmon River on a high ridge between two main tributaries to the Salmon, Bargamon Creek and Sheep Creek, but on the breaks of the Salmon River.

Big surprise. In the mail comes my sheep tag! Now to get prepared. Bob and I in those days had no horses, so we backpacked. We picked a site on the maps called Bear Point. It was located about 15 miles from the Darby Road, a road that runs from Elk City, Idaho to Darby, Montana. It is an old very primitive road that winds up and down over mountain ridges which one travels at about 10 to 15 miles per hour. The road passed over the high ridge between Bargamon and Sheep Creeks so our backpack from the road to Bear Point was relatively level, with no long steep grades, proceeding

179

along the ridge to the breaks of the Salmon River where Bear Point was located. There was a Forest Service trail along this ridge. Sheep normally live in very steep rocky country so the idea was to hunt the breaks of the Salmon River. The top of the ridge was at an elevation of about 8000 feet and the Salmon River below was at about 3000 feet. There was also a trail that went from Bear Point to the Salmon River, so the assumption was made that one could hunt sheep from Bear Point down to the Salmon River.

With everything prepared we arrived in Idaho around the 15th of September. This date also was the opening of Elk Season. Unknown to us was that the outfitter who had that area for outfitting had been convicted of illegal sheep hunting and had lost his outfitting license. The matter was still being adjudicated and no new outfitter had been given that area. Therefore, in retrospect we were hunting in an area with no licensed outfitter. That was probably what raised our chances of getting drawn for a sheep tag as no outfitter put in for the sheep tags for his clients for that area.

We decided to set up a base camp near the Darby Road where the road crosses Bargamon Creek. This was at a low elevation and would give us a place to return to and have a camp. We set up out outfitters tent with our stove and sleeping cots there. Not far from us, a few hundred yards was a camp set up by an outfitter, Archie George. There was a horse coral there and a few horses but as I remember no one was around. We finished our camp and early the next morning drove my Toyota Land Cruiser from this base camp up to the top of the ridge, about 10 miles, to the trail head for the trail to Bear Point.

As we hiked along the trail to Bear Point, Bob kept falling back behind me and was not keeping up. This was unlike Bob as normally he had lots of energy. Finally in exasperation, I asked Bob what was wrong with him. He finally admitted to me that the doctors had told him his tri-glycerides were too high and he was on a salt free diet. It was the middle of the afternoon and Bob was exhausted. There was a lake about ½ mile below the trail so I decided we had better make camp. I was very concerned about Bob and as we were starting to eat supper I threw him the saltshaker and told him, "Bob, if you expect to get out of here you must eat lots of this salt." He knew as well as I that he was in trouble. I had had an experience a few years before of heat prostration and salt depletion and I knew his problem. The exhaustion is terrible; you just cannot put one foot in front of another.

Bob put lots of salt on his food and we went to sleep camped by the edge of a beautiful mountain lake. In the morning Bob felt better and a discussion was held as to what to do. He said he would like to try to proceed awhile and see how he did. His recovery was marvelous. He did not fall behind me and we decided to keep going and arrived at Bear Point around the middle of the day. We set up camp and decided to make an evening hunt along a ridge to the northeast.

Our hunting method is to split up a little bit and hunt parallel to each other in hopes of driving game past each other. I was sitting on a rock outcrop with about 150 yards of view downhill into a large canyon type bowl. As it was starting to get dark, and I was sitting there thinking good thoughts as I usually do when hunting, a large black object suddenly appeared about 130 yards off with his nose in the air. It was a large Black Bear. My 270 Husquevarna Fabrinvabrinks came to my shoulder automatically and I squeezed off a shot aimed into his rib cage. The bear made a little jump and turn and went downhill. I went to where the bear had been and followed very quietly and slowly. I saw a few drops of blood but not much. There was no snow so I had a very difficult track to follow as bears are soft footed and don't leave much of a trail. Adding to my difficulty was the gathering darkness. Trailing a wounded bear in the dark is not something one likes to do, but my hunting code sense told me it was my duty to follow up now. I slowly and very quietly followed a speck here and a speck of blood there. My senses were in a very high state of tension with my vision and hearing and smelling at a very acute level. After about 80 yards or so of this, my system received a new shot of adrenalin when my vision detected a large black object about 15 yards off. Getting over my surge of panic I very, very, slowly approached the black object. It did not move when a rock was launched onto it. With more confidence I came closer and discovered a very dead bear.

I quickly removed the inners and propped the bear up in the air as much as possible. By this time it was almost fully dark. Bob never hunted till dark so I knew he would be nowhere around even though he probably had heard my shot. I worked my way back to the ridge and back to camp. I do not

181

remember using a flashlight. My rucksack always contained a flashlight and emergency gear so I may have used the flashlight; I do not remember, but I could have spent the night there if I had wanted to. Bob had a roaring fire going when I arrived at camp and we celebrated my bear kill.

After breakfast and discussion we went back to the bear and hung it up in a tree and skinned it. We did a nice careful job as I thought I would make a bear rug of it. I still have it today. About half way through the skinning process we heard a bull elk bugle across the canyon from us. There was a large patch of trees and brush surrounded by open country about ½ mile in diameter across and slightly below us starting about a half mile away. We listened to him bugle at about 15 minute intervals during the rest of the skinning and hanging process. We put a game bag on the bear meat, salted the hide and put it in a sack, picked up our stuff and proceeded down a little ridge toward the bull. At a point opposite the bull I gave a bugle myself. The bull immediately answered me. The hair on the back of my neck stood up. He was awesome and this was the first time I had talked to a bull elk.

Bob and I held a meeting and it was decided that I would talk to this bull and Bob would sneak down and cross the canyon below us and get up on that elk. This was our usual mode of operation to cooperate with each other. Then began a great learning experience. I had never bugled elk before. I tried to mimic him. When he would bugle first I would bugle like him only try to do one better. He would grunt three of four times after his bugle in very low tones. His bugle started on so high a pitch that is was above my hearing range. The pitch would then slowly descend lower until ending in its first grunt. Soon in answering him I put every bit of emotion into it as he did, including the grunts. The grunts were like moose grunts, which Bob and I had learned how to do while in Canada on a moose hunt. The challenge to each other became more and more intense. Sometimes the elk would bugle first and sometimes I would bugle first if he did not bugle in about 10 or 15 minutes. We did this for 1 ½ to 2 hours. I learned more about bugling that day then I have ever learned since. It was really great. My emotions were staggering. At any moment I expected him to charge out of his tree and brush patch and charge to where I was and mow me down. I still remember the intense emotions.

182

Suddenly it was all over and there was no answer. After a while Bob returned with the story that as he proceeded into the tree and brush patch he discovered it was full of cow elk. He thought the bull had 30 cows or so. He said every time I would bugle the bull would storm from one end of the patch to the other knocking his antlers on trees and raising a great ruckus. Bob tried again and again to get to where he could see the bull but he kept moving and chasing his cows to keep them confined to the patch. Eventually, a cow spotted Bob, gave the alarm and they were off and gone. We left, picked up the bear hide and returned to camp a lot wiser on the ways of elk.

We had a good meal and relaxed around the camp. Elk are best hunted early in the morning so our mode of operation is to wake up two hours or so before dawn, have a real good leisure breakfast that will stick with us all day, and leave camp about just before first light. Bob did not like to leave camp until he could see enough to tell where he was going. We proceeded up the trail intending to hunt the ridge where the bull had gone the day before. We split up as usual and I was on Bob's left. I heard a faint elk bugle off to my left down in a new watershed off to my left. I proceeded slowly down into some open large timber. The elk bugles were again about 10 to 15 minutes apart. At one point as I was descending I slipped off a log and fell on my behind about 10 feet down. I hurt a lot but I did not think too much about it. Years later a doctor told me I had broken my tailbone.

I listened some more; I did not answer but slowly went to the bugle. I intended to slow down even more as I thought the elk was still far away, but in the timber the bugles must have been muted as all of a sudden there was a large, six point to a side, bull elk, about 150 yards away in the timber. As usual, my 270 jumped to my shoulder. The elk was slowly moving through the timber from my left to my right. I placed the crosshairs slightly behind his shoulder and squeezed off. He dropped in his tracks.

As a side note, I was hunting with my 270 at that time with a variable 2 ½ to 8-power scope. I was hunting with the 270 because it was lighter for backpacking and I was to hunt sheep anyway. A 270 is a great rifle to hunt sheep with. I normally prefer my 378 Wheatherby Mag for hunting elk. I was hand loading my own 270 shells using 59 grains of Hodgkins 4831 and a 130-grain bullet. Since I had learned to always sight in my rifle before hunting each year the bullet always went where I wanted it to go. I sighted it in at about 2 ½ to 3 inches high at 100 yards. This would put it right on to within 4 inches anywhere out to about 400 yards.

I got up to the elk and he was a real beauty. He was magnificent, six points to a side and very well balanced. My bullet had hit slightly high and had shocked his backbone enough so that he dropped in his tracks. I finished him off with my pistol behind the ear. I propped him up as best as I could, expecting Bob to appear before too long, as I thought for sure he had heard my shot. We have always used a pistol signal. After shooting with a rifle, if we had got game we would fire two quick shots as a signal that we had killed something and that we needed help with the game. Usually, I just fired two quick shots into the animal's head killing two birds with one stone, so to speak, accomplishing finishing the animal off and giving the kill signal at the same time.

I always carry a small block and tackle and rope in my rucksack. Elk are very big and very hard to move. Elk are usually killed on steep slopes and this was no exception. I tied his head to a small tree, stretched him out and opened up the stomach and chest cavity to clean him out and get the cooling air to the meat. This is very important in order to have great tasting meat. I expected Bob at any time but he did not show up. Usually when we are looking for one another we fire a single pistol shot or give a moose grunt, which carries for some distance. The other person answers and we find each other by the sound of the grunts. One needs to be careful in country full of moose, however, as this signal to a bull moose is a challenge to fight.

Bob did not show up and just after I got started butchering, another bull elk bugled just below me out of sight. It took me about two hours or so to skin the elk. I did not quarter it because that requires two hatchets. I carry one hatchet and Bob carries another. One hatchet is used to pound on the other one in order to split the backbone for quartering. The bull continued to bugle all during the butchering process. When I was done I thought and listened for a while. I was very curious about what kind of bull it was so I moved toward it. I had come to sheep hunt, so if we got another bull quickly we could get to sheep hunting. Bob and I were used to shooting each other's animals. When we had tags to fill and were thinking about going home we usually filled each other tags. This was before this became a serious no-no to the fish and game departments. I moved slowly downhill and soon here was a large bull about 250 yards below me in a small clearing through the timber. Again without thinking my 270 jumps to my shoulder and I squeezed off a shot. The animal never moved. I squeezed off another into the same place and he then slowly moved off downhill. I went to the spot in a clearing where he was when I shot and looked carefully for blood. There was no snow so tracking was difficult. The trail led down a shallow ridge with small watercourse depressions to the right and left. I lost the trail about 300 yards or so down the ridge. I circled several times and moved off to the right, as there was no sign of a blood trail down the ridge. As I moved off to the right the terrain became very steep and there was no blood trail there either. After several hours of this and as it was by then late in the day and I had a ways to go to climb out of there I returned to camp.

Bob was in camp and I related my story. The next day we both proceeded down to the first elk. We usually would leave a trail blazed with a hatchet to show us the way. In later years we would use colored tape, which we would remove on the way out. We quartered the elk out and hung him up on a cross limb and put game bags on him. We then went down to where I had lost the trail of the second elk. Bob is a much better tracker than I am. He eventually picked up the trail to the left of where I had lost it. The elk had made a sharp turn to the left, got on an elk trail and moved out on a ridge to the left that had a point on it where the elk could watch his back trail. There he was bedded down on the point and quite dead. He was a huge white colored old bull. We were shocked when we saw he had only one antler. His other one must have been damaged when in the velvet in the spring as it was shriveled up and only about a foot long. The other antler was huge and massive. This elk would have made a great trophy, except it had only one antler.

His body was still slightly warm. We knew that the meat might be hard to keep since the body heat had been in him all night. We did not know when he had died. We butchered him and hung him up. There were two 270 holes in him about two inches apart just behind the shoulders but nearer to the bottom of the chest cavity than to the backbone. He had been hit rather hard with two 270 130 grain bullets but still had moved about 600 yards from where he was hit. I was disappointed that the elk had gone so far with two lethal shots in him in the lung cavity. I made a mental note that I would

185

rather hunt elk in the future with my 378 Weatherby Mag even though it kicked worse that a mule.

We put game bags on the elk and went back to camp. That evening I walked a little way downhill to look for sheep. That evening we had a discussion as to what to do. We had two bull elk and a bear down. We had had a great hunt. We had one sheep to go. It was decided that Bob would return to base camp and hire some horses to pack the game out, and I would continue to hunt sheep.

We followed our usual morning procedure and Bob left at daybreak for base camp. The Toyota was 15 miles away so he had a good hike ahead. I wandered downhill looking for sheep. I hunted for two days and saw nothing, not even a track. The hunt did not seem the same. When one is alone in the wilderness one has to have a much higher sense of self-preservation. Even a minor accident such as a fall can be lethal when no one else is around to render aid. I do not remember my broken tailbone hurting me or giving me lots of trouble, but it must have hurt a lot. I expected Bob back on the second day as he could walk out the 15 miles in about 6 hours and have plenty of time to find the outfitter and return. After one more day of sheep hunting, I became concerned and decided to walk out myself and find Bob. After all he still had his tri-glycerin problem and might have gotten into trouble.

I left in the morning and walked out. When I got to the road I still had 10 miles to go to walk to base camp. I expected somebody to come by on the road in a vehicle and I would get a ride. It never happened. I walked all the way, 25 miles. I got to base camp and there was Bob. He was getting ready to return to Bear Point in the morning. He related a story that the outfitter for the area had been terminated for illegal sheep hunting. Archie George, the outfitter whose camp was next to ours, had to get permission from the Idaho Outfitters and Guides Board down in Boise to go in and get our elk, since our elk were in an area outside his designated hunting area. In addition Archie had been kicked in the ribs by a mule and was laid up in the hospital. His son, just back from the Viet Nam War where he was a Marine, would take the pack string out to get our elk. I have forgotten the name of Archie's son. For this account I will call him the Kid. I do not mean to treat him with any disrespect. He turned out to be an excellent packer and companion, but I don't think he was much more than 19 years old. As you might expect, the war experience had sobered him a lot and he was quite quiet in his speech and demeanor.

We loaded the mules into the truck and drove up to the trailhead. We unloaded the mules and watched the Kid string up the mules. Bob and I were just learning about horses and mules in those days so we knew little of what to do. The Kid suggested we ride the mules on top of an empty packsaddle. Bob climbed up on a mule; as I was about to get on my mule the lead horse decided to move off. The string followed. Horse and mules are always excited and antsy when they first start up and do weird and unexpected things, especially, after being cooped up in a truck or barn. Of course, I learned all this years later when I had my own horses.

Somehow in the melay as the horses and mules got themselves all mixed up while still tied together Bob fell off the mule and got a half hitch of the lead rope of the mule behind him wrapped around his leg just below the knee. Bob was screaming in pain. The kid was trying desperately to cut the lead rope with his pocketknife and I was trying to catch the lead horse to stop the horse. We both succeeded about the same time. Bob however was in sad shape. He was in great pain and his leg was blue and squeezed down to the bone. Fortunately, the bone was not broken.

We held a conference and decided that I should take Bob to the hospital in Grangeville, and I would meet the Kid again tomorrow at daybreak to try to get the elk one more time.

I took Bob back to the base camp in the Toyota. Bob would scream every time the Toyota hit a bump, which was all the time as the road was full of holes. At base camp on the Bargamon I filled Bob up with painkiller and that helped a little, but he still screamed at me constantly to go slower as the pain of the bumps was killing him. I compromised between an appropriate speed and his desire to crawl. We stopped at Archie George's house to tell Mrs. George what happened. The ride to Grangeville took more than three hours. I took Bob to the hospital, bought some diner, filled the Toyota with gasoline, and returned to base camp.

At daybreak the Kid and I again loaded the mules and went to the trailhead. This time the Kid gave me a beautiful black mare to ride. As I look back over the years that I have owned lots of horses, that black mare was one of the finest horses I have ever ridden. It was a gorgeous ride out to Bear Point. The day was a typical fall Indian summer day for Idaho – pleasantly warm and very clear. My knees were not ready for constantly riding so we would ride some, walk some, and ride some more. We got to Bear Point and our camp towards evening. We decided to go out and get the bear meat. We found the bear and loaded it on a mule. By the time we had him all loaded it was completely dark and I could not see my hand in front of my face. My horse, however, had extremely good night vision and brushed by every branch, every tree, and every rock, that she brushed by on the way in. I never appreciated until then the intelligence of a horse. That horse had a mental picture of the trail we came in on and she never missed putting her foot exactly where she had put it down before on the way in.

At daybreak we took the mules down to the second lower elk and put the quarters in mannies and loaded the mules. This was a great learning experience for me as the Kid taught me to pack. I have used the knowledge gained that day the rest of my horse owning and packing days. The Kid turned the mules loose and we took the empty ones up to the first elk, and mannied and loaded that elk and turned the mules loose. I had asked the Kid if the mules really knew the way to follow us and he assured me that they always just follow the mare, especially, when they are loaded. Well, we returned to camp in late afternoon with the intention of reloading the bear and packing out that night. The mules did not show up. They were loaded and they had to climb up the steep timbered slope to get to the camp at Bear Point. In hindsight I now assume the Kid wanted them to take their own pace. I have since packed many elk out of steep canyons myself. It always is a tricky business and should be done quite slowly.

Well no mules. We unloaded the bear tied up the horses and mule, had supper and went to bed. The next day we went looking for the four missing mules and the following day also. Understand that those mules were the Kid's father's means of making a living and were very good and valuable mules. We found two of the mules the second day. We still had two more to find. The second evening a rescue party shows up. The Kids mother is very concerned about him, since he has just returned from the Viet Nam

War. That war still today has the reputation of ruining people so perhaps his mother's concern was proper. The Kid seemed very fine and stable to me. He was very concerned about the mules and did not want to return without them. I was by that time in great physical shape and the Kid was in fantastic shape. We hiked up and down those mountains continually looking for those mules. The rescue party helped us look the third day. They were unprepared for a wilderness ordeal and were not of much help as I recall. The next day another rescue party shows up. I think the Kid thought this was getting out of hand so he decided we had better return before his mother sent the Marines to look for him.

Thus late that day we left for the trailhead with our horses and three mules. Some in the rescue parties had horses and some had walked in. We still had two lost mules, which we had not found and were leaving behind. That ride back to the trailhead is the high point of my life. It was very cold, maybe about zero. The night was crystal clear and I could see lines of mountains for 100 miles to the East and 100 miles to the West from the top of this high ridge. Lines of mountains stretched forth from rank to rank, row upon row in the starlight. There was no wind. We had an elk and a bear in the pack string. The beauty and serenity was just awesome. I was riding a magnificent horse, and by that time was well used to riding. She would respond to the slightest neck rein or leg pressure. It was a night I never have forgotten, even to the details. We had been successful even though I had spent only two days hunting sheep. The others in the party were so cold they seldom rode their horse even if they had one. I was well prepared with a down jacket and woolens, warm and comfortable, but occasionally, I too would walk. It was magnificent.

We got to the Toyota, unpacked the mules and loaded them up and went back to base camp. The rescuers returned to wherever they had come from. Archie himself painfully was in camp with his broken ribs. In no uncertain terms the Kid was to turn around and go back out and look for those mules at daybreak.

The next morning I broke up the base camp, packed up, and went to Grangeville to get Bob.

Archie George became one of the premier outfitters of Idaho, highly respected among his peers and clients. Years later, I met him at an outfitters convention and we reminisced about the experience of his son and the lost mules.

It turned out Bob had found his brother Elks at the Elks Lodge in Grangeville and had a high old time nursing his leg. It was permanently damaged, however, in the tendon and never was the same after that. We stopped in Riggins to hunt deer for a while and to have our meat processed. We called Archie and he told us the Kid had found the mules right down at the lower elk kill. They apparently went back down there and waited to be rescued themselves. He said the meat had bone soured, which was not a surprise to me but still a disappointment, and that he had thrown it away. When we had finished hunting deer for a few days, we recovered our elk meat and went home to California. Thus probably the most memorable hunt of my life was ended. The highlight was, however, the starlight horse ride out from Bear Point, a beautiful, unforgettable experience

SIX

EMPLOYER LITTON

I completed my Masters Degree in Physics in February of 1959 and departed the University of California at Berkeley. I had only two serious employment interviews.

The first was at Lockheed in Sunnyvale near Moffett Field, an old naval air base. The striking thing about Lockheed was the seemingly huge sea of Engineers in desk after desk in a vast football field size room of a building. I just could not imagine myself working in such an environment.

This discouraged me somewhat, but since I had a wife and a little son I had to get very serious about a job. The next interview was with Litton Industries in San Carlos, California. I was not very impressed with the people Litton had sent over to interview me in Berkeley, but since they were interested in me, I went to visit their manufacturing plant. I was interviewed by several more people; it seemed to be interesting and was a small, cozy type of environment quite in contrast to Lockheed. The offer I got was $625 a month which as I remember was $25 more than Lockheed. I accepted the job.

Geneva and I found a one bedroom ground floor apartment in Redwood City where Geneva could walk about a half mile to El Camino Real and shop, and we moved in. We still had Geneva's 51 Ford, which I drove about 4 miles to work. My old 48 Chevrolet had broken an axle on a street in Stockton the previous summer and my father in law helped me tow it, and I left it at Geneva's folk's farm in Stockton.

191

Joe Hull the Director of Research became my boss at Litton. The Electron Tube Division of Litton in those days was divided up by product lines. There was a division which manufactured magnetrons, another carcinotrons, another Klystrons, and the Research Group which worked on new things. The General Engineering Manager, Paul Crapachetts, was a crusty old Engineer and he ran the whole thing like a boss rooster over a flock of hens composed of PhD Electrical Engineers which in turn ran each one of the divisions. It was a very exciting place to work. We were on the cutting edge of radar technology manufacturing, "tubes" for the Military of the United States engaged in a cold war with the Soviet Union.

"Tubes" was a term left over from early radio days where an oscillator or amplifier tube was made from glass with a vacuum inside to generate radio signals or amplify such signals. The tubes Litton made were made from metals and ceramics and were often huge devices weighing sometimes hundreds of pounds.

I have forgotten the name of the business General Manager who was responsible for the economic factors, but the Chief Engineer was Paul Crapachetts. He would gather his PhD Engineers together and have them report what was going on and grill them on what their problems were and what their proposed solutions were. We Engineers were all very young and sitting in on these meetings taught me a lot. The PhD types, I think thought it was below their dignity. After all, it's tough to lay out all the problems you can't solve and let everybody give you lots of ideas, most of which will not work.

This Chief Engineer and Joe Hull were both active Christians and went to the Peninsula Covenant Church in Redwood City. PCC those days was a very fine evangelical Church and these were very good solid men. I did not realize at the time just what a fine thing it was to be able to work for such outstanding men.

Geneva and I had been going to the Christian Reformed Church in Walnut Creek, east of Berkeley where, in hindsight, a large number of Berkeley graduate students of CRC persuasion had been attending. Looking back it seems remarkable that so many CRC graduate students, especially in Physics were attending UC Berkeley. Leaving Berkeley, Geneva and I just naturally looked for a CRC Church and we found one just starting up in Palo Alto. We were the sixth family to arrive at that CRC, and Rev Frank DeJong arrived soon after we did. He was a great pastor to be involved with in starting a new church. Rev. Frank DeJong had started several CRC churches is southern California and was very experienced.

RESEARCH GROUP AND CFAs

The Research Group Engineers at Litton when I started were just Joe Hull and me. More were constantly added as time went on. Joe had started the design of an Injected Beam Crossed Field Amplifier. Joe had built magnetrons and was just getting his PhD from Brooklyn Polytechnic Institute. Joe was older than most of the PhDs at Litton having got his PhD later in life. Joe taught me the rudiments of building a Radar Tube. These tubes were made of metal and ceramic and were actually quite involved and required quite a careful manufacturing processing effort. The parts to the tube were made of copper, stainless steel, ceramic and some other exotic materials. Litton had a reputation of building very fine high quality tubes which had very long lifetimes and were manufactured to a very high degree of precision. Litton philosophy was to build the last tube first. This meant that even on a research device like Joe and I were now building, was to be built to a very high standard of manufacture. In fact, if it worked and the military had need of it, even the research device we were making could be put into a military system and perform with long life.

Looking back, that was a very insightful principle, the disadvantage, however, was that the devices we made were very expensive. But then expense was no matter when possible warfare, people lives, and continued national existence were at stake. When I first came to Litton the cycle from conception to making a model of a new device was three months. That was clearly astounding and enabled Litton to make some very important devices for the US military. By the time I left Litton some seven years later, however, this cycle time had become a year. That meant that much more careful design and anticipation of all the problems had to be done before the tube was designed. That did not work nearly as well as the quick cycle approach as it is impossible to anticipate all the problems without a very extensive staff of top engineers like, for example, that was on the Manhattan project for the atomic bomb.

Joe explained to me the workings of the Crossed Field Amplifier, (we never did come up with a better name for it, I suggested Diabatron, but Joe would have nothing to do with that name as it is derived from the root word of devil, meaning crossed, as in crossed field amplifier). I soon was doing my own analysis of the device. The first one we built was an X band (about 7,000 to 12,000 megacycles or now days called megahertz, in honor of Hertz, a researcher of the past) model. It was about 8 inches in diameter and 2 inches thick and made of copper and weighed maybe 20 pounds. We used oxygen free high conductivity copper which has excellent vacuum characteristics. Litton was very particular of what material went into a tube. Any material put into a tube had to have very low out gassing properties even at high temperatures. We were really limited to copper, certain types of stainless steel, tantalum, and ceramic made of aluminum oxide. These materials also had to have nearly the same coefficient of thermal expansion, since in the manufacturing process they were baked out for 36 hours at 625 degrees Celsius. (Essentially red hot) Baking the device out at that temperature for that length of time is almost the equivalent of running over it with a freight train. It is a very tough procedure for any device and demands exacting manufacturing standards and control.

Our first CFA was finished about April of 1959. Joe conjured up a power supply, an old refugee from some military camp with almost no voltage regulation and big as a small truck. I have forgotten what it was called. Let's call it here a WS13. On the CFA device the cathode operated at about 10,000 volts dc. We had an electrode called the sole which was about 4000 volts above this, a grid about 0 to 2000 volts above the cathode to control the electron beam amperage, and another beam controlling electrode called the accelerator which operated about 3000 volts below the cathode. We had the electronics department at Litton design these regulated power supplies which floated with the cathode voltage. That department seemed to take forever to make those power supplies. It eventually got to the point that every day I would walk over to that department and ask the chief project engineer when my power supply was to be ready. He would say, "Tomorrow for sure". That would be repeated again the next day. I did that for weeks much to my great frustration.

One day I finally got my power supplies and hooked it up with the WS13. I had built an electromagnet to provide the magnetic field, including specially designed pole pieces of cold rolled steel to shape the magnetic field. The whole thing is a complex plumbing operation as waveguides for input and output, water for cooling, high voltage wires, and wires galore for measuring power level are required. Fortunately, Litton was nonunion so I could set it up by myself with no technicians required to help. I plugged it all in with several power monitors. The whole thing must have occupied 200 square feet. I got Joe to come and watch, and eureka! It worked! The dial on the power meter started to rise when I tuned in the right voltage. As soon as the accelerator voltage was raised to provide more beam current, because the cathode power supply, the WS13, was unregulated, the cathode voltage would drop when the beam amperage rose, and the beam would fall out of sync and the power output would drop. I would then raise the cathode voltage to get it back in sync and then more power! It was great. We had built the first Crossed Field Amplifier the world had ever seen. Joe was ecstatic. He soon had a paper off to Electron Devices publication announcing our success of discovery.

This was a first step in the rapid expansion of the CFA bubble at Litton. More Engineers were hired and additional tubes designed and built, funded mainly by the US Air Force out of Wright Patterson Air Force Base in Dayton, Ohio.

Joe wanted to come up with a large signal analysis of the CFA. He wanted to be able to predict power output and efficiency of the device. There was a small signal analysis in a paper by a college professor at the University of Michigan, Joe Roe. I, of course, had studied that paper, but it was somewhat obscure. The idea occurred, I don't remember if it was Joe Hull or me, to create a model to imagine to divide the electron beam up and concentrate the beam into many points in two dimensional space or rods in three dimensional space, and then calculate the motion of these rods, and the interaction of these rods with the electric field of the slow wave structure of the device. Then we could compute the power generated by the device.

Joe put me in charge of this project and we soon recruited technicians, secretaries, and others who did not seem to be absolutely needed in their regular jobs, and a part time summer intern student to whom Litton gave a job. (I later estimated that in a place like Litton, 30 percent of the people do 70 percent of the work and 70 percent of the workers do 30 percent of the work, so one can always find people who are not producing anything but keep their jobs because management has not yet discovered them or got around to laying them off. After all, laying people off and taking away their job is a very distasteful thing to do.) I gave each person a rod to calculate. Calculators did not exist in those days, so each person had the formula for calculating the force on each rod exerted by the electric field and so calculate the motion of the rod, and used a slide rule to do it. I had worked out the formula for the work done by each rod on the electric field so the power or amplification of the device could be calculated. Then the whole overall calculation would be advanced a time step and the calculation repeated with new parameters. I soon had a flock of about a dozen people doing this hour after hour, day after day. It worked great.

The summer intern we had was a boy wonder from somewhere and said we should do this on a computer. He must have been going to school where they talked about computers. None of us had ever heard of a computer before. Joe liked the idea so after a little research we discovered that the Standard Oil Company had a computer, an IBM 704, on top of a San Francisco skyscraper and would rent time on the computer to us.

Soon the boy wonder was trying to program the computer to do the project I had a dozen people working on. Of course, after the summer was over, boy wonder went back to wherever he came from and I was left with the project. My dozen were also disappearing as after all if they somewhat permanently stayed with me then obviously they were not really needed in their supposed job, and were superfluous, and if the management discovered this their bosses might lose them.

So I became a computer programmer. I loved it. My learning to program cost Litton a fortune. There were no books as to how to program so everything was by trial and error. I could only get on the Standard Oil computer between midnight and 6 AM so nights were sometimes spent in San Francisco. I usually got only one, two, or at the most three, turn around a night so progress was very, very, slow by today's standards. If I punched in on an IBM card a wrong symbol or left out a comma, that constituted an error and cost me a turn around. That also meant, however, that most of my time could be spent on tube design and manufacturing as debugging a program with only a few turn a rounds a day took very little of my time.

My time at Litton became very productive and soon Joe Hull thought I was a wonder boy too, now a man however, and could do anything. I soon had a computer program that computed the power output and efficiency of any CFA design at any frequency and power level, including space charge effects which my flock of people could not do. So when raise time came around, Litton gave me a stock option on Litton stock. When they gave it to me it was worth maybe $1000 a year; remember my salary was then about $10,000 a year, so it was a mild bonus. When I left Litton, however, five years later, Litton Stock had gone up by a factor of 32 times so my option eventually became worth maybe about $150,000, a huge sum in those days. (Remember, then a 3 bedroom 2 bath house cost only about $20,000.)

DISTRIBUTED EMISSION CFAs

After a few years Joe wanted to make a distributed emission CFA. He had experience in magnetrons which is a distributed emission device and had dreamed of making the first distributed emission CFA. So after completing the Injected Beam CFA computer program, I started in on the distributed emission CFA program. That was a much more difficult project, and it consumed a good part of my time for the next five years or so.

That DECFA program required a much more complicated analysis of space charge effects. Space charge is the force that each electron in the beam exerts on every other electron in the beam. The Poisson equation of electrodynamics is a mathematical statement of the electric fields caused by space charge. Thus what was required was the solution to the Poisson equation. I solved the equation by dividing the region in the model of the DECFA between the cathode and the anode into a grid of cells. My consultants from Stanford University suggested that the computation for the solution would be faster if we divided the model region into a 48 by 96 grid of cells. That size grid allowed us to create a fixed point Fourier transformation for the solution of the space charge equation that involved lots of common factors, and so would make the computation very fast. Thus I could count how many rods that were calculated to be in each cell of the grid and solve the Poisson equation for the electric field in each cell and, therefore, calculate the motion and trajectory of each rod as it moved through the interaction space. This really worked well.

However, it involved a huge set of computer calculations, and since computers in those days were much slower than now days, huge amounts of computer time were required to make the calculations which were huge and very expensive. I spent many, many, day after day, months, and several years writing and debugging this program. It was difficult to debug because I had nothing real to compare the results to. When I computed the results for the IBCFA program I had a real operating CFA's to compare to. There were no DECFA's in existence so I had nothing to which I could compare the calculated results. The electron trajectory equations were also complex. To simulate the beam, I had to use a large number of, "rods". This also required a very large amount of complex calculation and used a huge amount of computer time.

Since the program took so much time to run a search was constantly being made to find government computers which were not completely used so we could find computer time to run the program. Thus I traveled to sundry places to use sundry computers. I spent a fair amount of time at Wright Patterson Air force Base in Dayton Ohio. I eventually had enough confidence in the results of the program to design the electronics of DECFA's.

Joe then sold an absolutely aggressive CFA amplifier concept to the Air Force, as I recall to the Advanced Research Projects Agency. The Air Force thought they needed radar capable of distinguishing fake incoming Soviet missiles from the real thing. Apparently Soviet planners had decided to send over a huge flock of missiles simultaneously so as to overload US defensive weapons systems. Since nuclear weapons are expensive only some of the missiles would have war heads and so make that particular missile heavier.

So Joe sold the concept that we could build a Distributed Emission CFA giving a radar signal operating at 10 megawatts of peak output power with a 200 microsecond pulse length at an average power of 200 kilowatts. The very long pulse length would allow the radar signal to be frequency chirped over a huge frequency band so as to generate a huge amount of information about the incoming missile. The DECFA was the only device then known that would be able to do this at such a high power level with such a huge bandwidth.

In my mind and in my view the understanding and execution of this project became the defining event of my career at Litton.

Litton was contracted to receive a million dollars a year for three years to develop this tube. Remember this is about 10 million a year in 2010 dollars. This was a lot of money and making the device was a difficult but not an undo-able project.

Joe gave me responsibility of the overall electronic design but hired additional people to do the mechanical design. Tomas Tomacello, a very experienced tube designer was added. He was very good and we worked well together even though he was considerably older than I was. We designed a magnificent tube. It operated at S band, about 3,000 to 4,000 megacycles. The cathode voltage was about 60,000 volts. It was about six feet long and weighed maybe 250 pounds, all of copper, stainless steel, and aluminum oxide ceramic. It was designed to have water cooling inside the tube within the vanes, an oil cooled cathode with non-electrical conducting transformer oil, the input and output waveguide was pressured with freon gas, and with sulfur hexafluoride gas blowing on the windows for cooling. The whole thing was submerged in a tank of non-electrical conducting oil. It was an absolutely astounding device, and a horrible plumbing nightmare. It took days for a tech and I to hook up the plumbing. The cathode voltage had to be regulated with a large electrical current so a whole room, consisting of 400 square feet of floor space ten feet high full of high voltage capacitors, was required to provide the regulated cathode current.

The first severe problem I had was that nine months or so into the program, I discovered that everybody and his brother and sister were charging their time to my project. I was shocked. I discovered half the money was already spent and we had just got started. Soon I spent a lot of my time tracking down who was charging to my program and to get it terminated or soon all of the three million would have been spent and we had not even started to test a tube. In a place like Litton as soon as the word gets out that government money is available and one does not need to charge to overhead when one has nothing constructive to do, account numbers are discovered and charging begins for even anything that even remotely could be construed to be related to the project. Government auditors never seem to see if time cards reflect work actually done on the project or if someone is lollygagging or trying to drum up some idea that might have some application somewhere, and doesn't want to charge an overhead account for it. I believe widespread fraud against the United States Government is overwhelmingly prevalent in places like Litton.

Anyway the money was more than half gone and we had just hardly got started.

Joe now panicked and determined that we had to save money and economize. Here is the start of the making of a disaster. Joe had heard that our competitors, SFD (These letters represent three names, Sulome, Feinstein, and Drexler) had built a circular DECFA, (ours was linear) and that they did not heat the cathode so as to provide a source of thermal electrons for the beam, but depended on secondary emission of electrons banging back into the cathode to provide the electrons for the beam. Tomacello was just completing the mechanical design of the cathode with heaters in the cathode elements and the structural elements required to keep the cathode at about 1100 degrees centigrade for thermal emission of electrons. Joe ordered that cathode heating be eliminated. I protested to no avail as I believed that was taking a risk, and not covering all the bases for all eventualities. We had already provided in the design for cathode structural cooling and it would have been simple to continue. Well we stopped the design of the cathode and built the tube without cathode heaters, so depending only on secondary emission of electrons for beam generation.

The microwave power generated within the tube is propagated out of the tube up a ramp to a window that lets the power out of the vacuum of the tube into an S band waveguide pressurized with Freon and with sulfur hexafluoride blowing on the window outside the vacuum. I had concluded that the power level required a window of sapphire. That in itself would be a horrendous task. Sapphire has a very low coefficient of absorption of RF (radio frequency) energy so it would make a very low loss window. In addition sapphire is relatively strong, and about a five inch diameter window would be able to withstand the pressure of the gas against the vacuum. I had found a source where I could purchase 6 inch diameter crystal balls of pure sapphire which were grown from scratch. I had some windows made of sapphire. I don't think anybody else ever did that.

The cost of the sapphire windows was over $1000 each so the decision was made to make the initial windows out of beryllium oxide. Now beryllium oxide dust is quite dangerous and has to be handled quite carefully but they were assumed to work. I had some made and tested them to the breakage point and they broke at about 25 pounds of pressure so I thought they would work.

The first tube was built and my tech, Dave Sailor, who became a hunting friend, and I installed it into the oil pit. What a lot of work, but we were excited with anticipation of making it work. The tube arced. That is normal for most of the high voltage tubes we had built as sharp edges in a vacuum tend to have very high electric fields off any sharp point so normally there is a period of breaking in where these sharp points are melted off by the energy of a high voltage arc. For this tube because we had a highly regulated voltage which required a huge capacitor bank, every time the tube arced the huge amount of energy in the capacitor bank needed to be discharged. We did this with a very fast microsecond circuitry which detected the initial increase in amperage feeding the arc and then discharged the capacitor bank by the use of a huge set of metal balls separated from each other in a vacuum and then discharged by an arc generated between the metal balls, before the arc got fully started in the tube, thus protecting the tube. The discharge of the huge capacitor bank created a huge noise and shook the whole building. Soon we had visitors just to see what was going on and what was causing the huge noise heard a block away.

Well the arcing did not quit. Eventually, the tube was removed from the pit. I was gone at the time and lowe and behold the window was broken. Reflecting on this, I do not think we could have maintained the voltage in the tube with a tube full of neon or sulfur hexafluoride so as to when the window broke is a mystery to me. This caused quite a delay as Joe did not believe my window tests and all the tests were repeated and another tube built.

The next tube arced for a while as normal, but we observed no amplification of the RF signal. That is, the tube did not work. We tried everything we could think of but it just did not work. There never was any current amperage off the cathode, even with very long RF pulses. Well, I had acquired a new boss by then and did not directly report to Joe anymore and my new boss put me to other things. The money was now gone anyway. A lot of study and reflection was engaged in and the answer as to why it did not work lies in the dependence on secondary emission for cathode current generation. SFD, our competitor, did not build their tubes to the standards that Litton did. Consequently, SFD tubes had a lot more gas in them then Litton's did. It eventually turned out SFD even had a gas source within their DECFA tubes, something Joe did not know. Secondary emission requires a source of gas oxide to keep the secondary emission active from the cathode.

Gas in a microwave tube is unthinkable to Litton. Never would that ever happen at Litton. Litton had a long held reputation of high quality tubes that had long life. Putting gas in a tube is not only unthinkable, but is heresy, and even thinking of that could get one fired at Litton.

Thus this the supreme electrical mechanical creation of my whole life died a disaster, and a three million dollar boondoggle (at least a thirty million dollar boondoggle in 2002 dollars) was tied to my resume.

What a tragedy. I still believe today the device would have worked with an active thermal cathode. The military establishment would have been blessed with a pulsed frequency chirped radar that could have distinguished soviet missiles with warheads in them from those which do not, so the missiles with the warheads could have been destroyed and not the decoys. Well, of course, the USA never had an active war with the Soviet Union so one might argue that that radar was never really needed. Nevertheless, in retrospect it is a very, very great disappointment to me.

Well, dear reader, I write this to pass on wisdom and understanding. In retrospect, I should have fought for active cathode thermal emission and even got myself fired for absolutely insisting on it. When one knows and understands truth, there must be no compromise with what is not true. Lies and falsehood are the product of the Devil. Have nothing to do with lies and falsehood. If one tolerates falsehood there is a huge price to pay, one you cannot even imagine, and yes, this is very, very true in scientific and engineering things.

Another insight of wisdom is that when you think you have good intelligence from a source derived from a competitor; look at it carefully as they may have deceived you on purpose with incomplete information. Basing your actions on information derived from informers or intelligence agents is foolhardy when you have your own understanding of the physics of the subject.

DECFAs eventually became a very useful, valuable device for the Navy of the USA. They are used for the final amplifier output stage of the Aegis Phased Array Radar. The radar radiation elements are mounted as part of the superstructure of the cruisers or heavy destroyers used for fleet defense and are now used in many free world navies. These were all made by Litton competitors.

SONIC RESEARCH

As I reflect on things, I wonder what kind of corruption happened to Joe Hull. When I first meet him he was a man of very high integrity. Why would he subsequently tolerate the wasting of huge amounts of the government contract money on sundry crap, and not spend the contract money only on the tube creation so as to promote maximum chance of success, and do what was promised to the Air Force?

My last interaction with Joe adds to the mystery. Joe had sold to the CIA (Central Intelligence Agency) the concept that we could see into walls with sonic waves to discover what was in the walls, perhaps microphones. We got a contract and I was assigned to work on it. It took me a couple of months to understand the physics of sonic stuff. The frequency of the sonic source is important. Too high a frequency and one cannot see very far into the medium due to attenuation. Too low a frequency and back scatter destroys resolution. Joe had sold the CIA on the basis of the fact that we already had the power source machine for sonic waves at the right frequency. I calculated that the source we had was the wrong frequency and, therefore, would not work, and that we would be unable to make images of anything buried in any walls.

I made an appointment to see Joe. My new boss understood nothing of sonics. I met with Joe and explained what I learned. His response was I lacked motivation and to go back to work.

That was the beginning of the end of my employment at Litton. The CIA money got spent quickly, again by others and nothing was accomplished. Sonic imaging eventually became a very useful medical tool for doctors and hospitals as images can now be made of internal human organs and even of little yet to be born humans. It is also very useful for submarines in order to make images of underwater objects in front of the submarine.

Before this I had requested a new boss. My old boss in the CFA theoretical concepts was Se Paun Yu, an extremely intelligent, but very lazy PhD. He provided me with almost no guidance or direction whatsoever. That was normally OK by me but eventually I got tired of it and wanted to really work on something real. With Litton's suggestion and cooperation I had enrolled in what was called the Honors Coop Program at Stanford University where I would work ¾ of the time at Litton and attend Stanford ¼ of the time to work on a PhD in Electrical Engineering. After a few years of that when it was time to do a thesis, then I was to work for Litton ¼ of the time and go to school ¾ of the time. It was a very exciting program, and I had already been in it for a year and a half.

When finals came, however, I would almost not go to work for a couple of weeks as Stanford is a very tough place to do coursework and one must get A's in grad school, and this required an intense period of study before finals. Se Paun had no problem with all that and did not care what I did. I assumed that my new sonic boss would put up with that too. He didn't, and Litton terminated me on the day before Christmas in 1965. Joe probably had a hand in it too as I am sure I would have not been terminated without his permission.

That was the end of my relationship with Litton Industries. I was employed there seven years. That was a very productive time of my life.

.

SEVEN

MY OWN
BUSINESS

UNIVERSAL COMPUTER APPLICATIONS

Litton Industries decided the day before Christmas in 1965 that they did not need me anymore. I had a Christmas present of a termination sum and the holiday time to reflect on what I would do next.

A very professional lady by the name of Pat Vartanian had worked on the projects I was involved with as a computer programmer at Litton. She also was an old blue, was a graduate of the University of California at Berkeley, with a BA degree in Mathematics in 1961. She was extremely intelligent, hardworking, very competent, and completed her work very quickly and very skillfully. She was the person that by use of the grapevine told me Litton was going to lay me off a few days before it happened, since I had taken off the day Litton decided to send me packing, and I was not around to receive their usual dismissal procedure.

We had discussed the possibility of a programming, or software business. Her brother, Perry Vartanian, who was a decade or so older than her had started a business with some associates in the microwave device area which had gone public. Stockbrokers had got a hold of it and run up the stock price. Perry and his associates had then sold out for a large sum of money. She had hopes of doing the same thing. Of course, I was interested.

Perry, by the way, in his youth had invented a color television scheme which used a rotating mechanism screen in front of the main television screen. I believe he patented it and sold it a few times before other technology took over.

We rented a very small office on Welch Road in Palo Alto across the street from the Old Stanford Barn to give us a mail address and a beginning. Welch Road is on leased land of Stanford University, near the huge Stanford Hospital complex, and on the Stanford Campus, also near the Stanford Computation Center. We formed a partnership and filed the necessary papers for Universal Computer Applications, the name of our new business.

PHYSICAL ELECTRONICS LABORATORIES

I needed to feed my family so I looked for a job. I do not remember who suggested Physical Electronics Laboratories to me, maybe I thought of it myself as Bob Craig, who was the president and major owner had a duck hunting blind near one that a few friends and I had leased for duck hunting near Los Banos. I went to see Bob and explained to him I was starting my own business but was looking for work. Apparently he and one of his Engineers had had a little falling out, and he had just received a contract from the Navy and needed somebody to work on it, so he was interested in me. He must have made a few calls to Litton and then hired me in a few days.

Bob was a remarkable duck hunter. One beautiful sunny day things got a little quiet in my duck blind so I walked through the knee deep pond water over to his blind. He had lined up a string of cock sprigs in his blind, lacking only one more bird for a limit. It seems he only shot cock sprigs. That took a lot of skill. When a flock of ducks circles your blind and decoy setup at a very good speed, one must sit very still with one's head down hoping the flock will maybe look over your spread and try to land among the decoys. Ducks that have been shot at are very wary and very suspicious. Thus one must identify what kind of ducks are approaching the decoys, stay hidden, and in Bob's case identify only the cocks in the flock, which differ from the hens by the color of their heads, and shoot them before they get too close to the decoys, get spooked and then veer off. That takes a lot of skill. I shot any mallard and sprig that got close enough to me, and usually ended up shooting teal when I was near ready to go home. I was, therefore, very impressed with Bob as a duck hunter. It struck me that he must be a person of very high integrity and skill. He had been a professor of Electrical Engineering at Stanford before he founded Physical Electronics Laboratories.

The navy contract job at Physical Electronics Labs was to develop a power limiting device at a broad band of microwave frequency. One of the warfare counter measure techniques the USSR used was to blast the oncoming airplanes radar with huge amount of radar power so as to confuse and maybe wreck the receiver of the radar device on the fire control system on the attacking airplane.

Bob was in the business of making YIG (yttrium - iron - garnet) filters. These devises could filter out everything but a certain frequency that was tunable by the magnetic field applied to the YIG sphere in the device so that the enemy's radar frequency could be determined and counter measures invoked to jam the enemies frequency. They are also used in microwave spectrum analyzers. They came in a little box with a microwave circuit and a magnet with the key element being a very round and highly polished sphere of YIG.

This YIG when placed in a magnetic field would resonate at a particular frequency determined by the magnetic field, and therefore, propagate that frequency, which was roughly proportional to the magnetic field applied.

These were marvelous devices and Bob got a pile of money for each one. The problem was that only he could tune the device before it was shipped. No matter how many technicians he trained none of them could tune the device in any reasonable amount of time and Bob would end up tuning each one himself before it was shipped.

The project I was to work on had been a little started by the previous Engineer who I believe had worked with Bob to send a proposal to the Navy. The idea was to build a slow wave structure which would propagate a broad band of microwave frequencies, and somehow get YIG spheres coupled into the microwave circuit so that the power transmitted through the circuit would be limited. The power limiting occurred when the YIG sphere would saturate and only transmit out a limited amount of power.

Of course, as usual, I went to work and made lots of theoretical calculations and thought about the problem. To make it work at the proposed power level one needed to get the microwave electric fields of the slow wave structure as large as possible coupled to the YIG spheres, so the electric field needed to be concentrated. This also maximized the propagating magnetic field. The answer to this problem is to get the microwave signal to propagate within a material with a very large dielectric constant. They had attempted a set up to use a crystal material called rutile (titanium dioxide) which I recall, has a dielectric constant of about 80 or so. That I concluded would not work good enough so I built a slow wave structure of disks of strontium titanate, which has a dielectric constant of about 278 or so, with holes in the centers, so they looked like donuts. I stacked up the donuts of strontium titanate with alternating layers of Plexiglas. This made a neat beautiful full octave wide band pass microwave filter.

To find pure crystals of strontium titanate and fabricate doughnut type disks of the stuff is not easy as it is extremely brittle. Fortunately, my old hunting buddy, Bob Wire, had started his own business fabricating ceramics. I found a supplier of good pure strontium titanate crystals and Bob Wire's company made me some very beautiful very, very actuate crystal disks of strontium titanate with holes in their centers.

One of the problems that I never was to solve was to make a microwave broad band match from waveguide or coax into the propagating slow wave structure of strontium titanate disks. Making a broad band match where the microwave signal goes from propagating in waveguide to propagating within the stack of disks is a very difficult, very black art. One sort of has to imagine in one's mind how the electric and magnetic fields of the microwave signal are proceeding through things and imagine how they will radiate from one structure to the other without making a reflection, like a radar would from some object, which would cause a high voltage standing wave ratio. Using the mental picture then how does one make wires or what else to get coupling over a broad band of frequency from one structure to another? I started to use little loops of wire at the end of a coax structure but was never was able to achieve a nice broadband match.

Anyway, I got a match over enough of a limited amount of frequency so I was able to test the power limiting concept with YIG spheres in the holes of my doughnut disks. It worked, much to my professional joy. The throughput power was indeed limited. There is a certain amount of professional satisfaction in creating something the humans in the universe have never seen before. Of course, God has designed the universe. But within that universe to discover something that is new to mankind, and has never been done before by mankind in the universe gives a certain sense of satisfaction. Of course, it was not only me. Success like that required the money support of the Navy and its scientists, and then entrepreneurs and business people like Bob Craig to have the insight that something like that might work and then be useful to the military of the United States.

The overall contract challenge, it turned out, however, was that Bob Craig had promised the Navy a power limiting level of a tenth what I came up with. Now the integrity of Bob Craig really showed. He talked to the Navy and told them our results and gave back the rest of the money in the contract to the Navy. I never saw such integrity at Litton; in fact the opposite was true. Litton would just spend the money anyway even if the development concept was impossible to achieve.

I had been going to the office on Welch Road at lunchtime to work on the business of Universal. I usually left about 12 noon and returned at 3:00 or so and worked till 7 or 8. These were long days but Craig's project was very interesting and I was also developing at Universal a new cross field amplifier computer program that I could sell to the industry. Sometime in the spring I made a deal and sold it to General Electric in Schenectady, New York. I started to pick up jobs of professors at Stanford who needed programming help. Pat also picked up a bunch of work, so soon we were very busy. Pat still worked for Litton too so the time she had to work on her projects was limited, and she sometimes turned her project contacts over to me.

Sometime in the September when Bob Wire and I were planning our first elk hunting trip to Idaho I realized I really could not work for Craig and still work on my own and take time out to elk hunt. So I parted with Bob Craig and Physical Electronics Laboratories on good terms.

We had lots of interesting work at Universal. I wrote programs to interpret spacecraft data, programs to interpret infrared spectroscopy and remotely identify from satellites, rock types, trees, and crops, even diseased crops; statistical programs to predict what type of employee counties should hire for police officers, other statistical analysis programs and what not else. Pat picked up a large job from the Hoover Institution at Stanford.

BALFRAM

Pat had also picked up a job with a Stanford professor who was consulting for Cargill, a major grain player and exporter in the commodity markets. They had been accused by the government of manipulating the wheat market, and the professor was hired as a consultant by Cargill to prove they had not. The graduate student working on the wheat problem for the professor liked our work and recommended Universal to a research type in Operations Research by the name of Paul Chaiken, at Stanford Research Institute (SRI). That started off a very large piece of very interesting programming work I did for Paul. I worked on programs for Paul for maybe the next seven years.

Working for Paul I wrote a program which Paul called BALFRAM. (Balanced Force Requirements Analysis Modeling). That program modeled military forces and their interaction. The computer program grew and grew. It became a very huge program that eventually became essentially a programming language where the user could model the interaction of military forces of most any type. We applied it to scenarios like the Korean War with amphibious and vertical envelopment, World War III in Europe with USSR tank forces invading France and Germany, with a sea battle affecting supporting logistics, including nuclear submarines and air craft carriers. I was provided with the data on sundry kinds of USSR submarines, US submarines, USSR aircraft, US aircraft and what not else. We modeled an invasion of China with highly maneuverable tank armies. We modeled lots and lots of very interesting scenarios, some of them classified top secret.

One of the most interesting events of my life occurred with the development and application of this program. President Nixon had started bombing North Viet Nam in hopes of bringing the Viet Cong Communists to the conference table. College students around the country started to riot. Stanford had its contingent. The rioters thought they would picket the Stanford Computation Center. So here am I, yours truly no less, passing through these protest mobs with my computer output under my arms delineating military scenarios using top secret data supplied by the United States Military. Of course, everything was coded, but nevertheless, all of that which they were violently opposed to was walking by right in front of their eyes and they had no perception. I still am amazed that I got away with it. But I did it day after day being very cool about everything.

One day I wandered over to the computer center. Student rioters were milling around; up showed two busloads of Santa Clara County Sheriff's deputies. They all filed out of their buses with full riot gear and huge nightsticks into the computer center parking lot. I looked and saw real fear in those deputies' eyes. I said to myself, "GET OUT OF HERE NOW". And I did, quickly. I read in the paper they made a sweep and bashed a few heads and hauled a lot of rioters off to jail. They might even have got me if I had not run quickly.

One day the rioters picked up rocks, as the Stanford University landscaping scheme is full of sundry rocks, and destroyed $3,000,000 worth of glass windows. Next quarter, Stanford instigated a window fee of big bucks for the students. If no windows were broken the students got the fee back. That worked and no more windows were broken by student rioters.

I eventually installed this program or a version of it on the computers at Quantico Marine Headquarters near Washington, DC, CINCPAC (Commander in Chief Pacific) in Hawaii, and in Taiwan at the Republic of China's intelligence agency.

We worked for anybody that walked in the door. One memorable project was when a gentleman who had started to develop a program for placing DIPs (Dual Inline Package) and their electric circuitry on circuit boards including several layers of boards. He wanted me to take over his program and write it for him. But he had no money. I made a deal with him for future profits from this program as I usually am willing to take a risk, but in this case sort of against my better judgment.

I had bid on a public broadcasting TV station fund raiser for several hours (maybe a half dozen) of very expensive computer time ($1000 per hour type rate) on a CDC (Control Data Corporation) very fast computer. I had sort of done that to help the TV station out with a charitable contribution. I got the time very, very cheap as nobody else bid on it, but I did not then have a plan as to I how I would use the computer time.

So thinking I would use the computer time, I worked on the gentleman's program for free with high hopes of selling the program someday to somebody. I would make the computer runs and the gentleman, let's call him Sam, would go over the results. I usually stopped at the CDC computer center and ran it at night on my way home. I would pick up the results on the way to work and show the results to Sam in the morning, and every day Sam would have huge changes to the program. Eventually I had used up all my purchased computer time, and I did not see, after a huge amount of work, that we were incrementally making much progress. I suggested we hang it up. Sam was rather sad and disappointed about that, but I then became a bit wiser. I have often worked for nothing. Sometimes it subsequently pays off and sometimes it doesn't.

The BALFRAM project ended do to some complex political intrigue at SRI sometime in late 1974. In my view that was very unfortunate as Paul was getting very interested in N-Staged game analysis. The US Air Force had developed a program called, "Sabre Grand", where allocation of air resources in an air battle scenario was accomplished by the mathematical methods of game theory. We studied that a little and became very interested in using game theory and including it in the methodology of the BALFRAM program. The methods of game theory are rather complex and quite involved, but with high speed computers the methods could be astoundingly powerful to analyze battlefield scenarios between two antagonists like in a game. But it was not to be. The project was terminated.

DEC COMPUTERS

Without Paul and Stanford Research Institute's business things got a little slow so we looked around for some new projects. Pat had made contact with a sales lady at DEC (Digital Equipment Corporation). DEC was making some really great mini-computers. The decision was made for Universal to get into the business of selling DEC computers with Universal software on them and selling complete work force ready computer systems. DEC had developed a computer language called DIBOL. We purchased the source code for payroll, accounts payable, accounts receivable, inventory control, and such, from a supplier in Los Angles. We then modified the source code for each individual client to meet individual client's needs. We became good at DIBOL programming. Universal became what was called an OEM (Original Equipment Manufacturer) for DEC. Soon we were selling mini-computers to different kinds of small business. We often got sales leads from DEC.

This caused a fundamental change in the Universal business plan and business operation. One does not fully understand the whole ramification of a new thing until one actually does it. The whole financial structure of Universal had to change. The machines cost us in the $10,000 to $20,000 range or so. DEC wanted to be paid 10 days after they shipped the machine. We then received the machine and delivered it to the customer. The customer did not want to pay until 30 days after the system was completely operational. This means I had to get involved with banks.

Banks are a rather strange thing of a business. They usually seem to be very incompetent and stupid. It took me a long time to understand this as it usually is just plain hard to believe. It probably comes about because they are highly regulated and so follow very strange rules which seldom make any business sense and which makes them seem to be insane.

I would go across the street to Fritz, the manager at the Wells Fargo Bank, and borrow the money to finance these machines. I had known Fritz a long time and we had a good business relationship. He would mutter under his breath, "This is not bankable", but he always gave me the money.

Of course, now, the pressure was on. The business changed from writing rather fun, sometimes complex computer programs, to one of how can I make this customer pay quickly. So I would work night and day at the customer's facility to get the system operational and working to the customer's satisfaction. Then turn around get a night's sleep and do the next one. This after a while was not a lot of fun.

DEC often shipped a machine that would not work. A DEC maintenance crew would then show up and work on it to get it going. Sometimes that took a long time. I soon learned that DEC shipped any machine even close to being finished out the door when the calendar quarter was near the end, as DEC wanted to book as many sales as possible to make their quarterly financial statement look good. Bookkeeping rules counted a machine on their books as sold when it was shipped. My response to that was never to order a machine during the last month of the quarter. It seemed very strange to me that I must game the system to protect myself.

Then one day we get a letter from DEC that the backlog is now 90 days and that any machine ordered today would be delivered out into the future, out as far as 180 days. This seemed to put us out of business as how could we wait six months to get our customers machines. Then I discovered an outfit in Florida that would ship me the same machines in three days at a cheaper price that I had paid DEC, even with DEC's complicated discount system for OEM's. It seems that outfit had placed a huge volume order with DEC and got a huge discount and, therefore, got their machines from DEC pronto.

Well it took a little while to sink in but I soon came to believe that DEC had thrown their OEMs like us, who they had so carefully nurtured over the last few years, overboard off the DEC ship, like one would do to a dead rat. I then understood that I needed to be much more astute and really understand the evil ramifications of dog eat dog capitalism. Business is a lot of fun and a great challenge but one needs to keep one's wits about him and never trust anybody, especially large corporations.

It is the nature of large corporations to change personnel periodically. So after carefully building up a relationship and understanding with a person at a large Corporation, that person then leaves or gets promoted and the new corporate person who lacks the understanding that was previously established, does things that can devastate a small business which has become somewhat dependent on the large Corporation.

I digress and explain a strange phenomenon one does not expect from dealing with large corporations. Everybody I encountered at DEC seemed incompetent. I was mystified by this as DEC was a very large computer manufacturer of outstanding machines. One day I read an article that discussed the problem where if a company is expanding and growing at a large rate, then as soon as employees becomes competent at a job, he or she is promoted to a new job where the employee is now incompetent. Thus almost everybody at the corporation is incompetent. Weird indeed.

Well we still had a new quick supplier of DEC computers, but then we not only sold DEC computers but others also, especially Tally printers. There is always competition out there so one could not raise prices too much without losing business. But it eventually came to the point where the more computers we sold the more money we lost. The fundamental problem was that because we sold turnkey systems we were committed to make them work for the customer. If the customer then hired a new employee, and that employee screwed up the files, it was yours truly that went out to the customer site and fixed the computer system. Soon I was working night and day fixing past installations and it was not fun anymore.

Bill Gates at Microsoft came up with a much better business plan a few years later. You bought his software cheap and you were given an 800 number where you could wait hours on the telephone for somebody to talk to. Marvelous. If I had had the gall to do that I could have gotten my eight hours of sleep at night.

Pat wanted her brother Perry to get into the business with us. Perry was, of course, a highly talented very capable addition to the operation. Perry was soon selling systems to sundry customers.

Financial complications eventually disturbed the mutual trust Pat and I had long enjoyed and disputes arose between us as to which suppliers to pay with the limited cash flow Universal had available. Eventually from great frustration, I set up a different bank account to pay the suppliers that in my sole judgment must be paid first. Then mistrust became huge and the business trust between Pat and I completely fell apart.

We had hired a young male programmer. Pat had a somewhat close relationship with him as he worked mainly on her projects, and that may have complicated the understanding between us. Universal thus started to fall apart and things devolved into a lawsuit. Soon we both got tired of paying attorney's fees, and we split and terminated Universal Computer Applications, Pat taking some business and I taking some, mainly those each was, respectfully, working on. This all happened in the spring of 1976.

About the same time in our search for new business, I wrote a proposal to the Air Force Office of Scientific Research (AFOSR) to study and write programs for the analysis of noise in Cross Field amplifiers. Also a gentleman by the name of John Hubbard and I had come to an agreement for him to sell turnkey CPA computer systems to CPA's (Certified Public Accountants). Our agreement included him getting paid when the system was completed and the customer had paid for it. Of course, we provided the office space and other facilities for him and our contacts for obtaining DEC computers.

Things became financially very tough for me. My last mini-computer project was one that Perry had sold to the Truckee Donner Public Utility District in Truckee, California. I took Geneva and the children to Truckee where I put the teenagers, Sheridan 19, Brenda 17 ½, and Crystal 15 ½, to work building the District's data base. One of them or me was on the customer computer 24 hours of the day building the customer power meter data base into the machine. It was a lot of fun as we rented a place to stay, and then played on Donner Lake during the day with our water skiing boat, and worked at night on building the data base. Cindy 11 ½, had a CRC Navaho friend from our church along. Cindy seemed to collect friends like that. The girl's father was doing something at Stanford. That project, it turned out, was to be the last of me and customer mini-computers.

MANAGED COMMODITY ACCOUNTS

I had traded commodities starting in about 1968. I had done some trading and had worked on a trading methodology on and off for years. Now I worked on it a little more seriously as I had time on my hands. Paul and I still went out to lunch a lot and stayed in contact with each other. Paul was using a broker by the name of Allen Nicol. Nicol was always looking for somebody to manage money for his clients and tried to talk Paul into it. Paul told him, "Jerry Kooyers does the same thing that I do."

Nicol had a Canadian client by the name of Al Bueckert. Nicol introduced me to him and all of us went out to lunch and talked. Bueckert at the time was involved in corn hedging for some Canadian operation. He agreed to pay me $300 a month to provide the commodity trading signals to Nicol from October to December of 1976. That caused me to formalize my system and be disciplined about it. I was to give Nicol the buy and sell signals.

I thought I needed a new business structure so I bought a quickie California corporation from a guy in Los Angeles and named it UCA Systems, Inc. It became organized on December 7, 1976, a date that in hindsight (Pearl Harbor Day) was an accident but might have been auspicious.

Nicol liked my trading system with the signals I gave him so in the middle of December Nicol said he would put clients on my system. In the week just before New Years Day Hubbard sold three CPA computer systems using DEC computers. In the first week of January the AFOSR (Air Force Office of Scientific Research) called me up and said they would give me a $50,000 contract to study noise in Crossed Field Amplifiers. Wow! The Lord Jesus had given me a new business beginning with three product lines!

The business then became very successful. We were fortunate to catch a soybean move right off in about the end of January. Nicol's clients started to make lots of money and Nicol signed up everybody he could. I made the computer calculations for the trading system every day and had Nicol

217

monitoring the futures markets. He would call me up when something needed to be done, such as when commodity futures contracts needed to be bought or sold using the stop points I had provided.

I also worked on the AFOSR contract. A good friend of mine from Litton, Elden Shaw, who had a PhD from the University of Utah, had become a professor of Electrical Engineering at San Jose State University. Elden started to consult with us one day a week and worked on the Air Force contract. I also put my son Sheridan to working with Elden to do Elden's programming. Sheridan was taught some very good programing methodology by an employee we had for a while by the name of Mathew Haar. Haar was a PhD student in Psychology at some University in Palo Alto that I had never heard of. However, he was an extremely good programmer and taught Sheridan a lot of very good stuff. Haar also became a commodity client. We made him some money trading to support his education. Those were heady times.

I concluded that I really did not have time for the CPA business, so I gave it to Hubbard. He had been doing all the work anyway and he could buy DEC computers as well as me, especially since I was no longer interested in buying and selling DEC computers.

1977 became a very profitable year. I still had lunch every day with Paul Chaiken, so he was following my huge success very closely. We decided that Paul would join the business. Paul had been full of very innovative ideas and I thought that he would generate lots of good ideas to contribute to a very successful long term business.

I gave Paul an office across the hall from my office in the same building we were in. I provided him some perks and gave him the use of a new Cadillac. I had hired three or so full time employees plus son Sheridan, daughter Crystal, and Mathew Haar part time. The employees processed the paperwork of the client commodity futures trades, and Sheridan, Haar, and I did the programming. The markets closed before noon California time, so I had afternoons to work on the research contracts and do programming. We created a very good efficient client reporting system that was one of the best in the industry.

Lots of large and small brokerage companies had severe, "back office problems" in those days. UCA went way ahead of everybody with beautiful computer generated monthly statements. Of course, we had our own mini-computers we had bought from DEC, so in those days we were on the cutting edge of computer methodology. We also had access to the Stanford University very high speed main frame computers for any involved calculations.

Paul suggested we hire his brother who had a PhD from someplace and was an expert on combustion, especially in coal fired plants. I thought it would be a good idea to expand our government contracting research business so I went ahead and hired Paul's brother, Dave Chaiken. Dave was motivated to move to California and join UCA because his wife had a form of cancer which Dave expected to be treated at the Stanford University Hospital which had a great reputation for treating these types of cancers.

Wow! Things were really heady with very high expectations. In hindsight it seems I was shooting for the moon.

The commodity money management business is a very difficult business. My huge success was based on solid scientific statistical analysis. Nevertheless, in the statistics, extremes can occur which make huge successes as well as failures. My costs were huge as you can well imagine with all those employees.

In the late spring of 1978 things were not going well and eventually a disaster occurred in the cattle market so that the clients lost lots of money and continued to lose money. I was facing financial disaster so I decided to lay off most all of the employees including Paul and his brother, and as I remember, kept only Jackie, my leading office lady, and jack of all trades. I had no choice. I did not have a reserve of capital as I also had put all of my own capital and company profits under client fund management also, so I lost lots of capital funds too, so I had to bite the bullet and just lay them off. It was sad indeed.

Since this is treatise on wisdom, understand that putting my earned capital into trading funds was a huge mistake. When you have the remarkable fortune to make a lot of money fast, take the money and salt it away, such as in land or gold or art works. Such are hard to sell quickly. That way you preserve some of your fortune for the future and maybe retirement.

The last half of 1978 was survival mode with the commodity business limping along, but with the scientific research business continuing to maintain minimal cash flow; I was provided with a little take home money.

JUDGE LOOKING FOR A BRIBE

Paul's brother did not take being laid off well. I had explained to him I had no choice as the money was gone. I encouraged him to take all his work and proposals he had written with him and go somewhere else.

After about a year later he filed a lawsuit alleging a one year verbal employment contract. That was not true. He sued me for $100,000 direct cause and $1,000,000 for mental distress on his wife who was suffering from cancer. I went back to my old UCA attorney Burris to defend me and UCA. We went through all the legal nonsense. By the time of the eventual trial, (I had moved to Idaho), we were finished with depositions, and what not else lawyers do to maximize their fees. Eventually, we end up in Santa Clara County Superior Court for a jury trial. We start jury selection. We select a juror. The judge calls a recess. Burris tells me the judge wants this case settled now. We negotiate. My attorney, Burris, comes up with new legal wrinkle so we have an edge. I say no, Dave Chaiken is lying, and I want the jury to determine he is lying. We select another juror or two. The judge calls another recess and takes the attorneys to his chambers for another talk and tells them to settle or else. My attorney tells me the judge thinks it should be settled for $17,000. I say no, no, Dave Chaiken is lying. We select more jurors. Judge calls another recess. Now it is just me and the judge in the judge's chambers.

He is a nice friendly Hispanic guy. I went to high school in San Jose with mostly Hispanics, have always liked Mexicans, so we have a fun conversation talking about the birds and the bees and what not else along with some very good coffee. Hispanic men on the whole have a fine sense

220

of humor so we have an enjoyable conversation and get to know each other a little bit.

My attorney tells me that that judge has lots and lots of power so I must do as he says or I could end up losing big time. So I write a check to Chaiken's attorney for about $17 grand and write my attorney another check for about $17 grand. Ten years later I read in the San Jose News that this judge, Aguilar, was his name, goes to federal prison for bribery! So, NOW I UNDERSTAND! I am just too dumb, and too stupid, and too naive, to read the judge, and understand that that judge had wanted a bribe no less!

Wow, dear reader, things are not always as they seem. I suspect, contrary to what you are taught, that there are lots of crooked judges out there. I know that most attorneys are crooked. You must not trust any of them. Actually, I am glad I am dumb, and stupid, and naive about the wiles of the world or maybe I would have suspended my moral commitment to the Lord Jesus and bribed that judge for a few grand and saved myself maybe 30 grand! Praise Jesus I did not. Jesus protected me. Jesus always protects me! After all, as one of my commodity trading clients used to say, whether he won or lost in a bunch of trades, "It is only money."

On the other hand, do not ever expect to receive justice from the judicial system of the United States. The party with the most money always wins. That Chaiken trial was the only exception to that rule in all of my experience. In that case, at that time, I had more money than Chaiken did, but the judge wanted a bribe, and I did not offer one, so I lost.

LEGEND IN MY OWN TIME

Now back to 1978 and the commodity futures business. In January of 1979 as it happens, something started to happen in the commodity markets. No one knows anything but the markets in this case, all the commodity markets, grains, livestock, metals, all started to rise. Soon the clients that had not terminated and were still with me had large positions in lots of different markets. The positions started to make lots of money and soon the positions were producing very huge profits and nobody knew the cause of the price increases.

Then the Chinese army invaded Viet Nam. Wow a real shooting war! Now the cause was known and the markets accelerated making huge even bigger paper profits for the clients.

Then an astounding thing happened. The Chinese called off the war. Unheard of! They just called off the war and gave no reason, and their armies went home. The markets collapsed. We gave back a lot of the paper profits before I got the clients out of the markets, but nevertheless, the clients made a large sum of money. Since my fee system was designed to get 25% of the profits, UCA was again receiving lots of nice cash flow.

Some of my brokers were utterly amazed. The amount of profit the clients had generated in just a few weeks was astounding, even though we gave a huge amount of paper profit back. This event was a large part of the reason that I became a legend in the money management business and this in my own time, no less.

1979 became a very good, very profitable year for the clients and UCA. Jimmy Carter was President and almost everything was being screwed up. This is great for commodity markets as uncertainty causes people to store up inventory and buy lots of stuff. The markets really gyrated around. Gold started to really develop an astounding bull market. We just bought gold contracts and more gold contracts. I had increased the size of the client initial deposits because of the lessons learned in the cattle fiasco of 1978, and of course, became much more conservative; nevertheless, the market's gyrations generated huge profits for the clients.

Sometime in 1980 the epitome of performance accrued which in hindsight was the most elegant of all of the UCA performance in the commodity markets. We had built up a maximum position in gold contracts. Gold had rapidly moved up from about $400 to $800 an ounce. I was on a dog and pony show road trip at some brokerage firm down in Atlanta, Georgia when the top came. I had hired Paul's old broker, Bob Sebilian, to do the actual trading for me, especially because I needed someone when I was on the road.

Bob was an extremely good, outstanding man. He had been a Major in the Marines, and been very badly shot up in the Korean War. He later was head of security for the Marines nuclear arsenal on Guam. Paul Chaiken said he was the only honest broker he ever knew. Every year at UCA we celebrated the Marine Corp birthday with a cake with Bob bringing his sword to cut the cake.

I had developed from an insightful suggestion from Paul, a concept from queuing theory, that when the markets were in an exhaustion phase, when they went up faster that 3 sigma times the square root of the number of days in the price move, it was time to sell. I developed the method of selling one fourth of the position on any day this 3 sigma root n occurred. It worked perfectly in the gold action and we sold maybe $100,000,000 (one hundred million dollars) worth of gold at prices greater than $850 an ounce. The price of gold did not go above that price again for the next 30 years. The clients just made a stupendous amount of money from that one trade, and this added to the legend of UCA. I even had one client change his car license plate to IMMGOLD as we had done our gold trading on the Chicago IMM exchange.

Bob Sebilian executed the trades flawlessly. He was an extremely good employee. Unfortunately, Jackie did not like him, and she did not fully cooperate with him. I had no talent as to how to resolve personal conflicts like this. It was very unfortunate as Jackie could have learned much from Bob. Bob and Jackie ran my business while I went wandering around in Idaho, wasting time, but having fun, mining, rafting, and farming. Bob died young not long after he left UCA, and after I moved the back office (ie the overhead operation) to Idaho. Bob's stomach had been shot up too much in the Korean War so he had lots of severe health problems, especially eating, but you would never know it from talking to him.

MOVE THE BUSINESS TO IDAHO

I had moved to Idaho in July of 1980. Geneva and I had bought about 110 acres on the Salmon River in 1979. In 1981 I decided to move the back office operation to Idaho. Jackie did not want to move to Idaho but she said she would come for about 6 months or so and train any new employees. We built an office building on the ranch and bought a DEC VAC 750 computer which cost me about $250,000 - an extremely nice machine which worked really well.

I hired a really outstanding local Riggins lady. She worked for Geneva cleaning house. I was looking for people to hire, and had settled on a man who looked good to me. I hired Dave, but since Geneva thought very highly of Debbie Shaw, I hired her also. Jackie soon said that Debbie could run circles around Dave. It turned out that Debbie had been the valedictorian of her class, but had married her husband, Leroy, right out of high school.

Debbie was simply outstanding. I soon saw I could trust her to do the trading, so I let her do the trading and take care of everything of the back office, so I again could wander around the country, visit the mine, or hunt elk.

Dave told me a fib one day so I laid him off. As usual, Geneva was very, very correct and very, very insightful about Debbie. Debbie traded millions and millions of dollars' worth of contracts and never made a mistake. I every once in a while would make a mistake that would cost me $10,000 or so. Debbie never made a mistake. She was a genius and a very sincere, hard worker, and a Christian besides. Her IQ must be out of sight.

Jackie, after she trained Debbie returned to California and went to work at a brokerage firm. She had lost her Christian faith. That seems unfathomable to me. Her mother had developed Alzheimer disease and she would take off an afternoon or so from the Palo Alto office to visit her mother in Oakland. She would come back to the office in tears and cry and cry, sometimes all afternoon. I was very poor at giving sympathy and it was not appropriate for me to be intimate in any way with her anyway, so I did not know what to do to help her. She decided she would take six months or so off and go to Switzerland to a Christian retreat type thing called, L'abre, where they lived very primitively in a chalet in amongst the Alps, and sort of went back to nature, where perhaps she might find herself. Jackie was of the hippie generation so that type of thing appealed to her. It did nothing for her, and she had come home minus her Christian faith. What a wreck. It still is unfathomable to me. I later heard she went off the deep end and made a tragedy out of her life.

The Christian life is seemingly like that. God brings trials and tribulations into our lives to test us, to see if we really belong to Him or not. These trials and tribulations are not fun and sometimes are very difficult to handle. But through trials and tribulations we must go. God loves us and wants to make the excellent Christian character even better. So here come trials and tribulations. Jackie did not make it. Very sad. Indeed.

Debbie after a few years decided she would become a missionary with her husband, so she left my employment. They joined YWAM (Youth with a Mission) and went to the Korean Olympics as well as working in Seattle and Riggins with YWAM.

I had become a little wiser about employees so I consulted with Geneva and looked around and hired a very competent Riggins lady, Alberta Rainwater. Alberta was managing the Salmon River Motel in Riggins and it was obvious that she was doing an outstanding job. She also did the books for the Assembly of God Church. Debbie trained her, and Alberta did a very quiet nice outstanding job for me until I closed the trading system down.

BATTLE FITIGUE

As happens in the commodity trading management business, things for a while do not do well. I lost clients and the business did not generate nice profits. We had to go through the mine lawsuit and the stress of that did not help. The big house troubles and the stress of that also did not help either. However, then along came the drought of 1988.

As usual, things are just moving along and the waiting game is being played. Rain in the mid-west stopped and the grain markets started to move up. Of course, it can rain any day so the markets fluctuate. The drought continued and we started to build a very large position in grain contracts. Soon we had the maximum position I would take for the clients, and the drought continued. Geneva's sister and her husband had long planned a vacation trip to eastern Oregon, and we were to go too, so I had promised Geneva I would be out of the grain markets by the time of the trip. I knew that the probability of the drought lasting past the end of July was low, so I had given her that promise. Well the Friday came before the trip and the technical signals by the system were also given to get out. On that Friday I started to get out of some of the positions of some of the clients, but was wasting time talking to brokers. All the computer models of the weather predictions in the United States indicated the drought was to continue. I was slow and inattentive and did not follow through on my promise to Geneva to get out. Sub-consciously, I really wanted to stay in anyway and earn more profit. I was guilty of greed, a huge mistake. That afternoon after the markets closed I trained my daughter, Cindy, who was working for me then, to trade commodities.

Well it started to rain in the mid-west on Saturday and it rained and rained and rained. Some Midwest internally generated weather pattern just happened out of nowhere in the central United States. Lots and lots of farmers and lots of churches were praying for rain. Monday the markets are down limit and we cannot get out. Soybeans went down limit for three days in a row and we cannot get out. Cindy did a very good job and eventually got us out of all of our positions by midweek. But the clients had lost most of their profits.

That essentially ended my commodity trading career though the business was not fully terminated for another five years. I had suffered what is called battle fatigue. When a soldier has been in a fox hole too long and dodges bullets too long he becomes worthless as a soldier. That happened to me. That experience finished me off. It takes lots of steel nerves and courage to confidently trade commodities with high risk most of the time like I was doing. After that event I just did not have it any more.

A good example of battle fatigue is the submarine war during World War II. There are lots of factors to consider in such a war, but I believe a very important factor was how the selection of submarine commanders was accomplished. By the end of the war the United States had sunk all of the Japanese ships of the Japanese navy and merchant marine. United States' submarines sunk thousands of ships and at the end of the war the Japanese had none. But also the United States sunk almost all of the German submarines in the Atlantic and so was able to support the United States armies in Europe logistically and win the war. Now the difference in technology between the Japanese, Germans, and the United States weaponry isn't much. So what happened?

I believe one of the most important factors was that the United States gave each submarine commander about five missions. During the first mission the submarine commander learned how to effectively use his submarine and fine tune his crew. During the second, third, and fourth missions he sunk lots of Japanese ships. By the time of the fifth mission the commanders' submarine had been attacked by Japanese destroyers and he had spent 36 hours or so most likely right on the bottom of the South China Sea being attacked by depth charges, giving most of those submarine commanders a severe case of battle fatigue. After about five missions the US submarine commander was promoted to a desk job, and his submarine turned over to a new commander.

In the German navy the commander was sent out with his submarine again and again until he did not come back. There are stories of German submarines near the end of the war just lying on the rocky sea bottom off the coast of Ireland and Scotland. Once in a while the commander would raise his periscope and watch the allies ships go by, since it is easy to rationalize why an attack could not be made. That is battle fatigue. It does just not seem worth it to go after an enemy ship one more time since I might get sunk. The commander's nerve, courage, and psychological strength are gone.

This happened to me. I got battle fatigue, and I just could not do it effectively any more.

I had gotten into a legal contest with the Bank that financed the construction of the Big House. That Bank was conducting a massive loan fraud scheme. That is covered in another chapter. We had filed a Chapter Eleven Bankruptcy as part of the legal contest to save the house. Before the rain came, UCA clients had about five million dollars in new grain profits. In the normal course of events UCA would have collected about a million dollars in fees over the next six months or so. With all that money all of the debts would have been paid off including the Big House and the Ranch and the legal contest would have been a piece of cake. But that was not to be.

DIEING RICH BEFORE YOUR TIME

As an interesting side story here, it has been said that a commodity trader who dies rich, dies before his time. That actually happened to one of my clients. Some crazy type got the drop on him and his wife in a remote part of Montana where they had a small ranch. He was a retired Green Beret military officer. The crazy tied them up and shot them both in the back of the head. The crazy then went on a spree back to the mid-west. About eight months later he was apprehended at a burglary site. He had with him a tote bag with the name and address of my client on it. That very competent sheriff of the mid-west county called up Montana and ran my clients name through the system.

The crazy was extradited to Montana, and Montana to their great credit, did not mess around. The crazy was tried, convicted, and executed by the Montana legal system about a year later. But that murdered client of mine died with all his huge drought profits! The fee that I collected when the broker closed down the account was huge too!

As another indication of what was happening, in the middle of July I went down to Boise and bought a brand new 1988 ¾ ton diesel Ford pickup with cash. I did not even try to mess around to finance it. I did not even deal over it! I just paid what the dealer wanted! I just wrote him a check!

After the 1988 drought lots of clients got disgusted after losing their huge trading profits, and slowly the business died away, as I did simply not have it any more. Reagan and Bush ran the country well and there were very few real good trading opportunities based on government incompetence. The business just kept slowing down while I was concentrating on the fight to just survive in the big house legal contest. The government had taken over the criminal Bank. Suing the government does not work.

About 1993 I just stopped trading and stopped sending out client statements and just terminated the trading business of the very few clients left.

So thus ended the commodity futures business of UCA Systems, Inc.

EIGHT

FUTURES TRADING

My Futures trading career started about 1968. I was short a group of stocks in the spring of 1968. They were sinking rather nicely and I had a nice profit. I was short stocks like Scientific Data Systems and General Electric. One day out of blue sky President Johnson decides not to run for reelection for President of the United States. The market interpreted this to be extremely bullish. Stocks went straight up for six weeks. At first I did not believe it as that jerk Johnson's departure really could not be that bullish. But the rally fed on itself and up it went including all my shorts. I got them unwound at a smarting loss and made the mental resolution that I would not trade stocks again. And I never did trade stocks for the rest of my life, until now at least which has been 32 years, until this year, the year this was first written, 2000.

MCCAIN

At Universal Computer Applications, which afterward in this book I will call UCA, we acquired a client in the Food Research Institute at Stanford University. I believe it was a Professor by the name of Gray at Stanford that was consulting for Cargill, a very large exporter of grains. Cargill had been accused of manipulating the futures markets in grains and had hired Gray to help them prove to the United States Government that they had not manipulated the grain market.

My Partner in UCA, Pat Vartanian, had been doing most of the work writing computer programs for a graduate student by the name of McCain who worked for Gray. McCain would come by the office once in a while, and I became acquainted with him. He was a very young 19-year-old boy genius from New York. As I remember he was one of the youngest persons ever to get his PhD from Stanford. He would talk awhile and check on the progress of the project, and wander across the street to a brokerage firm located in the old Stanford Horse Barn, now the location of Wells Fargo Bank.

I started to go along with him, as we sometimes would get a spot of coffee or an ice cream cone. Wes always checked on the price of silver and the British Pound and other commodities. Wes was a quiet fellow but I have always been one to ask questions so I kept quizzing him on what was going on. Silver was a carrying charge market, meaning that prices are increasing out into the future on successive monthly contracts, reflecting the interest cost to otherwise hold the silver represented by the contract. The Government was trying to hold the price of silver at no more than $1.29 per ounce as our coin money was based on silver, since if the price of silver went above that price it would pay speculators to melt down the coin money creating problems for the country.

This whole process was just a license for speculators like Wes to just coin real money. One would buy silver in the spot market, usually from the Government supply, and sell the silver futures market making money with no risk by earning the carrying charge premium. It took on the look of a sure thing. The United States Treasury was selling its huge stock of silver in very large quantities, and speculators were making lots of money with no risk. Wes just knew that eventually the treasury would fail in its efforts to control the price of silver.

This contest was fascinating to watch, and Wes started to give me a blow-by-blow account every day of what were the latest happenings. We would read the latest news bulletins and other stuff that all brokerage firms have around. Wes, as I said, was a boy wonder, and he and his friends and associates at Stanford who had started a small pool or joint account together to speculate in silver, had another wrinkle. They would borrow British Pounds to buy the silver! The Brits Government in those days seemed to be run by a bunch of stupid jerks who believed that devaluating the British

Pound would lead to British prosperity. Well every once in a while the Brits would devaluate the Pound by 15% or so. Again this was just a license to just coin real money. Wes and other speculators like him and his friends would constantly sell British Pounds and borrow British Pounds knowing the stupid Brits would devalue again. The Brits just could not win. Speculators would wage war on the Pound and the Brits would accommodate and pay off the speculators, and then the speculators would do it to the Brits again.

I watched Wes and his associates make a fortune. I mean hundreds of thousands of dollars. This was a lot of money in the mid 60's; all by a few not yet dry behind the ears Stanford graduate students. I was fascinated. I started to think there really was something to this commodities business. They were called commodities in those days; now days they are called futures.

PAUL CHAIKEN

Wes had a friend by the name of Paul Chaiken. Paul worked at the Stanford Research Institute, afterward herein called SRI, an independent research center with loose name ties with Stanford University. Paul was doing some research at SRI that was funded by the Office of Naval Research in Washington D.C. Paul was quite frustrated by the lack of programming support he was getting at SRI and Wes recommended us at UCA as capable programmers that could help him out. That began a very deep friendship and business relationship between Paul Chaiken and me. I started to work for him and SRI as an independent consultant type contractor doing Paul's computer programs.

Paul was also a commodities trader. Wes knew him quite well and it may well have been Paul that got Wes and his friends into commodities trading. I do not recall them telling me how they had met. Paul and I would go out for lunch, first at a local restaurant and eventually to Bob's Big Boy in Mountain View, about 15 minutes away. We would discuss the progress on the computer program I was writing for him. Paul would also stop at a brokerage firm to check on commodity prices. We spent a lot of time talking and became real good friends and Paul became my commodity trading mentor.

We started to go out for lunch every day, and we spent two to three hours doing it. Paul would stop at the brokerage firm, in a shopping center near the Palo Alto High School, and, "do his numbers". Paul had a broker who Paul said was the only honest broker he had ever met. His name was Bob Sebilian, more about Bob later. We would stop there every day except when Paul had an important meeting to go to. Paul would calculate a statistical index, which he used in his futures trading. I eventually used a similar one, which I will discuss later.

Paul was Jewish from New York City. Paul had an Uncle who had a seat on the New York Mercantile Exchange. Paul told me lots of stories about his Uncle who was the largest potato dealer in New York City, having made his fortune during World War II buying and selling potatoes. Paul's uncle's theory was to buy potatoes in Maine at whatever the market price was there and sell them in New York at whatever the market price was there. Any profit in the business would be made in the commodity futures market.

The futures market profit would be obtained by the information and knowledge available in the cash markets, which Uncle knew from his cash business. This became known as the "Uncle" factor. This became an euphemism for insider knowledge and understanding in any commodity futures market -- all very legal in the commodity and futures markets.

Paul participated in his Uncles futures ventures. I would get firsthand accounts of the potato battles, and I became an active trader of potato futures on the New York Mercantile Exchange.

I do not remember what my first futures trade was. I slowly started to trade. I made a little money, lost a little money. Successfully trading of futures contracts is very difficult. Fortunately, for me I had little money to lose at that time so I did not incur any big losses in those early years. Nevertheless, I never made any money that I would manage to keep.

As an example, I will tell you the saga of a somewhat ordinary experience that seemed to become routine as time went by. I was very short of money, probably between projects or having lost most of my trading capital on my most recent venture. I could see a potato move coming, especially after a discussion with Paul. I took the $1000 that I normally would have given to Geneva for household expenditures for the coming month and put it in to my trading account. I pyramided my futures positions and within two or three weeks had the account up to $30,000. (Does this remind you of Hillary Clinton's Cattle venture?) I gave Geneva the $1000 for the month and thought to myself, "I am finally getting this right". Remember this was in the late 60's when $30,000 was a lot of money. In fact the $1000 I gave to Geneva each month covered all of our expenses, and we lived in a house in the upper class sections of Los Altos Hills, today worth maybe $4,000,000. Today it would take maybe $5,000 to cover those same expenses. I took that $30,000 less the $1000 and started trading grains. Two weeks later my funds were gone and I owed my broker about another $1000 as my account was under water, in the hole. By that time I had done a little work for somebody or collected some receivables so I somewhere found the $1000 to pay off my broker. That is futures trading. It is fairly easy to make money in futures trading; it is very difficult to keep it.

Robbing the family expense budget to fund a futures venture was not the thing to do and I never did it again.

Paul was a real visionary and predicted the coming of financial futures. In the late 60's and early 70's we had only agricultural and metals futures to trade. Paul told me stories of once owning 5% of the outstanding copper open interest and how he liquidated his position to make a small fortune. Paul's theory was that the only way to make money long term in the futures markets was to aggressively pyramid. Paul was my mentor and taught me a very great deal about futures trading.

Once, I do not remember the details now, I accumulated a large position in rapeseed futures contracts trading on the Winnipeg Grain Exchange in Canada, perhaps a few percentage of the open interest. I had made a huge paper profit, but getting out of the position was difficult. I made money but not nearly what might have been made if I had had more experience trading in markets where I had become a dominant trader. The higher ups in the broker firm where I was trading did not seem to know what I was doing. My local broker got very nervous, but he was making good money, as commissions were routinely $50 to $80 per contract in those days. Today with modern computers commissions are a fraction of that. My broker started to call me the, "Rapeseed King".

STATISTICAL QUALIFIER SYSTEM

Great ideas and inspirations come; it seems, out of the blue. Perhaps one has been thinking about the general subject for some time, and in a moment of vision, a grand idea is conceived. Then perhaps the vision is lost because of distractions or the press of duty or job or family or friends, and the vision is aborted. My consulting, programming business usually became very dead during the Christmas/New Year holiday season. The phone just did not ring and most people went out partying. It happened the holiday season of 1970-1971. All the conception of my own commodity trading system started as a vision, became conceived, and was reduced to a procedure during the week between that Christmas and New Year's Day.

The System, as I will call it, is a collection of procedures and mathematics. Years later in promotional literature we called it the, "Statistical Qualifier System". The system has four facets to it. The first is a statistical calculation, which produces a, "signal"; the second is called, "structure" and is essentially a pattern recognition template, the third is a set of trading rules, and the fourth is a money management theory. There should have been a fifth, which I never conceived, which should have been how the system would interact with the world, and what to do if the world is watching you. I have never written this whole thing down before, thus so as to never have it be lost to posterity, I write it down here. My hope is that I can remember it all. It made me, my family, and my clients a lot of money, and became THE defining successful venture moment of my life.

I had been learning a lot about commodities from my dear friend Paul. He used a nine day statistical comparison procedure which really is what is called in mathematical terms a convolution. Every day he would calculate a change in an index of all the futures markets. He never gave me the basic theory of what he was doing. I will give mine later. He would algebraically add up all the open to close differences in the commodities prices and all the close to close differences. Paul used one tick in wheat as his unit of measure. All the changes relative to wheat were added up. He counted them in the number of, "ticks". A total each day of say +59, or −179 ticks as the change from open to close, or the change for close to close. Paul's method worked very well as it was a very simple short hand way to compute by hand what he wanted to know, which was, how is the market as a whole changing? He never told me where he got this system or how he thought it up.

Paul would compare the last nine days of open to close difference as a set. This is a very small sample from which to make any statistical judgment, but one has no choice, as this is all you have. Nine days to Paul was very significant. Why I am not sure. Perhaps it is an approximate two week interval. If the open to close sum of all the ticks for today compared to the last nine days was greater than 1 ½ sigma then today was called a signal. A buy signal if the change was negative and a sell signal if the change was positive. Therefore, tomorrow would be a day to buy commodities contracts or a day to sell commodities contracts. Sigma stands for the standard deviation of the nine day set of numbers.

Why open to close rather than close to close? I never figured that out. It just worked. Perhaps it is a measure of the buying or selling pressure occurring on that day.

Paul thought he was measuring the buying pressure going on for the day. The assumption perhaps was that the buying pressure would dissipate the next day and selling pressure would take over.

I was much more mathematical than Paul. What Paul was doing was a differential convolution filter being passed over the day to day data. I was operating on and had access to the cutting edge of computer technology in those days with several user accounts at the computer center at Stanford University in Palo Alto. I created a geometric index of all commodity contracts. This is a product of all; let's say n, commodity prices together. The index then is the nth root of the product of all the prices.

The change in the index is the sum of all the partial derivatives of each commodity with respect to the time interval. Or in delta type mathematics the delta i (i being the index) is the sum of the all the changes in the commodity prices. I would use the waited sum of the last four contracts of each commodity. I eventually had the whole thing programmed in a computer language called Basic on a computer where I could call up the commodity data supplier company computer and get all the price data and make the calculation.

The index changes were input to the Stanford University computer. I did not think nine days had any special significance so I had the computer calculate 6 day, 7 day, 8 day, etc., etc., up to 12 day intervals. I found that greater than 12 did not seem to have much meaning and that 6 was problematic but I used it anyway. I used the rule that I had to have at least two of this set to be greater than 1.37 sigma. This came about after I did large numbers of samples and came to the conclusion that I needed a signal on the average every 5 days in order to have meaningful trading. When I used the rule that any two of the set of 6 to 12 being over 1.37 sigma created a signal, I got a signal every 5 days. This was done over many years of data. This constitutes the first facet, computing a "signal".

What is the meaning of signal? I have concluded that being forced to act at some point in time greatly assists the decision making process. It forces one to act. The oversold and overbought condition of the market has some significance, but it is very hard to generate some consistent theory as to why what one is doing is meaningful. In the early days I had great confidence in it; I know Paul did too. Today I am not so sure. Forcing me to act was probably more important. Also, obviously, if the market sold down all day in a very significant way, is not tomorrow a good day to buy? Prices are certainly cheaper in that case than yesterday.

The second facet to the System was structure. Little arrows would be put on a day-by-day bar chart under the day following a buy signal and over the day following a sell signal. I would look at these charts and interpret them according to the set of rules. Maybe I will perhaps list the whole set of rules. The rules were such as buy on the third buy signal that is at a higher price level than the last two signals. To buy a commodity the buy signals must hold and not be violated and the sell signals must not hold and be violated for at least three weeks. I could look at a chart and make this judgment. I always wanted to get the computer to make this decision but I never got around to doing it. It would have been a tedious program to write, as humans are better at pattern recognition than computers. Structure was very important. Structural analysis was done whenever a signal was generated to decide what to buy or sell the next day.

Get out rules were based on structure. Any position that violated the buy signal on which it was established by ½ sigma was to be liquidated. Once a position was established any subsequent signal must be violated two days on the close to liquidate the position. A fail safe out, which should be the worst case, is 3 sigma. Sigma is again the standard deviation of the price volatility, based on the open to close price change. This can be computed by a convolution integral over any time period.

The fourth facet was money management. Paul believed that pyramiding was the only way to make any real significant money. My thinking on the matter is that in any linear system the buys and sells will generate a normal distribution of results. Since we are dealing with random "white" noise, (the markets themselves in their price changes from moment to moment are purely random or white noise) any linear system dealing with the white noise will also be white noise. Thus when one employs any linear system, to consistently make net profits one would have to be very good at picking winning candidates for a trade before the trade is made.

In my time in the 70's most commodity trading advisers used a moving average system. A moving average is also a convolution of the day to day price moment in this case the convoluting function is a rectangular pulse or square function. For example a 6 day moving average convoluting function would have a value of one (1.000) the last six days and a value of zero elsewhere.

I came to the conclusion that Paul was indeed right and that to consistently perform one must make profits exponentially and not linearly. In my system I decided to make money exponentially and lose money linearly. To do this one must add to positions based on profits or pyramid.

Pyramiding has the reputation of being very dangerous and has an associated high risk. That is essentially true. The problem then is to control the risk. I eventually settled on a formula where if I generated 7 sigma of profits, I would add to the position. Markets usually do not react more than 3 sigma in any normal sell off. In fact one of the liquidation rules was that if a market sold off more than 3 sigma from a new high close, the position was to be liquidated. Also margins required by brokerage firms are about 3 sigma.

A severe problem occurs when the volatility in the market changes. Sometimes a news event or anticipated price action will cause an increase in volatility. Sigma is a measure of the volatility and in this writing I use the terms interchangeably.

For example, let's say wheat has been trading with a sigma of 3 cents for months. News comes out that the Russians are starving and they start buying wheat in huge quantities and selling their gold. The price of wheat starts to rise rapidly only now the sigma is 5 cents. If you are pyramiding with a 3 cent sigma and the market reacts with a normal 15 cent sell off, the new 3 sigma, you are going to be wiped out. Thus successful pyramiding must be very sensitive to changes in volatility.

My pyramiding rules required a price to be, "in the clear", that is no sell signals holding, and required 7 sigma in profits to add each new contract. I originally calculated that 6 sigma would be adequate, but I arbitrarily picked 7 to have a little margin of safety. Even then lots of, "campaigns", that is serious pyramiding efforts, would end in severe loses.

The key to successful long term profitability was to treat every new position as a pyramid campaign until the position proved itself a loser. Many, many times, I would add one contract or so and then the position would prove to be a loser and, of course, I would lose more from having tried to pyramid then if I had not tried at all.

In order to have pyramid action close to a mathematical continuum one needs to start with at least five contracts. That is a rather large position for most normal managed accounts so small accounts started with three. With five contracts a price move of three sigma would generate 15 sigma of profits. This for example would be enough to add two new contracts if one is adding contracts based on seven sigma of profits. The ideal pyramid campaign would start with a position of five on a buy signal. Usually the price then moves up and down for a while. Sell signals develop above the market and buy signals below the market. Once the price is through the sell signals and is moving up, "in the clear", contracts are added on the close every day seven sigma is generated. If a sell signal occurs, buying is stopped until again the price moves above the new sell signal for two days on the close. On buy signals contracts can be added with the rule that there must be seven sigma behind every added contract. The assumption has been made that initially seven sigma was behind each contract in the initial trade.

This is a very dynamic entertaining trading system. My clients used to get very excited when a campaign got serious. Good campaigns have a life from three to six weeks. Sometimes I would have positions go from five to 35 contracts, (35 was the arbitrary maximum I invoked to control very severe risk, being seven times the initial position) and produce huge profits. All one needed was one big campaign a year to generate 50 to 100% net gains for the clients for the year.

It turned out that 63% of my trades were small losers; about 32% were small winners, and 5% significant winners. If I could do that we made 50% to 100% per year on account size.

I return now to the history of the system development. I traded my own accounts from the conception of the system in January of 1971 to the fall of 1976. I made a little money and lost a little money, probably a net loser, I do not remember. Nothing serious happened, however, as I was changing things and learning. 1976 was a very tough year for me. My partnership with Pat Vartanian was falling apart. The more computers we sold the more money we lost. Her brother, Perry, who had sold one of those legendary Stanford type start-ups for a ton of money, informally entered the business. Finally, we just split up in lawsuits. Then we both got tired of wasting money on attorneys and just quit and split, she taking some business, I taking some.

MANAGED ACCOUNT BUSINESS

I had few clients and lots of time on my hands. I wrote proposals to the military services and had a salesman trying to sell mini-computers to CPAs. A broker who handled Paul's trading account tried to get Paul to manage money for him; his name was Alan Nicol. Paul told him, "Go see Jerry Kooyers, as he trades the same way I do".

Al Nicol was always looking for someone to manage commodity money as he knew he could not do it successfully himself. We talked. He introduced me to Al Bueckert, a Canadian from the Vancouver area in British Columbia. Bueckert agreed to pay me $300 a month for a three months trial of The System. That was a minuscule amount of money, but it forced me to become very disciplined in computing the numbers and giving the orders to buy and sell to Nicol. This was about the 1st of October of 1976. The trial was to last until December 31, 1976, all of this for $300 a month.

I wanted my system to be successful so in typical scientific fashion I tested it. I had time on my hands that fall and I devoted all my time to it. I went over all my past charts. I created trading campaigns for every tradable commodity. I hand worked through each campaign, calculating the loss or gain for the last five years or so. From that I generated a distribution of results. It was a skewed normal distribution with a tail to the profit side, as you would expect from the pyramid successes.

I created my own smooth function from what I could estimate as the results. I then used a random number generator to generate this function. I could then take samples from this distribution function that was random over the function. I then had the Stanford University Computer simulate results from a large number of trades from this random distribution I had created. I had the computer do millions of simulated calculations of simulated trades and computed the resulting distribution of profits. I wanted a confidence level of 0.50 for at least 100% gain per year and a confidence level of 0.05 for ruin, ruin being defined as going down 50% (the client losing half his money) and, therefore, quitting. I ran calculations varying my parameters to achieve these results. I was satisfied that my system would work and produce these results. I selected the account size, which is the amount of

242

money the client was supposed to deposit with his brokerage firm, so as to give a 50% chance of gaining at least 100% per year and a 5% chance of going down 50% from any high.

On December 7, 1976 I bought a quickie California Corporation and named it UCA Systems, Inc., as a name for my new business. During the Christmas holidays my computer salesman sold three CPA mini-computers. On January 10 of 1977, the Air Force Office of Scientific Research gave me a contract for $50,000 to study noise in Crossed Field Amplifiers. On January 15th, Al Nicol decided he liked my trading system enough to put one of his clients, William Richardson, an old man from Rhode Island on my system. Wow, the Lord is gracious; the Lord had given me a new beginning!!! A new corporate company with three operational product lines!!!

A few trades later in late January an initial position was established in Soybeans. It turned out as we discovered later a contest was developing in the Soybean market between two major players. My system, of course, does not know that; it just establishes a position based on the calculations. We just added and added Soybean contracts. Richardson's $40,000 account had made $120,000 dollars in profits by late April. Al Nicol started adding new accounts as fast as he could convince people to do so.

I started to become a legend. Al Bueckert in Canada started to add clients as fast as he could. Everybody wanted a piece of it. I decided I would branch out to other brokerage houses and started signing them up too. It was very heady stuff. I was off to being a very successful commodity trading adviser.

My fees were based on the concept that the adviser was entitled to 25% of the profits. I derived my own system for getting that amount. My fee was a percentage of the money under management, but the percentage varied each quarter depending on what percentage of the profits had been paid out in fees. It was very unique and generated a large cash flow for UCA Systems, Inc. It was based on the theory that any fee was too high if the client was losing money, but no client objected to paying huge fees if he was making huge profits. So I keep the fees small if I was losing money but had large fees when the clients made money. It worked. It worked very well and with the Soybean profits, and with lots of new clients the cash flow to UCA Systems, Inc. became astounding.

PRYAMIDING FUTURES AS A WHITE WHALE

Here follows a poem of sorts that describes a futures pyramid and the psychological pain involved, using similar words as in Moby Dick pursuing an insane quest.

It's a white whale, I say -- a white whale.
Skin your eyes for him, men:
Look sharp for white water;
If ye see but a bubble, sing out.

Avast, in the dim,
Yonder to the rim,
A spout,
Shout ye lubbers.

Careful now,
Count the risk.
Ready the 'poons,
Make liquid the rope.

Reach deep within ye;
Rouse courage,
With confidence approach the yawning abyss.
When ready do not miss.

Wait for the moment,
A gentle roll
Pounce with all your might;
Yet, if a miss, in a wave quickly hide.

Now! Drive it deep.
Hang on for the ride.
Watch out to cut the rope
If a sound for the deep.

Men! He's coming our way.
Drive another deep,
And another on the rise,
And more and more!

We've got him!
Careful now,
Keep the trim,
Not sideways to the wind.

Ah! The great taste of success!
Oh! We be sized
Greed, fear, pride, guilt, satiated.
Yikes! Now appears the disaster brink!

He's for the deep!
Cut the ropes!
Quickly, cast off all.
We be had!

Count the survivors.
Are any left?
The deep is black indeed.
We've seen the elephant.

Indeed, a futures campaign with huge profits and the emotions involved are really a vision of the elephant. "See the elephant", for those of you who have not encountered the euphemism is a term from early North American explorers where being out in the American Wilderness quite a time and surviving was counted as, "Seeing the elephant."

NINE

THE SUMMER OF "81"

The summer of 1981 started, as I recall, with a nice move in sugar that generated nice profits. I remember walking up to where the Big House would eventually be located. It was a favorite place to be, look at the mountain walls, the meadows, the river, and thinking, what a great blessing I was receiving from the Lord to generate such profits and be in such a beautiful place. This seemed to be quite a time of joy and even euphoria.

Euphoria dear reader is a time of very high vulnerability. I will try to discuss that subject later in this thing.

In hindsight such a great time of material gain had both blessings and problems. Problems occurred when such profits stirred up the promotion juices of my brokers (those who raised money for my program) and these brokers started to rain down new clients in unbelievable numbers. We had had two very good years in a row (up about 100% in 1979 and about 160% in 1980, and now it looked like we would have another year in excess of 100%) This flood of new clients was not necessarily a blessing because to sign up clients after a run of profits only sets those clients up for the next downdraft which could possibly destroy their equity and cause them to eventually quit while in a losing state.

All of this was well known to me but I seemed to be able to do little about it. If one did not sign up clients after a run of profits, one never signed them up, and since the business needed new clients to grow and prosper, the compromise of what I really knew to be the right thing, which would have been to temporarily stop signing up new clients, as contrasted with the signing up new clients. The signing up of new clients then continued.

This, of course, is a corruption. Most brokers could care less about the right thing to do. They only wanted to sign up clients when they could, and the best time for that was when I had made their other clients money, the more the better. If I was going to continue to have a business relationship with these brokers, I needed to accept their new clients. Life seems to be full of compromises like this. As Bill Gothard (His organization was originally called, "Institute of Basic Youth Conflicts".) once said, a man struggles with his conscience. It would really be nice to have the courage to do the right thing all the time. And to you my readers I pass on this wisdom, DO THE RIGHT THING ALL OF THE TIME NO MATTER WHAT. Sure you will probably pay a short term price for this, but in the long run and in the struggle with your conscience, you will come out ahead.

PEAK OF REVENUE GENERATION

To give you the reader some idea of what was occurring, I was at that time, which proved to be the peak, generating an average of about $10,000 per day in income, or on an annualized basis about two million a year. For those of you who read this sometime in the future after 1981, consider that starting Engineer salaries, of a bright young Engineer just out of college, was about $2000 per month, and gold was priced at about $200 per ounce. And this was all before anyone heard of Bill Gates and the income he eventually generated.

As I have said, this was the peak, or the maximum expansion of the balloon of this futures management business of mine. When something like this is beginning to peak, of course, one has no expectation or perception of this peak, and last of all, to even think that this glorious thing will ever end. Normal human presumption believes and expects the boom to go on forever. Since the purpose of this writing is to pass on some accumulated wisdom to grandchildren, great grandchildren, subsequent posterity, and to you dear reader, consider everything very carefully when you have hold of the tail of a seemingly tamed tiger. It would seem proper to stay awake nights thinking about all the bad things that might happen, and to anticipate all the possible outcomes of the scenario you are in, and to carefully weigh them in the balance of judgment. This of course would rob you of your sleep, your peace of mind, and maybe even give you the shakes. That, however, is the price you must pay if you are to continue in your success or to be a King, especially in awesome success like I was experiencing.

The spring went on into summer. We, meaning my family and my friends, went on many very nice white water rafting trips. Hells Canyon, Lower Salmon, the Main Salmon, we did them all, what a summer. Both Al Buckert and I did trips with clients. We gave the trips away and invited the clients along. The Main Salmon River trip I was on cost UCA about $10,000, but within 6 weeks had generated $50,000 in new business. Al did a broker only trip to better the relationships with the brokers. Al, as you recall did marketing for UCA.

In July the markets became inconsistent and we started to lose money for the clients. Ronald Reagan was now 6 months into his presidency and perhaps anticipation and execution of his new policies was occurring. In August it was even worse. I was traveling quite a bit with vacations, the motor home, and river trips. Al was in charge of operations during some of the time. September came and we started to lose big time and clients started to quit. They just kept on quitting through December.

It all seemed that since Ronald Reagan had become President, he amazingly did what he said he was going to do. Few people believed it, least of all me. We had become hooked on Jimmy Carter and his previous pseudo democrat compatriots (that includes Nixon, Ford, Johnson, and Kennedy) who had been seemingly inflating forever. Who could have believed it? Well I should have, because I was subscribing to the Bank Credit Analyst from somewhere in Canada at a very high subscription rate, and they had it right on, and though I read it, thought they were correct, and yes knew they were correct, simply did not believe it in my heart of hearts, because I did not act upon such wise information.

Ronald Reagan had lots of help from his Chairman of the Federal Reserve Board, Paul Volker, the predecessor to Alan Greenspan; both of them came from the same mold. Maybe I might be giving Reagan too much credit, but I do not think so.

The lesson for you my children is that when you pay for good advice, have considered it carefully, have understood that you can rely on their expert advice, use it. Use it carefully and wisely. When one looks around at the world and is trying to decide what to do, real good advice is very precious. Seldom does one receive good sound measured advice, as very few people really know what they are talking about, and this includes lawyers and doctors.

Probably the greatest consistent need of my life was good advice. In my experience lawyers are especially bad at giving advice. Lawyers are simply hired guns (mercenaries) who sell the gun they have in their holster to the highest bidder, or the next guy with money that enters his door. A bankruptcy lawyer sells bankruptcy stuff, a criminal lawyer sells criminal stuff, a tax lawyer sells tax stuff, and so on and on and on. If at all possible get lawyers out of your life, and never, never, never, ever, vote for a lawyer in any public election.

You might think this hyperbole or maybe I have some grievance against attorneys. Believe me attorneys are far worse than I have said. The very hypocrisy of the thing is vast, black, and deep. Attorneys are part of the third branch of government. This third branch has awesome power and can put you in prison and take away your life, and take away your assets and ability to make a living. They report to no one but their higher court and courts act very slowly. They are all buddies, so no one, even by their code of ethics can even speak ill of another attorney or judge.

Yet in all this they make a living and gouge and rob the public and innocent people. As one attorney told me, "Attorneys are a very great luxury". How true. The weapon of the system is money. He who has the most money always wins. I have never seen an exception to this rule, except the time the judge in my case was looking for a bribe from me, and I was too dumb and innocent to perceive it.

Tell me dear reader; is this legal system superior to the old medieval system of trial by combat? At least in the medieval system the loser usually died so that the winner improved the overall gene pool by generally increasing warrior skills. At least in a trial by combat one could estimate his chance of losing and decide the contest was not worth it and concede defeat. Attorneys never concede defeat until they have drained and milked the combatants of every dime it is possible to extract. Then of course they "settle". Dear reader the hypocrisy of attorneys and the legal system is vast and deep. Avoid them at all costs. Like Jesus said, "Settle with your adversary before he takes you to court and you pay every last penny".

This advice principle probably has a very large extended meaning. Advice from pastors reflects their seminary training or the latest course they have taken. The CPA the latest lecture he went to. Look for good advice carefully. When you find it, it is very precious. Try to use many advisers, but consider the biases in the advice.

My father gave me very good advice on a number of occasions, but yet his advice was limited to what he knew from his experience. Many times I needed advice beyond his experience and of course he could not give that to me. This, of course, ought to be obvious, but one usually does not think about that when asking for advice. The best advice probably comes from dear Christian friends who really love you enough to tell you the truth. There are very, very few very true friends like that. Treasure them very highly.

LOVELY DAUGHTER CINDY

My very lovely fourth child, daughter Cindy, had become involved with a man now her husband and father of her four beautiful children in the fall of 1980 and in the spring of 1981. The relationship did not at all seem right to Geneva and me. Guy was not a Christian even though June Cook claimed she had led him to Christ in her Sunday school days. Cindy became 17 years old on May 24, 1981.

Sometime in the late spring Cindy announced that she was tired of her parents and she was headed to Boise to look for a job. She headed into town. At the time it seemed to me to be somewhat innocent and I thought she might wander around a bit and come to her senses. We somehow got word that she was at the Carlson's and Geneva and I decided we had better talk to her. We went to the Carlson's ranch house and Kim (also called Carmen), Guy's sister gave us a lecture that we should not be imposing our religion and moral standards on Cindy.

We somehow figured out that Cindy was at the Berg Ranch (Carlson property on the north side of the Salmon River maybe five miles upriver from Riggins) We went to the Berg ranch and met Gail and Mick Carlson, Guy's parents. By that time I was becoming angry about their involvement rather than their cooperation, which I had every reason to expect from a neighbor. Mick took a real swing at me which I am sure would have knocked me cold if I had not ducked. It is the only time in my life that anybody seriously took a swing at me. Of course, dear reader in grammar school I engaged in the usual little boy stuff of fisticuffs.

I left to call the Sheriff and went to the house at Lake Creek, about two miles away. I called the Sheriff and they said a deputy would be out shortly. Meanwhile Geneva, who had been talking to Gail, had walked to the Lake Creek house. She remembers praying all the way asking the Lord to remove Satan out of the Carlson's and the situation. Somehow, Joe Anderson, the High School principal also came along with the deputy. I met the deputy and Joe, who then went and talked to the Carlson's. I had found Geneva by then. The Carlsons then seemed to become quite mellow and Cindy went home with us.

The decision was made to send her to California. I took her to California against her protests and she lived with my sister, Marcia. Cindy started to work for my business, which still had an office in Palo Alto, California. Her supervisor was Jackie Crane. Jackie was an interesting person who eventually lost her faith. Again since you readers are to be passed on wisdom, let us digress and think about Jackie and the losing of her faith. The Christian life for some Christians is full of trials. Those whom God loves He disciplines and tests. It seems God takes great pleasure, but no, not pleasure now, but ultimate pleasure in the result, in sending men women through trials and tribulations which test their faith to make them even better, stronger, holier, more committed Christians, and more intense lovers of God.

To some, and to all unbelievers, this seems perverse, and to very many people, a great source of protest. If you doubt this, read Fox's Book of Martyrs. Many outstanding Christians were crucified, burned at the stake, imprisoned, starved to death, stoned, put to the sword, etc. etc. Now it is very important to remember that we, and that includes me, do not understand this. We know that God loves us and intends everything for our good, our benefit, and our growth. However, our perspective must be to the eternities. Anybody who is crucified, crucifixion being a very cruel, inglorious, miserable, humiliating experience, usually thinks this can't possibly be from God. And many people usually say it's not and blame the Devil. Nevertheless, dear reader, understand that God is in control, and not one hair of your head will fall without the will of God. Therefore, when God puts you through a trial, thank him and use the trial for your own growth and maturity.

My employee, Jackie, had a mother who had Alzheimer disease, a very sad thing where the memory is destroyed and the persons so afflicted becomes eventually unable to even take care of themselves. Jackie would come back from visits to her mother in tears, tears, and more tears. At that time I little understood God's testing me and so would have had little counsel for her even if it would have been appropriate for me to try to council her. Jackie did not make it as a Christian. Let this be a real warning to you my dear readers. Thirst for God is the most important goal of one's life. No matter what the trial, no matter how bad it gets, God still loves you and is in control. He really intends it for your benefit. This is faith. Faith is seeing the unforeseeable. Your vision must be into eternity and not in the present age. Jackie could not take it, flipped out into the American culture, abandoned Christianity, and disappeared out of our lives.

Jackie had called me one day and said Cindy needed to return home and needed her family. I, of course, love Cindy very much, missed her, and wanted her home myself. Therefore, in hindsight, I did a very foolish thing. I listened to Jackie, and contrary to Geneva's opinion, invited Cindy home. I extracted a promise from her that she would not marry Guy without my permission. That promise was soon forgotten.

My brother Neal and his wife Martha visited us in the first part of September. Neal walked around the ranch for exercise once in a while, and reported to me that a horse was tied up behind the ranch in the brush. The day before, early in the morning, Susanne had told me that Cindy was gone and not in her bed. We looked around a bit and soon Cindy came in the house and said she had been for a walk, which was unusual as Cindy seldom went for just a walk especially early in the morning. The next day Susanne again told me Cindy was gone and not in her bed. I put two and two together as the saying goes and suspected something was up with the horse. I immediately got on my motorcycle, a Honda XR250, (a real good dirt bike) found horse tracks going up the Elkhorn Creek Road and followed them. I got to the end of the road and started up the Elk Meadows trail. I of course was traveling very fast and was gaining rapidly on Cindy as it was just getting light. (I measured later that I could cover three times as much distance on a dirt bike on a trail as compared to being on a horse) I have often times wished I had been a better motorcycle rider as I eventually came to very narrow, very dangerous steep places to take my bike. I just could not make it, so I eventually quit. I walked and ran a little way and realized that I could not hope to gain on a well-conditioned horse going uphill and stopped exhausted. My last effort was to call Cindy very loudly. My call echoed up the canyon but I heard no response. I knew she was near as the horse tracks were very fresh. Years later Cindy said she heard my call.

This began a real saga. I returned to the ranch and reported to all what had happened. My brother Neal left for his continued journey after breakfast. I discussed Cindy's leaving with Geneva and with my mine manager Dan Cook.

The next day word somehow came up the grapevine that Cindy had not shown up at the rendezvous with Guy. The Carlsons were becoming very worried. Dan suggested a helicopter to look for Cindy. How very terrible, my very precious beautiful rebel daughter Cindy who just turned seventeen years old was lost in the wilderness, all by herself, with no food, not knowing where she was going, into an area she had never been before, however, it was said with a real good horse, said to be Mick Carlson's best mare. But of course, at that time Cindy had had very little horse experience.

MINE DISASTER

This excruciating painful confusing situation was interrupted with a radio call in the afternoon from Ladene Bedard, the wife of the miner, Glenn, at the mine. She said the miners had not returned for supper after setting off the late afternoon round. She said it sounded bigger than normal. For those of you not familiar with mining, a round is a set pattern of drilling holes in the tunnel face. The face is the wall in which you are trying to advance the tunnel through solid rock. After drilling the pattern, the holes are filled with dynamite, wired together with electric blasting caps so the blast goes off in a set sequence, which happens so rapidly that it sounds like one big blast. Setting off the blast advances the tunnel about five feet by dumping the rock shattered by the blast into the middle of the tunnel, where it is then mucked up by a mucking machine, dumped into a mine car behind the mucker and hauled outside the mine.

Dan came to me and told me about the radio call from Ladene, that she seemed worried and that all might not be right at the mine. We agreed then to dispatch Rocky Wilson, our mine foreman and general troubleshooter and all around fixer of anything to the mine. The mine was about 21 miles away from the ranch over a very treacherous road, over a 6,000 foot pass, in many places a four wheel drive road. Rocky took my Honda 250 dirt bike motorcycle so as to get their quickly. Rocky made the trip in less than an hour and in the process burned up the motorcycle engine. The trip normally takes two hours in a four wheel drive truck. Rocky called on the radio when he arrived at the mine, said things did not look right and suggested that Dan come in to the mine. Dan and I left for the mine shortly thereafter in a pickup truck.

Rocky had met a neighboring miner, Arty Johnson on the way in to the mine and suggested to him that there was trouble at the mine and that he might need help. After calling us on the radio Rocky and Arty went to the mine portal and from later testimony at a trial went into the mine tunnel to see what happened. Rocky testified later that he and Arty found the air compressor running and went into the tunnel about 400 feet to a place where the tunnel forked. This was called a Why. Rocky took the right hand fork to where the day box was located and Arty took the left. They then came back to the why. Arty reported that he had found Glen's body in the tunnel and that he was dead. Rocky reported that he found that the day box had exploded and that Morgan Owen, the miner's helper was nowhere to be found. Rocky said they should get out of there now, but Arty wanted to go back to the day box to see if he could find Morgan. Rocky agreed to wait at the why while Arty went to look. Arty returned and said he found nothing and both proceeded to leave the mine. They never made it. Both collapsed about 60 feet from the mine portal. They both had carelessly proceeded into the mine where in fact a lethal concentration of carbon monoxide was present.

All miners are required by law to have with them a "self-rescuer". This is a canister device carried on a miner's belt so that if you ever get near a fire in a mine where carbon monoxide might be present, you place the mouthpiece from the canister in your mouth and then you breathe through the mouthpiece and it eliminates the carbon monoxide by catalytic combustion. If Rocky and Arty had simply put their self-rescuers on they would have been fine. In fact neither had them on their belts. Arty paid with his life. Rocky recovered from acute carbon monoxide poisoning, and was rescued, the only person so rescued from a mine in the previous 10 years in Idaho, a large mining state.

Dan and I arrived at the mine about an hour and a half later. We talked to Ladene and discovered that Rocky and Arty had not returned either. We went to the mine portal and could see Rocky and Arty lying in the tunnel. Dan perceived immediately that the men had been overcome by carbon monoxide and put on his self-rescuer and proceeds into the mine. I waited at the portal. I went into the mine a little way. Dan reported that Rocky was still alive but that Arty seemed in worse shape. Dan proceeded into the mine to look for Glenn and Morgan. I thought that I could escape the 60 feet out of the mine if I got poisoned so I went into the tunnel. When you know your friends are in bad shape, I guess no matter what, I would have helped them. I grabbed hold of Rocky and tried to drag him out of the tunnel. He is quite a heavy man, maybe 280 lb. or so, so I made progress slowly and with much breathing. I remember that this concerned me, but I kept dragging. I dragged him past Arty and was halfway to the portal when Dan came back and reported that Glenn was dead, most likely poisoned by carbon monoxide and that Morgan could not be found but that the day box had exploded. Dan helped me drag Rocky out of the tunnel. We immediately went back and dragged Arty out of the tunnel. Dan gave both of them a dose of smelling salts. Rocky moaned but Arty did not. We placed Rocky in the pickup with several doses of smelling salts while he made slight moans. Dan took Rocky in the pickup to the cook shack to warm him up as both Rocky and Arty were cold to the touch. I then proceeded to give Arty the resuscitation procedures I had learned in first aid classes. Mouth to mouth did not seem to work until I discovered that he had swallowed his tongue. I had finally to force my fist down his throat to grab his tongue and force in out of his throat. For me this first experience was quite difficult, but I was pumped very high with adrenaline and probably at that time could have accomplished anything no matter how repulsive. Once I got his tongue out of the way I was able to get air into his chest. I did this for a half an hour in the black dark of night all by myself. The autopsy report later revealed that he had sand and water in his lungs. My guess is that when he lost conscious and fell down his head fell into about one inch of water in the bottom of the tunnel. This prevented him from getting air in his unconscious state and he swallowed his tongue. I finally concluded there was no hope for Arty. I committed him to the Lords mercy. Arty had chosen to be my enemy. He had caused us needless trouble and now he was dead. I do not remember any emotion but sadness.

I walked in complete darkness of very black night back to the cook shack about a half mile away. I remember rather complex emotions about death and God's sovereignty in life as I groped along a very, very black trail. I remember being, it seemed, intensely lonely, yet my spirit seemed to completely interact and trust God.

Dan was still trying to warm Rocky up and get him breathing better. A little later people started to show up, eventually a lot of people showed up. Somehow the word had gotten out that a mine collapse had occurred and we needed workers to help the rescue. Morgan Owen had been a river guide for me and had lots of river friends. Many of his river friends showed up as well as the Riggins Ambulance Service and other volunteers.

The Idaho County Sheriffs deputies showed up and the deputy wanted to go into the mine. Dan had reported to me that his self-rescuer had not heated up when he was in the mine so he said he thought that the carbon Monoxide was out of the mine. The diesel air compressor had been running all the time and was blowing fresh air into the mine. The deputy and I went to the why, discovered Glenn's body in the left hand fork, the deputy then pronounced him dead and we returned to the why. The air valve was closed at the Y and I proceeded to open it as I wanted as much air in the mine as possible. The valve opened with a tremendous noise. You could have scraped the deputy off the ceiling. He virtually became unglued. He was ready then to leave the mine, so we left, to no ill effects.

This particular sheriff's deputy was a very brave man. He was in the Riggins area for maybe only a year or two. He had made a major drug bust and nabbed two very dangerous types, and also stopped Riggins only bank robbery cold. Every other deputy who was in the area for years never had any excitement like he had in the little time he was there.

Some crooks robbed the Riggins bank, and fled up the Salmon River Road in a stolen yellow pickup. The sheriff's office called us and asked us if we had seen it going past our ranch where we were living. They also called Gail Carlson and she reported it was just going past their ranch up the Allison Creek road. The deputy goes by in hot pursuit. He gets on the CB radio and tells the loggers up the road what's going on. They jackknife a truck across the road about 12 miles up. The robbers take time to switch vehicles and so when they encounter the jackknifed truck the deputy is right behind them. The robbers jump out of their vehicle and a fire fight with guns begins. The deputy gets one in the leg and the other two run down a canyon on foot leaving the money behind. Rumor had it the bank gained in the process as they recovered more money than they lost! The sheriff sends a helicopter and one robber surrenders at the Bullion Mine down the canyon and upriver a ways. The other gets away but on foot with no boots, jacket, or gun according to what the sheriff himself told me when they proposed to evacuate the canyon the next day. Geneva and the kids left for town and my son Sheridan and I stayed at the ranch. At night we turned the generator off in those days, and I remember the night as extremely dark. We locked everything securely and slept with our guns in hand.

Three days later the robber stole another car in Riggins and escaped to McCall. He must have walked right past the ranch in the dark and continued his 30 mile lonely walk, cold and very hungry. When he got to McCall he bought a goose down coat and stopped at the Red Steer Drive Inn for a hamburger. A cop spots him and another hot pursuit begins. The robber again abandons his stolen car at the end of a logging road and escapes on foot. Later he steels a motorcycle in McCall and eventually is spotted by an FBI agent in a law library in Boise. That story itself would make a movie. That was the only major robbery in memory in Riggins.

So let's continue the events at the mine. The Riggins ambulance team took Rocky to the McCall Hospital. After about 24 hours Rocky became conscious and started to recover. It seems carbon monoxide poisoning has psychological effects. It took a long time for Rocky to fully recover.

That very day of the disaster, in early afternoon, the mine had a visit by MSHA, the federal Mine Safety and Health Administration. The inspector was still in McCall that evening and he arrived at the mine at about midnight. He proceeded into the mine about 250 feet with his carbon monoxide detector, where he pronounced that the mine had a lethal concentration of carbon monoxide and officially ordered the mine closed. We left.

Nobody slept that night at the mine. In the morning we had breakfast. The mine safety inspector then led the way into the mine and officially opened the mine for the purpose of recovering the bodies. The deputies put Glenn and Arty in body bags. They found no more of Morgan's body than a piece of bone about the size of a half dollar, and a piece of one of his boots. Otherwise Morgan had been vaporized. His remains left a slight scum on the walls of the mine. A mold later formed on this scum. Morgan left his silhouette on the ceiling of the tunnel above the day box. He apparently was bending over the day box when it exploded.

The day box probably contained about two boxes of dynamite and two sacks of prill, a mixture of ammonium nitrate and diesel fuel, now days called ANFO. This was placed at the end of a spur tunnel, which was about 4 feet wide by 7 feet tall, against the terminal face.

The great mystery of all this is what caused the explosion. Dynamite does not go off without a cap placed in the dynamite. The caps do not go off without an electric jolt. It is very much against the safety procedures to have a cap in the dynamite away from the face where the round is to be loaded. When Dan and I inspected the face later, the round was about half wired. All the holes were loaded with dynamite and priell. Priell is cheaper than dynamite, so it is used when you can, but dynamite is necessary to set off the priell. On the other hand priell seems to make much more carbon monoxide than dynamite. We surmised that Glenn was wiring the face and had sent Morgan back to the day box with the excess dynamite in a yellow bucket. None of this dynamite should have had a cap in it. Both Glenn and Morgan were well trained by Dan and other experienced mine people we had had at the mine at various times. All Morgan should have been doing was placing the dynamite back into the day box and the caps back into the cap box.

So in order to have an explosion some very extenuating circumstances have to occur. In order to get electricity into the caps a lightning bolt has to occur outside the mine and the juice go up the mine rails to the daybox, or Morgan has to scrape the wires connected to a cap on his water proof coat to generate a static charge. This seems very improbable.

The electric detonator which was normally used to set the caps off was at the Y or maybe at the portal, I don't for sure remember. There should not have been a cap in the dynamite anyway. If there was they were violating the rules. It was a clear day that day with no reported lighting.

Maybe Morgan killed himself on purpose. This seems very unlikely. Morgan was 19 years of age, very well adjusted, had lots of friends, and was well liked. He had only been on the job about 3 weeks and seemed very eager about the job.

So how did Morgan get caps into dynamite and set them off with an electric charge? I have thought about this on occasion for 15 years. I write this in March of 1997. I have prayed many times for the Lord to give me a revelation. I have now come to the belief that that may be an improper prayer as I am beginning to believe we should not desire to know the future, as that seems to be the devils work. Since a vision into the past may be of the same nature, I now no longer seek it with great passion. My judgment now after 15 years is that we were sabotaged. I have refused to believe this all these years as that seemed just too painful and full of all kinds of deep, deep, complications. Probably the biggest regret of my life is that I did not hire a failure analysis company to come and analyze the explosion. They quoted me $5,000, and at that time, the mine just did not have the money, but in hindsight I could have, and should have, found the money somehow.

There just does not seem to be any other answer than sabotage. I have thought about it many, many times. How do caps get into dynamite and electricity get into the caps at a day box where this kind of thing is just not done? Sure Morgan was inexperienced. Still he was trained, and if anything a miner is trained to do he is certainly trained to respect dynamite. It is a very fearful thing just to handle it, especially for someone new who has not handled it before. We have all learned from the TV that dynamite is bad stuff and can kill you.

Someone suggested that the MSHA guy told the miners to do something or change some procedure which caused the accident. Dan as you might have observed was at the ranch thinking about Cindy rather than being at his post at the mine. Normally he would have always been at the mine for an MSHA inspection as this agency has great power and could easily have put us out of business. It seems improbable for MSHA to have told the miners to do something quite unsafe, but in this age where many of us mistrust the government and its bureaus, this idea can take root.

Well, we had some enemies. Arty and his wife were some. Al Osborn who got me into the mine in the first place, left with very bitter feelings. He is quoted to have vowed after he left the mine that he was going to have a miserable winter and everybody around him was going to have a miserable winter. Dan on my instructions had managed on a very clever ruse to get the compressor back from some men Al had sent to take it from the mine. The compressor belonged to an investor in Washington, and I felt that Al had no more claim to it than I did since I had been leasing it.

As I said the idea of sabotage raises very, very painful ramifications. At this time there is no proof. It will be left to God's judgment. Sabotage seems the only reasonable explanation. The explosion occurred after a long Labor Day holiday weekend. This was the first time the day box had most likely been used after the holiday. We had no caretaker at the mine that week end and nobody of the mine staff was there.

Is there a lesson for you dear readers? Yes, try in all of life to make as few enemies as possible. Remember we all are depraved and fully capable of yes, murder. Jesus said he who hates his brother is guilty of murder. It is only by the grace of God we do not murder each other. Real reprobates like Arty and Al are only restrained by the thought of being caught and the possible consequences. If they think they will not be caught, they are not restrained.

DISASTER REFLECTIONS

Geneva said I was a different person after the accident and much more reflective as you might imagine. It took a while to get back to my normal self. In retrospect this might have had a great influence on my trading. Trading in fact continued very badly and we lost almost all of the clients during the next year and a half.

Morgan's funeral and Glenn's funeral were both conducted at the Salmon River Community Church by the Mormons, as they claimed these young men as theirs. By the way, Dan was the local Mormon Bishop. Dan, observing Glenn's body at the funeral, pointed out to me that Glen's lips were blistered. That would mean that he had probably used his self-rescuer. The self-rescuer was near Glenn's body in the mine, like it was discarded.

Dan and I surmised from the evidence we saw that Glenn most likely heard the great explosion, went to investigate to see what happened to Morgan by going down the tunnel about 300 feet to the Y and going 300 feet up the other tunnel to the day box. Somewhere he put on his self-rescuer. He probably did not find any evidence of Morgan and returned to near the face he was about to blast to get something. The self-rescuer became very, very hot which it does when carbon monoxide is present. He must of then took it out of his mouth, became even more poisoned, lost consciousness and died.

Now miners are trained that when the self-rescuer gets hot it is working and never, never, take it out of your mouth if it is hot no matter what. Dan's theory was that Glenn could have just put his self-rescuer in his mouth and just walked out of the mine with no ill effects. Glenn was young, somewhat impetuous, and in the confusion of not finding his friend Morgan perhaps just became ill disciplined.

There is a lesson in this for you dear children. When you have a dangerous job, get yourself trained, and disciplined as to safety procedures. Be mentally prepared to do what you need to do in case of an unexpected event. It is somewhat like running a major rapid on a whitewater river. By watching the rapid for a length of time you plan and time your moves of each stroke of the oars at a time. When you are in the middle of the rapid with lots of noise and people screaming you do not have time to think or change your course of action. You must mentally be prepared to make all the right moves in their right timing, and in the right sequence, to execute the oar powered water moves properly, and avoid a rock, a hole, or a flip. Glenn and then also Arty died needlessly.

I was astounded, although perhaps I should not have been, by the difference between the funerals of Glen and Morgan and that of Arty Johnson. Glen and Morgan were claimed by the Mormons and the funeral was conducted by Dan Cook, the local Bishop, and other local Mormons. The funerals were depressing to the extreme. They spent their time talking all about the good things in Glen and Morgan lives. Everybody was very, very sad. It seemed these young men had no hope whatsoever. In Mormon theology one must apparently do lots of good, and since these young men died young and had little opportunity to do lots of good, they were destined for oblivion. The funeral events were really very, very sad.

In contrast to this was Arty's funeral. The Catholics claimed him. Arty was a real beer drinking reprobate with a not very good, in fact let's call it bad, reputation. Yet his funeral was full of hope, resurrection, and life. The priest said so many good things about Arty; I got to wondering if it was really Arty in the casket! The Catholic approach was full of hope, concern for the survivors, and salvation. What a difference. If any you dear readers have swallowed the Mormon nonsense, you be warned that Mormon religion is really of the devil and is out to destroy people. It is, in the final analysis, a very depressing religion, especially for women.

The accident made national news as three men were killed in a mine accident. Mine accidents have a large profile. The news people showed up in a helicopter - quite a show. They talked with me for a half an hour and then we went "live", meaning that the interviewer asked questions while the video cameras were running. The whole demeanor of the interviewer changed, like an actor going on stage. In retrospect they were trying to set me up to be some kind of news casualty. The grief of losing my friends came through and I lost control of myself and started to cry. This of course was not very manly in my culture, but the news types must have taken it in stride and made a grief story out of it.

There is a lesson in this for you dear grandchildren. Be very, very careful in front of news cameras. You do not know the agenda of the news generators, and they may be out to get you for no other reason than to make you look very bad for news generation at your expense.

The trip back to the ranch with Dan later that day was very emotional. I knew the mine was finished and that I was finished with mining. This was a mental emotional decision which was independent of future circumstances. Sometimes it takes such an event as that to just finish something off so that you never even consider it again. I had received the cure and never again would I even desire to look for gold or mine for even the greatest possible payoff. I was finished.

The sheriff's search somehow found Cindy. They and the Carlsons worked together somehow. It has never been explained to me. The Sheriff asked me what was to be done with Cindy as the Carlsons were now apparently very embarrassed. Some friends, sometimes church friends, Pat and Shari Merek, people who later bought the Main Salmon part of the rafting business, must have thought they would make good substitute parents for Cindy and invited her to stay with them. Cindy liked the idea and since Geneva and I had turned Cindy over to the care of the Lord Jesus when the mine accident occurred we just accepted the idea. In hindsight I was probably exhausted by the mine tragedy and did not want to think about such a complicated matter. Cindy had really made her own decision to run away and leave her parents; there was no reversing it without a great deal of spiritual energy and for what anyway. She was going to do it her way and do her own thing no matter what. Geneva and I just prayed, "Lord she is all yours, watch over her and keep her".

A lesson for you dear children is to be very careful of do-gooders, and be very careful that you do not become do-gooders like the Mereks. They are nice people but really meddlers poking themselves into others peoples business in their great pride since they know they can do better in parenting than her parents. I believe that if Cindy would have had to go out into the world alone to make all of her own decisions she would have come to her senses. There is nothing like going out into the cold, cold world by yourself to find it is really not a very nice place and realize your parents really do love you and go back and talk and listen to your parents. Between the Carlsons, the Mereks and other sundry do gooders, Cindy drifted into a relationship with Guy, and with Guys parents' full approval, eventually marrying Guy in the spring of 1982 in Las Vegas, Nevada, with the presence of the Carlsons and Jungerts, neighbors from French Creek as witnesses, when she was still just seventeen years old. They must have lied about her age. She never even told her parents about it or invited her parents to the wedding.

Dan Cook seemed to take great delight in telling Geneva and I all about this to our great grief. May the Lord rebuke all those people who delighted in hurting us.

Years later, Cindy told me she got on a wrong trail, missed the rendezvous spot, and ended up somewhere now in the dark of night maybe on top of a mountain. There she encountered a Good Samaritan type who let her sleep in his tent, so she was not too terribly cold and exposed. In the morning he told her where to go. So she then on her Carlson faithful, but now hungry horse, arrived at the rendezvous spot, but Guy had already come there and left to look for her. This is real fun, but it makes a spectacular story about attempting to elope -- the talk of the town for quite a while. Yes indeed, the Lord Jesus Christ answered our intense prayers and watched over her. Praise you Jesus! Thank you Jesus!

Construction of the big house started that fall a few days after the mine disaster, and that is another story in another chapter. So was ended the most remarkable summer of 1981. It began with Euphoria and ended with Disaster.

Big House om the Salmon River of Idaho about 1990

TEN

THE BIGHOUSE

An account of the Big House leaves one in a quandary as to where to begin. In order to understand what happened one has to begin with a study of economics and banking. That seems just too much in a simple explanation of what happened. However, I will need to proceed in just that manner in order for you, dear reader, to understand this saga.

In 1981 financial life had become very successful with an unbelievable amount of money flowing into my business. It seemed such a flow was going to continue for a long time as I had a very fine set of Brokers raising money for me and client performance was very good, one Broker even calling me a legend in my own time.

This can be very heady stuff and one even starts to think one is invincible, and even think very little of the time about God even though it has been quite obvious that God is omnipotent and in control of everything. And perhaps even potentially more devastating, one starts to think more highly of himself than he ought to think.

Thus, the thoughts of a new dream house for Geneva, a house to be kept for family posterity for hundreds of years, to be built on the Ranch on the Salmon River of Idaho. Preparations for a house had been going on for a while with pipelines and buried electrical lines going to the potential site. A hydroelectric system had been contemplated, and the dam, pipeline, and power house for it had been built. The pipeline system, fed by a dam on Elkhorn Creek, which gave a 300 foot gravity head, also had a potential for a fine gravity head irrigation system. Most everything was in readiness so thoughts turned to a new house.

A fine office building had been completed with about 2,000 square feet of space on the lower story which I occupied with my employees. The upper story with a precast concrete floor was a vehicle, shop, and storage building of steel construction with bays for vehicles and a third floor of lofts over half of the upper 2000 square feet for sundry additional storage. It was and is a very fine building. All my businesses were run out of there during the next 15 years.

The spring of 1981 had produced huge profits for the clients, so then as always happened, the Brokers get excited and lots of new clients had been signed up. The summer, however, had not gone well. Ronald Reagan had become President in January, and the United States economic system was significantly changing. Even though I was a Ronald Reagan fan, the consequences of the economic changes occurring were not at all obvious, and I had not even considered the potential effects, but had subconsciously assumed the stupid government actions of the Carter years would just continue. Those Carter policies had created huge swings in the prices of commodities and, consequently, also in the commodities futures markets and, of course, the volatility had created great opportunities for trading which greatly benefited the clients.

During the summer I had taken lots of vacation time with family, friends, and clients on river rafting and other trips, and had turned the management of the trading over to Al Buekert, an early client who then had become an associate of mine, whose prime responsibility was raising money in Canada. Things had not gone well with the trading, as the markets had stopped trending, and clients were terminating their accounts because they were losing money in large amounts.

In the first part of September the mine disaster occurred at the same time that seventeen year old daughter Cindy had decided to run away with her boyfriend, Guy Carlson. Thus, there was lots of stress and other potential warning signals. But good ideas die slowly so I again turned to Bruce Shoo to construct the house.

Bruce was married to a cousin of Geneva's and lived with his family in Grangeville about 50 miles to the north. Bruce had built the office building, remodeled the white house, remodeled and finished the red barn house, and built the dam, pipeline, and powerhouse, so I had had lots of experience with his construction skills, and he had done well and I was satisfied with his workmanship.

TAX LAWS

The tax laws of the United States were complicated in those days, and they still are to this day in 2008, very complicated. We had sold a very fine house in Los Altos Hills in California in July of 1980, and had a large capital gain subject to income tax. Another house needed to be built in order to avoid the capital gains tax on the house, which was huge. The new house construction needed to be started within a year and completed, as I recall, in two and ½ years. Thus the new house construction had to be started in 1981.

I had been in contact with a friend, Glen VanderSluis, who was an architect. Both of our families had attended the Palo Alto Christian Reformed Church before we left to attend the Peninsula Bible Church in about 1976. Glen was a graduate of Calvin College and Calvin Seminary, and had done additional graduate work in a California Seminary leading to a PhD in order to be a professor in some seminary. Somewhere along the line he had lost interest in that profession and had gone back to being an architect, his old profession before going to seminary. Glen had joined an architectural firm in Grand Rapids, Michigan, where he had designed for them College dormitory buildings. He had come out to the west coast to run an office for the firm in Menlo Park, California.

I discussed the dream house with Glen and told him we wanted to build a very nice house and spend about $400,000 on it. That was a large sum in those days for a house, but I wanted to avoid the capital gains tax on the house we had sold. Because of the time constraints in the tax laws we had to design the house at the same time that it meanwhile was being built.

In retrospect that is a very bad idea. An old saying is, "Too soon old, too late smart". The United States tax laws are a huge cause of many, many terrible problems. When one becomes wise he completely disregards the tax laws in his contemplated operations and planning of life and just pays the government what it demands and goes on living. That is a very hard lesson to learn. Legally avoiding taxes is a fine art but the pitfalls have terrible consequences. The Tax laws of the United States are still a complete, absolute horror, and just financially destroy the unsuspecting, the naive, and the simple minded.

Glen designed the house and Bruce proceeded to build it even while Glen designed it. Glen sent up plans to Idaho piecemeal. The first inclination that I had a serious problem was when the architect fees got to $65,000. Normally, architect fees are about 7.5% of the total cost of construction. When Bruce saw the plans, when they were nearing completion, he estimated the cost of the house not to be $400,000 but $600,000. The architect fees indicated maybe a cost of maybe $850,000. I, of course, was astounded and just did not believe it could really cost that much.

Just for the record, and getting ahead of myself, ultimately I spent $1,150,000 on the house and it still was not finished. Ray Hamill once told me Yankie and MacAlvain, the people who eventually acquired the house, spent another $350,000 to finish it. That is a grand total of $1,500,000 in 1980's dollars. That is an astounding amount of money for a four bedroom four bath house.

It turned out the house was massively designed. It was more like a commercial building, perhaps like a college dormitory. The foundation was massive with lots of concrete and probably earthquake proof as Glenn designed for California. The complicated design put Bruce in way over his head, but I did not fully appreciate or understand that. Construction kept on going until the money I had allotted for the house was gone. I was also investing and spending large sums on the mine and the river rafting company, so as the foundation was being completed, I was coming up short of money.

BANKING IS A STRANGE BUSINESS

Let's digress a little and talk about banking. Banking is a strange business. It seems over the years of my interaction with bankers, that bankers are the most incompetent, the most dull, and the most unimaginative of all the types of businessmen I have ever encountered. Of course, there are exceptions and sometimes one encounters a competent banker. It seems this phenomenon is caused by the nature of the business. Bankers rely on past performance to determine the future payback potential. Now days, all investment disclosure statements have a disclaimer that says past performance is no indication of future performance, yet that is exactly what banking is based upon. Bankers obtain all kinds of paperwork from you that prove to them that you can pay back the loan. Yet the past is no indication of the future, so one's ability to pay back the banks' loan is based on luck, the competence of the borrower, and the future state of the economy. All this makes banking a very tenuous business.

Yet our whole national economic system performance and job creation depends on banking. Huge, terrible depressions and economic failures, with very terrible consequences for huge numbers of innocent people and bystanders have occurred because of what is sometimes called, "Bad banking practice". The consequences of these recurring past failures are that the government has established regulatory institutions whose responsibility is the preservation of the money system through sundry controls on Banks, which in the end, unfortunately, have their own very evil consequences.

Ultimately, however, the few bureaucrats responsible for regulating the money system cannot out think millions of other humans whose greedy goal is to make money, sometimes through nefarious means.

Understand that money can be created out of nothing and be annihilated just as easy. For example, suppose you have a little eatery and you print up a bunch of little certificates that say they are good for a meal at your eatery. Then suppose the people who have these certificates use them to trade with each other, say in eggs. Suppose a neighbor has a few chickens and he gives a dozen eggs to another neighbor for one of the meal certificates. Eureka! That is it. Your little certificate has become money suitable for trading eggs or anything else for that matter. Everything now goes along fine until you take a vacation and close your eatery down for a bit. Now the certificates are presumed to become worthless and you have a run on your meal certificates as people try to cash them in. Money value, such as these certificates, just depends on the confidence people put in the certificates.

271

Money can be created out of nothing. Suppose you buy a house. Assume one year later the market value of your house goes up by $100,000. You want to buy a boat and a new car so you go down to the bank and borrow $50,000 on the increased value of your house. Viola! You have just created $50,000 of money out of the hot air of the hot housing market. This money goes around the whole system buying things and eventually this excess money creates excess demand for goods, and the price of goods rise, and you then have inflation, meaning that the purchasing power of the money unit went down.

The government has empowered regulators to try to control the amount of money that is created by the banking system. It is the duty of these regulators to preserve the purchasing power of the money, but they are also under great pressure to create as much money as possible so as to have an expanding economy and an increase in the number of jobs available for the people. All of this balancing is not an easy task and quite susceptible to sundry political pressure.

SAVINGS AND LOAN INDUSTRY

The savings and loan industry as it existed at that time in the 1980's was part of this whole money banking supply system. Before about 1980 or so the savings and Loan industry was a quiet conservatively managed system where people would save money, put it into a Savings Bank, and the Bank would lend the money out to people who wanted to buy or build themselves a house.

Congress for some reason in the late 1970's decided to loosen the controls a bit and, hopefully, provide more money for more home buyers. Now with the new legislation, Savings and Loans could lend money to sundry other borrowers, and invest in sophisticated money instruments in the housing industry, and also lend money to builders of homes and commercial property.

The American capitalist system gives a tremendous opportunity to fast buck operators to make money from sundry schemes. Thousands of entrepreneurs studying the system can come up with sundry intricate ways to make lots of money.

Over the last century one of the best ways to make a lot of money and get rich was to create a product or service, create a public stock company to market that product or service, and juice the price of the stock of that public company, then sell out the stock to the public and, therefore, pocket a lot of money.

A person by the name of Charley Knapp got control of a little Savings and Loan Company in Stockton, California and set about to make a lot of money.

Because of the new looser controls on the Savings and Loan industry, he was able to conceive of a scheme that resembled a Ponzi scheme to create the illusion of huge earnings for the company, called State Savings. Normally, in the old days, an S&L got its money from little ma and pa depositors spread over the country. But Knapp's company, State Savings, and its eventual holding company, Financial Corporation of America, wanted more, so he created a sales force that went after "brokered" deposits, meaning deposits from groups of people, or brokers who would bundle together a sum of money, divide it into $100,000 lots, the maximum insured by the United States government in the new law, and deposit such in State Savings.

Now Knapp spread the word that he would lend money to almost anybody by relaxing lending standards. The market was hot in the 1980's and there was lots of demand for money to build houses, shopping centers, commercial buildings, and what not else. Interest rates were high, and State developed what I call a Ponzi Scheme in honor of Charles Ponzi who is credited with first conceiving of the scheme in Boston where new investor money was used to pay off previous investors, about 100 years ago.

What State did was to enter into a loan commitment agreement with a contractor or builder where the builder would sign papers making a legal contract, indicating intent to borrow a given amount of money to build say, an office building. State set up a system such that the money was supposed to be paid to the owner/borrower, contractor, or his suppliers. As he built the building a voucher system was used where the builder would summit a voucher to State and then State would pay the supplier the amount of money indicated by the voucher. This voucher had to be signed by the builder. Then, of course, the builder would have in fact borrowed the money from State and then would begin paying interest on the amount of money that State had paid to the supplier.

State would enter into commitment agreements like this with almost any contractor or builder who supplied the necessary paperwork. The very lucrative payoff to State Savings was that the builder was charged a fee for the loan commitment. Thus if an agreement was made to borrow say $1,000,000 a 5% fee or $50,000 would be charged the builder up front when the commitment was signed. The builder did not actually pay this amount; the amount instead became part of the loan amount on which the builder would then pay interest.

Now the real interesting part of this Massive Loan Fraud Scheme comes into play. The regulators allowed these S&L's to operate with as much as a 50:1 asset to capital ratio. The regulators wanted at least a 25:1 ratio, and theoretically could close down any S&L that had a ratio greater than 25. Sometimes they did close down the small ones, but the big ones in some ways were too big to close down as closing down a large S&L could cost the government a lot of money and could have a ripple effect on the whole economy through the banking system.

Capital is the amount on the company balance sheet that represents the amount of net worth of the company. Assets for an S&L are the sum total amount of all the loans they have issued and paid out with actual money to customers. This total is the Assets of the S&L.

What Knapp did at State Savings was to charge the loan customer a 5% or even a 10% loan commitment fee and immediately credit State's capital account the amount of the fee. Thus without any loan being funded State's capital to asset ratio would go down, and State could then make even more loan commitments to the next borrowers who showed up at its door --- thus the Massive Loan Fraud Scheme. Knapp could show huge company profits just by making paper loan commitments with no actual loans being funded.

The profits were reported in the company financial statements and the illusion of State making a lot of money was created.

Once Knapp and State Savings got hooked on this, the sky had no limit and State Savings made thousands of loan commitments totaling billions of dollars. The paper profits of State Savings skyrocketed with these paper loan commitment fees. This then resulted in investors buying the parent company's stock and so drive up the price of the stock of the holding company, Financial Corporation of America.

To keep this great illusion going, eventually some of these loan commitments have to be funded. So then Knapp hired an army of salesmen who would scour the earth for money deposits to State Savings. The United States government guaranteed depositors savings accounts up to a maximum of $100,000, so lots of dividing up of larger sums of money into accounts of the $100,000 level occurred.

WILD CAT MASSIVE LOAN FRAUD SCHEME

Thus conceived is the, "Wild Cat Massive Loan Fraud Scheme". Make loan commitments to anybody, search far and wide for depositors, drive up the price of FCA stock, and use the inflated stock price to buy up more S&L's.

Knapp and State Savings spent little time and money managing the back office. Loan papers were just put into boxes and just stacked up in warehouses. It became a complete chaotic zoo of an operation.

Now that you have a little understanding of State Savings and its loan fraud scheme, let's return to the story of Gerald and Geneva Kooyers.

We started building the Bighouse in September of 1981. A year later it became clear that we had to stop construction and wait for funds to be generated by our commodity trading business or get a construction loan to finish the house. I started making inquiries and looked for a lender. The Bighouse was a project few banks and S&Ls were interested in. It was remote and had almost nothing to be compared with, and so was difficult to bank. Someone, I do not remember who it was, it might have been the wife of my river rafting company partner, Phyllis Carmichael, who was in the real estate business, suggested State Savings of Stockton, California. I contacted State Savings and supplied them with all the paperwork they requested.

State was extremely slow about responding and delayed months before giving an approval to a $400,000 construction loan, the amount the builder, Bruce Shoo, said would complete the house, less, of course, the fees on the loan. State would charge me a fee of 10 points, or $40,000 for the loan. That was outrageous, but they were the only Bank that seemed interested in making the loan, so I agreed to it.

The papers were ready to sign about the end of January 1983. Geneva and I traveled to Grangeville to sign the papers. We discussed our serious misgivings about signing the papers and committing ourselves to a construction loan. Borrowing money is always a long term risky business and normally should be avoided. We did not have inner peace about it and discussed our lack of peace. State had taken almost three months to get the paperwork for the loan to me. That in itself should have been a huge warning to me that State was essentially incompetent or worse. On the other hand, the little experience in dealing with S&Ls that I had, had been very good, so how was I to make the judgment that that S&L Bank outfit was probably incompetent or had serious unknown problems, or was indeed conducting a massive, Wild Cat Loan Fraud Scheme?

We were under a lot of pressure from the builder, Bruce Schoo, as he, of course, wanted to keep building on the house. At that point we had already spent about $250,000 on the house and all that had been accomplished was the very complicated foundation. That in itself should have been a warning to me, as in hindsight that was probably unreasonable for just the foundation. Nevertheless, we signed papers and Bruce went to work.

State Savings hired an engineering firm in Boise, JUB Engineering, to come up and inspect the work progress and issue their estimate of how far the construction had proceeded. I would then issue vouchers to Bruce for him to be paid. At first things proceeded with little problem, but soon the voucher just would not be paid, and Bruce would come to me and say he had not received his money and asked me for money, as he, of course, had to pay his employees and suppliers. I often just paid him and other suppliers without giving them a State Savings voucher, and so bypassed the loan, since State seldom paid anyway.

Eventually, I learned the State Savings system. It turned out there were seven desks occupied by seven different people that my voucher went over before it got paid. I eventually, through a lot of detective work, obtained the phone numbers of all seven desks. I would call them every day to ask that my voucher be put on top of the pile and please pay it today. It was almost a full time job chasing low level functionaries in the State Savings bureaucracy by telephone trying to get them to pay a voucher. It was a complete chaotic zoo of an operation.

Then State sent an inspector from Stockton, California to come up and inspect the progress. I was absolutely dumbfounded by his approach and demeanor. If I was asked to characterize it, I would say State must have recruited this inspector from the State of California mental hospital institution in Stockton. He was completely irrational and normal words most people use had unique meanings known only to him, and that was impossible to understand.

As I later looked back on it and now understand State's problems, the inspector had to find any reason, even irrational ones, so as to have any excuse to not pay the vouchers. As I look back on it, State had no money to fund the loan commitments they had made, so any excuse, any delay, any behavior, even irrational feigned insanity, or stupidity was used so as to not have to pay vouchers.

This whole scenario was beyond my understanding. In hindsight, I should have thoroughly investigated State Savings and found out what kind of institution they were. I had traveled to Stockton and visited their headquarters, but it made no impression on me except for its huge size and vast number of employees.

Let's digress again in this account. The purpose of this writing is to pass on to you dear readers a little wisdom. Perhaps in the course of your life you can apply this wisdom and avoid some of the huge devastating pitfalls of life.

CASH FOR TRASH

The first thing to understand is that when something is going wrong and not up to what was expected to happen, make a thorough investigation and find out what is going on. Even hire some competent experts. The not paying of the vouchers should have been thoroughly thought through by me. Why would a Bank not lend you the money they had promised to lend? Think deeply. It should have been obvious to me they had no money even though they had 8000 employees and rented half the office buildings in Stockton, California to house them. I should have seen the light, and pulled the plug and stopped construction, and filed a lawsuit right there and then! NOW!

Instead I had been influenced by an article I had read which suggested the best ploy was to finish the project and then sue. Again, thoroughly thinking through the scenario would have indicated that that was the wrong thing to do. It was wrong because if I spent my capital building a big house which belonged in the toy category of assets, I would have no capital left with which to trade. After all, trading is what makes my income, and if I had no capital to trade, I was not going to have any income. Liquidity is of extreme importance in one's business. When one becomes illiquid, one becomes stuck and subject to failure no matter what huge amount of assets one has.

My sense of ethics, derived from my Christian commitment, told me I must pay the suppliers even if State Savings was not going to pay them. I had no ethical choice. Nevertheless, the project should have been stopped so the money hemorrhage would have been stopped, and let the new chips fall where they would have fallen.

Well the house construction continued. Bruce and other suppliers would leave the project if they were not paid and once they got paid they would come back to work. The cost overrun caused by these starts and stops in construction because of State's slow pay was huge. It was horrible. It almost seemed obvious that State wanted the project to fail. How could a big Bank like State not understand that? Was that State's actual intent, to make the project fail? That thought seemed absolutely unfathomable to me. A bank actually wanting one of its loan projects to fail? Yet now, almost 30 years later, as I have read the histories of State and American Savings in several books, that is exactly what State Savings intended. The employees at State Savings even had a name for the process; they called it, "Cash for Trash".

Again a digression, State had some interesting schemes that had some interesting names. One was, "Cash for Trash", another, "Buy Sell". State developed procedures where if a project was failing, they would demand that a new builder/borrower come in and buy the old failing project of some other builder/borrower in order to get a new loan commitment for a new project. Of course, State would provide the money to buy the distressed failing project. Yet no money would change hands! Think about it. Builder A gets loan commitment. Builder A is charged a fat loan commitment fee. Builder A starts building his project. He collects a few voucher payments, but subsequent vouchers are then not paid by State and he puts his own money into the project. Eventually, the builder tires of this or runs out of money and he defaults. State either starts foreclosure or otherwise gets the property. State then has the new builder B, in order to get his new loan commitment, agree to take over the foreclosed property. State then has cleared off its books the supposedly bad loan and incorporated it into a new loan commitment and earned a huge new fee! This was called "BUY SELL", by the employees making the actual transactions at State Savings.

I believe now after 25 years that State actually wanted my project to fail. Their intention was for me to dump my own money into the house, then for me to default, then for them to take it back, then for them to give it to another borrower for their book cost, which was probably less than half the real money actually spent on the project, collect a new fat fee, and then for them to repeat this for the next sucker. All this to show imaginary huge paper loan commitment fees, so as to show huge paper profits, so then to drive up the price of FCA stock. Yes indeed, a massive loan fraud scheme that makes Ponzi look like an amateur. Yet all of this was approved and regulated by the government of the United States of America!

Well back to our story. As 1984 came it was obvious that the house could not be completed with the $400,000 loan amount, and I made a request to State to increase the loan amount. About the time the increased loan amount was made along with more points to State, State changed their rules and said 20% of the total loan amount would be withheld until a certificate of completion was issued. That ate up almost the total amount of the new $100,000 commitment. That was the last straw. I understood the house was not going to be completed, and State, now called American Savings had sucked another fee out of me. My business was also slowing down and cash flow was not as it had been so I finally stopped the construction.

SUE AMERICAN SAVINGS

I then went to Stockton to find an attorney to start a lawsuit. Needless to say several law firms made it their main thing in life to sue State, now called American Savings, after a merger with a Southern California S&L. It seemed American Savings collected lawsuits like a dog flees. Later, I read in the Wall Street Journal that when the time came for American to be liquidated by an agency of the United States government, American was paying 100 million dollars a year just to attorneys to defend American from lawsuits from other attorneys. Most of the lawsuits were by builders like me.

Well, we get a preliminary hearing before a Stockton judge. My attorney was astoundingly unprepared and did not educate me at all as to what to expect. The judge wanted to set up a court supervised escrow account where I would pay into the court a monthly payment equivalent to what I would have to be paying American if the house had been completed. By this time I was getting a little wiser and just knew that would be the last I saw of my money. Once the court saw my $6,000 a month piling up I just knew the court would give it to somebody, probably the judge's attorney friends. I never made a payment and the lawsuit faded into oblivion.

Learn a lesson from this. Once you see your expensive attorney unprepared, get rid of him. Lazy and unprepared attorneys are essentially thieves. They will rob you. They do not care if you win or lose, and only are out to collect large fees from you for doing nothing. Being unprepared is a dead giveaway. If he is unprepared it means he expects to lose. After all, why should he work on something when he does not expect the work to benefit his client?

LIFE IN THE BIG HOUSE

I decided that since that Bighouse had sucked up almost all of my trading capital and all the money out of my corporate retirement plan, I should at least live in it for a few months. So Geneva and I and daughter Kim started to camp out in the Bighouse in the fall of 1985 and, as time went by, completed more and more of it myself to make it as comfortable as possible. Geneva has a huge talent for decorating and finishing. She made it into a very lovely home. It was indeed an extremely lovely home. If one counted decks and the garage it had over 12,000 square feet of space. It was magnificently finished with solid oak doors, exquisite tile in the solarium, beautifully designed fireplaces with lovely decorative tile, and decks with unusually beautiful views of the Salmon River and the Salmon River mountains. The house was positioned for supremely lovely views out of the windows. The beauty of the place warmed ones soul. VanderSluis had indeed designed an exquisite house.

The house was magnificent. Not only did it have 12,000 square feet but it had a three car garage, furnace room, meat processing room, walk in freezer and cold storage rooms, downstairs secret storage rooms under the room intended for hot water storage, large downstairs room intended for a library, pool table and game room. It had an indoor pool of unique design where the major structural component is an upside down deck cantilever, of Olympic length with slanted Pella windows to received solar heating. There is an equipment room for pool and spa heaters, both electrical and propane, hot water heaters, both electrical and propane, connected in series, the low voltage equipment storage, controls for lawn watering and sidewalk electrical heating. This house had everything one could think of.

There are three bedrooms on the main floor with a well laid out laundry room for storage and clothes distribution with pool showers, and both electrical and propane clothes dryers, and an entrance to the main level of the pool and spa.

The kitchen had a commercial propane stove, an electric stove, and large amounts of kitchen storage with a breakfast nook, also a large dining room with exquisite Dutch delft blue tile fireplace and a large family room with an elevated fireplace. There was also a cabinet door to the dumb waiter that went down to the food storage room below the kitchen and the walk in freezer and walk in cooler in the meat processing room below.

There is a very large bay window that gives a huge view of the Salmon River a mile downstream to the Manning Crevice Bridge. It was custom made as no supplier would sell a bay window that large. The view is magnificent from anywhere in the family room or dining room. There is an outside deck all around the family room on three sides. One can walk all around the outside and take in the magnificent views of the Salmon River and the mountains. Outside of the family room fireplace was a built in barbeque system with its own chimney. In the garage in this same chimney tower structure, below the family room, is a garbage burning unit.

One of the central structural components of the house is the chimney tower. Within the chimney tower are four chimneys which serve the furnace room, the room behind the furnace room with its own wood stove, the dining room, and the room above the dining room which was my home office above the dining room and kitchen. Within the tower are cold air outside air ducts to serve each of the fireplaces so that warm room air is not used to feed the fire in the fireplaces.

On the top floor is the master bedroom. It has huge windows to view the mountains and river, and it has large walk in closets. It had two shower heads so two can shower at the same time in a large shower, two stools, two sinks, and an elaborate Jacuzzi bath tub. A deck was outside the bathtub area giving views of the mountains. From the home office room on the top floor through the upper story of the solarium was a long deck out over the family room and lower decks. From that deck I watched the game across the river; from there I shot rock chucks in the field above the house.

The Bighouse

Geneva and I spent many an exquisitely romantic warm moonlight night out on that deck enjoying the spectacular quiet scenic beauty with the soft background murmur of the Salmon River rapids and the astounding circle of the beautiful line of mountains to feast our eyes upon.

One of the magnificent central features of the house is the solarium. When one came into the solarium from the huge custom made front door, one walked up stairs of beautiful white tile, with green tree tiles here and there, to the main floor. The roof of this room was above the top story so plants of various types could be grown in this solarium greenhouse in the center of the house. One would walk through greenery to go into the house. An additional greenhouse room extended out to the south of this solarium at the upper ground level.

The custom made front door has a large etched glass center piece of grapes and grape vines with the Bible verse, "I am the branch, and ye are the branches". All of the doors in the house are of solid oak.

The living room entrance was off the main home entrance and down a few steps. It was a very large room with a truly magnificent fireplace of exquisite rock from Livingston Montana of Pink Travertine. It has its own wet bar with a sink and refrigerator. Geneva's very beautiful organ with huge base tonal speakers and grand piano were in this room. The full length north side wall had a wall of windows that gave a truly grand magnificent view of the Salmon River.

The house electrical system was designed to be run by a computer. All switches were low voltage and one could control any circuit or group of circuits from any switch in the house. At night as I climbed into bed I could glance at the bank of low voltage lights along side of the bed and turn any light, water heater, space heater, or motor off or on at the touch of a finger. To the best of my knowledge, nothing exists like this yet even after almost 30 years in the rest of the whole world.

My son Sheridan, just out of the University of California at Davis, with a degree of Electrical Engineer was the main designer of this system. He was assisted by an Electrical contractor out of Boise. I finished building this system all by myself after Sheridan had left and gone to work at General Electric in San Jose, California in about late 1984.

This was before the invention of the PC, the Personal Computer. Sheridan designed the system to be run by a microprocessor, the forerunner of the PC. (Personal Computer) We were way ahead of our time.

I put line frequency meters around the house. It turned out that none of my sensitive electronic equipment required sixty (60) cycles per second power. The power system in Europe runs at 50 cycles so all my computers and electronic equipment ran fine. My hydro electric generator system which again Sheridan and I built operated from as low as 48 cycles to as high as 63 cycles. The Pelton wheels, which I had obtained from a renegade (meaning polygamous) Mormon in Montana, had the characteristic of producing more power as the wheel slowed down. The system produced about 35 Kilowatts at 48 cycles and 18 Kilowatts at 63 cycles. I had not expected that as everything I had read indicated I needed a control system to keep generating power at 60 cycles per second. It turned out that the control system that Sheridan had designed was not nearly as reliable as just ignoring the system and hoping it would not break down. Even breaking down as often as once a year because of electronic control problems, was a lot less desirable then as not breaking down at all when the whole thing was just ignored, but watched carefully for potential problem.

Thus just glancing at a frequency meter told me the level of power being produced and whether we needed more or less load. Geneva was trained to glance at a frequency meter and turn stuff off when she wanted to run the electric clothes dryer or any other stuff requiring significant power. At night as I was retiring to bed a glance at the meter gave me the input to switch on or off water heaters, space heaters, flood lights or anything else to sort of balance the power being produced with the load. I had a bank of 24 switches by the side of the bed, another bank near the front door and another in the control room, so I could turn anything off or on from anywhere else.

The system was astoundingly reliable. It was a lot better than the power company power in town. The only thing that shut it down was extremely high water during spring snow melt when lots of sand and sticks came down the creek which would clog the water intake system. During spring flood it became a lot less work to just shut the system down for a day or two and go to the backup propane or diesel generators.

AMERICAN SEIZED AND BANKRUPTCY

American, now having been seized by the government of the United States was turned into a two headed, "Good Bank", with the good assets, and a, "Bad Bank", with the bad assets such as mine, and turned over to the Bass brothers of Texas by the government for a song. The Bank decided to foreclose. I found a very fine bankruptcy attorney in Boise, Terry Meyers, who later became the bankruptcy judge for southern Idaho. We filed for a Chapter 11 Bankruptcy in April of 1986 to stop the foreclosure process. We filed in the name of Elkhorn Enterprises, an Idaho proprietorship of Geneva and me. Thus my trading and commodity trading management companies, UCA Systems, Inc., Moria Corporation, and Queston Systems, Ltd were unaffected by the Bankruptcy filing.

The bankruptcy court system in the United States grinds very, very slowly, so things went on very, very slowly and we continued to live in the Bighouse and make no payments to American and continued to finish it. Terry Meyers had been able to get me to be appointed to be my own trustee over the assets of Elkhorn Enterprises, so I continued in business just like I had before. I even did my own monthly financial reports sent to the court. It worked really well and as time went on and on, we lived in the house and continued to work on it.

The court hearings of course, were held in Idaho so American's attorney had to fly up from Stockton for every hearing, lots of them in Moscow, Idaho, not an easy place to get too. I ran American's costs up as much as I could, as by this time I clearly saw American as an evil adversary even though they had been seized by an agency of the government and given to the Bass Brothers of Texas. In lawsuits it is important to run up your adversary's costs, as that detours them a little bit.

In a couple of years Meyers had a Chapter 11 plan worked out which crammed down American, but not nearly enough, as it turned out later. My business had not been going well, as I had been served up with a severe, almost terminal case of battle fatigue in the summer of 1988, which is discussed in another chapter, which left me unable to function as the outstanding legend in my own time commodities trader I once had been. I understood that the plan Meyers had carefully derived now would not work, and so I rejected it. Meyers then decided that he could, therefore, no longer continue as my attorney.

Then began the difficult task of finding a new bankruptcy attorney. Geneva and I prayed and traveled around interviewing attorneys. The situation looked hopeless as by this time we had little money. We then discovered in Lewiston an all-purpose attorney, Dan Radakovich, who sometimes did bankruptcy work. Dan, it turned out was of Serbian ancestry. The cultural nature of a Serbian is that of a warrior. The Serbs have fought the Muslims to a standoff for centuries. Dan is a real tenacious fighter and has no sense of compromise at all. He just stands and fights to the bitter end or until his opponent is worn out, or destroyed, or his client runs out of money or is destroyed.

He fought the American attorney's right into the devil's tar pit. We eventually got a Chapter 11 Plan approved which crammed down American a lot more than Meyers did and then into a scenario we believed we could handle. In hindsight they should have been crammed down even more as at auction the house sold for about $170,000 whereas we had crammed down American to $400,000.

But then my business continued to further deteriorate and with my capital gone it did not seem to make sense to continue to make payments to American even at the reduced crammed down level. All of the rest of the Plan we could handle, so I stopped making payments to American, and eventually American then foreclosed again.

American, when it was State Savings, of course, did its paperwork very shabbily. The two acre parcel on which the Bighouse was located did not have recorded deeded access. By this time I clearly saw American as an evil adversary, so I figured to let them foreclose and then deny them access.

Eventually, a foreclosure sale was held in the family room of the Big House itself. As I recall, after a lot of high powered advertising about six bidders showed up as well as over 70 people. It was a BIG event, an important real estate agent, media, and community event for Riggins. The bidding stopped at about $148,000. The auctioneer announced that that was below the unannounced minimum bid set by American, and so was rejected. Eventually, American negotiated with the three highest bidders and American then sold it to Ron Yankee of Boise for an unannounced amount, which I later discovered to be about $170,000. Just think of it, a house which had actual construction costs of about $1,150,000, plus lots of sweat labor of Geneva and me, was sold for $170,000. If my attorneys had crammed down American to $170,000, that would have been a loan amount I could have even handled.

Dear reader, there is a real wisdom insight here; never over estimate how low a price can go for a troubled asset.

WISDOM OF BIGHOUSE

Well dear reader, as the purpose of relating this tale is to pass on to you a little wisdom, let us review the lessons learned.

One)   if you embark on the building of a huge toy, which in fact is what an exquisite beautiful house is, have the full amount of the construction cost and then some in the bank. Plus you must create an endowment fund to pay the taxes and upkeep on such a thing. These are things I never even thought about as I just presumed on the future, that the money would just arrive to complete, maintain, and pay taxes on such a thing. The tax assessor of Idaho County thought he had found a real bonanza when he came to assess the house. He thought it might be worth $1,500,000 so the taxes were $15,000 a year. The insurance man in Grangeville wanted $10,000 a year for just fire insurance. The costs for such a thing required a high income. High incomes do not last forever unless maybe it is based on a conservatively managed endowment. To afford the taxes and insurance one needed $500,000 in a 5% yielding fund alone.

Two)   thieves and criminals are everywhere.   One of the great disadvantages of growing up in a nice Christian home with loving parents and good neighbors is that one starts to think most people are nice people.

Nothing could be farther from the truth. Most people are greedy thieves, and full of wickedness. A lot of people put on respectable airs and act, (to outward appearance) righteous, but really are just thieves waiting for an opportunity. Since most large American corporations are run by such people, often the line gets crossed in their dealings with the public. It takes extremely good, highly ethical people to run such corporations. Whenever you suspect such a corporation to be shading its ethics, avoid such corporations and their products. Life is just too short to be destroyed by unethical corporations. Banks and brokerage firms should be held to an even higher standard yet. People who handle your money and lend you money must be of the highest ethical standards. Be very careful when you sell something like a business. Chances are you will seldom see your money in dealing with most people unless you get cash in hand. In hindsight when I first suspected State/American Savings to be incompetent or run by people with a criminal mind, I should have quickly terminated the relationship. That would have taken courage and cost me a lot, but there is never any substitute for doing the right thing now. As the scriptures say, when you are trapped by your own foolishness, or encumbered by a foolish commitment, FLEE! And I would add, DO IT NOW!

Three) never underestimate how low in price something can go. I had built the thing, and was very proud of it and its exquisite beauty. Beauty is in the eye of the beholder, and is not necessarily shared by everybody. If I had been of a more criminal mind, I could have trashed the place and made it look ugly. That would have reduced the price even more. Given that American was a bunch of thieves, even though the government had seized it and given it to the Bass Brothers, I might have thought how I could make that place as unattractive as possible, and saved any money I had for the eventual foreclosure sale. That would have been a much better overall strategy.

Fourth) lower your expectations of good intentions of friends and relatives. All through this mess I thought some friend or relative would come and help me out. I did get a brief commitment from a brief acquaintance for $100,000 later on when I was trying to save the ranch. People pass judgment on you and write you off as foolish or that you deserve what is happening to you and will not help. Children are especially disappointing. After all, eventually they would have inherited the property, and yet took absolutely no interest in saving the property. Not one of my children even discussed the possibility with me. (Kimberly should be excused as she was too young.) In the early 1990's through buying of timber, because of my knowledge of the futures markets, I had created a huge windfall. A wisdom lesson here -- do not expect to participate in the windfall of any friend or associate or family member. When a windfall happens, the recipient absolutely thinks this was because of his or her own efforts and talents, and he or she surely deserves it!

Well that is the saga of the Bighouse. A fantastic thing of great beauty located in one of the most beautiful settings in all of Idaho. There is an old saying that it is better to have loved and lost, than to never have loved at all. So all in all the experience of building such a thing of such exquisite beauty, enjoying Geneva's outstanding ability of beautiful interior design of form and color, and to then have lived in it for seven years was worth more than all the pain involved and even the pain of losing it. I thank the Lord Jesus for the experience, and look forward to an even more beautiful place for life with my Lord Jesus in eternity.

ELEVEN

EIGENS

As I add up all the experience in my life, including several minor careers and entrepreneurial ventures, I want to pass on to you wisdom and the most important things of life I ever learned. I want to pass on to you my understanding of human life, the purpose of life itself.

Understand the things that I will tell you, they could change your life so that you will have a very abundant, happy, satisfying life, and yes, life eternal. So think carefully about the things I will tell you. I will give you the basics first, these may seem complicated, but if you understand, you will be highly rewarded. The reason I am telling you this is for you to understand the purpose of your life on earth. I want to pass on to you all that I ever learned.

I will need to coin a term. It is essential in order to give you these concepts, for you to understand all that I will tell you. I have searched for a word to describe all that I want to place in the concept and cannot find one. The term I coin is Eigen, which I will define.

When one does scientific research, one looks at the facts and from them devises a theory or a model, and really, theories are just models and models are just theories. The model uses known concepts or descriptions that one already understands. Then the newly created theory or model is used to devise new understandings and insights. If wrong or inconsistent results are obtained using the model, then the theory or model is changed to reflect new observations or understanding. As time goes on, and the theory evolves, one gets closer to the actual truth that may exist. So, I present to you an understanding or concept that I will call Life Eigens. I have thought a lot about it and I believe it represents a better model and understanding of human life than anything else yet described by mankind.

I am also a student of the Bible. The Bible contains the Old Testament, the scriptures of the Jews, and the New Testament, the Christian scriptures. Muslims, also accept the Bible, and Jesus, the focus of the New Testament, as a prophet. I believe the Bible to be the Word of God and as such is reliable for teaching and instruction. The Bible gives us revealed truth as opposed to scientific observation and deductive and inductive derivation to find truth. I use Bible revealed truth to assist in the generation of the theory or model I present to you.

We humans are of the animal species that goes by the scientific name of Homo sapiens, sapiens. We are of a specific form, substance, and behavior determined by our chemically structured genetic code, which is written into each and every tiny cell which make up our bodies.

Our genetic code determines who we are and how we operate. When a human tries to operate outside of what the genetic code mandates, that one become troubled, psychotic, neurotic, and destructive to one's self. Let me establish for you in your mind the fact that Homo sapiens, sapiens mate for life. It is set within our genetic code. We are like some geese and other species that mate for life. Understand that humans are programmed by our genetic code to mate for life. If you disagree, well OK, but you, if you act on your own contrary principle, will pay a price, a price you cannot now anticipate unless somebody like me tells you the corruption and the cost.

Eigenvector is a mathematical term but the root of the word has been used to describe cultural effects as in eidos or eidolon. In mathematical physics eigenvectors are used to describe the mathematical basics of a system, or in quantum mechanics the solutions to the Schrödinger Equation. The solutions to this equation are basic to all chemistry and other quantum interactions. The use of the principles of quantum mechanics drive chemistry and this has produced all the chemicals, drugs, and many other marvelous things and inventions of our modern culture.

Eigenvectors are that upon which the rest of the system can be described. Let me postulate to you then that all of the functions of human life can be described on the basis of four Life Eigens which would be similar to four eigenvectors of a life simulating system. One might also consider terms like dimensions, or basics, or degrees of freedom, or modes of life, or perhaps spheres of life, or perhaps the best term, functional dependencies of life, but none of these terms are adequate enough to describe the whole scope of human life in all of its complexity.

I, therefore, postulate to you that the full human life is a total combination of magnitudes and complex vectors and interactions of four Life Eigens, of functional dependencies in their various quantities, combinations, and conundrums of each. I do not mean a scalar combination, but some complex multifaceted vector and tensor representation and combination of these Eigens, like eigenvectors would be of a physical system. The Eigens of life are what all of human life can be referenced to and all of life composed. All the functions and manifestations of life are composed from the Eigens of life. So let me coin this new term and call them Life Eigens.

Let me postulate to you that the first essential thing, or what I call an Eigen, or Eigen of life in man is man as a spirit. The first Eigen of life is then life of spirit. Your spirit is a person. You as a person are a spirit. Spirit is something few moderns think deeply about. The Christian Bible representations of spirit are wind and air. Spirit is something one does not know where it comes from or where it goes. The Hebrew Christian Bible says one manifestation of God is as a spirit, and is called the Holy Spirit. The Westminster Catechism says, "God is a spirit, infinite in being, wisdom, power, justice, holiness, goodness, and truth."

The Bible says man also is a spirit and when a man dies his body returns to dust and his spirit returns to God who gave it. So your spirit is a thing of God which God gave to you to give you existence and an identity. A man's spirit is transcendent. That is, a man's spirit is not part of the universe. A man's spirit exists as a thing of God, which God gives. Since a man's spirit transcends the universe, this means that your spirit is outside as well as inside the universe with its created matter, energy, time, and space. Therefore, your spirit existed with God before the universe was started or came into being, before time and space was, or began, or is, outside of time and space, or what some might infer, before what some call, the Big Bang!

And, your spirit exists now in eternity, outside of the universe as well as inside the universe, independent of time, space, energy, and matter.

The second essential Life Eigen of man is that of the human body which lives within the universe and is part of the universe. This Eigen includes all that is involved within the universe, in eating, in living, and in meeting the needs of the body. A man has and is a body. This is the realm of physical existence. It includes all that we can see or touch. It includes all the things we can observe – stars, planets, the entire observable universe, and that part of the universe that is outside that part of the universe that can be observed. The unobservable part of the universe is beyond what telescopes can observe. Telescopes can observe out to where the beginning of time is observed, but beyond exists the universe which cannot yet be observed until more time passes. Second Eigen includes all the laws of Physics, the so called Big Bang, all that exists in what let's call the real world, or the world of living and observation. This Eigen of a man exists in the universe, and is contained within the universe, and does NOT transcend the universe.

Your body started with an immense amount of information coded in organic chemicals from both your mother and your father, which then combined and formed a cell which then became a living organism which then multiplied the cells within itself, and using this information from your mother and your father grew you into a person with a body. This body is the second Life Eigen, which lives in time and space, and is confined to time and space, and is limited to time and space.

The Hebrew Christian scriptures, the writings of what are called the Old and New Testaments, Muslims also recognize these scriptures, hereinafter, I will call them the Bible, say God breathed into the dust, and Adam, the first man, became a living soul. So God breathing a spirit into a body of dust makes a man, who then has a soul. So into the dust (which is our body), our second Eigen, God breathed a spirit, our first Eigen, and the third essential functional element, our third Life Eigen, our soul, (which consists of our mind, our will, our emotions) develops and grows from this insertion of spirit into dust. So God breathed your spirit into your initial single cell within your mother which then became alive in itself, grew and multiplied the cells, and God then formed you into a man, or, of course, a woman. I use the term, man, as generic, so it includes women.

This third essential functional element Life Eigen, that of the soul, is all that is involved in the cognitive processes or the result of cognitive process. Thinking, planning, the realm of imagining, calculating the results of some plan, creating images in one's mind, all of this is done in this third Eigen. Business decisions, intellectual operations, government, making money, all of that is included and involved in the realm of the third Life Eigen.

You might think of life in the third Eigen soul as one vast computer program. The program itself consists of words, statements, coding, in the old days consisting of IBM cards, or in your brain lots of molecules, electrical impulses, memory storage, and neuron connections. This real physical stuff is in the real world, the realm of the second Eigen, but this computer program when executed generates stuff in the abstract, which has meaning in itself, independent of the actual words, statements, or coding. The same thing occurs in your brain. All the molecules, electrical impulses, memory storage, and information coding, in your brain generates stuff in the abstract. This abstract does not consist of real physical stuff, but stuff, so to speak, out in the ether.

All of this abstract, all of that which is generated, is in the third Eigen, that of the soul. This is the realm of the mind, you can dream, create something in the abstract, perhaps an image, but perhaps something of that image cannot even exist in the real word. This is the third Eigen, the life of the soul. This is life of imagination, of your will with its plans and programs, and your emotional responses to physical stimuli. This soul develops and grows, learns and matures as the rest of the body grows and matures.

The last and fourth essential functional element Eigen of life is that inner essence being of a man, in the modern translations of the Bible called heart. The heart Life Eigen is the center of the being, the center of self-awareness or awareness of existence, and lies deep within the extension of the spirit of a man. This inner essence being becomes more clearly manifested when a man is confronted with serving God or not. The Bible says when a man becomes a Christian; the man becomes a new creature in Jesus Christ, and is given a new cleansed, purified heart. When a man commits himself and starts to serves God, the life of God moves into the man, and the man receives a renewed dimensional functional quality to life, and life has new extended meaning, and in my terms, a new, renewed, or made over fourth Eigen purified heart.

In the Bible, in the book of Romans, the apostle Paul, that great apostle of the Christian Faith, says that the Old Testament descendants of Jacob, called Hebrews, have their hearts circumcised, that is, the filthy or hardened part of the Hebrew person's heart is removed by God by spiritual circumcision, or the putting off, or the cutting off, of the sinful nature, as Paul stated it. The great prophet of the Hebrews, Moses, in the Old Testament part of the Bible, says God circumcises the repentant Hebrews' heart. Normal body ceremonial circumcision, the cutting away of the foreskin of the male sexual organ, for the Jew then, is an outward sign or symbol of what God has done in the Hebrew's believer's heart. The Bible uses the term heart meaning an inner essence, or inner being of a man.

God gives to man this fourth Eigen new, renewed, cleansed, purified heart; it starts with and is generated from the gift of faith that is deposited in the man. The cleansed fourth Life Eigen grows as the life of a man of God matures; its primary attribute is love, love of God and love of fellow man. In the Christian theological view, God gives the Christian a new or renewed or purified heart, the Christian then grows, becomes a complete whole person, and becomes sanctified, sanctified meaning to be put to the proper use. The man then becomes a complete whole human person, as God intended, when this fourth Eigen heart life grows and dominates and rules the man's existence.

All of these Eigens extend into eternity, that is, life beyond the cosmos, life beyond time and space itself that our bodies now live in. In our body resurrection after our death, God gives us a new renewed physical body in a new creation, our spirits, souls, and hearts extend into this eternity, and our fourth Eigen heart, which is really only a seed in this present life, expands and grows tremendously as we enter into eternal fellowship with God, this our Lord, Jesus.

The Bible tells us that in the original Garden of Eden (garden of bliss), intended by God for the first man and woman and all subsequent mankind, God planted four kinds of trees. He planted trees that were good for food, planted trees beautiful to look upon, the tree of knowledge and of knowing good and evil, and the tree of life. Amazingly, here we have the four Life Eigens. Beauty as input for our Eigen one spirit life, food for our Eigen two life in the body, knowledge tree for our Eigen three soul life, and the tree of life for our Eigen four life of love. This demonstrates that our life in its whole completed four Life Eigen form, was to be fed by the fruit of four kinds of trees. We absorb the fruit of these trees as we eat of each. As we mature and grow in life, we, of course, eat food, but we also absorb beauty, especially beauty of spirit. We absorb knowledge and increase in the knowledge of good and evil, and we absorb the life of God, the life of the Lord Jesus, as we feed on, absorb Jesus, the only begotten son of God, and grow and mature in our fourth Eigen, which dominates our loving eternal life.

Let's try to understand a little of the Eigen spirit thing. Our spirit, our first Life Eigen, is similar to a cup in that it is meant to hold God's Spirit. Another word for this second Eigen spirit cup might be vessel, like a ship is a vessel. It is meant to contain something, or haul something. Another word which might better describe the nature of this cup might be temple. A temple was used in ancient times to designate the home or place of a god. So in us too, that is, our spirit Life Eigen part of us is meant to be the temple of God. This temple is especially developed within a Christian. Man's spirits are meant to hold God's spirit. From our spirits with interaction from our hearts come our motivations and attitudes, as well as our intuition, conscience, and communion, so when our spirits hold God's Spirit, our attitudes and motivations reflecting our renewed heart, our renewed, purified inner essence being, which is powerfully influenced by the presence of God's Spirit, become more like God's attitudes and motivations.

Our spirits are involved in worship. In some very mysterious way, which is very difficult to understand, God gives to humans a taste of worship in the sexual act between a man and a woman. This was reflected in many ancient pagan religions, where the sexual act between a man and a woman, usually done near or in the god's temple, was counted as some part of the worship of the god. Temple prostitutes were present at many ancient god temples, so that when a man came to worship the god, he engaged the temple prostitutes. Undoubtedly, this was a corruption promoted by Satan himself, who is the prime angelic enemy of God, to capture and destroy man through false worship, or the worship of the evil demons. Satan and Satan's cohorts the demons goals are also to occupy men's spirits and then corrupt and take possession of them.

Nevertheless, there is a truth in this principle, which Satan meant to indeed corrupt; which is that the sexual act between a man and a woman has some sort of spiritual root in worship. Now in a very mysterious way when a man and woman become united together, not only do their bodies entwine, but then their spirits entwine, as well as then their souls entwine, so that a man's spirit, which is like a cup, begins to hold part of the woman's spirit when sexual union takes place, and the woman's spirit starts to hold part of the man's spirit. As this communion continues and grows the spirits of the man and the woman absorb more of each other's spirit, and the thoughts of their attitudes, motivations, and faith become entwined.

The Old Testament Scriptures say that in the union of a man and a woman, they become one flesh. The New Testament scriptures confirm this with Jesus teaching the same concept and adding, "What God had joined together let no man separate." What is meant here, in all likelihood, in the message that when man and the woman become one, since, of course, they cannot occupy each other's body, become one not necessarily in the body of flesh, but become one in the spirit, and through their spirits one in the soul, and perhaps even one or at least similar in their hearts. Not exactly, of course, but similar, as each are absorbing of one another or becoming like one another.

In the ideal situation this happens between a man and his wife. Their spirits became entwined. They start to have similar thoughts and think along similar lines. They begin to absorb each other's attitudes and motivations. They became one in the spirit. They become mates, mates with their bodies, mates with their souls, mates with their spirits, and mates with their hearts.

This is a very great mystery. One does not really understand the process. After these many years of life I think I understand a little. Since I now understand my spirit is like a cup meant to hold God's spirit, and my spirit cup holds part of my wife's spirit, in many hours of contemplating I started to think about this matter, and analyze as to why this should be. This mystery periodically would set me to thinking. As the years went by and I studied the matter I think I have now started to understand it a little bit, and,

298

therefore, now try to pass this understanding on to you my dear reader. As I develop this Life Eigen theory for you, the process may become somewhat understood.

To begin to understand this Eigen theory I present to you lets go back to man's beginnings and start from there.

ON THE BEGINNING OF MANKIND

There is overwhelming evidence from genetic studies, archaeological studies, and anthropology studies that modern man appeared on the earth suddenly, in complete modern, extremely complex form, genetically identical to us modern humans about 30,000 years ago plus or minus a factor, or between maybe about 20,000 to 100,000 years ago. This is a very, very, extremely small amount of time in what seems to be the history of the Earth. The evidence is there, and as the years of time go by it will become obvious, regardless of what others may now try to tell you.

The universe that we observe, that in which we live and exist, is a four dimensional space time continuum. Measurement of space and time depend on the state of the observer and not on what is being observed. This is a consequence of the Theory of Relativity, a theory well established by observation and consistency. It turns out the quantity of time, and yes even the quantity of space itself, measured by any sequence of events, therefore, depends on the state of motion and the gravitational state of the observer relative to that being observed. Therefore, given that time and space dilate by known and perhaps unknown processes, depending on the state of the observer, 30,000 years may or may not be as long as 30,000 years seems to us at the present time.

Another possibility is the passing through the earth and solar system of some massive gravitational wave, or some localized dilation of time and space, or other phenomena not yet understood, which dilates time and space, or which may have even reversed the direction of time, meaning that time may have run backwards, for a season. If we assume that the conditions of the earth have remained essentially the same for the last 30,000 years, an observer on the surface of the earth would have measured time of approximately 30,000 years, each of those years like those we now experience.

The inescapable conclusion, because man, in extremely complex form, appeared suddenly without traceable antecedents, is that man was caused or formed by some agency. You cannot escape that reality, and that agent I will define to be God. Now then, what agent or what God did this, and for what purpose? Any very careful logical study of the matter, based on all the written and oral traditions of mankind, will conclude that the Hebrew Christian God, the same God also claimed by the Muslims, Mormons, and others, is the only representation of God that is at all reasonable from sensible examination of mankind records and observation.

Let's call the animal, Homo sapiens, sapiens, (the scientific name), human, to make the nomenclature short and simple, or as I said before, man. The human genetic makeup, a chemical coding system, which determines everything there is about that human, stores an almost incalculable amount of information. This information is stored in a complex molecular structure in each teeny cell of the human body. Scientific studies are slowly beginning to understand how this genetic code system works. It will probably be a very long time before it is fully understood.

But let me give you a little head start jump on this whole business. Let's skip any explanation of the processes and go right to the bottom line. Certain chemical reactions occur in our brains where certain enzymes (chemical compounds) controlled by our genetic makeup can make us happy, sad, confused or what else. Somehow our brains through our soul with its third Eigen ether fog interact with our spirits and our hearts to produce chemicals in our bodies that drive our sense of happiness, dread, well-being, anguish, etc. It drives our sense of morals, of what is right and wrong, of what is fair and what is not fair, of what is trustworthy and what is not trustworthy. In a very complex way we do not yet understand, the electromagnetic flux in our brains, determined again by our genetic code, processes the decisions we make. Our sense of consciousness and our sense of self seem to be some product of the integrated quantum state existing in our brains.

In the process of becoming a Christian or growing in one's Christian walk of life, an actual change occurs in our genetic makeup, and certain unused (or subdued) combination of genes which are part of our genetic makeup, wake up. When the Lord Jesus comes into your life, and through your spirit which then directs your soul with input from your new,renewed or cleansed, purified heart, heart meaning your inner essence being, and the soul through your brain accepts the Lord Jesus as ruler and God of your life, chemical reactions take place producing chemicals which then go throughout your body, similar to viruses, directing the cells with the change to the genetic code, telling all these genes that you belong to Jesus.

The genes in our cells are designed with such an immense number of genomic interaction structures, such an immense amount of coded information, that even when we are in the depraved, lost state, latent codes are in our genes, so that when we respond to the love of the Lord Jesus, derivative interactions of these genes wake up so as to produce that immense sense of well-being that accompanies a para dyne conversion to follow the Lord God Jesus.

In other words, in everyone's brain there is a latent capability to accept Jesus, and if our spirits, awakened by God's Spirit, say yes, Jesus, I am yours, then these latent genetic places are woke up so that the chemical reactions take place, which precipitate electromagnetic patterns, and quantum states, which produce the extreme sense of well-being and quietness of spirit that accompanies a para dyne shift in our commitment to serve God. Some people, of course, come to know God slowly, perhaps even over a number of years, but this chemical, electromagnetic, and quantum reaction still takes place, but more slowly.

You might say, "This is all nonsense". How can all the information stored in my brain, stored in my cells, survive my death when I return to dust and physical nothingness? Let me give you a brief physics lesson. There is a theorem in physics, derived by one of our great 20st century physicists, that all the information in a black hole is stored on the surface of the black hole.

For those of you who may not have thought about black holes, a black hole is a stellar mass usually bigger than the sun, (large because small black holes radiate their energy away by quantum transactions and disappear) that burns up all of its hydrogen, helium, and other fuel and collapses because of gravitational interaction of its own mass, even contracting time and space within the hole itself. In fact, some theories suggest that within a black hole time stops and space flows. At the center of the galaxy we live in, the Milky Way, there is an immense black hole. Almost all galaxies have immense black holes at their centers.

What's left after a black hole collapse is to a great extent unknowable since one cannot see into a black hole. A black hole cannot be escaped from. It can hardly be defined since one cannot get information out of a black hole. We can only see its event horizon, which has a diameter, dependent on the mass of the black hole, which is the point of no return as you enter a black hole. Even light at the speed of light cannot escape from a black hole.

Because the universe has a very large mass, which seems to have been created by quantum mechanical interactions in the very early universe, it too is essentially a super huge black hole. Therefore, viola! All the information within the universe exists on the surface of the universe! Now I am not going to offer here any proof of this postulate, as that is not the intention of this writing. But something like that is undoubtedly true as the Bible says that all your deeds, everything you have ever done or even thought, are collected in books to be revealed at the last judgment day before Jesus Christ.

Now since a huge flux of neutrinos (tiny nuclear particles) produced by the sun and other burning nuclear fires pass through your body every microsecond (estimated to be 100 billion per second) continuously on their way to outer space, all an observer needs to do is to collect all the information this huge flux of neutrinos obtains from you as it passes through you, and deposit it on the surface of the universe. Thus all the information of every human that ever lived and will ever live is deposited on the surface of the universe.

All your memories, everything you ever did or thought, are deposited on the surface of the universe where they can be read by an outside observer, yes, by God, the Lord Jesus Himself. Now don't take this as any kind of accurate scientific description. I am giving you a preview of what physicists may know a 1000 or more years from now, given that the Lord Jesus tarries in His return, and yet waits for more people to come to know him, and God does NOT in the meantime terminate the universe.

Now if you are a confirmed and dedicated evolutionist with the understanding that everything that has ever occurred come about by random chance, random chance being the basis of the theory of evolution, you should consider now the words of modern microbiologists, who say that the complexity of the information stored in each animal or plant cell seems to have a hidden agenda over and above any randomness.

Consider the question of how much time it takes to generate an ordered state from a random state by random processes. One of the fundamental principles of the universe is entropy. Entropy is a measure of the randomness of a system and is related to the direction of time. By direction of time is meant whether time goes forward or time goes backward. All the physical laws of the universe work just as well with time going backward as time going forward. In fact some nuclear reactions, at extremely small space dimension, where even the fabric of space itself becomes fuzzy, are best explained by time going backward.

Physicists have concluded that the early universe had an extremely low state of entropy. That is, the early universe was in a very highly ordered smooth state. As the randomness of the state of the universe increased, the entropy of the universe increased. It takes time for randomness to generate itself.

Physicists and astronomers have concluded the universe is about 10 to the 10th earth years old. That amount of time is very extremely small compared to that amount of time which is needed for any amount of randomness to produce order by the laws of physics of statistical mechanics. In other words the system is so complex, that to expect randomness, after the original smooth ordered state decayed by randomness, to again produce beautiful order as required by the molecular genetic structure of plants and animals in the extremely young age of the universe, is impossible.

Consider for a moment this time scale. The universe seems, given the assumption that the observer is and has been in a state of very little space curvature, to be a little more than 10 billion years (or 10 to the 10th) old. (In fact the best estimate is about 1.37x 10 to the10th) 10 billion years is 10 to the 10th years, or about 10 to the 17th seconds, or 10 to the 23rd microseconds. Or in other words the age of the universe in microseconds is about 10 to the 23rd.

Roughly, by any calculation of statistical mechanics, if any randomness was to create order it would require way in excess of 10 to the 100th years or the equivalent of 10 to the 113th microseconds for any reasonable probability of that to happen. Yet in order for the order we observe, for example, as in any one cell animal to happen by random chance, that order has to occur from disorder again and again many, many times over. Thus the universe is far too young for any kind of order to come out of randomness. Therefore, to believe that randomness or random chance produced the genetic structure of homo, homo, sapiens takes a lot more faith then to believe God, or some agency of God, made it.

Over the centuries Christendom has been involved in a continuing controversy concerning the extent of God's sovereignty, that is, God's rule and control in the universe. All of this controversy certainly would be avoided if God's creation of the universe was better understood. The Bible starts off with the statement that, "In the beginning God created the heavens and the earth". Just a straight forward understanding of the reading of this text establishes two facts. One, the universe had a beginning, and two, God created it. So God existed before the universe and outside of the universe. Therefore, God transcends, or is outside and inside the universe, or better put, God exists separate from and yet encompasses the universe, and therefore, God is outside the universe as well as inside the universe. As the old theological statement of the Westminster Catechism of the Presbyterian Church which I once memorized said, "God is infinite in His being, wisdom, power, justice, holiness, goodness, and truth." That statement certainly agrees with the Holy Scriptures of the Christians. So God is infinite and transcends the universe.

The apostle Paul in the book of Romans in the Bible, writes that God has left enough evidence in the creation so that man is without excuse --- God's power and divine nature have been clearly seen, being understood from what was made.

Now then, scientific observation has well established the theory first postulated by Albert Einstein of what is called the Theory of Relativity. A corollary of that theory, directly established by that theory, is that both time and space, as well as energy and mass, began at the beginning of the universe. Thus it cannot be contradicted that an external force, (Christians believe that that force is God), created or started the universe at that instant in the beginning of time, space, energy and matter. So God made the universe and made it out of nothing and the apparent reason He did so was to just enjoy it. God also then made man just to enjoy her and him, that is, enjoy you too, and enjoy all of mankind.

It is very difficult for humans to imagine or understand a place where there is no time and there is no space. Space and time are intrinsic to our existence. We just cannot understand a place with no room to be in, or a time where there is no time to be in. Yet God dwells there and observes the universe with us in it from such a place.

Therefore, since God dwells outside time and space, God observes your beginning, at your birth, and every moment of your life until the moment of your death, so to speak, all at the same time, or in different words, in all of God's observable scene. This would be somewhat like a picture painting where we observe all the things in the picture at the same time. Artists have painted pictures of accounts of battles where the armies are painted into the scene including most of the important events that took place during the course of the whole day of battle, and painted everything into that one scene. Similarly, all of the events of your life from birth to death are presented to God in one scene. And since God is also painting the scene, He can change the elements of the scene any way He wants to.

So God can certainly vary the events in your life to suit His own purposes. Perhaps at 52 years of age you encounter an event that requires certain psychological preparation. Therefore God goes back into your childhood and has your mother give you a spanking at six years of age, because of some mischief you performed, so that when you encounter an event at 52 years of age your memory brings back the psychological impressions of the previous spanking so you now perform as you and God intend.

Now we cannot understand this. It is just beyond our understanding, yet it must be true if God indeed dwells outside of time and space, and made the universe for his own pleasure, and made it just to enjoy fellowship with you and me.

This understanding then negates any serious controversy in the discussion of predestination or foreknowledge, or for that matter, any discussion of free agency. Obviously, we who dwell in time and space, have a free agency in time and space to do anything we please bound by the constraints of time and space. Yet the results of this free agency may certainly have been already determined by God. This cannot be understood in human terms, yet it is obviously true.

In the context of this discussion then, the Biblical statements such as, "Your name was written down in the Lamb's book of life before the foundation of the world", can be understood. God wrote my name down in the Lamb's Book of Life long before I was born, before the beginning of the universe with its beginning of time and space, energy and matter. God wrote my name down outside of time and space, and I already now live with God outside of time and space.

In all of my life on the earth as I wandered around in sin and degradation the angels of God waited, so to speak, for my decision that I would love God, to be made sometime during my life in time and space. Does that mean that I was predestined to love God? Yes and no. All my life I had the free agency to reject God, though in retrospect that seems impossible. In no way was I coerced to love God. As I said before, all this is impossible to understand in human logic terms.

Contemplate then for a moment your life as it relates to the universe, the place where you are now living. We all must face death, the end of our life on earth, and the consequences of eternity, or perhaps as some have called it, the afterlife. Consider then the universe, its beginning, and its end.

Essentially the Inflationary Big Bang Theory for the origin of the universe is based on the understanding that in a very short time after the beginning of the universe, maybe about 10 to the -32th seconds or so, quantum mechanical reactions occurred forming pairs of quantum particles such as to cause the creation of negative energy. Since energy has mass and negative energy has negative mass, huge gravitational type relativistic forces, were generated that, therefore, expanded the fabric of space so that three dimensional space we live in expanded to a huge extent. This was caused by the vast generation of net negative energy which, of course, according to the relativity theory has negative mass. After an extremely short period of time due to the cooling by expansion of the universe, subsequent quantum interactions took place that generated positive energy along with the termination of the generation of negative energy. Reactions then took place so that most of the particles in space annihilated each other. But left over from these interactions was a net mass, in comparison to the initial amount of quantum particles, a very, very small positive amount, of which came the huge, by then universe. Almost all of the quantum particles generated in this process had annihilated each other. The very small left over positive mass particles was smoothly spread over the universe, but again due to very slight variation in quantum interactions, localized groups were formed due to the attraction forces generated by the slight local curvature of space, caused by the positive mass/energy of the left over particles. Thus particles and energy with mass accumulated together into clumps.

Understand that in a black Hole for example, the curvature of space is so strong that space in a black hole is warped almost into nothing, so contemplating the opposite, a negative black hole, which occurred in this early universe due to the huge negative mass/energy, expands into an almost space infinity, going from a highly curved space to flat curvature so that we now have almost flat curvature, meaning very little curvature, in the three dimensional space of the universe in the regions between particle clumps.

So the universe expanded immensely shortly after the beginning and passed to the point of almost zero curvature as the remnant mass in the universe was then spread evenly and very thin over the universe. The mass/energy of the universe then slowly coalesced into clumps which were the beginnings of stars and galaxies.

Now, of course, as we look out into the universe with telescopes, since light travels at the speed of light, we can only see out to where light from these initial stars and galaxies has had enough time to travel from where they were formed to us where we observe the light now. Thus as was discussed before we can see out only about 1.37 x 10 to the 10th years. How far the universe extends beyond that which we can see is an interesting field for physicists to figure out. Some have estimated from the small amount of curvature now present that the size of the universe is about 10 to the 80th times the size of the observable universe. This would give the present size of the universe as about 10 to the 90th light years. The determination of the total mass of the present universe would also give an indication of the approximate total size of the universe.

Now since the universe was formed by quantum interactions, and as is the nature of quantum interactions, there is the possible likelihood that since the overall quantum state of the space gravitons are in some quantum gravitational state above a ground zero, perhaps a metastable state, these quantum levels may at some time collapse to the ground state. That, of course, would cause the universe to collapse into itself in a blinding flash, in an instant, and become nothing just like the universe was before being started from nothing.

This picture of the possible end of the universe is very much like that described by the apostle Peter in the Book of 2nd Peter in the New Testament of the Bible. Peter said the heavens and earth will pass away in a roar and intense heat in an instant. Since I believe the Bible to be true and trustworthy, I believe that is how the universe will come to an end, at some instant when we least expect it.

In the meantime, let me; therefore, present to you the basic understandings of the successful life, that is, life with God Himself. This is the God that made you for His own pleasurable purpose. Any careful logical examination of religions or of human philosophies of life, will lead to the inescapable conclusion that the Hebrew Christian God is this agent of creation and life. Therefore, herein, as the logical extension of my understanding, I give you the information you need to come to know this God who made you.

THE PLAN

The question arises, what is God's Plan?

308

First you need to recognize that we, that is, you and I, are fallen creatures. Even if you do not accept the literal nature of the story of the Garden of Eden in the Bible, and the eating of the forbidden fruit by Adam and Eve, let me present to you a plausible scenario of what a creator might undertake.

If you or anyone else wanted to create a creature for fellowship, you would initially, unless you are of some perverse nature, make something like a man and make him very good. You would give him an initial flawless genetic code. Let's assume you have been playing and experimenting with genetic codes for a half billion years or so, and have hit on a set that would give all that would ever be needed to make a functioning animal, that could hold part of your spirit, that has all the potential that would ever be needed to develop into a creature that would give you sweet fellowship. So, like any good Engineer would do, you give the object of your creation a test.

The test is to find out if this creature, the object of your creation, if it is to be all that you intend, is then to give it free choice, or in technical terms, let's call it free agency. But buried in that free choice, is that if they chose wrong, they cannot be allowed to develop into extremely powerful eternal beings that do things completely contrary to your overall objective. Thus you make a simple test. The test is, "Thou shall not eat of it", - a very simple test indeed. You want to know if they will heed you, listen to you, and make lovely fellowship with you or not. And perhaps more important, will they become your adversaries or not?

Now you must, therefore, include, in that food, which has been set forward for the test, a virus or other such agent, that has the capability of making sure that the object of your creation, perhaps man, if he and she fail the test, will terminate itself, so that this object of your creation cannot achieve, what you have determined beforehand, would be completely contrary to your intentions.

Thus understand that the brief Biblical account of Adam and Eve in the Garden, being offered the food which you have forbidden them to eat, by an adversary which you have also have allowed to exist, is perhaps such a test. This embedded virus type agent is absorbed by the object of your creation, through the fruit which they have eaten contrary to your specific instructions, and indeed the virus like destructive agent spreads throughout this object of your creation, now man, and infects the genetic code of this race of men, so as to make sure man's physical life is terminated at the proper time.

Also, included in this test, in the event of test failure, is knowledge of good and evil. So this virus like agent not only insures the death of the recipient but also imparts to it a sense, or knowledge of right and wrong, of what is fair and not fair, of what is morally right and what is morally wrong. Thus the object is given capability of making choices so it has the capability to regenerate into the pretest state, or better yet, into an even more advanced and wonderfully higher quality state, having seen and encountered evil, and therefore, has really come to intensely hate evil.

Now then, the object of your creation can continue to choose either good or chose evil. You want only those who choose good, and are committed to doing and following good, to come into eternal fellowship with you. After all, why would you want nasty wicked people around you giving you trouble all the time?

I again want to remind you that I use the traditional generic use of the word, man, to mean the race of men, thus meaning both men and women.

But you desire fellowship with man you have formed; only now he has failed the test. You have put a lot of effort into designing this creature and you originally have made him near perfect and very good. So how do you now accomplish new perfection? You must renew him or make him anew. He must be made over. So you conclude to make a lot of them, give them a variation in the scope of all the genetic codes that might be available, and then select the ones who really come to love you and will be forever faithful to you for eternal fellowship.

So thus you have a new revised plan, which undoubtedly you have anticipated.

Now let's look at this whole process from the view of the created object, that is, man, you and me. We must recognize that we are fallen creatures. We have received a genetic code which defines everything we are from our fathers and mothers and it contains the damaged genomes of genes corrupted by a virus or some other agent at the fall of our original parents.

We now have within ourselves the original imputed or inherited corruption now called sin, caused by the corrupting agent or virus. So we have a nature, passed on to us from our parents that given a choice will choose sin and evil over good. We must recognize this, understand this, and be then resolved to do something about it.

First we must repent. Repentance is recognizing that you and I are a sinful fallen creature, and that you and I sin, and given a choice we will choose sin. God has said that sin leads to death, and your genetic code insures that you will in fact die a physical death. So the first step is to tell God you are sorry for your sins, and that you do not wish to continue in doing sin, that you hate sin, and want to repent. You go to God and you repent, and you tell God you repent. You ask God to come into your life and work on you, so that this sin problem can be fixed. Like any good Engineer you want to fix the problem.

The next thing to do is to try to understand something of the nature of the God who made you and desires fellowship with you. God, to reveal himself to you, has had some of his servants over the years write about Him so as to reveal himself to you and other men and give man a little understanding of God. Thus, first, God picked a group of people, some children of Abraham, a man of faith whom God then spoke to. The descendants of Abraham over the centuries have written down what they learned about God, and created what we call today the Bible, a written account of what God told men and some of His dealings with men.

The underlying object and goal of these writings is to present to us, the modern race of men, a very special man, a man chosen of God, identical, of the same substance as all men, but, God Himself in the form of his creation, a man. Thus we have the God-man, Jesus Christ, fully God and fully man. This man, Jesus, is of the same substance as God, and therefore is equal to God in everything, and yet fully man. Understand that if you wanted to communicate and fellowship with ants, the thing to do would be to become an ant. Therefore, God too, to communicate with the object of his creation, became a man just like us, just like you and me.

This man, Jesus, received his genetic code from one single woman. The rest of his genetic code was implanted by the Holy Spirit. This person, the Holy

Spirit, is another manifestation of God acting in the realm of the spirit, and therefore, can interact with the spirit of a man to motivate the man to accomplish God's goals. So a woman of this race of men, a highly chosen woman, became the mother of this Godman. This woman gave the Godman her genetic code and the Holy Spirit supplied another genetic code, which gave to this Godman a perfect human genetic code, so as to enable this man to again make the choices that the first man Adam made. Understand that if this Jesus child was conceived by her mother by some unknown asexual process, the child must have been a woman, as only X chromosomes can come from a woman mother, and all females have double X chromosomes. But the child was a man; consequently, His Y masculine chromosomes could only have come from the Holy Spirit, by a creation process we do not understand.

This man Jesus thus was born into the world, lived as a man with all the temptations available to a man, helped raise his mother's additional children subsequently fathered by His stepfather, so as to have all the problems and temptations of raising children, and supporting them through gainful work, being tempted by all of the village damsels, yes, even being tempted by the village prostitutes, being tempted by material things surrounding him, tempted by the powerful Roman forces which tramped through his village, tempted by business opportunities and the achievement of wealth, and yes tempted by the Devil himself, yet this man, Jesus, did not sin. The man Jesus lived perfectly and chose to live perfectly. This man Jesus demonstrated that it was capable of being done.

Then this man Jesus proved what a real man of God will do. This sinless man Jesus freely gave his life and tasted and suffered death potentially for all of mankind, so that any of mankind could be saved to eternity, and given the eternal never ending life God intended in the beginning, but now only to those who will absorb this life of Jesus into themselves, so that they too become perfect, like unto Jesus, and in eternity, in the next age, dwell in the place prepared for them by Jesus. So then, these are to have sweet fellowship with Jesus, now in fact a taste in this present life, and then on into completion, in this the eternal eternity.

In His horrible sacrificial death, in which Jesus freely gave Himself up to death, having been put to death by crucifixion by the Roman authorities at the instigation of the Jewish leaders, Jesus descended into hell itself. He went into that depth of ugly, horrible, fiery black torment, which had been set aside by God for rebellious spiritual beings called angels, to pay the price God's justice demands for the sin of you and me.

So, we are saved. I now belong to Jesus. You may now belong to Jesus. He paid my price. I am now his child. You can be his child.

In the Bible in the Book of Romans, it is written:

> "If you will confess with your mouth, Jesus as Lord, and believe in your heart that God raised him from the dead, you will be saved."

This is the essence of faith and shows clearly how you can become a child of God. Confess before men that Jesus has become the Lord of your life and that you will follow him and are committed to loving him and obeying him and all his commandments.

When you believe in your heart that God raised Jesus from the dead, you have received from Him a renewed cleansed purified heart, heart now being a word that means your essential inner essence being. Thus you take into your spirit, heart, and soul the fact that Jesus rose from the dead, and that you too will rise from the dead, and be given a new body on the last day when Jesus will meet you in the air, and take you to live with Him forever in eternity.

Your response, and mine, is to love God. How can I not love the one who bought me, paid my price, and rescued me from the eternal damnation and the death I so deserve because of my sin? So, now I must follow the commands of Jesus. Jesus said I am to love God with all my heart, strength, spirit, and soul, and I am to love my fellow humans as Jesus loves me. Therefore, I fully, freely, give myself to God and fully give myself to love.

God then starts a work in my life so that I become like Jesus. This is a complex and arduous process. It has fits and starts. I sin, but when I discover the sin, or a brother or sister points out a blind spot of sin, or sometimes when I have deliberately sinned because of a temptation I had chosen not to resist, I repent. I ask God to forgive me, heal me from my sinful choices. And God does. Slowly, as my life goes on, I seemingly make better choices; I fall into temptation less and less. I slowly let love permeate my life and I slowly start to love the unlovable people around me. I slowly have compassion on those not as fortunate as me. I slowly start to share my life, my material things, and my spirit with those with whom I come into contact. God works in me so that I become what both God and I want me to be.

And I invite the Spirit of God to make His home in my spirit, and live in my spirit. I then live life in the spirit. I pray in the spirit, talk to God in the spirit. I heed the words of Jesus and strive to get all hypocrisy and lies out of my life. I let God work on me from the inside out, from my inner essence being, into my spirit, into my soul, and into my body.

The Spirit of God himself tells our spirits, is a witness to our spirits, gives evidence to our hearts, that you are, and I am, a child of God. That same Spirit makes intercession before God for us in accordance with the mind of Jesus. Nothing then separates us from the love of God.

So in this way our life in our bodies, our life in our souls, and our life in our spirits, directed by our renewed inner essence purified being, called in the Bible our heart, our fourth Eigen, becomes filled with the love and life of God. So we walk with God, walk in truth, and walk in love. And our love overflows so we love our fellow man.

This love bestows to us our life in the fourth Eigen, where resides our heart. Fourth Eigen life continues to expand and anticipate life in a new renewed body with our souls, spirits, and renewed purified hearts in the age to come. In this account I have already introduced the Eigen concept. Let's develop this concept a little more.

But, before I go on to explain this Eigen theory, let's look at the question of how we understand what we know. There are three sources for information and understanding. The first is investigation and establishment by observation in the real world or the world of the second Eigen. This would include scientific experiments and derivative understanding of experiments and observation.

The second source of understanding is that of logical analysis. A process of logical conclusions derived from observing what is true and then by logical extension and inference, other conclusions of what then must be true can be derived. In the realm of this third Eigen, that of thinking and contemplating, a source of information and understanding is in what one writer called, using a new term he created, praxeology, or the study of the general theory of the laws of human action, of which for example, economics is the best developed branch. Confirmed theories of how humans act and behave with logical extension can be a source of information and understanding.

The third source of information and understanding is revelation by God and from God Himself. God has at certain times in the past spoken directly to certain individuals, or used spiritual beings called angels to communicate to human individuals. Some of these individuals wrote down what God communicated to them. The Bible contains such communication. Such communication comes from God Himself and is information and understanding that one cannot know except by revelation from God.

This Eigen theory stuff I am presenting to you comes from interpretation and understanding the written Word of God, the Bible, and therefore, is something you cannot discover by scientific study and analysis, or by logical extension of known understanding.

Christians are promised the witness of the Holy Spirit, a manifestation of God, to the Christian's own spirit. This effect is impossible to quantify and is taken by faith.

EIGENS OF LIFE

As the concept of Life Eigens is herein developed, understand that the perspective is that the Hebrew and Christian scriptures, called the Bible, are taken to be the word of God, correct and accurate in everything contained therein, and reliable for instruction and practice. Therefore, quotations given from the Bible are instructions from God Himself, and, therefore, have power and authority. It is my intention to be as truthful and faithful to the words and concepts of the Bible as I know how.

The Hebrew Christian scriptures in the book of Genesis, or beginnings, tell us that God planted a garden in the East in a place called Eden, as a place for man to live. These scriptures tell us about a river from a plain or steep of Eden that divides into four rivers that water the Garden of Eden and four kinds of trees that grow there. Now it is possible that this story describing Eden is an allegory. But a lot of scripture is a real account of real events and has been recorded for us to receive an allegorical meaning. This is meant to instruct us and then to develop us into beings who come to know God.

The four kinds of trees in Eden are, one, pleasing to the eye, two, good for food, three, tree of knowledge, and fourth, tree of life. The rivers came from one source, seemed to have divided into four rivers, and then watered the Garden of Eden.

A real important question is why does God expend words telling us in these scriptures, in the beginning of the Bible, describing the beginning of man, about trees and rivers? This is a very compelling question. Given the normal perspective of our culture one would think there are far more important information to impart to mankind than stories about trees and rivers. One must thus conclude that these rivers and trees are very important to the understanding of mankind from the beginning.

The trees are more obvious than the rivers. There is the tree of life. That obviously, from the prospective of my Christian Eigen theory is life in the fourth Eigen, which is life in Jesus, the life of our inner essence being, which gives eternal life. The trees good for food are for feeding the second Life Eigen, physical life, life in the flesh, life in the body, life in the real physical creation existence. The trees good to look upon appeal to the spirit, and so would feed our sense of beauty, feed our spirits the first Life Eigen of our lives. And, of course, the tree of knowledge feeds our life in the third Eigen, our life in our souls, life in our imaginations, plans, programs, and things we would create and understand.

God anticipated here a great danger. If indeed, the man whom He created, could dream up, design, make or construct most anything, and I conclude today that man collectively is able to do just about anything, and there is nothing that these men cannot do, therefore, if God gave man such a soul, so that he would have this capability, then of course, God must build in death, that is, termination of this creature, otherwise if the creature were to embark on an evil path, and there was nothing the creature could not accomplish, the result would be quite disastrous. Therefore, the fruit of the tree of knowledge, must have in it the seed virus or agency of death, so that this creature man, as he feeds his soul, and develops his latent huge potential in mind and will, developing in the capability to do both good and evil, must be put to death.

So what is the purpose of this Eigen theory stuff I have suggested to you? When an engineer or scientist starts out to do something or understand something, he observes the facts as he understands them and creates a theory or model. Then he can try to understand the subject better by putting his facts into his theory and extend it to new more accurate understanding. This Eigen stuff is a theory by which we can try to better understand what life is all about. That is how you should understand this Eigen theory.

God has put us on the earth for a purpose. That purpose is seeking fellowship with man, yes with you. An American pastor of some note has said,

> "The purpose of life is to come to know God. If a man has lived life and has NOT come to know God, his life has been wasted."

That in my experience is very, very true. So I give to you this Eigen theory so you might better understand life, and how God interacts with you, so as to produce for you eternal life and fellowship with the Lord Jesus, how you too can come to know God.

The Hebrew Christian scriptures say man was created in the image of God, and these scriptures give several descriptions of the appearance of the likeness of the Glory of God. The descriptions of this likeness of the Glory of God are almost impossible to understand, and it is very difficult to give them useful meaning. The occurrence, however, of very similar images in several places in this Bible give the clear understanding that the appearance of the Glory of God includes four somethings, usually a face or image of an ox or calf, an image of eagle, an image of lion, and an image of man -- here again the four Eigens. Careful study of these images in several places in the Bible leads to the understanding that the face of the ox or calf is associated with the second Eigen body of flesh, the eagle face the first Eigen spirit, the lion face the fourth Eigen ruler of love, and the man face the third Eigen soul with its knowledge. I have coined the term Eigen so as to have a theory upon which to hang a possible understanding of the dimensionality, scope, and functions of life.

There is a very interesting reference in one of the old Hebrew scriptures of the prophet Ezekiel to Cherubim, who are angels of God, and serve God directly. Ezekiel describes an image of the Glory of God, and mankind is made in the image of God, where the foursome has four faces, that of a man, that of a lion on the right, the bull on the left, and the face of an eagle. But when the cherubim's glory is described they have faces of the cherub, man, lion, and eagle. Therefore, let us draw the conclusion that cherubim are also Eigen foursomes. Observe now, however, that the face of the bull is replaced by the face of the cherub when describing cherubim. Therefore, here we have again the four fold nature of the beings of God's creation, where cherubim are foursomes with Eigens of spirit, soul, heart, and instead of a body of flesh as represented by the bull for mankind, have a body represented by that of a cherub.

So let's us consider these Life Eigens a little.

Most people in this world live mostly in the flesh or the life in the second Eigen. They live to eat, sleep, and satisfy the needs of the body. Some poet has said,

> "Into this world to eat and to sleep,
> And to know no reason why he was born,
> Save to consume the corn,
> Devour the cattle, flock and fish,
> And leave behind an empty dish."

Some men, and perhaps there are some women, live only to feed their sexual desires. Young men have a huge sex drive and some live only to satisfy it. King Solomon, king of the Jews about 3000 years ago, had over 1000 wives and concubines. I guess he could afford them all, but one wonders what the purpose of all that was. After all how many women can one man service in one night even if he is a superman? A modern, popular, and talented basketball player has claimed to have slept with over 3000 women. One wonders what the purpose of that was also.

Some people live mainly in their minds. They spend their time in intellectual pursuits. They almost ignore the needs of the body, and live in the world of thinking, planning, imagining, and writing books. Some clergymen are like that, spending almost all of their time studying, reading, and thinking. Their lives include years and years of education and then years and years of studying the classical languages, theological works, reading and studying. The result of all this can be one or two sermons a week preached to a few people in the pews.

Some people spend all their time thinking of nothing, emptying their minds so as to get in touch with their spirits. The Rajneesh types, the eastern religions where ultimate reality is silence, "shoonyta", or nothingness, have much of this. They search endlessly for meaning in and through their spirits, ignoring the needs of the body, emptying their minds and just dwell in as much nothingness as possible so as to get in touch with their spirits. Someone who has studied Australian aborigines say they do that. As these people sit around a fire and stare in to it, they are thinking of absolutely nothing. I have done some of that too, sitting around a campfire, staring into it and thinking of nothing, being mesmerized by the dancing flames and the warmth of the fire.

So now let's try to understand the concept of heart or inner essence being a little. The term heart as used in English translations of the Hebrew Christian scriptures refers to the inner essence of ones being, the center of ones being. And, in an anthropomorphic way, God also has a heart. For example, when God considered the destruction of mankind by the flood, we read in the book of Genesis:

> "Then the LORD saw that the wickedness of man was great on the earth, and that every intent of the thoughts of his heart was only evil continually. The Lord was sorry that He had made man on the earth, and He was grieved in His heart. The Lord said, "I will blot out man whom I have created from the face of the land, from man to animals to creeping things and to birds of the sky; for I am sorry that I have made them. But Noah found favor in the eyes of the LORD.""

So the intent of the thoughts of man are evil continuously. God's heart was filled with pain and was grieved that he had made man. After the flood, after the destruction of all mankind except for Noah and his family, Noah built an altar and made an offering to God. Again from Genesis:

> "Then Noah built an altar to the LORD, and took of every clean animal and of every clean bird and offered burnt offerings on the altar. The LORD smelled the soothing aroma; and the LORD said to Himself, "I will never again curse the ground on account of man, for the intent of man's heart is evil from his youth; and I will never again destroy every living thing, as I have done".

So the intent of man's heart is evil from his youth. Yet we have the promise now that God will never again destroy mankind as long as the earth exists. So how is God to preserve mankind and deal with the problem of the continuous evil intent of man's heart? The Hebrews, that race of men that God chose to be God's special people, were given a promise, if they repented and returned to Him, in the book of Deuteronomy:

> "Moreover, the LORD your God will circumcise your heart and the heart of your descendants, to love the LORD your God with all your heart and with all your soul, so that you may live."

There we have it. God circumcises the heart of the Hebrew. What does this mean? Like the act of circumcision where the foreskin of the male sexual organ is cut off, so as to promote cleanliness, the figurative foreskin of the heart is cut off so that the heart may be cleansed, purified, and purged of the intent of the heart of man to do evil continually. Then people may love God with all their heart and soul. The great apostle of Christianity, Paul, also a Hebrew, in the book of Romans writes:

> "For he is not a Jew who is one outwardly, nor is circumcision that which is outward in the flesh. But he is a Jew who is one inwardly; and circumcision is that which is of the heart, by the Spirit, not by the letter; and his praise is not from men, but from God."

So Hebrew circumcision, (the Muslims also practice circumcision), is an outward act, the cutting of the flesh, that corresponds or is an outward sign, to an inner act by the Spirit of God to circumcise the heart of the Hebrew.

Now the apostle Paul says to mankind in the book of Romans:

"But what does it say? "The word is near you, in your mouth and in your heart" — that is, the word of faith which we are preaching, that if you confess with your mouth Jesus as Lord, and believe in your heart that God raised Him from the dead, you will be saved, for with the heart a person believes, resulting in righteousness, and with the mouth he confesses, resulting in salvation."

So there we have it. With our heart, our inner essence being, we believe, and it is counted as righteousness, that is, giving us right standing with God. Our heart, our inner being, then believes that God raised Jesus from the dead.

When a person becomes a Christian, he or she becomes a new person and is given a new heart, a cleansed heart, a purified heart. He is like the Hebrew in that the Hebrew has his heart circumcised, or the filth cut off, while the Christian is given a new cleansed, purified heart, in other words, a pure sincere, heart. So, our heart, or inner essence, our fourth Life Eigen, is an essential part of our being from which comes faith, and is the essential driving force in our God loving being.

So the question is; does our heart produce evil intent continuously, or does it produce intent for love of God, and then as a follow on, love for our fellow human beings?

Let me suggest then, you and I want to, and are to, live life abundantly in all four Eigens, with the goal to maximize our fourth Eigen life – that is, the life of LOVE in our inner essence being. Our most fervent desire must be to want to live eternally with God Himself, that is, with the Son of God, Jesus our Lord, in fellowship with this our Lord Jesus. We are commanded to love God with all our strength, soul, spirit, and heart.

It is very significant that when Jesus was asked about this loving of God, Jesus responded with a foursome statement, that He added a fourth to the Old Testament statement, that is, to love God with all our strength, our souls, our hearts, and our minds. Let me suggest to you that Jesus is trying to communicate to you and me that there is abundant life, and it has four somethings, four aspects, four dimensions, four fundamental modes, four functions, four vectors, or according to the understanding I am trying to give you, since none of those terms are adequate, four Life Eigens.

So now let's go back and again consider the beginning of man as recorded in the Bible. The scriptures say the Lord God planted a garden in the East, and from the root meaning of the word Eden, on the delightful plain, or valley, or steppe of Eden, where He put the man whom He had formed. We have discussed the trees God planted so now let's look at the rivers that watered the Garden of Eden, or garden of delight with its trees.

Names of places are often reused again and again for new places in new areas. South of the little town of Mendocino in California a few miles is the very little town of Albion. Albion, of course, is another name for jolly old England, probably of Roman origin, so here the same word was applied as the name to the river below Albion and the little village of the same name on the flat ridge above its bank. The same thing was done in ancient times so that the names of the rivers of Eden were used again and again by subsequent peoples, and the names given to other rivers in other places, and then to places in the land of Mesopotamia. So let's look at the roots of the words that were used as the names given to the rivers of the Garden of Eden, so as to try to understand what message God is giving to us about the beginnings of mankind and the Garden of Eden and its rivers.

The account says a river flowed from Eden and divided into four rivers to water the garden. The root of the word Eden is delight, plain, steppe, or flat area. So the message is that a river flowed from a delightful plain into the garden where the man was placed, and there it divided into four rivers to water the garden.

The first of the rivers in the Garden of Eden was named Pison, or Pishon. The root meaning of that word is to increase, multiply, overflow, or to make grow around the land. The biblical account says the Pishon winds around the whole land of Havilah where there is good gold and precious stones. The root meaning of Havilah is circle, land, distant, perhaps sandy. So the River Pishon winds around the wonderful very rich land of the garden and waters it.

The second river is the Gion, or Gihon. The root meaning of the word Gihon is to burst forth, arise from the east, swift, or impetuous. The Gihon winds through the land of Cush. The root of the word Cush seems to have been completely indistinct or undefined. Perhaps the meaning is intended to be indistinct, so Cush may mean an indistinct place that is not defined.

The third river is given the name of Hiddekel. The root meaning of this word is active, rapid, vehemence, sharp, rapid velocity flow, swift, or arrow, going east. It is on the east side of Asshur, the root meaning of Asshur being a region of vegetation associated with water.

The fourth river was called the Euphrates. The root meaning of this word is sweet river, long river, fruitful river, good to cross over or swim in, or good and abounding river. It is the mightiest of the four rivers.

What are we to make of these four rivers with the names given by the scriptures that water the Garden of Eden, in the description of the beginning of man? Why does God through these scriptures spend time telling us about rivers that water a garden? Let me suggest to you there is a much deeper meaning to these rivers names then just geographical locations. The graphical descriptions, if applied to presently existing rivers make no sense at all, since, obviously, the names have been reused and applied to subsequent new rivers observed by mankind. Obvious also is that, the character of the land has changed greatly through the centuries and we now have no idea where the Garden of Eden was located.

Let me suggest to you that these four rivers, described to us, were to water symbolically the four kinds of trees that were put in the garden to provide sustenance to the man put in the garden. The Pishon is symbolic of watering of the trees, the fruit of which was good for food, that is sustenance for the physical body, that of the second Eigen. The watering by the river causes fruit to grow which when eaten causes bodies to grow and multiply in the very rich land of the Garden, of Havilah, which is also very rich as symbolized by the gold and precious stones, and all that is needed by mankind. Man with his physical body is to increase in number and multiply and become abundant, and feed on the fruit of the trees good for food.

The Gihon is symbolic of the watering of the trees beautiful to look upon, trees associated with the spirit of man as it bursts forth, arising from the east, meaning arising from God Himself, swift and impetuous. The Gihon winds around the whole of the land, as the spirit of man also has no boundary, an indistinct place as the root of the word Cush implies, and is transcendent. So the watering of the spirit of man knows no boundaries. This river then is symbolic of watering the trees of the garden that appeal to the First Eigen, the spirit of man.

The Hiddekel (sometimes translated Tigress) is symbolic of the watering of the trees that are associated with the soul of man. This river is active, rapid, vehement, flowing swiftly or like an arrow. The Asshur name associated with it suggests it has the vegetation of the kind that would not be found along a river. It flows to the east, meaning that in being watered or nurtured, the soul of man is to seek God or find God, this being the meaning of flowing to the east, or flowing to God. The prefix of the first part of the word means very. The meaning of the name is then very sharp, very rapid, very vehement, etc. This river then is symbolic of watering that tree in the garden -- the tree of knowledge. However, with knowledge comes knowing good and evil, and once man knows evil, there is death, the consequence of eating the fruit of this tree of knowledge of good and evil.

Let me suggest to you that the fourth river, the river called the Euphrates, is symbolic of watering the tree of life. The tree of life is watered by sweet water, long life water, fruit producing water, flower, and beauty producing water, abounding water of the river of life. It is intended to be the mightiest of the four rivers and is to water the tree that feeds the fourth Eigen of man -- that of his heart, or inner essence, so that man would be abounding in love – love of God and his fellow creatures.

Of course, the tree of life is symbolic of the Lord Jesus Himself. We, who are fallen creatures, are to absorb the life of Jesus, to become like him with all of our four Eigens.

Thus we have from the beginning of scripture a message that man functions in four realms that he operates in four realms that he is to be fed by fruit of four kinds of trees, which are watered by four kinds of rivers. The conclusion is obvious. Man is a foursome or man functions as a foursome. Man has four Life Eigens -- Eigens from which all of life can be composed, even into eternity, the life beyond the life we now live in our physical bodies on the earth. This sets forth our complete existence as a human, or as I have used the term, complete existence as a man, meaning woman also.

Jesus in His life on earth told some marvelous parables. These parables were meant to explain some very complex, very important, very interesting subjects. In order to really captivate His listener's interest, Jesus told the concepts in parables to make the hearer really think about what Jesus is saying, and to really examine the truth that Jesus wanted to convey. So too, about 2000 years later, these written accounts of these parables are meant to cause us to really think deeply, to really analyze the message conveyed. Remember that it is God, the creator and sustainer of the universe, God Himself, talking to us, and instructing us in these parables.

So we have the parable of the sower. This parable explains a part of Four Eigen Life as it is impacted by the hearing of the word of life. From the Book of Mathew, Chapter 13:

> "That day Jesus went out of the house and was sitting by the sea. And large crowds gathered to Him, so He got into a boat and sat down, and the whole crowd was standing on the beach.
>
> And He spoke many things to them in parables, saying, "Behold, the sower went out to sow; and as he sowed, some fell beside the road, and the birds came and ate them up. "Others fell on the rocky places, where they did not have much soil; and immediately they sprang up, because they had no depth of soil. "But when the sun had risen, they were scorched; and because they had no root, they withered away". Others fell among the thorns, and the thorns came up and choked them out. "And others fell on the good soil and yields a crop, some a hundredfold, some sixty, and some thirty. "He, who has ears, let him hear."
>
> And the disciples came and said to Him, "Why do You speak to them in parables?" Jesus answered them, "To you it has been granted to know the mysteries of the kingdom of heaven, but to them it has not been granted. "For whoever has, to him shall be given, and he will have an abundance; but whoever does not have, even what he has shall be taken away from him. "Therefore I speak to them in parables; because while seeing they do not see, and while hearing they do not hear, nor do they understand. "In their case the prophecy of Isaiah is being fulfilled, which says,
>
> 'You will keep on hearing, but will not understand;
> You will keep on seeing, but will not perceive;

For the heart of this people has become dull,
With their ears they scarcely hear,
And they have closed their eyes,
Otherwise they would see with their eyes,
Hear with their ears,
And understand with their heart and return,
And I would heal them.'

"But blessed are your eyes, because they see; and your ears, because they hear. " For truly I say to you that many prophets and righteous men desired to see what you see, and did not see, and to hear what you hear, and did not hear.

"Hear then the parable of the sower. "When anyone hears the word of the kingdom and does not understand it, the evil comes and snatches away what has been sown in his heart. This is the one on whom seed was sown beside the road. "The one on whom seed was sown on the rocky places, this is the man who hears the word and immediately receives it with joy; yet he has no root in himself, but is temporary, and when affliction or persecution arises because of the word, immediately he falls away. "And the one on whom seed was sown among the thorns, this is the man who hears the word, and the worry of the world and the deceitfulness of wealth choke the word, and it becomes unfruitful. "And the one on whom seed was sown on the good soil, this is the man who hears the word and understands it; who indeed bears fruit and brings forth, some a hundredfold, some sixty, and some thirty."

Jesus thus explained this parable to His disciples so we do not, therefore, have to guess or study in great detail to establish its meaning. The sower is Jesus. Jesus is the creator God of the universe, and let me suggest to you that Jesus sows the word of truth, as the parable indicated, into people's hearts, the fourth Eigen of our existence.

Jesus says that the seed that fell by the side of the road represents those that hear the word but do not understand it and evil or the evil one snatches it away. Let me suggest to you that this occurs in the realm of the spirit, in the first Eigen. The evil one operates in the realm of the spirit. So when the word is sown in the heart of a hearer, evil manifests itself through the spirit Eigen and the word is snatched away. That person has his spirit dominated by the evil one, or one of the evil one's cohorts and the word is snatched away.

Jesus says that the seed that is sown in rocky places represents those that hear the word and receive it with joy but they have no root, because when persecution and affliction arrive, they fall away. Persecution and affliction occur in life in the real physical world, the realm of the second Eigen, the life of the flesh. Life in the flesh has its good times and its bad times. Sometimes we Christians encounter real persecution and it gets tough. We would rather be approved by our friends and those in positions over us than be devoted to Jesus and seek His approval. Afflictions of all types sometimes hit us. We run out of money, we get sick, our loved ones get in trouble, or get sick, and we can't take it and give up, and sometimes even curse God, or blame God for our troubles. Then we fall away because of first Eigen troubles in the flesh, caused by our living our life in the real world.

Jesus says that the seed that falls among the thorns represents those who hear the word and receive it, but the worries of the world and the deceitfulness of riches choke off the word and it becomes unfruitful. Worries and deceit occur in the mind, in the third Eigen, that of the soul. Let me suggest to you that the corruption of the world system, that which occurs in the third Eigen, is that which chokes off the fruitfulness of the word sown in that persons heart. Worries, not trusting God to take care of you, and the deceit of trusting riches to take care of you, choke off fruitfulness.

Jesus says that the word sown in the good soil, that sown in a good and receptive heart, the cleansed, purified heart of the fourth Eigen, that sown which is not snatched away out of the heart by evil in the first Eigen realm of the spirit, that not found lacking by the shallow soil where persecution and affliction occur in the second Eigen, and that not choked off by worries and deceit in the third Eigen wherein is the soul, produces much fruit, some a hundredfold, some sixty, some thirty.

Jesus, before He gives the interpretation of the parable to the disciples, quotes the prophecy of Isaiah, to explain why men and women do not all become fruitful in the kingdom. Jesus tells the disciples that it has been granted to them to know the mysteries of the kingdom of heaven. So we too, to those of us who believe that Jesus is the anointed One of God, God Himself in the flesh, it has been granted us to understand the mystery of the kingdom of heaven. And to those who do not believe, it has not been granted to understand the mystery of the kingdom of heaven. We believers are to hear with our minds, we are to see with our spirit eyes and perceive, we are to understand in our hearts, and then Jesus heals us. Jesus heals us of our brokenness, and heals us of our inadequacy. Jesus works in us to make us complete whole human beings as God intended us to be from the beginning.

So why is it that those who do not believe keep hearing but do not understand, keep seeing but do not perceive? Jesus says those hearts are dull. So how is the heart of the unbeliever dull? Because it has not been washed or sprinkled by the blood of Jesus, that blood which washes away all sin, and makes the heart clean. Jesus says unbelievers have ears that scarcely hear and have closed their eyes. Eyes are a symbol of the spirit so Jesus is saying these unbeliever's spirits are closed, that is their spirit, which is like a cup, which was meant to hold God's Spirit, is closed and will not accept the spirit of God to come and inter into the cup of the unbelievers spirit. Jesus says, otherwise, if they would hear with their ears, see with their spirit eyes, and understand, I would heal them. Here again we have a four Eigen operation. We hear with our second Eigen body, see in the spirit with our first Eigen spirit eyes, understand with our third Eigen mind as part of our soul, and our fourth Eigen hearts are washed with understanding, and then our whole four Eigen life being is healed.

Let me suggest to you that this whole salvation process, this whole healing process is a four Eigen happening, and we would do very well to understand the four Eigen nature of mankind. That understanding will do us well in our spiritual growth to maturity or as Jesus says, "I will heal them"! Jesus gives us a very interesting insight here and that is that the heart gives understanding to the mind. Or from the concepts I am giving you, the fourth Eigen heart gives understanding to the third Eigen soul.

That the heart gives understanding to the mind is a very important concept for our culture. People whose hearts reject God often in up in corruption or in insanity. Political leaders often seem vulnerable to this. The pride of success with an uncleansed heart often leads to disaster.

The example of the parable of the sower presents an opportunity to understand the Eigen theory and why the term Eigen has been chosen. The state of almost all of those who become unbelievers is not due to any particular Eigen, but in some combination of the Eigens. This is how eigenvectors work in the engineering and scientific world. A value of a complex vector is some combination of the magnitudes of the basic eigenvectors of the system. So too is the unbeliever. His lack of faith and cleansing usually comes about partly from unbelief, partly from troubles, trials and persecution, and partly from worries and deceit accumulated in the world system.

All of life is some complex integration based on combinations of the elements of the four Eigens. Even the washed who have had their hearts cleansed and purified by Jesus, and, therefore, are children of God, temporarily sub scum at times to unbelief, to trials and troubles, and to worries and deceit. This is the battle of life of the Christian. He or she has been washed, been born again in the spirit, and holds God's Spirit within his or her spirit, but then also must continue to live yet in the fallen state. But knowing and understanding what it is all about enables the believer to live and walk before the Lord blameless, and have that blessed hope of eternal salvation.

TABERNACLE

Let's look now at another very, very interesting account in the Old Testament. Moses, that great prophet of the Hebrews, was commanded by God to build a tabernacle. Moses had led the children of Israel, called Israelites, or sometimes called Hebrews, by the powerful hand of God, out from Egypt, where they had been slaves to Pharaoh, the King of Egypt. Moses had first encountered God directly when he was sheep herding in the wilderness, having fled from Pharaoh. Sheep herding then as it is now still is one of the lowest occupations known to man. Moses lifestyle, (According to the Roman historian Josephus, Moses had once commanded the armies of

Egypt and was second only to Pharaoh himself), had sunk to the bottom. Moses is wandering around in the desert wilderness with his father in law's sheep and saw a bush that burned but was not consumed. He turned aside to see this sight. God spoke to him from this bush, and that started a relationship with communication between God and Moses.

The tabernacle that Moses was commanded to build, subsequently, became the place where God spoke directly to Moses. It then became the center of Hebrew worship of God. Priests, the intermediaries between God and the individual Hebrew, performed ritual services of sacrifices and feasting with the worshiper and his family. The tabernacle thus became an integral part of the methodology of how the Hebrew came to worship, to know and understand God.

Four hundred ninety (490) or so years later, Solomon, the son of David, King of the Israelites built a temple in Jerusalem patterned after this tabernacle. This temple then became the focus center of Hebrew worship of God. This magnificent temple was destroyed by the Babylonians about 490 years later, was rebuilt again with the help of the Persians and then again destroyed by the Romans about 490 years after that in the year 70 AD.

God gave the appearance that He dwelt in the tabernacle and then again in the temple by the presence of the visible Glory of God in the likeness of a brilliant cloud. While the Hebrew Israelites were wandering in the wilderness, a huge cloud by day and a pillar of fire by night was above this tabernacle built by Moses.

So what is this tabernacle all about? Let us take a look at the pattern of the tabernacle and try to get a little understanding of what the pattern is of this tabernacle, and what the subsequent temples were all about. Let us look at the tabernacle from the outside and proceed to the inside. God commanded Moses to be very careful and make the tabernacle exactly as the pattern he was shown on the mountain by God Himself.

First was a courtyard surrounded by a set of tent type walls hung on pillars. The Hebrews were wandering in the wilderness moving about from place to place so all of this was all portable. The Israelites dismounted it and carried it along with them when they moved from place to place, and they were commanded by God to carry it on their backs with the use of poles only and not to use carts. This courtyard was a rectangle that enclosed an area of about 150 feet by 50 feet, or about 50 meters by 16 meters.

The courtyard walls of animal skins were hung on poles and posts so as to enclose the courtyard. Toward the back of the courtyard was a tent building about 15 feet high made of vertical arraigned boards overlaid with gold with a tent type roof top of animal skins draped over the top and walls, ordinary drab looking on the outside, but very beautiful on the inside. In front of the tabernacle tent building was an altar for offering burnt sacrifices to God, and about halfway between the tabernacle building and the altar was a large basin of water for washing the feet and hands of the priests who served God doing the ceremonies connected with this tabernacle.

The tabernacle portable building had two rooms with a curtain separating the first room from the courtyard and a second elaborate veil curtain separating the first room from the inner room. In the first room was the golden table of show bread, a seven branched gold lamp, and a golden altar for incense, all made of wood and overladen with gold. This room was called the Holy Place. The inner room, called the Holy of Holies, contained two gold statues of angels, called cherubim, that stood above a box, with faces looking toward the box, and wings bent down toward and pointing to the box which was overlaid with gold inside and out.

The box was about 48 inches long, 24 inches wide, and 24 inches deep, with feet and rings for poles to be inserted for carrying when on the move. The box, called the Ark of the Covenant, or the Ark of Testimony, had a thick solid gold lid, which seems to have been attached to the gold cherubim. Inside the box were the tablets of stone on which the ten commandment law was written by the finger of God, which was given to Moses on the top of the Mountain, a jar made of gold which held some of the manna, the white seedy food deposited on the ground provided to the Israelites by God when the Hebrews wandered in the wilderness, and the Rod of Aaron, the brother of Moses the High Priest, a stick of an almond tree wood that overnight produced buds, leaves, and almonds so as to prove that Aaron was the chosen high Priest of God.

This is a very brief description of the tabernacle. God gave Moses very detailed and complete instructions as to how this thing was to be built, which seems to be quite complicated, and it seems that this tabernacle was extremely important, and became the place where God gave the impression of dwelling, when He was among the Hebrews in their wanderings in the desert. It became the center of Hebrew worship of God and the center of the perceived presence of God.

The magnificent temple built by Solomon about 490 years later was patterned after the tabernacle. That temple had a series of enclosing courtyards surrounding the temple building, all in stone, the inner one for Israelite men only, then outside that of the women, then that of the gentiles, which meant everybody else not a Hebrew. It seems the water basin and the altar for sacrifice were larger and made of heavy bronze, as these, of course, did not need to be carried about. The tabernacle portable tent top building was replaced by a building in which the cherubim statues were now quite large, about 15 feet high, whose face and wings again pointed to the lid of the same Ark box, also called the Mercy Seat.

So what is this all about? Let me suggest to you that here is a rather astounding picture of a shadow image of the tabernacle of God in the eternities, and since mankind has been made in the image of God, here also is a shadow image of mankind, and the essential representation of how man is to worship God.

Again, astoundingly, we have the four Eigens. The Eigens as I have defined them are four modes for the function of a human, or the four realms in which a human, a man or woman, functions. The tabernacle and then the temples became places where God was formally worshiped. People would bring their sacrifices to the temple and feast before God, sharing their feast with the priests who served the temple. The priests were intermediaries between the worshiper and God, and were responsible for the care of the tabernacle and the temple, and to perform the ceremonies for the benefit of each worshiper.

So we too, now that the formalities of tabernacle and temple worship have been terminated by God, as we want to come to know God and come to worship God, we approach God within and through our four Eigens. The courtyard let me suggest to you is a representation of man in the flesh, what I have called the second Eigen. This is the life of the body, life in the real world of the created universe. In the real world we are to be washed so as to become clean before God as indicated by the basin of water in the courtyard. In order to approach and come near to God a sacrifice is required offered to God in the real world as indicated by the presence of the altar of sacrifice. As we approach God, attempt to come to know God, attempt to come to worship God, life in the real physical world then in our relationship to God is about having a sacrifice, a sacrifice offered in the real physical world, and being washed in the real physical world, so as to become clean, and, therefore, acceptable to God. The sacrifice that we Christians claim, of course, is the cleansing power of the sacrificed body and blood of our Lord Jesus, our faithful savior. Jesus, our High Priest, has brought His own blood, the blood of His own sacrifice.

The holy Place, within the building behind the first curtain, behind the wash basin, is a representation of the operation of the soul, the functions of the soul, the third Eigen in our relationship to God. In this Holy place was the table for the show bread, also called the bread of the presence, which the priest put in order every day, indicating the necessity of daily soul food, the lamp stand for providing light to the soul, for which the priest provided lamp oil every day, for the understanding by the soul in its thinking and knowledge process, and the incense resin censor where also the priest replaced the incense oil every day.

Incense is a symbol of prayer. So here in this Holy Place are representations of the operation of the soul, our third Eigen, in relationship to God, in its worship of God. Mental food in the form of daily bread bringing knowledge, light for insight and understandings of the mind, and prayer to God generated in the mind, all to develop a soul relationship with God. These need to be replenished or operated every day. Just as the priest comes in to the Holy place every day to put in order or replenish the supplies of the bread, lamp oil, and incense oil, so we too are to replenish every day, in our relationship to God, in our worship of God, our food for the soul, light for the soul, and prayers of the soul. This shows us how the Christian is to worship, and grow and develop his or her soul in relationship to God.

In the Most Holy Place behind the next curtain from the Holy Place just described, are these gold cherubim, two of them, statue images of spiritual beings, indicating the spirit nature of the place, or as I have defined it, the realm of the first Eigen, the realm of spirit. The wings of the angels in the Solomon temple filled the whole room and overshadowed the box also called the Ark of the Covenant.

In the tabernacle the angels were attached to the box lid, and overshadowed the box lid. There was a small gap between the wings of the two angels above the Ark, so that the wings did not touch. There, God told Moses, God dwelt, in the gap between the wings, and there from that gap God spoke to Moses. Here then is a shadow picture of your spirit, your first Eigen, it too is of nothing, just like a gap. But the gap between angel wings, a representation of your spirit also, overshadows an ark box.

Let me suggest to you that this Ark Box is a representative picture shadow of your heart, your fourth Eigen inner essence being. The lid is a thick plate of pure gold indicating the absolute extreme value of your heart, the supreme importance of your heart. Inside the Ark Box, which is a picture shadow of what is inside the Christians heart, is first, the table of the law, the Ten Commandments. The prophet Jeremiah prophesied and wrote that in the last days, the days we are now in, and the Christian era, the laws of God would be written on the believer's heart. The Bible New Testament Book of Hebrews, chapter 8, quotes Jeremiah:

> "This is the covenant that I will make with the house of Israel:
> After those days says the Lord:
> I will put my laws into their minds,
> and I will write them on their hearts,
> and I will be their God,
> and they shall be my people,
> and they shall not teach everyone his fellow citizen,
> and everyone his brother, saying, "know the Lord",
> For all will know me,
> From the least to the greatest of them,
> For I will be merciful to their iniquities,
> and I will remember their sins no more."

Thus we have the new covenant promised by God. God writes his laws on our hearts.

The second thing inside the Ark Box was a golden jar of manna. Thus as we worship, God feeds our hearts with spiritual manna food. The Israelites in the wilderness were provided with manna food every day. Every day the Israelites went out from camp and gathered the manna from the ground for their daily food, but were not to gather on the Sabbath day, the day of rest. So we too will not gather daily manna food once we pass on and enter God's rest, but now our hearts are fed daily with spiritual food from God. When Jesus taught His disciples to pray, He taught them, "Give us this day our daily bread".

The third thing inside the box of the Ark was Aaron's stick of almond wood that budded. There was a disagreement among the Israelites as to why Aaron was chosen as high priest. Some disputed it so Moses had the leader of each Israelite tribe cut themselves rods of almond wood and they were all bundled together and placed before God. In the morning only Aaron's rod had budded, putting out leaves and almonds, proving that Aaron was chosen as High Priest. This stick being put in the Ark Box is a picture of being chosen, chosen by God. So you too, in your inner being, in your inner essence heart being, in your fourth Eigen, God has put evidence that you have been chosen by God. You belong to Him. You just know you belong to Him, your heart tells you, "I belong to Him."

Thus we have an astounding picture of the shadow image of man who was made in the image of God. There your heart, which is like a very, very valuable box, contains the law of God written in spiritual stone, spiritual daily manna food from God, and God provided evidence that God has chosen you to be His.

Around and above overshadowing this heart box is a room where there is a gap between angel wings. This is a place, a gap between the wings of your guardian angels, where your spirit, which was given to you by God, has a dwelling place, and communicates to your heart and your soul. And then there is a curtain that separates your spirit room from your soul room. The curtain indicates fuzzy filtered communication between your spirit and your soul, sometimes open and sometimes closed, sometimes with light from the lamp stand and sometimes not.

In the picture room of your soul is daily mental food for knowledge as indicated by the table of show bread, daily light to guide your path in life as indicated by the lamp stand, and daily communication through prayer to God as indicated by the altar of incense.

Then there is a curtain that separates your soul room from the real physical world outside where you are washed in regeneration as preparation for worship, and a sacrifice has been made to God on your behalf, of course, the precious life, body, and blood of your Savior, Jesus Christ.

What a beautiful astounding picture of the human life as it relates to God, and how your worship and knowing God is manifested.

In the days of the tabernacle use the priest was to go daily into the Holy Place to put in order the bread, and replenish the lamp oil and incense oil. Once a year the High Priest was to open the curtain to the Holy of Holies, taking the incense altar with him, taking a bowl of blood from the bull sacrifice, seeing by use of the light of the lamp stand, and sprinkle the Ark Box with blood from the animal sacrifice. The writer to the book of Hebrews in the Christian New Testament of the Bible explains this picture. (Please understand that these Biblical pictures often have several messages, meanings, and applications.)

The Writer of the Book of Hebrews in the Christian New Testament scripture tells us this tabernacle that Moses built is a representation, a shadow, not the real thing, of a Tabernacle in Heaven, in the eternities. In the Tabernacle of the Eternities, the High Priest, Jesus Christ, our Savior, once for all appeared and presented his blood in the Heavenly Holy of Holies and passed through the heavens sacrificing Himself for the forgiveness of the sins of his chosen ones. The Writer of the book tells us that is why the Old Testament Hebrew High Priest appeared only once a year in the inner room, the Holy of Holies, the Holy Spirit of God showing by this that the way into the Heavenly Holy of Holies was not yet open while the Old Testament Tabernacle was still standing or had standing. So, now that the Moses earthly tabernacle and subsequent temples are gone, having been destroyed, by Philistines, Babylonians, and Romans, and Jesus has appeared on the earth, and eternally offered his blood of the New Covenant in the Holy of Holies of the eternities, we believers in His Name are washed clean and forgiven of all of our sins, and made perfect before God, and now, therefore, belong to our faithful Savior Jesus Christ, and there is open access to our fourth Eigen inner being, our heart, into the Heavenly Holy of Holies in the eternities.

Stupendously astounding! Praise God! Praise you Jesus!

What an amazing picture. Jesus, a man just like us, yet fully God, God in the flesh, has become our High Priest, knowing all our weaknesses, has ascended and passed through the eternal Holy of Holies in the heavens and sprinkled his own eternal life giving blood on each one of our fourth Eigen hearts so as to make us perfect before God.

Here has just been laid out for you the amazing, powerful Christian Gospel, and an understanding of it was presented to you by an understanding of this Eigen theory I have been trying to communicate to you.

GLORY OF GOD

But let us go on and consider now additional evidence of our four Eigen functioning and existence. Let us consider some additional Biblical writings.

In the Bible are several descriptions of the Glory of God. Let's look at one of them. In the book of Revelations is a very interesting picture of the Glory of God. Since man was created in the image of God, let's look at this Glory of God in order to understand something of mankind.

The word picture painted by the Apostle John, who wrote the Book of Revelation, while in the spirit, looking into heaven, is that of a throne, high and lifted up, and one seated on the throne. Around the throne are creatures who do not cease to say,

"Holy, Holy, Holy is the Lord God, the almighty, who was and who is and who is to come", and, "Worthy are you, our Lord and our God to receive glory and honor and power, for you created all things and because of Your will they existed, and were created."

Before the throne appears the Lamb of God, slain since the foundations of the universe were laid. The Lamb has seven horns and seven eyes, which are the seven Spirits of God sent out into all the earth. This is, of course, Jesus Christ, the son of God Himself, the Godman.

Surrounding the Lamb are four living creatures, covered with eyes all around, which indicates they are very powerful spiritual beings. Surrounding the four living creatures are 24 elders, seated on thrones, clothed with white robes, holding harps and having gold crowns on their heads. Surrounding the 24 Elders are myriads and myriads of angels. In front of the throne is a multitude no man can number from every tribe, peoples, nations, and tongues, clothed in robes, washed white with the blood of the Lamb, with palm branches in their hands.

What are we to make of this picture? First, it is a picture of the gospel of Christ, the central tenant of the Christian religion. The multitude that no man can number are those men and women saved from destruction and judgment, washed clean of their sins by the blood of the Lamb, and have been ushered into eternal life to have fellowship with God by and through the Lamb, Jesus Christ, the manifestation of God Himself.

Similar pictures of the Glory of God are presented in the Old Testament scriptures. It seems that we can understand the meaning of thrones and elders and angels but what are and why the four creatures? These creatures have six wings like angels so they are powerful spiritual angelic like beings, but they are around the main throne and the Lamb.

Let me suggest to you that again we have a message about the four Eigens. John says that the first creature is like a lion, the second is like an ox or calf, the third has the face of a man, and the fourth is like a flying eagle. The lion is symbolic of one who rules, so I suggest to you representative of the inner essence ruling heart of a being, the fourth Eigen. The ox or calf is representative of the flesh or the Eigen of the real world of matter, energy, time, and space. The face of the man is representative of the operations of man's civilization, thinking, planning, the doings of mankind, all that takes place in the soul of mankind, in the imaginations of mankind. The flying eagle is representative of the spirit Eigen. The spirit moves about anywhere, seemingly effortlessly like a soaring eagle going about everywhere. These four creatures surrounding the throne indicate God rules supreme in all four Eigens. God not only rules over his creation, but rules supreme in the thoughts, minds and souls of mankind, and rules supreme in the spirit world and spirits of mankind, and rules supreme in the inner essence of mankind, their hearts.

As John watches this scene, the four creature beings call out four horses. The Lamb opens the seals of destiny, and as the first four seals are opened four horses with riders appear going forth. From the Old Testament scriptures we are told that horses represent messengers sent out to patrol the earth.

So the first creature, that of the lion, with a voice of thunder says, "come", and the white horse, a messenger, goes forth to conquer and conquering, the rider with a bow and crown. Later in the book of Revelations the white horse messenger is identified as an agent of the Kingdom of Jesus Christ, so the white horse messenger goes forth conquering, but I suggest to you that this conquering occurs in the fourth Eigen, that of the inner essence or heart of mankind. The white horse messenger is adding men and women to the Kingdom of Jesus Christ as it patrols the earth with its bow and crown, and it does this in the inner essence heart of mankind or what I call the fourth Life Eigen.

As the Lamb opens the second seal of destiny, the second creature, that like of an ox or calf calls, "come", and a red horse messenger goes out, the rider with a great sword, was granted to take peace from the earth, and that men would kill one another. Let me suggest to you that men killing one another occurs in the second Eigen, that of the flesh or the real physical world. Men have power to kill one another, to eliminate one another. The red horse messenger thus goes forth through the earth not only giving man power to kill each other but power to engage in all kinds of sinful, shameful acts to destroy one another. Men have power to corrupt themselves and become slaves of sin and corruption.

As the Lamb opens the third seal of destiny, the third living creature, that with the face of a man calls "come", and a black horse messenger goes forth and its rider has a scale in his hands and a voice in the center of the living creatures says, "A quart of wheat for a unit of money and three quarts of barley for a unit of money and do not damage the oil and the wine." Here we have trading transactions. Men trade with one another --- men making money and conducting business affairs and men cheating and taking advantage of one another, and stealing and defrauding one another. This happens in the third Eigen, that of the soul, that of the mind, will, and emotions -- again, a source of corruption of mankind.

As the Lamb opens the fourth seal of destiny, the fourth living creature, the creature like a flying eagle, says with a voice, "come", and an ashen horse or pale horse messenger goes forth; the rider has the name of, "death", and Hades following with him. Hades is the place of the dead, or the abode of the dead, and the spirits of the dead are what is in Hades. Authority was given to the ashen horse rider to kill with sword, famine, pestilence, and wild beasts. As men die of sundry causes their spirits are collected in Hades.

Let me suggest to you that ultimate death is death of the spirit, the second death as described later in John's book of Revelation. So in this Eigen, that of the spirit, ultimate death occurs.

So here again in this astounding vast picture of the Glory of God there seems to appear the four Eigens as I have suggested them. God's Glory and Power has four aspects to it, as the four living creatures that surround the throne would indicate. Man created in the image of God also has four aspects to him or her, four Eigens as I would have you understand, four modes of your life, four integrated partitions of your life, four functional relationships in your life, four Life Eigens.

So here understand a little of the whole picture. The Lamb opens the seals of destiny, the four living creatures that serve God call out messengers that go forth into the earth. The messengers in their respective function of their Eigens have power to conquer, have power to take peace from the earth, have power to enable men and women to conduct affairs and business, and have power to kill.

Here it seems we have all of the human experience in perspective. Men and women live lives in the flesh, eating, sleeping, consuming, suffering corruption and degradation, and historically have spent much time killing one another. They trade with one another and some become rich and acquire goods and honor through civilization and competition. They enjoy beauty and become puffed up and proud. They write books, engage in intellectual pursuits, and indulge in the arts. In all of this the spirit of God here and there enters into the spirits of sundry men and women, cleans and purifies their hearts, and they come to acknowledge God and to love God. It all seems to be a huge stage play where each one seeks out each one's own destiny. Some choose to be washed clean by the blood of the Lamb and join the multitude before the throne, and others sink into the oblivion of their sins. Some emerge as that multitude before the throne in white robes of righteousness in eternal fellowship with the Lamb, and others are left in Hades for the ultimate destruction of their spirits on the day of the final judgment.

That is it! That is the human condition! Yes indeed! Oui! Oui! Oui!

I hope I have convinced you that you are a complex four fold person, functioning in four realms, in four Eigens as I have defined them. The scriptural evidence is overwhelming. Man functions in four Eigens.

Let's sum up the application of the Eigen concept and how the concept applies to living one's life. One of the reasons the term Eigen was coined was that the word eigen has been used in mathematical physical science as in the term eigenfunction. So Eigen can be thought of as a term for functional relationships. Thus the four Eigens of life can be understood in how the totality of life functions, and that man has four functional interacting complexities in the operations of his or her life.

Consider now then your heart, what herein has been called your fourth Eigen. Your heart is defined to be your essential inner essence being. The direction of your life, the form, quality, and quantity of your life is set within and comes out of your heart. Your heart is your essential inner you so out of this heart comes the manifestation of the essential you. Your fourth Eigen heart functions to give overall direction and quality to your life. Remember from the tabernacle illustration that your heart is located in the room of your spirit, in the tabernacle called the Holy of Holies, in a golden box with a thick solid gold lid overshadowed by your spirit. It was intended from the beginning that God's spirit is to have an effective presence there within your spirit. But now in the contrary corrupted fallen human state, there is the presence of the spirits of sundry demons, whores, gigolos, and what not that you have invited or allowed to have a presence within your spirit.

Remember what God said of mankind before the flood, and restated after the world was destroyed by the flood,

"The thoughts of men's hearts are only evil continually."

What are the thoughts of your heart? Let your mind examine your heart. That is probably the most important thing your mind can ever do.

Now consider your spirit and why there is a distinction between your heart and your spirit. The primary purpose of your First Eigen spirit is to hold God's Spirit. But also your spirit can hold and then be influenced by, or be even controlled, by other spirits, such as even evil spirits. It is possible for your heart and mind to direct your spirit to only hold God's Spirit and not any evil spirits. This is very important and can only be accomplished by prayer, that is by asking God to rid your spirit of all evil spirits, and that only the pure and holy Spirit of God be present in your spirit. This is mysterious and it is not obvious how this comes about. God's Spirit interacts with your spirit and the overshadowing of your spirit with God's Spirit on to your heart brings about this interaction so that God's Spirit is deposited within your spirit by interaction and commitment from your heart.

God promised Moses that the hearts of the Hebrews and their descendants would be circumcised; meaning that the filthy corrupted part of the reformed and rededicated Hebrew's heart would be cut off, so that the heart of the Hebrew could respond to the prompting of the Spirit of God. The great apostle of Christianity, the apostle Paul, said the Christian's heart is cleansed or renewed by God when a person becomes a believer in Jesus Christ. This cleansed and purified heart then also can respond to God's Spirit and facilitate the deposit of God's Spirit into the spirit of the Christian.

342

The apostle Paul says that each Christian's spirit is built with other Christian spirits into a spiritual edifice, like stones which are built up into a massive building, with Jesus Christ as the chief spiritual cornerstone. This is indeed none other than the temple of God. So your spirit becomes part of the temple of God, and God Himself dwells within you! Yes, God then dwells within your spirit.

One of the activities of your spirit is to provide motivation. In some complex way that is unfathomable to understand, the Spirit of God moves into the spirit of a man, and the man is then motivated and given strength to accomplish tasks in the real world. And, of course, in the contrast, like humankind before the flood, when God said,

"The thoughts of man's heart are only evil continually."

Evil motivations also come out of the spirit directed by the thoughts of the heart, and these result in evil thinking and then evil deeds. And, of course, Satan's captives produce evil continuously.

The function of the third Eigen soul is to process the intents and thoughts of the heart and to provide the thinking, planning, and commitment of life, so as to provide implementation. The soul takes these thoughts of the heart of the man and puts wheels under them. The soul, of course, directs these actions. Just like as God said of man before humankind, (except for Noah and his family), was destroyed by the flood, so the evil intent of the heart results in evil motivations of the spirit, and then evil thinking and then evil deeds, producing a community of people that so grieved God that they had to be destroyed.

The function of the body, your second Eigen, is to provide a home and place for existence of your soul within the universe. The body is composed of flesh and blood and is nourished by food and absorbs, grows, and so provides for the existence of the soul. The needs of the body - food, and the satisfaction of sundry drives of the body, are inputted to the soul so that in the thinking and planning done by the soul, the soul seeks to satisfy these needs of the body.

Consider now in sequence the progression of how the Life Eigens must dominate your committed Christian life. Consider first the opposite where the flesh dominates.

When you let life in the flesh, your second Eigen life, the Eigen of the real world and the body, dominate your life, then the needs and demands of the body dominate your whole existence. You live to eat, you constantly search for promiscuous women or if you are a woman, search for men that will give you protection and pleasure, and ignore the consequences. You search for and participate in anything that gives you bodily pleasure, and you hope satisfaction. The cries, demands, and needs of the body connect to your soul, so that your soul life is only to meet the needs, cries, and demands of the body.

Greed and the search for wealth and money or power over others occupy your thoughts. Everything you plan has the purpose of acquiring more wealth, property, or power. Thoughts and schemes are generated so that you even create secure places where you can hide money and assets from spouse, and family or business partners or your employer. You even entertain thoughts of taking advantage of friends and family.

Your soul hardly knows you have a spirit, and your attitudes and motivations are captured from your spirit by your soul, and are then determined by your soul, which then become servant to the body's demands. And your spirit, which came from God, completely ignores God, and your fourth Eigen, your loving life with God in your inner being, does not even hardly exist. Again, so with you, like God said about mankind before the flood, "Every intent of the thoughts of his heart is only evil continually."

The consequence of such a life is death. Not only in the age to come but death starts here and now. Slowly your life becomes boring as you search for more and more pleasure and you are not satisfied. Eventually, nothing satisfies you. Your life becomes more miserable as you realize that your expectations are never going to be satisfied. You fight the consequences of your actions and behavior and you start dying before your time. Death pervades your whole existence and you wonder why you are still alive, and you wonder what the purpose of your life is. With some, it comes to wishing he or she were dead. This is life dominant in the second Eigen, that of the body of flesh, it leads to death.

The contrary existence, life in abundance as Jesus calls it, which leads to eternal life, is to have as the goal of your life to maximize life in your fourth Eigen, that of the life of God within you, within your inner essence being, your life of love. Your four Eigen life will have an eternal perspective. Life in four Eigens is all about love. God is love and you must become love. You love God intensely, you love Jesus Christ intensely, you love the Holy Spirit intensely, and you love your fellow humans, because how can you love God who you have not seen if you cannot love your neighbor who you have seen? This fourth Eigen functional heart dimension of your complete life is to dominate everything.

Remember the tabernacle shadow picture of what you as a child of God possess within your fourth Eigen heart inner essence; first, manna sustenance from God given daily, second, principles from God as to how to live your life, and third, evidence from God that you are His and belong to Him, that you have been chosen by Him. So, of course, he loves you intensely.

A very important sequence is that this fourth Eigen heart which loves must give loving input to your first Eigen, your spirit. Fourth Eigen love flows out into to your first Eigen spirit so that the functions of your spirit – faith, motivations, attitudes, and holding God's Spirit, reflect the love you are passing up from your fourth Eigen inner essence heart. Your spirit overshadows your inner essence being so your inner essence heart partnerships with your spirit and both become dominated by love. Your motivations will then reflect love and your attitudes will then reflect love.

Your first Eigen spirit then directed by your fourth Eigen heart must dominate and control your soul, your third Eigen. This third Eigen, your soul, is your mind, will, and emotions. So your heart and spirit are dominate over your soul so that love is reflected in your mind will and emotions. You control yourself so that you think loving thoughts. Your will, which is your plans and programs you intend to carry out, reflects love, love of God and love of your fellows. Your emotions, which may start as a physical stimulus from your body, are controlled in short order by your mind, so that your emotions are under control. You must not let your emotions get out of control so that you commit foolish acts. You must get your thinking process in control of your emotions. Discipline yourself so that anger, wrath, envy, jealousy, and other mind type emotions are under the control of your thinking mind and not your mind being controlled by your emotions.

Your mind, will, and emotions, which are your soul, your third Eigen, must control your body, your second Eigen. This is very important in that this final step, where your soul controls the acts of your body, which are manifested in the real physical world where family, friends, relatives, and the citizens of the world, are watching you.

If you have that correct sequence so that your fourth Eigen love from the heart or inner being, communicates love to your first Eigen spirit, which then dominates your third Eigen soul, which dominates your second Eigen body, which is then manifested to the world, then you are a witness to the work of God who is living within you, at home with you in your spirit. You become a very, very, very lovely creature. People, whom God has also destined to become loving people, will observe you and want to become like you, for they will see what they deep down inside themselves, want for themselves.

Not everybody will respond to the beauty of character they see in you. Many, many people are captives of that enemy of us all, Satan himself. Remember that the scriptures teach that the wicked are a ransom for the righteous. Thus Satan's captives belong to him and, therefore, they are hopelessly lost to him, and you are freed from Satan's control because there is a ransom, and the ransom has been PAID. Thus do not look down upon Satan's captives or think you are better than they are, because you are not. Only by God's grace are you not among Satan's captives. But Jesus has bound Satan so that many can come to know God like you have come to know God. So be a very faithful witness in the world so that many, many others also can come to know God like you have. So live your life in your body as a sacrifice to God, being a faithful, true, beautiful, very loving, witness for the work of God in your life.

Well, I have given you the results of a lifetime of interaction with God, and of how I came to know God and to deeply love God.

Now that I have given you an understanding of the Eigen Theory, let us go on to some applications for living our lives.

TWELVE

THE SPIRIT WALK OF LIFE

I present to you the Christian walk of life and how the Christian interacts with other Christians and the world. First, however, I want to consider a little more of our first Eigen, our spirits, which was initiated in the last chapter.

Our spirits are transcendent, that is, are not part of the created universe with its characteristics of time, space, matter, and energy. Our spirits are a thing of God which God gave to you to make you a person. The basic principle from the scriptures is that the intent of God was that our spirits were primarily meant to hold God's Spirit. But with the complete free agency God also gave to man, this intent has been corrupted so that spirits of men can also hold spirits of demonic powers.

Christians are built by the power of Jesus Christ into a huge edifice of spiritual stones that make up the spiritual temple of God, the Almighty, the one and only God. Jesus himself is the chief cornerstone of this temple.

The human spirit is like a cup or other kind of vessel meant to hold God's Spirit. In the records of the Old Testament of the Bible, in the historical record of the Hebrews, many accounts are given where a person is filled with the Spirit of God and then enabled to carry out difficult tasks in the real world. Examples are King Saul, King David, Samson, Gideon, and others.

The Spirit of wisdom was given to those who originally built the tabernacle in the wilderness after coming out of Egypt with all of its intricate design and uniqueness. The Spirit of Moses is placed on the 70 elders that are to govern with him. The Spirit of God came upon Balaam when he was hired by the Moabites to curse the Hebrews but instead was moved by the Spirit to bless the Hebrews. Joshua was filled with the spirit of wisdom when he was commissioned to conquer the land of Canaan.

The Spirit of the Lord came upon Othniel the son of Kenaz, as he judged Israel and went out to war. The Lord then gave Cushan-rishathaim king of Mesopotamia into his hand, so that he prevailed over him. Cyrus king of Persia, in order to fulfill the word of the Lord by the mouth of Jeremiah the prophet, the Lord stirred up Cyrus' spirit, so that he sent a proclamation throughout all his kingdom returning the Hebrews to Palestine. There are lots of examples like these where the Spirit of God moved into the spirit of a man, and then the man was motivated to do great things.

In the book of Job it says,

> "But it is a spirit in man, the breath of the Almighty that gives him understanding."

Yes, that is it. The spirit of man gives him understanding.

Isaiah, in the prophecy concerning the coming Messiah says,

> "The Spirit of the Lord will rest on Him,
> The spirit of wisdom and understanding,
> The spirit of counsel and strength,
> The spirit of knowledge and the fear of the LORD."

And,

> "It will come about after this:
> That I will pour out My Spirit on all mankind;
> And your sons and daughters will prophesy,
> Your old men will dream dreams,
> Your young men will see visions."

And in another place,

"Thus declares the Lord who stretches out the heavens, lays the foundation of the earth, and forms the spirit of man within him."

(As a comment here, how could Isaiah possibly know that the Inflationary Big Bang Theory, the theory that most present day physicists accept as correct for the beginning and design of the universe, say that space was and is being stretched out and now scientific observations have proved without much doubt that space is still being continually stretched out? The accuracy and time invariant scope of the Hebrew Christian scriptures is simply astounding.)

In another place,

"I will pour out on the house of David and on the inhabitants of Jerusalem, the spirit of grace and of supplication, so that they will look on Me whom they have pierced; and they will mourn for Him, as one mourns for an only son, and they will weep bitterly over Him like the bitter weeping over a firstborn."

Given these quotes it becomes understood that God's Spirit moves into that of a man and can drive the man's being to do great tasks or give him spiritual insight or understanding to do great things. In some very interesting way that is unfathomable to understand, the Spirit of God moves into the spirit of a man, and the man is then motivated and given strength to accomplish tasks in the real world.

The cup of the spirit concept implies that a man's spirit cup can be added to by sundry other inputs so the spirit cup is partially filled by sundry spirits as the need arises.

In the New Testament Christian era the Spirit of God also acts within mankind. In the book of Corinthians we read:

"Now there are varieties of gifts, but the same Spirit. And there are varieties of ministries, and the same Lord. There are varieties of effects, but the same God who works all things in all. But to each one is given the manifestation of the Spirit for the common good. For to one is given the word of wisdom through the Spirit, and to another the word of knowledge according to the same Spirit; to another faith by the same Spirit, and to another gifts of healing by the one Spirit, and to another the effecting of miracles, and to another prophecy, and to another the distinguishing of spirits, to another sundry kinds of tongues, and to another the interpretation of tongues. But one and the same Spirit works all these things, distributing to each one individually just as He wills."

Thus here we have a little understanding of how God's Spirit interacts with a man, and of course, a woman.

Another quote,

"For even as the body is one and has many members, and all the members of the body, though they are many, are one body, so also is Christ. For by one Spirit we were all baptized into one body, whether Jews or Greeks, whether slaves or free, and we were all made to drink of one Spirit."

And,

"Now may the God of peace Himself sanctify you entirely; and may your spirit and soul and body be preserved complete, without blame at the coming of our Lord Jesus Christ. Faithful is He who calls you, and He also will bring it to pass."

And one more quote:

"Now the deeds of the flesh are evident, which are: immorality, impurity, sensuality, idolatry, sorcery, enmities, strife, jealousy, outbursts of anger, disputes, dissensions, factions, envying, drunkenness, carousing, and things like these, of which I forewarn you, just as I have forewarned you, that those who practice such things will not inherit the kingdom of God. But the fruit of the Spirit is love, joy, peace, patience, kindness, goodness, faithfulness, gentleness, self-control; against such things there is no law."

Let us now proceed from this understanding that God's Spirit within us can enable men and women to accomplish great tasks to the consideration of the contrary to this, that is, the absorption of evil spirits which can destroy the life of the man or woman.

In this account, it has been presented that our spirits are like a cup, meant to hold God's Spirit, and also generated has been the understanding that the sexual act between a man and a woman in some mysterious way provides for union between the man and the woman. So like their bodies, their spirits and their souls become entwined, and that through the sexual act, in some spiritual process we do not understand, the man's spirit becomes part of the woman's spirit, or the cup of the man's spirit receives part of the woman's spirit, and the woman's spirit becomes part of the man's spirit, as also the cup of the woman's spirit receives part of the man's spirit.

So, here we have discovered the essential reason why the law of God so strongly condemns fornication and adultery. As each human violates these prohibitions, that human adds to his or her spirit little pieces of each spirit he or she collects along the way. Each, prostitute, each one night stand, each drunken encounter, each affair, each promiscuous encounter, the spirit of the other is added to his or her spirit. Eventually, as perhaps sexual encounters multiply, there seems very little room for God's Spirit. The guilt becomes so overwhelming, and the conscience becomes so callused, that the human finds it very difficult to come to know God, so that God's Spirit could indeed be even added to his or her spirit.

In consequence, that human becomes very hardened, and comes to oppose God in everything he or she can conceive. They are want to become the enemies of God and come to hate God. They eventually become irrational in their hatred of God and become captives of Satan, that evil being whose goal is death for as many men and women as possible.

This partially explains the mystery of why advocates of free love and sexual promiscuity, seem so adamantly, irrationally, opposed to God, whereas, other sinner types who oppose the law of God, such as thieves and murderers, seldom seem to become those in violent opposition to God and of Jesus, God's goals and programs.

God's Spirit within me keeps evil spirits out of me. The most effective prayer I ever made was to ask God to prevent all evil spirits from witnessing to me or influencing me. My prayer was that only God's pure and Holy Spirit was to witness to me. It worked. I was no longer confused as to what to do in very difficult situations.

As has been discussed, in the sexual act between a man and a woman, in some spiritual way we do not understand, the woman's spirit becomes part of the man's spirit and the man's spirit becomes part of the woman's spirit.

Consider then the terrible results of fornication. As a result of a sexual encounter the woman's spirit is added to your spirit, or the man's spirit is added to your spirit if you are a woman. Can you imagine the consequences of a whore's spirit being added to your spirit? Every evil spirit that ever entered into that whore, because of performing some sexual act, can now have access to your spirit. Can your bosom take on evil after evil and not be become evil itself? No way! The scriptures say the whore's path leads to death and destruction, and her path leads you down into hell itself.

Can promiscuous sex with college or work friends or a pick up at a bar be any different? You do not know what kind and how many sexual partners he or she may have had. Evil spirits may have been collected from sundry places and now they have access to you, to your spirit. If you absorb evil spirits in some sexual play how can you keep out other additional evil spirits invited into you by the evil spirit that came to live within you?

Demons, another name for evil spirits, now by extension become manifested in your life as insanities and irrational thinking. These demon insanities have access to you, and you can start down the path to insanity yourself. Indeed, fornication is terribly destructive.

Understand that the Apostle Paul's imperative for the Christian believer is there are only two choices, (1) complete chastity, or (2) one man and one woman in paired monogamous marriage. He received this command from Jesus Himself, who quoted the book of Genesis where Jesus said:

> "In the beginning the Creator, God, made them male and female, and said, "A man shall leave his parents and be joined unto his wife, and they shall become one flesh". So they are no longer two, but one. Therefore, what God has joined together, let not man separate."

The Christian Scriptures say to the believer:

> "You are a temple of God and the Spirit of God dwells in you. If any man destroys the temple of God, God will destroy him, for the temple of God is holy, and that is what you are."

We must take these warnings very seriously. The Scriptures also say:

"Christ Jesus Himself being the cornerstone, in whom the whole building, being fitted together, is growing into a holy temple in the Lord, in whom you also are being built together into a dwelling of God in the Spirit."

Continuing another quote:

"You are not in the flesh but in the Spirit, if indeed the Spirit of God dwells in you. But if anyone does not have the Spirit of Christ, he does not belong to Him. If Christ is in you, though the body is dead because of sin, yet the spirit is alive because of righteousness. But if the Spirit of Him who raised Jesus from the dead dwells in you, He who raised Christ Jesus from the dead will also give life to your mortal bodies through His Spirit who dwells in you."

Another statement of Jesus Himself is:

"He who overcomes, I will make him a pillar in the temple of God, and he will not go out from it anymore; and I will write on him the name of God, and the name of the city of God, the new Jerusalem, which comes down out of heaven from God, and My new name. He, who has an ear, let him hear what the Spirit says."

What marvelous statements of our life in the spirit as part of the temple of God the Almighty.

In this our life in our bodies we must walk according to God's Spirit. For with the Spirit of the life of Jesus Christ, we are free from the condemnation of sin and death. God sent His son, the only begotten of God, of the same substance as God, to be condemned as sin in the body of His flesh, so that we who walk according to God's Spirit are free from sin and death. We are free. We have received life eternal. So, to sum up, the Spirit of Him who raised Jesus from the dead, dwelling and living within your spirit, gives eternal life to your mortal body.

THE WALK OF LIFE

Let us now look into our walk of life on earth and how you will interact with God - this God who made you and wants fellowship with you.

The Christian's walk in life begins with the gift of faith. This can begin in a number of ways - perhaps a huge disappointment, such as your spouse running off, bad financial decisions which have left you devastated, or a close call with death. Perhaps you needed to grieve or have been grieving for a while. Perhaps someone who has been very close to you passes away. Maybe your mind just got you to thinking, and you just wanted to find out more about God. Maybe one day you remembered Bible stories from Sunday school when you were a child. Whatever the event, within you, your soul and your spirit, are restless, searching. Then you hear the Gospel of the Lord Jesus preached, perhaps over the radio, or a friend takes you to church or a friend or even a stranger encounters you and tells you the gospel of Jesus, or perhaps you just started reading the Bible. Whatever the event or the psychological reflections of the event, your mind asks you, "What is the purpose of my life, or why am I living". The event causes you to stop and think. All of a sudden your inner essential self, in the scriptures called heart, tells you there is God.

Whatever the stimulation; you now come to understand and believe there is God. This is the gift of faith manifested in your heart from within your spirit. Eventually you will understand that God is seeking you and He found you, and you responded, and you believe. This is faith. Understand that Jesus, a man like you, yet very God of very God, is the person of the Godhead, through the Spirit of God, seeking you.

Peter, the leader of Jesus' apostles, wrote a marvelous book in the Bible that tells us what to do with the faith we have been given. Faith begins and develops in your first Eigen, the Eigen life of your spirit. Your inner self, your heart, through your spirit, by the prompting of the Spirit of God, tells you God is real, and though you do not completely understand, God's love overshadows you, and you start to understand in some very subtle way God is seeking fellowship with you. You respond and you believe.

Peter's book describes a progression of qualities to be added to your faith, and Peter says to pursue them diligently. He says to be diligent to first add to your faith moral virtue. God is revealing Himself to you and God is the God of love and truth. God wants you to be morally good. You may be in the depth of moral degradation, full of sin and disgusted with yourself, or maybe you have lived such a life of sin it is hard to even know what moral virtue is. It does not matter. It matters not into what depth of sin you have fallen. You must now read and understand God's law and listen to God judgments on sin and wrong doing and resolve within yourself that you will reject sin, and you want to live a morally good life.

So you repent. You do this in your mind. Carrying out this mental commitment to moral virtue in the real world sometimes is very difficult, but do not give up regardless of your ongoing mistakes. God will gently help you regardless of your past. This carrying out of this mental commitment happens in the third Eigen, the life of the soul, which includes the mind, will, and emotions. You make up your mind and decide to be committed to moral virtue.

All sin begins in the mind. You see a woman and lust after her, or if you are a woman you envy and desire some other person's husband to look after you and take care of you and give you pleasure. You observe some wealth or property and you want it. Sometimes you may be seized with anger and want to damage someone severely. Perhaps they have done you wrong and you think they need chastising. Or you envy someone. All this occurs in your soul which is the mind, will, and emotions, your third Eigen. Therefore, your soul needs to take control, and put a stop to such thinking. This is the process of adding moral virtue to your life; it is done in your mind. Peter says to do that diligently.

Peter says the next thing to do in this progression is to add knowledge to your moral virtue. That is, to study or try to understand God's laws and the nature of God, and how God interacts with mankind. We are to diligently add to our moral virtue, knowledge. Knowledge includes the understanding of God's purpose for your life, studying how God interacts with people and how God instructs people. Knowledge and understanding are vast things to be accumulated. Our primary source of knowledge about God is the Bible and God's created universe. Real sincere Christian brothers and sisters, pastors, and priests, are also a source of knowledge and understanding. In our age there are books without end. Tremendous amount of knowledge is available to you. Knowledge, like moral virtue occurs in the soul, your third Eigen, the Eigen life of the soul. Wisdom is a product of knowledge, applying knowledge so as to live life skillfully.

Peter then says to diligently add to your knowledge, self-control. Self-control essentially means that your mind controls what you do. When you are provoked, or disturbed by some event, you do not respond with anger that leads to rage, or envy, or anything else that leads you to verbally or physically damage someone. Especially, this is true with children. Children can be quite damaged by thoughtless words or blows that were undeserved. Self-control means your mind takes over your emotions after a short interval, so that you do not let yourself sin in your anger or envy or other emotion. Again, self-control takes place in the soul, your third Eigen - your Eigen Three life is in your soul, which consists of your mind, will, and emotions.

Peter then says to diligently add perseverance to your self-control. Perseverance is to be consistent in your responses, to act in the real world steadily and work at being consistent in your responses. This occurs in the second Eigen, the real physical world, or the realm of the body. It means to go ahead steadily, do not wavier in your consistency, and practice your Christian life consistently. Practice your moral virtue, accumulation of knowledge, and self-control consistently. Practice this so that you have a consistent response in the real physical world, the world of the second Eigen.

Now Peter says to add godliness to your perseverance, and do it diligently. Godliness means to act in this world the way God would act. Godliness means to take on the character of God. Study Jesus' responses to events or words in His life; how He interacted with people; there is your example of Godliness.

The last of the Eigen two real world attributes that Peter says to add diligently to Godliness is brotherly kindness. That word really does not need any explaining. Brotherly kindness is really just kindness to everybody, especially Christian brothers and sisters. Being kind to the unlovable or difficult to love people is sometimes very hard. Yet Christians are called upon by God, here through the words of Peter, to be kind, especially to one another fellow Christians. Kindness makes for a happy life. Treating other people with kindness usually results in them treating you with kindness. And when we get treated with kindness and respect it seems to create in us a sense of self-worth feeding our happiness. Yes, treat everybody with kindness so that they too are encouraged in their Christian faith, or an unbeliever may observe your kindness and is attracted to it and seeks to find out from you what is the reason for your kindness and may then discover that you are a Christian, and then seek to become a Christian himself or herself.

The last of Peter's progression is love. Peter says to diligently add to brotherly kindness love. Let me suggest to you that the love that Peter is talking about occurs in the fourth Eigen, our life with God. This is the life in our most inner being, called our heart, or the very center of our being, the heart of our being. We are commanded by God to love God with all our heart, soul, strength, and spirit, and our neighbor as our self. God is love. And we are to live with God in love, love here in this life, and love throughout eternity. This means that our fourth Eigen love in our hearts is to dominate our whole being and this love permeates down to our spirits, and to our souls, and then our physical life of real action in the real world.

When this, our fourth Eigen, called the heart, dominates our life and especially our life with God, we are filled with love. Then this fourth Eigen heart life dominates the third Eigen soul and fills our soul with love. Our attitudes and motivations within our spirits fed from our hearts then reflect love. Our minds, wills, and emotions reflect love and so with our souls in control of our bodies, we act with love in the real world of the second Eigen, doing deeds of love in our physical life on the Earth.

Now that I have given you the Eigen concept as applied by Peter, let's proceed to how to achieve love in all of our life, in our foursome functional existence, that is, in all of our four Eigen existence.

FEEDING ON JESUS

Jesus gives us some astounding words on how we are to feed upon him, to feed upon his life. He wants us to feed upon Him, the fruit from the Tree of Life, so that we will not die, and instead have eternal life. I want to quote Jesus at some length to give you an understanding of what Jesus commands the Christian to do. The scripture quotes I give you are from the New American Standard version of the Bible, used here by permission.

359

Jesus said, as recorded in the book of John:

> "Truly, truly, I say to you, unless you eat the flesh of the Son of Man and drink His blood, you have no life in yourselves. He who eats My flesh and drinks My blood has eternal life, and I will raise him up on the last day. For My flesh is true food, and My blood is true drink. He who eats My flesh and drinks My blood abides in Me, and I in him. As the living Father sent Me, and I live because of the Father, so he who eats Me, he also will live because of Me. This is the bread which came down out of heaven; not as the fathers ate and died; he who eats this bread will live forever."

Jesus is not talking about cannibalism here, but about inner food, inner sustenance that which we are meant to live upon. We are to absorb Jesus. This is a metaphor for living on Jesus' body, soul, spirit, heart. The scriptures say, "Have the mind of Christ" We are to absorb the mind, will, and emotions of Jesus. We are to absorb Jesus, absorb his motivations, and absorb the attitudes of Jesus. We are to absorb Jesus, just like our bodies absorb the bread and the wine when we partake of Christian communion. That is a ceremony when Christians remember Jesus death and resurrection. We are to absorb Jesus' love and life into our hearts.

Jesus explains that the process is analogous to his own relationship to the Father. He lived by feeding on the Father, and we are to live by feeding on Jesus. As He told his disciples in the upper room, before his death through crucifixion,

> "I in you and you in Me."

God gets our attention when we fall into what some call a wilderness experience. For those of you maybe not familiar with the use of the term, some examples of a wilderness experience might be when you lose all of your lifetime accumulated assets, or when your wife out of the blue changes the locks on your home and files divorce papers on you, or when your husband says he is leaving for another woman, or when you suddenly acquire an incurable disease that debilitates you, or when you get falsely accused of some crime and you are not able to defend yourself or prove your innocence. There are lots of other wilderness experiences and what the Bible calls trials and tribulations, some are not nearly as bad as those listed above, and some are worse.

God puts us in wilderness experiences where we seemingly cannot cope, in order to humble us, so that we might learn not to trust in our own resources, but to depend on God. I have found that the quickest way to become humble is to be thoroughly humiliated, which happened more than a few times in my life. Therefore, if you are a Christian, but pride rules, have self-pride in your life, wait a while; God will have you humiliated. God resists the proud but gives grace to the humble. If you need it, God will certainly humble you.

The 5000 or so men plus women and children to whom Jesus during His ministry on earth miraculous fed bread and fish by the Lake of Galilee in Palestine, followed after Jesus the next day around the lake to find Jesus, because, as Jesus said to them:

"You were fed and you want to eat some more."

Some of these people reminded Jesus that Moses fed everybody in the wilderness with manna, a miraculous food, so Jesus should now feed everybody too, to just prove that He is just as great a prophet as Moses. Just think, no more work, no more scratching in the earth to grow food. Jesus please, just gives it to us. Just give us food, they told Jesus, like Moses did, and we will make you King. Jesus reminds them that it was not Moses but God who gave the manna food to their fathers.

After Jesus had told them these words, they say:

"Lord, give us this food."

Jesus answers and says to them:

"I am the bread of life; he who comes to Me will not hunger, and he who believes in Me will never thirst. But I said to you that you have seen Me, and yet do not believe. All that the Father gives Me will come to Me, and the one who comes to Me I will certainly not cast out. For I have come down from heaven, not to do My own will, but the will of Him who sent Me. This is the will of Him who sent Me, that of all that He has given Me I lose nothing, but raise it up on the last day. For this is the will of My Father, that everyone who beholds the Son and believes in Him will have eternal life, and I Myself will raise him up on the last day."

When those people heard what Jesus said they started to grumble.

> "Yesterday He fed us, but today He is not going to give us anything to eat."

He says we must eat him! Come on, he is a man like us; we know his father and mother. How could He come down from heaven?

> "Therefore the Jews were grumbling about Him, because He said, I am the bread that came down out of heaven. They were saying, is not this Jesus, the son of Joseph, whose father and mother we know? How does He now say, 'I have come down out of heaven'? Jesus answered and said to them, Do not grumble among yourselves. No one can come to Me unless the Father who sent Me draws him; and I will raise him up on the last day. It is written in the prophets, 'And they shall all be taught of God.' Everyone who has heard and learned from the Father comes to Me. Not that anyone has seen the Father, except the One who is from God; He has seen the Father. Truly, truly, I say to you, he who believes has eternal life. I am the bread of life. Your fathers ate the manna in the wilderness, and they died. This is the bread which comes down out of heaven, so that one may eat of it and not die. I am the living bread that came down out of heaven; if anyone eats of this bread, he will live forever; and the bread also which I will give for the life of the world is My flesh."

After those words of Jesus, those people who heard Him started an argument:

> "How can we eat him? How can this man give us His flesh to eat?"

So Jesus said to them:

> "Truly, truly, I say to you, unless you eat the flesh of the Son of Man and drink His blood, you have no life in yourselves. He who eats My flesh and drinks My blood has eternal life, and I will raise him up on the last day. For My flesh is true food, and My blood is true drink. He who eats My flesh and drinks My blood abides in Me, and I in him. As the living Father sent Me, and I live because of the Father, so he who eats Me, he also will live because of Me. This is the bread which came down out of heaven; not as the fathers ate and died; he who eats this bread will live forever."

After these words of Jesus, then the disciples of Jesus grumbled. Some disciples leave and will not follow him anymore. The twelve, those later who became apostles, who were then also disciples of Jesus, do not leave. The apostle Peter, says you, Jesus, are the Christ, You are the Holy One of God, the Son of the living God. You have words of eternal life.

What decision will you make? Are you feeding on Jesus, assimilating Jesus? Do all the Eigens of your life, your life functions, seek to absorb Jesus? Do you try to live your life in the flesh as Jesus would? Do you try to think good thoughts and dream good dreams as Jesus would? Do you examine your attitudes and motivations to see if they are assimilating Jesus attitudes and motivations?

Jesus has promised the Holy Spirit to those who ask. By far, the most important step in this whole Jesus assimilating process is to ask God for the life of Jesus to come into you. Ask Him to send His Holy Spirit to come into your spirit and witness to your spirit. Ask Him to feed your four functional Eigen being with His life. He will not deny you. He will work on you from the inside out.

To this point I have instructed you in the basic tenants of the Christian life and how you are to live life. Let us now take up the subject of living in the real world with other people.

LIFE IN THE WORLD

The Christian scriptures say we are to fellowship with other believers. As we associate with other believers we come into contact with organized religion. As our lives encounter organized religion we encounter real severe testing of our faith, our walk of life, and its associated problems. I want to share with you an incredible insight which I believe will help lead you to life eternal, and avoid the snares and pitfalls of the Devil who seeks your destruction through organized religion. What I present to you in the following I have found to be extremely important, and what was in fact the prime turning moment in my life when I really started to come to know and trust God. I first heard the beginnings of these ideas from a brilliant, young, very thoroughly thoughtful, very humble student of the Bible. He since then has gone on to bigger, more acclaimed academic pursuits.

For about forty years I have thought about and applied his profound insights. I now present many of his own words to you with my modifications and development along with some application of these ideas.

Jesus severely warned his disciples and through them you and me about the leaven of hypocrisy of leaders who put themselves in spiritual authority over us. During Jesus days on earth they were called Scribes and Pharisees, but in our day they are Christian leaders, such as Elders, Deacons, Priests, Bishops, Pastors, Ministers, and yes, even Popes. One might even extend these principles to our national political leaders. Hypocrisy is an evil deceptive thing. This race of men of ours loves lies and hypocrisy. It has been said that the art of governing is the art of lying. All really successful political leaders of men are very good at lying. Jesus hates lying. Jesus said, "I am the truth and the light." Let's take a look at hypocrisy.

Hypocrisy has four forms. Let's go to the words of Jesus and take a look at the real ugly depth of hypocrisy. Jesus said:

> "Beware of the leaven of the Pharisees, which is hypocrisy."

Substitute Christian Leaders for Pharisees and you will understand this concept. The question we have to begin with is, what is hypocrisy? Many make the mistake of not understanding what really is the hypocrisy Jesus is talking about. Many tend to think of hypocrisy only in terms of not practicing what they preach, the false pretense involved in telling other people how they ought to live their lives, but not consistently living with what they claim are their beliefs, and false pretense, perhaps insincerity. This is what most people think of as hypocrisy – insincerity, pretense, and not practicing what they preach.

Jesus' warning is to:

> "Beware the leaven of the Leaders, which is hypocrisy."

It is the hypocrisy that characterizes leaders that he is warning against. However, most leaders are not insincere people. They usually are not characterized by false pretense, or by lying. Most are highly moral, religious men who live consistently and sincerely with their own beliefs. So then, what is this hypocrisy, because Jesus has condemned these Pharisees, and let me suggest to you many of our own leaders – yes, those who live consistent, sincere lives of religious practice – for hypocrisy?

Most people's concept of hypocrisy is all wrapped up in the first three forms, insincerity, inconsistency, and pretense. Some leaders may have these in their lives, but nothing so characteristic of them, that we could say,

> "This is the leaven."

What does Jesus really mean by hypocrisy? Let me suggest to you, it is hypocrisy of the fourth kind, not pretense, not insincerity, not inconsistency, but play-acting, acting out a role.

The word hypocrisy comes to us from the Greek. It refers to an actor who is acting out role. Jesus said that the leaven of those leaders is the fact that they approach their life as actors on a stage, or as actors, period. They somehow come up with their own definition of righteousness; that standard which is set up for approval and acceptance that they have conceived in their own minds. They have in effect, written a script for themselves, of what consists a righteous man, and what he must be.

> "What does a righteous man do? Well a righteous man does this. He fasts, he tithes all that he gets, he keeps the law, he prays five times a day. He doesn't smoke, he doesn't drink, and he doesn't go with girls that do."

He doesn't associate with sinners; he keeps himself clean. They define what a good Christian does by these rules. In fact the Pharisees of Jesus day had written out very, very, minutely detailed scrip for themselves. They were meticulous in their desire to keep the law and in that they were utterly sincere. But what Jesus is condemning is the fact that they had approached it as actors.

> "Here's my script. Now I must perform."

Let me most assure you that this is the hypocrisy that Jesus condemns.

There are four dangerous human corruptions with this play acting hypocrisy, this leaven of corruption of many Christian leaders. And, to follow them you may very well lose your Christian faith. The first thing is that this play acting doesn't accomplish the purposes of God in your life. God's purpose for your life is that you would be a righteous person from the inside out, that is, in and from your heart, a cleansed purified heart, that of your essential essence you in your fourth Eigen, not that you act righteously. God's purpose is not that you would do a good job of acting out a role of righteousness. God's purpose is that you would be genuinely transformed in your inner being, in your heart, in your fourth Eigen, so your new cleansed purified heart directs your spirit with love, and your soul is transformed by the renewing of your mind.

God's judgment of us comes on the basis of who we are. Are we righteous or are we not righteous? Do you belong to Him or do you not belong to Him? It doesn't do us any good to be unrighteous people who do a good job of acting righteously; no matter how sincere we are, because we stand condemned as wicked, unrighteous people. This is exactly Jesus' criticism of the Pharisees, and by extension to our Christian leaders, and perhaps by even more extension to even you!

Jesus said:

> "Woe to you, scribes and Pharisees, (Author - Christian Leaders?) hypocrites! For you are like whitewashed tombs which on the outside appear beautiful, but inside they are full of dead men's bones and all uncleanness. So you, too, outwardly appear righteous to men, but inwardly you are full of hypocrisy and lawlessness."

Now realize that Jesus is not talking about people whose lives are inconsistent with their beliefs, but He is talking to people whose lives are utterly consistent with their beliefs. He says:

> "You know what you are like? You are like tombs full of dead men's bones. You look OK on the outside, but when you get down to inside who you really are, you are dead, wicked, evil people, worthy of condemnation, worthy of my judgment."

He is not talking about people like a politician who runs on a platform advocating high morality, and engages with prostitutes. That is not the kind of inconsistency that most leaders are involved in. Most are highly religious, highly moral, utterly consistent men. But Jesus says, they are like tombs full of dead men's bones. They sincerely act out a facade of righteous, but inside they are wicked. So the problem is that play acting hypocrisy does not accomplish the purposes of God, therefore, it is of no benefit to you and me. The people who will enter into eternity, into God's presence, will be those who are genuinely righteous from the inside out, not the people who have performed righteously by acting out their own, or someone else's conceived role of righteousness.

A major problem with play acting hypocrisy is that ultimately it leads to self-deception. This is what Jesus taught in another parable of a Pharisee and a tax-gatherer. The Pharisee in that parable thanked God that he was not like other men, who did not tithe and act righteously as he did, when in fact he was exactly just like other men. That Pharisee had the same genetic code and he had the same inherited corruption so he was just like other men. That Pharisee completely deceived himself. Play acting hypocrisy leads to this self-deception; it is a tremendous obstacle to real Christian life. What man will seek a doctor when he thinks he is in good health? What man will accept the mercy and love of Jesus when he does not think he needs mercy? On a number of occasions, in interacting with the leaders who asked him why he associates with sinners, Jesus said:

> "It is not healthy people who need a physician, but sick people."
> "I did not come to call righteous men but sinners to repentance."

Jesus was saying, I am a doctor, and if you do not need me, OK. Jesus here is being sarcastic. Jesus knew full well that they needed him desperately, that they were indeed wicked people.

There is another problem with play acting hypocrisy. Hypocrisy, play-acting, is the opposite of faith and without faith it is impossible to please God. With play acting hypocrisy, it is impossible to please God because play acting hypocrisy is the opposite of faith. Faith comes into your spirit and renews and cleans your inner being, your heart, your fourth Eigen. Having your second Eigen body play-acting a script prescribed by your third

Eigen soul is not the result of faith which activated in you a new cleansed and purified inner essence fourth Eigen heart.

The act of faith would ultimately strive to do what Jesus would do, depending upon the presence and power of God to produce a genuine response of righteousness. A man acting on faith trusts and depends upon God working in his behalf to transform his inner being heart to make his responses what Jesus responses would be. He works out his salvation with fear and trembling because God is at work within him.

In what seems a similar way a hypocrite will work out his salvation with fear and trembling. The hypocrite is play acting, and is counting upon his acting ability demonstrated out in the world of his second Eigen flesh. The man of faith is striving to act righteously, but is counting on the work of God in his renewed, cleansed, and purified heart. He is depending on God's gift of faith to him to be God's transforming power in his inner being.

The difference, very subtly, but very simply, is where is your inner being heart, within your spirit? Do you go about striving to live righteously, having taken your stand in dependence upon your acting ability out in the real world, or are you striving to be righteous, having taken your stand upon the work of God, expecting, as God has promised, He is going to transform you and work through you, and accomplish for you what you cannot accomplish yourself?

This distinction spells out the difference between life and death, between eternal well-being and eternal hell and damnation. This definition here is the most crucial distinction in all of Christianity. This distinction you must heed in order for you to be a real genuine Christian, and have life eternal.

There is a huge fourth problem with the hypocrisy of play acting. The corruption is that inevitably a person who is acting out his righteousness as a role will have a distorted concept of what righteousness really is, or what really is that behavior that meets God's approval. Jesus said to the Pharisees, the religious leaders of His day,

"You blind guides, who strain out a gnat and swallow a camel".

368

What Jesus means by that is that those leaders, who are extremely meticulous to make sure they tithed exactly one-tenth of absolutely everything they received, yet those same men were totally unaware of gross instances of lack of compassion and lack of justice in their lives. And not just lack of compassion and lack of justice, that if they knew about it they would condemn, they were totally unaware of gross injustice in their lives that actually was condoned by their teaching and doctrine. According to their scrip you could engage in this lack of compassion and justice and still consider yourself a righteous man, knowing full well what you have done, simply because they rather than God had written the script. And when they write the script, they distort what righteousness really is.

All play acting hypocrisy will inevitably distort ones concept of righteousness, so that it is not God's concept of righteousness. And it will always distort in the direction of external acts or ritual, in the second Eigen flesh of the body, as opposed to inner qualities of being in the fourth Eigen inner essence heart.

Which is easier to do, act out compassion, or to act out ritual? But how can one act out compassion? You can fake it, you can counterfeit it, and you can stir up a feeling inside that you call compassion, but real compassion is much more difficult.

So, inevitably, because we want our role to be as easy as possible, to be attainable, to be possible to live like a righteous man, we define our role in such a way that it is attainable, and that will always be in the direction of outward acts in that second Eigen flesh. But if we write our script to simply include sundry righteous acts, thinking that if we do them, that's what it means to be righteous, and we write love and justice out of the script, then we also strain at gnats, and we swallow camels. And that is hypocrisy.

So now you have come to understand what this "hypocrisy" is that Jesus condemns. But there is another question. Why does Jesus refer to it as the "leaven", the leaven of the leaders? Leaven was a little lump of bread dough saved from an old batch after it had fermented. Its effect is like yeast, to make the new dough rise in preparation for baking. This little piece of dough from the last batch has the effect of being able to influence the entire lump of the new dough. Jesus is using this phenomenon as a metaphor for the hypocrisy of play acting leaders. He is saying the hypocrisy of the play acting leaders is like that. It is very contagious. It will suck you in; it will influence you, without you knowing it. There is a tremendous pull from the hypocrisy that leaders engage in that tries to get you to join them in the same hypocrisy, and it is very difficult for you to resist.

Why is that so? In order to understand this you have first of all to understand that the play acting is not just the hypocrisy of an individual. It is hypocrisy institutionalized, hypocrisy formalized, put into a formal set of doctrine, a formal set of teaching, a widespread definition of righteousness that a large group of people agree upon, usually a large group of very influential people. They are the "cool" people in society, and if the "cool" people say:

> "This is what a righteous man is like, if you want to be an admirable person, here is how you will act".

Then you are dealing with a much greater force than the hypocrisy of anyone individually.

So, you and I are confronted with vast institutionalized hypocrisy -- in your life in the world on a huge scale, in your religious life, and in your political life.

A problem with humankind is that most have a perverted desire to be respected in the eyes of other men. We have a misplaced desire to be acceptable in the eyes of men. Most of us, in fact, would rather be respected by men than by God. We would rather be acceptable to men than acceptable to God. Jesus warns us do not go that way. Jesus warns, do not fear men, fear God. It is ridiculous to fear men. If men do not approve of you they can kill you, but they can't do anything other than that. That is the extent of their power over you; but if you are reckoning with God, consider that God, if he disapproves of you, has the power to throw you into hell, where there is weeping and mashing of teeth. And, the consequence of hell is that you will be eternally terminated in fiery torment.

So you can see the power this "leaven" of institutionalized hypocrisy has when you understand that you do not normally fear God; you do not naturally fear God. Most of us respect too much people's respect of us. Because of that, if I as an insecure person, really desirous of love, respect, admiration and approval by a group of people around me, have that group of people hand me a script and say, "If you're going to be worthy of our respect and our approval, here's the script you must follow", there is a tremendous pressure to do exactly that, to perform. And you will. You will play out that role and join those people in the same hypocrisy that characterizes their lives. Then you will have one more person giving credence to their hypocrisy, and the thing snowballs.

> "Well if a million people agree that this is righteousness, that this is the right way to believe and think, who am I to argue?"

There is a tremendous pull that just sucks people in and captures them and keeps them there. That is what Jesus is teaching:

> "Beware of the leaven of the leaders, which is play acting hypocrisy."

Beware of the leaven of the play acting Christians, which is hypocrisy. Beware of the leaven of the play acting politicians, which is hypocrisy. You must not take this warning lightly.

Let me confront you with a very simple question. Are you acting out your life? Are you acting out what you conceive of as a life of righteousness with other people as an audience, or even with yourself as an audience? Or are you, in fact, striving to live a righteous life utterly dependent upon God, utterly dependent upon God's Spirit working in your behalf? Are you utterly dependent on God's work, expecting, as God has promised, that he is going to come into your life and transform you from the inside out? Are you counting on that, is your life based on that?

The difference is extremely subtle. No one can tell you if you are a hypocrite. You can't be absolutely sure you can know if you are a hypocrite. But you have to know that the difference exists, because that difference is the difference between life and death, heaven and hell, condemnation and eternal well-being.

God has promised to Christians that they have the Holy Spirit as a witness within their spirits. Your spirit will then feed this witness into your heart.

371

The Holy Spirit will teach you what you ought to say and do. The Holy Spirit who lives within your spirit will teach your spirit what righteous deeds to do, and your spirit will feed your soul. We have a promise from the scriptures that God will write his laws on our hearts. Now this is not the written code as some would advocate. No, this law written on the heart is spiritual law of Jesus, in fact, the law of the new covenant. We must ask God to do this spiritual writing.

Well then, you walk with Jesus. The Westminster Catechism that I remember from my youth asked the question:

"What is the chief end of man?"

The answer is to:

"Glorify God and enjoy him forever."

So, we will walk with Jesus and enjoy Him. Assimilate Jesus; forsake any script given to you from anyone with which Satan through men would enslave you in what Jesus called play acting hypocrisy. Assimilate Jesus into your spirit and into your soul.

The issue of hypocritical Christian leaders is a complex one. I do not want to leave you with the impression that all leaders are hypocrites, because they are not. I want to warn you to be very careful and to be a complete skeptic. We all are sinners and that includes all Christian leaders. The Catechism also said:,

"All men are depraved and come short of the Glory of God."

Yes indeed, we are all sinners, that is very, very true. All men are subject to corruption so you must not expect too much from any man or man's institutions.

Some of the greatest tragedies I have ever seen in my life is where men who have given their whole life on earth to serving an institution, perhaps a church institution, and then they discover when they are old, when their life is almost finished, that the institution they lifelong served was taken over by what they considered its enemy, and that the institution itself was corrupt, and was corrupt all along. What a tragedy.

Jesus gave a parable of the Kingdom of God; He said this is what the Kingdom of God is like. A sower went out to sow his field with mustard seed. Then up came a tree and the carrion birds of the air came and nested in it and made their homes in it. Jesus was describing his own Kingdom on earth. Mustard is a low growing, pretty green plant with yellow flowers that fills the whole field uniformly. In the parable the field is human kind, so the sower, who is a symbol of Jesus, sowed His kingdom among humankind with the intention it is to be like a uniform field of pretty green plants with yellow flowers.

To understand the parable one needs to understand the symbols. The tree is a symbol of a power structure. Carrion birds are a symbol of evil. So the interpretation of the parable is that this Kingdom of God, which Jesus intended to be like green plants with pretty yellow flowers spread out in a field, meaning lots of nice righteous Christians spread over the whole Earth, none subservient to one another, none dominate over another, each blooming in spiritual beauty, instead up came as a power structure dominated by evil men who make their home in the power structure, like vultures in a dead snag, and rule over the place to satisfy their own ends, feeding on the carrion of humankind.

Jesus is describing His own Kingdom! His own Church! Do you get it? Jesus said My kingdom will be dominated by men who seek their own ends and are agents of the evil one, the enemy, that is, Satan. Wow! What a parable! You and I would ask, "How can this be?"

Remember God works in very mysterious ways that to us mortals seems often unfathomable. Yet remember, God is in control and will accomplish His goals. God will use even evil men to accomplish his goals, which is to find and bring into His eternal fellowship, His own, those who belong to Him.

There are a couple of other disturbing things about the Kingdom of God on the earth which you should understand. There are righteous God fearing men who follow all the principles I have presented to you herein, but work for and diligently serve institutions that have an ideology that by any definition that one would derive from basic principles, is hypocritical and corrupt. This too is a tragedy.

These men either have not thought seriously about what they are doing, or who they serve, or have been taken in by hypocritical ideology, and adopted it as their own. Don't you do this! If you have come to know God, and live life with the fourth Eigen of love driving your existence, but serve an institution trapped in its own ideology, consider that God's judgment on that institution may involve you, and you may pay a very difficult, terrible price. So be warned.

Also be careful what institutions you support. Again, many evil men, or even just careless men with little principle, make their homes and derive their incomes from institutions that are supported by Christian brothers and sisters. Many para church institutions adopt ideology that outwardly appeals to the Christian community, and they derive their support from the Christian community, but exist mainly to financially pay off those men who run this institution. You need real wisdom to know whom you should support. Again, ask God for wisdom. Prayerfully consider to whom you give your financial support. It is not a simple or easy matter, and requires lots of prayer.

Along the path of the growing of my Christian faith I found another very, very important principle. There are a lot of church leaders, Christian professors, pastors, priests, and others that will tell you that to be a real Christian you must practice certain forms of activity or disciplines in your second Eigen body of flesh. Through the centuries lots of groups were led by leaders and even monks that taught that you must fast, eat a very simple diet, take cold showers, live a very austere life, and such. Now none of these practices are to be condemned in themselves as any person that wants to practice them may, and may get benefit from the practice, but the point to be made is that there is absolutely no value whatsoever in the hope of earning favor with God by such practice.

A modern Christian list of disciplines might be a routine of daily Bible reading, Bible study or scripture memorization, routinely practicing meditation, a regularly scheduled time of prayer, regularly giving thanks before meals, tithing everything you earn, regular church attendance, fasting at regularly scheduled times, or daily confession of sins, and lots of others I could add to this list.

Now we are not to confuse this with moral discipline. It is important to understand that God is pleased with righteous moral activities, such as compassion, kindness, goodness, being sexually faithful to your spouse, not committing fornication, not stealing, being truthful, being honest and other such moral imperatives, and such as what the Bible calls the fruits of the Spirit - love, joy, peace, kindness, patient, goodness, fruitfulness, gentleness, and self-control.

Jesus gave a simple definition to His ministry, it is simply to,

> "Call sinners to repentance."

The Bible gives us a profound dialog between Jesus and the religious leaders, the scribes and Pharisees.

After the tax collector, Levi, also called Mathew, came to know Jesus; Levi invited all his friends and gave a big party for Jesus. The religious leaders of the Jews, known as Scribes and Pharisees, started to grumble, saying,

> "Why do you eat and drink with tax-collectors and sinners?"

Jesus answers and says,

> "It is not those who are well who need a physician, but those who are sick. I have not come to call righteous men but sinners to repentance."

The Pharisees respond,

> "The disciples of John often fast and offer prayers; the disciples of the Pharisees also do the same; but Yours eat and drink."

Jesus answers them,

> "You cannot make the attendants of the bridegroom fast while the bridegroom is with them, can you? But the days will come; and when the bridegroom is taken away from them, then they will fast in those days."

The purpose of Jesus parable is to make a statement about what is motivating the disciples of Jesus. The motivation for their religious activities is not duty, or obligation, but love and devotion to Jesus.

Jesus' disciples operate on an entirely different basis. It is not a desire to seek favor in God's eyes by religious activities and disciplines, any more than attendants of a bridegroom would fast to seek favor in the bridegroom's eyes.

The disciples already have Jesus favor and love. What dictates activity here on out is the circumstances. Do we have reason for joy or mourning? Religious activity then becomes an expression of one's love and devotion to Jesus.

The Pharisees claim is that they see no evidence of repentance as Your disciples do not practice religious disciplines as we do, but Jesus claims on the contrary, you do see evidence of their repentance and their seeking to find favor with God to the extent that you see love and devotion to Me.

My disciples are turning from their rebellion and approaching God on a radically new and different basis from the one that motivates you. They love me, they are devoted to Me, and that in and of itself is evidence that they have repented from their rebellion and they are, in fact, seeking to find favor in God's eyes.

Jesus, you must understand, changed the rules.

Jesus was granted unique authority from God. Jesus claimed to be the Messiah and that is exactly what He is. Messiah is not some fancy title, but meant that all of God's favor and blessings were centered in Him, and authority was given to Him to grant them to whomever he chose. Jesus claimed to have this incredible authority.

> "I am the way, I am the truth, I am the life. I am the bread of life. I am the door."

Jesus taught his disciples the absolutely correct way to find favor in God's eyes, and that is love and devotion to Jesus.

This new way of approaching God in other places of the scriptures is called, "The new covenant", as against the old covenant that God made with Moses with its written law. The apostle Paul wrote:

> "Not that we are adequate in ourselves to consider anything as coming from ourselves, but our adequacy is from God, who also made us adequate as servants of a new covenant, not of the letter, but of the Spirit; for the letter kills, but the Spirit gives life."

So this New Covenant that Jesus describes makes us adequate through loving and serving Jesus with devotion.

Jesus then goes on and states that not only are religious disciplines not necessary in order to give evidence you're seeking after God's favor, but religious discipline is inappropriate. Jesus then tells the Pharisees and bystanders another parable:

> "No one tears a piece from a new garment and puts it on an old garment; otherwise he will both tear the new, and the piece from the new will not match the old, and, no one puts new wine into old wine skins; otherwise the new wine will burst the skins, and it will be spilled out, and the skins will be ruined. But new wine must be put into fresh wine skins."

 What Jesus is saying is that religious discipline practice is as incompatible with the new covenant as new, unshrunk cloth is with old shrunk cloth, or as new wine is with an old wineskin. Just as it is impossible to put new wine into an old wineskin, it is impossible to take the new approach to seeking God's favor, which the new covenant involves, and express it by means of the same religious discipline, which expressed such seeking of God's favor under the old covenant.

Religious discipline, which has its only motivation and rationale in the old covenant, is in no way appropriate for expressing your seeking of God's favor by faith, by your trust in Jesus, in the new covenant. There is one and only one motivation for religious discipline, and that is to earn God's favor, to justify yourself in God's eyes. If that is true and the new covenant came along, which eliminates any need for earning God's favor, then it eliminates the need for religious discipline which had as it's only rational to earn God's favor.

To enter into the new covenant, claiming to trust Jesus, and to have faith in Him in order to find favor in God's eyes, and to go on living a life of religious discipline is a contradiction. It makes a lie out of your claim to faith. You claim to be trusting Jesus for your justification, but yet you are using religious discipline to earn your justification. That is a lie. Religious discipline is as incompatible with faith as an old wineskin is with new wine.

Jesus ends this encounter with the Pharisees with another very, very profound statement.

> "And no one, after drinking old wine, wishes for new; for he says, the old is good enough."

This is a warning and a statement into human nature. Just as a man who drinks old wine and enjoys the fragrant bouquet and flavor of the old wine, and prefers it to the harsh taste and lack of bouquet in the new wine; so fallen human nature would prefer the mellow taste and bouquet of legalism and religious discipline to the radical strong, harsh taste of faith in Jesus. Faith is too radical. Faith has too much adventure in it. There is not much security in faith.

Legalism, religious discipline on the other hand, is very mellow. It is very comfortable. It feels good. It feels right. It feels natural to us. How can anything that feels so good be so wrong? That is going to be the normal propensity of the fallen human person. If it was up to our taste we would all opt for religiosity, religious discipline, and legalism over the life of faith. We would choose religion over eternal life, if we were left to ourselves, and that is what Jesus presents as a warning to us;

"Be careful. Watch yourselves."

Realize that you have this propensity in yourself and guard against it. Don't you dare reject the new covenant, the life of faith, and the eternal life that will come from that faith, just because it doesn't feel good, just because it does not seem natural to you. You will follow your tastes at the peril of your soul. So be warned.

In the light of this scripture in the fifth chapter of the book of Luke, there is one and only one conclusion we can come to: Religious discipline, motivated by a desire to earn God's favor, is incompatible with being a Christian and should be eliminated from our lives, putting in its stead, a confident trust in the mercies and grace of God with devotion to Jesus.

The conviction that those who are spiritual will engage in religious disciplines and that in order to grow you must subject yourself to religious discipline, is a false doctrine. It is not a conviction arising out of biblical Christianity, it is convictions arising out of the unbiblical traditions of that form of Christianity you will find powerfully prevails among many, many churches, and yes, even us.

In the immortal words of the comic character Pogo:

"We have met the enemy, and he is us."

THIRTEEN

WISDOM, EVIL AND OTHER CONSIDERATIONS

This Chapter contains miscellaneous stuff; the intent is to pass on wisdom accumulated from a lifetime of interacting with people, and yes, with God.

Dear reader, consider from the new American Standard.

Psalm 55

Prayer for the Destruction of the Treacherous.

FOR THE CHOIR DIRECTOR; ON STRINGED INSTRUMENTS. A MASKIL OF DAVID.

1 Give ear to my prayer, O God;
And do not hide Yourself from my supplication.
2 Give heed to me and answer me;

3 I am restless in my complaint and am surely distracted,
Because of the voice of the enemy,
Because of the pressure of the wicked;
For they bring down trouble upon me
And in anger they bear a grudge against me.

4 My heart is in anguish within me,
And the terrors of death have fallen upon me.
5 Fear and trembling come upon me,

And horror has overwhelmed me.

6 I said, "Oh, that I had wings like a dove!
I would fly away and be at rest.
7 "Behold, I would wander far away,
I would lodge in the wilderness.

Selah

8 "*I* would hasten to my place of refuge
From the stormy wind *and* tempest."

9 Confuse, O Lord, divide their tongues,
For I have seen violence and strife in the city.
10 Day and night they go around her upon her walls,
And iniquity and mischief are in her midst.
11 Destruction is in her midst;
Oppression and deceit do not depart from her streets.

12 For it is not an enemy who reproaches me,
Then I could bear *it;*
Nor is it one who hates me who has exalted himself
against me,
Then I could hide myself from him.

13 But it is you, a man my equal,
My companion and my familiar friend;
14 We who had sweet fellowship together
Walked in the house of God in the throng.

15 Let death come deceitfully upon them;
Let them go down alive to Sheol,
For evil is in their dwelling, in their midst.

16 As for me, I shall call upon God,
And the LORD will save me.
17 Evening and morning and at noon, I will complain
And murmur,
And He will hear my voice.
18 He will redeem my soul in peace from the battle
which is against me,
For they are many *who strive* with me.
19 God will hear and answer them—
Even the one who sits enthroned from of old—

Selah.

<blockquote>
With whom there is no change,
And who do not fear God.
20 He has put forth his hands against those who were
at peace with him;
He has violated his covenant.
21 His speech was smoother than butter,
But his heart was war;
His words were softer than oil,
Yet they were drawn swords.
</blockquote>

<blockquote>
22 Cast your burden upon the LORD and He will sustain you;
He will never allow the righteous to be shaken.
23 But You, O God, will bring them down to the pit
of destruction;
Men of bloodshed and deceit will not live out half
their days.
But I will trust in You.
</blockquote>

What a comforting Psalm. These words are properly interpreted as words of David, and then prophetic words about Jesus, and now I use them as my words too.

Evil is a great mystery. Pastor Ray Stedman at Peninsula Bible Church gave a very interesting sermon on the mystery of evil. I have thought about the nature of evil since that sermon, especially, after I encountered strange human behavior I did not understand. The understanding and definition of what constitutes evil is what defines a culture. Cultures which have a different understanding of evil, and what constitutes evil, that is different from God's definition of evil disappear. One could do a whole study on this to prove it, but that is not the intention of this writing. Examples would be almost forgotten Indian tribes of the Americas, ancient kingdoms in the Middle East, and African tribes. Most are not remembered anymore and very many are completely forgotten.

Christian, Jewish, and Muslim, cultures now dominate western civilization in the earth. These cultures are all based on God's definition of evil, or a corruption of God's definition, originally given to the ancient people of Mesopotamia.

THE INTERACTION OF EVIL

Let me discuss a definitive understanding of evil in the context of my personal dealings with the Cooks. By the Cooks I mean June, her sons Dan, and Dave, and Dan's son John, who married my wonderful, precious daughter, Crystal, and became my son in law.

To you children of them, and grandchildren and great grandchildren, and some of you are my own grandchildren also, this may be painful, but I write these painful words for instruction, and to give everyone wisdom and understanding, and to teach a deeper understanding of what constitutes evil. Using an example makes for much clearer understanding than a theoretical discourse.

The 55th Psalm of David expresses my thoughts and reflections about the matter and conflict. The mystery of evil is very great and most people do not understand it or even want to understand it. We are saved and given righteous standing before God by the precious blood of Jesus, and the purpose of that salvation is to give us the freedom and the power to be righteous and act righteously. As Jesus said,

> "Blessed are those who hunger and thirst after righteous,
>   for they shall be filled."

Indeed, let us thirst after righteousness.

It is very difficult and not appropriate to accuse anyone. But I want to pass on to you dear reader, WISDOM. So, that said, what are exactly the encounters of which I would imagine that I might lay before the Cooks? Let us consider that question. I cannot think of a word to describe it, but its nature is a combination of envy, desire to put down those around, and to have power over those around. It is a complex thing, and when I was in conflict with the Cooks, I did not understand it or even consider that real evil might dominate basic Cook thinking. It is only now after 20 years of reflection and consideration of the matter and watching the mannerisms of my son-in-law, John Cook, and his father, Dan Cook, and their interaction with those around them, that maybe I have come to understand it a little.

It has as a part of it the nature of humor. It is manifested in the way they treat each other, and the fun of performing a trick on each other. It is really a basic cultural thing. Let me give you some examples I have observed during the last few days of when I write this, October of 2002.

I gave an old 1964 Ford pickup to my son-in-law, John, the son of Dan Cook, as a present for my grandson Warren Cook. It needs a new clutch and has not been run for 7 years so it needs to be towed to Emmett, Idaho. It will not fit on my tow dolly so a trailer is needed to haul it to Emmett. Dan and Dave have a suitable trailer but will not lend it. Ken Cook, John's brother has a trailer that is too small but John is about to elongate it much to the opposition and anguish of Ken's wife. Ken will say nothing about it to John and John will modify Ken's trailer as a matter of presumption and sport with Ken, but also of course, accomplishing the task of getting the pickup to Emmett.

Another example is that a worker, Ray, is working on the outside deck of my daughter Cindy's house. She needed some supplies from town for this deck for Ray to continue working. Dan has been working for them as a helicopter mechanic. Cindy was busy making some telephone calls but would get the stuff as soon as she was finished. Out of the blue Dan offered to get the stuff Ray needed. Instead of going to town and getting the stuff, Dan takes Cindy aside and wants to work on helicopter part ordering. Cindy tells him to go to town and get the stuff. Dan leaves. Dan wanders about town doing sundry errands. Two hours later Cindy goes to town and Dan is still there, but once he sees Cindy in town immediately gets the stuff and takes it to Ray. What's going on? Ray wastes two hours waiting for stuff at Cindy's expense of the cost of wages.

I submit that this is a basic cultural expression. Subconsciously, Dan wants to exert power over Ray. They have known each other for years. It is a form of humor to them to make someone wait in frustration completely ignoring the loss of productivity and pain it causes others besides Ray. I submit that this is evil. Of course, in these two cases it seems rather harmless, but in more serious cases the evil is manifested more deeply. In my case it resulted in great evil, which I like David, pray that it will be judged and punished, but may God have mercy on their souls.

What is the root cause of this cultural evil? Two suggestions come to mind. I have no proof for either, just conjecture. The first is possibly the Nez Perce heritage. The mother of old Warren Cook, the grandfather of Dan, this woman would be the great grandmother of Dan Cook, was a Nez Perce Indian. The native tribes of northwest America had a huge cultural problem with envy. The cultural expression of the Potlatch is a remedy these native peoples used to alleviate the bad effects of envy. The rich men of the tribe would periodically hold a Potlatch and give away most of their wealth, primarily of horses, wampum, and such. The tribal leaders understood that the tribe would have great difficulty cooperating in defending itself from enemies and other threats, if envy was allowed to hold sway over a large portion of the tribe, consequently, the Potlatch. A cultural heritage could have been generated through these generations, passed on from one generation to the next, of basic uncontrolled envy of anybody with more worldly goods.

The second is the heritage of Mormonism. Dan Cook is a practicing Mormon. That religion has a huge emphasis on material goods and that the righteous become wealthy; if one is not wealthy he must be not righteous. Wealth in that culture is acquired through the ownership of much property and many wives. One Mormon is automatically envious of the next who has acquired more wealth and women. This internal subconscious view then is transmitted at others, especially, if that person is not a Mormon, as, of course, that person must have acquired his wealth by nefarious means.

Let me state another example. Dan Cook gave my daughter Crystal, John Cook's wife, an old antique sewing machine which had belonged to Dora Gerber, the person from whom we had acquired the mine property. (Therefore, it really belonged to my mine partners and me) When John and Crystal were leaving the place they had rented up on Cow Creek, near Lucille, Idaho, John created a large burn pile of stuff he was going to dispose of by burning. His brother Ken and his wife Angela retrieved the machine from the burn pile, took it home, and fixed it up beautifully. One day Crystal saw it at their place and believed that Ken and Angela had stolen it from her, and really could not believe that her machine had been stolen. I don't think she realizes even today (September, 2002) what happened. Crystal is a very forgiving person, so she probably just gave it over to the Lord.

You, dear reader might wonder, what is the point of all this. The point is that a habit of this kind of behavior can be generated from cultural outlook which when applied to a serious matter becomes a great evil.

In my case Geneva and I had bought a 110-acre ranch from June and old John Cook, Dan Cook's parents, for $250,000. (Old John then died a few weeks after he moved off the ranch) We paid $50,000 down and financed the rest with the Cooks on a land contract. In hindsight the contract was designed by the Cooks to cause us, the buyers, a great problem so as to have a balloon payment in 15 years, because built into the contract was a restriction on the amount of maximum reduction in principal that we could make in any one year. Since the principle could not be paid down except at a slow rate, this almost guaranteed a balloon payment at the end of 15 years. We spent about $900,000 of our own capital on improvements to the ranch -- pipelines, roads, hydro electrical system, buildings, and telephone systems. We also spent $1,100,000 (about $400,000 came from a savings bank run by criminals) on a dream home separated from the ranch on its own two acres, yet access to the house was controlled by the ranch.

The thought never entered my mind that the Cooks would intend to deprive us of our ranch if they could, and not renegotiate the contract at the end of 15 years. Like Psalm 55, Dan and I were friends; we went together through the terrible tragedy of the death of three men at the mine. Our spirits had melded together through that tragedy. I had paid Dan Cook well. The Big House (the dream home) is discussed in another chapter.

After my financial difficulties, the question eventually came to extending the loan on the ranch. Think about it. We had been paying them $20,000 or more a year for 15 years and yet still owed them about $130,000, but we had invested $900,000 in improvements and they wanted to just take it back! June Cook and her sons just said nyet, no, never! No matter what we proposed to them, it was rejected. Terrible additional pressure was put on Geneva and I through the community and through our church. (June attended the same church we did).

June sued and we ended up in court. We had a special hearing for settlement before a justice of the Idaho Supreme Court, which the district court had ordered so that a compromise could be worked out. I was able to obtain from a friend, Kermit, Wiggins of Cambridge, Idaho a commitment for $100,000 for the Cooks. That plus the proceeds of a timber sale from the ranch timber would pay the Cooks off. This was offered to the Cooks at the hearing. Their answer was nyet! No answer, no consideration, no counter suggestion, no nothing, just nyet! NO, NO, NO.

That rejection told me that I was dealing with a situation I did not understand, beyond my comprehension, and with which I had no idea how to deal. In hindsight they intended to rob us of a ranch, for which Geneva and I had spent about $2,000,000, for a debt we owed them at that time of about $170,000, including all the past interest, the interest being more that the principle initially owed. The greed of that act was incomprehensible to me. It was also quite irrational and beyond any normal persons expectations. It has the substance of insanity.

To defend ourselves and delay the matter we did another bankruptcy. This made the Cooks very, very angry. Even my Son-in-law John Cook got involved and moved the pastor of the Riggins Community Church, Fred Emery, against us. Fred was put under a lot of pressure by the Cooks and their friends, and Fred then put me under a lot of pressure and acted to have me removed from the elder leadership of the Church in Riggins. All this was intended to generate pressure to force us to cave in to the Cook demands that we in essence let them rob us of the ranch. It was a terrible, terrible, sad time for Geneva and me.

I still cannot understand to this day the irrational expectations of the Cooks, and their multiple front attacks to achieve their irrational goals no matter whom they hurt. It was a very wicked evil and ensnared Fred Emory the Pastor, and my son-in-law John Cook, into participating in its evil execution.

Well to complete the story, we eventually found a company to finance the ranch and pay off the Cooks. My attorney, Dan Radakovich, said he never saw such an anguished evil countenance as on the person of June Cook when the papers were being signed to pay her off. I still today can see her face and remember her grimace while I sat in her attorney's office watching her. She indeed was quite angry and flabbergasted. Why should one be angry when one is to receive $210,000 in cash including interest to the very day, plus all costs and all of her attorney fees paid by me, so the contest cost her nothing, and she came out completely whole? I leave it to you dear reader to figure it out. I was just sad. Sad to see a person so affected. My attorney may have understood it, but I did not.

The final act was that the finance company immediately sold the debt to Ron Yanke, a very rich bottom feeder, who I, myself, had introduced to all the aspects of the ranch in an attempt to sell it to him. He knew what he was doing, had lots of fancy attorneys on his staff, and they prevented me from selling the ranch once I had it refinanced. I concluded the matter was hopeless, gave up, accepted defeat, got evicted illegally, clearly against Idaho law by Yankee's fancy lawyers, and Geneva and I left the ranch to go on to better things in life the Lord Jesus intended for us.

In hindsight and to so pass on to you Christian wisdom, in the beginning why did I just not let the Cooks have everything and go somewhere else and start over? That is a very good question. Why not let God deal with them? Why not turn the other cheek? As Jesus said, if someone steals your coat, give them your shirt too. Yes, why not? After all, God has said, vengeance is mine, I will repay. But understand, dear reader, that this is very, very difficult to do in the heat of the battle. But you, dear reader, consider it carefully if you are faced with a similar situation.

BURY THE BODY

Returning to the Cook question dear reader, which by asking is intended you learn from this, is why does irrational greed overwhelm ones thinking? Greed is a terrible thing. Now I do not call greed the normal hope to make a profit from a situation, maybe even a very large profit. No, greed, as a very good friend of mine, Paul Chaiken, defined it, greed is the attempt to get more out of a situation than you can rationally expect. Now he was a futures trader so he knew all about greed. But why would June Cook and her sons attempt to, in essence, legally steal a property in which I had invested $2,000,000 Plus the $250,000 purchase price? If they had been successful, how would they have buried the body? That expression comes from an old cliché in the commodity business where it is said,

"If one makes a killing one must bury the body."

What is meant by that is if one has a huge profit in some situation one must liquidate or sell out in order to convert the killing into real cash. That is not always easy.

It is one thing for Yanke and his cronies to legally steal something, after all they are quite practiced at it, and maybe consistently get away with it, but quite another for June Cook and her sons to pull it off. No, the lesson is to control ones greed. June and her sons may have a heritage of cultural envy, which produces inordinate greed; so you who are her offspring must be especially aware of this, and recognize it within your genetic self, and so protect yourself from its evil corrupting effects.

I give you another example. Dan Cook has sold a restaurant he owns in town called, The Cattlemans, several times, each time taking it back. Roger Laughlin and his wife bought it and worked it for almost 10 years making payments to Dan. Eventually, when Roger could not make a few payments, Dan took it back. Roger was quite bitter. One day he explained it all to me and probably is still quite bitter. Eventually I expect Dan will do something like that to someone who will not accept it without spilling blood.

There are a number of unsolved murders in Idaho County that have occurred over the years. I suspect the roots are in this behavior. Ray Hamill once told me the couple that was murdered in Grangeville about 10 years or so ago (1992?) had ripped him off. He was probably not the first to be ripped off by them nor the last. Eventually, someone took enough offense at them to do them in. It was very cleverly done. Apparently, they were murdered in their sleep and the house was set fire and then burnt down. Little evidence was left for the cops. The cops once in a while say they know who did it but do not have enough evidence. I suspect the people of Grangeville are glad the murdered people are gone and even will tolerate the presence of the murderers.

Eventually too, I suspect, Yanke and his cronies will get their reward. They have just left just too many bodies lying around in several States. It might amuse you dear reader to know that Yankee's investment in Micron Corporation declined by about $50,000,000.00 (fifty million dollars) within six months of robbing me. Micron stock price has never recovered those levels. I think the Lord must have a fine sense of humor.

About five years later Yankee died of cancer. He was younger than me. In few years June Cook died of cancer. I suspect she little enjoyed her $210,000.00. May God have mercy on their souls.

You dear reader will be much better off and you will have considerable reward in heaven, if you commit yourself to treating the people you do business with great respect and consideration. If someone cannot make the payment he or she owes you, give him some slack, work it out, or even write it off. The Lord will bless you and your business. In the long run people will remember you as a good person. You will be well spoken of. Remember the proverb that when the wicked perish the righteous rejoice. I doubt few lament the passing of June Cook and her Sons except perhaps their offspring, though I suspect they will secretly rejoice. There was a recent resident of Elk Lake Road who sold his place and left the country. The neighbors actually held a big party to celebrate that departure.

INTERACTION WITH RAY

I WRITE THIS IN AS IT WERE, REAL TIME. Here it is the 4th of June 1997 and my eyes are very wet from the tears of joy I shed today. It came about because of a morning spent with Ray Hamill at the Summervilles Coffee Shop.

After Geneva and I left Riggins in January of 1996 (At the end of the ranch loss disaster.) we spent the time in California and traveled several times between California and Riggins. After losing everything, it was a time of grieving. We worked at my brothers Gordon's insurance business and visited and played with our California grandchildren. Gordon was extremely generous and paid us for work. Geneva became a customer service representative and I a computer network consultant and insurance salesman.

We grieved because we had lost what seemed like everything we owned. I was greatly humiliated and humbled through this by the Lord. Yet we needed to grieve and heal. A great spiritual struggle occurred between me and the Lord. All my dreams and aspirations had died. All the dreams and visions I had of what the Lord was going to do had died.

Again I struggled with the Lord one more time, and went seeking another attorney to harass Yanke one more time. Since the Lord don't talk to me face to face like He did with Moses, I struggled again and again of what to do and what the Lord wanted me to do. To be robbed of all of one's assets and property legally, leaves one helpless. So then one can curse the legal system and curse ones enemies. Then like King David one can call down the Lord's vengeance on one's enemies. After all,

"Vengeance is mine says the Lord."

The struggle went on and on for a year and a half. And the Lord did nothing.

The telephone cable caused the problem to not go away. After all, if I had found a job after Geneva and I left Gordon's insurance business, or had not left Gordon's insurance business, or if things had become hunkie dorrie in California, I would not have left California and returned to Idaho. Geneva and I had also taken a month of holiday, met Dan and Mary Cook (different Cooks who were friends and lived near Lucille, Idaho) on the Colorado River in Arizona and spent most of April wandering around Arizona, Nevada, and California. Geneva and I enjoy wandering around very much.

The telephone company attorney had written me a letter. I responded and talked to her on the telephone. It seemed strange the telephone company was trying to contact me. The thing just would not go away so I could forget about it.

Returning to Idaho, I had to decide what to do. A great struggle with the Lord ensued. One option was to file a criminal complaint against Ray Hamill for breaking off the lock on the telephone cable termination where it connects to Citizens Telecom. Ray had in times past represented himself to be a Christian. After again struggling with the Lord many, many times, it seemed at least I should talk to Ray before I talked to the DA or the Sheriff of Idaho County.

I finally called Ray up and he seemed quite excited to meet with me. We met at Summervilles Restaurant and talked for maybe 4 or 5 hours. I came to think that Ray maybe really did love the Lord, and that he most assuredly was a Christian brother. He said he did not break off the lock but that the telephone company did. I called Ralph Mckinzie, the state director for Citizens and after some research, he said yes they had broken the lock, which was a great surprise to him. Ray and I had prayed together.

Now I had an even bigger problem. I decided to have peace about it and wait. Geneva and I went down to California for a couple of weeks as Geneva had made a commitment to Gordon that she would not leave his employment such as to cause him trouble. Well Gordon's business had really slowed down, he had hired his step daughter in law, and he did not need us anymore.

We returned to Idaho and I had another talk with Ray at the house in Riggins. Again we talked for 5 hours or so covering everything -- all the gory details about the Cooks, the Ranch, the Yankes, etc. etc. This was very painful, but in hindsight necessary to communicate our feelings to each other. In the process I shared with him my dream of the Everest Project. (EP) He immediately jumped upon that and said that he had studied and prayed about it considerably, and come up with the idea to give Geneva and me $20,000. (Which he would get from Yankee) This amount he said was twice what the EP needed and confirmed to him that this was the right number that he eventually had peace about. I of course went once more into the history of the ranch, that I had spent in excess of $2,000,000 on the ranch and house, and that I had had offers of $1,200,000 for the ranch alone, that I once had screwed up a sale which would have netted Geneva and I $500,000 etc. etc. etc.

The meeting was interrupted by intruders of sundry sort; we were meeting at the house in Riggins. Two weeks went by and we meet again today at Summervilles. In the meantime, the Lord had seemed to have convinced me to just give the telephone system over to Ray for whatever. I am committed to be a man of peace and since it seemed that the Lord had killed every deal I tried to put together again and again and again, I just accepted whatever the Lord would do.

At the meeting with Ray I wanted to clearly establish that I am committed to moral excellence. He stated he is also committed to moral excellence. I one more time went over what the Cooks had done to me and what Yanke had done to me so he understood my belief of the facts of the whole matter, which is that I was robbed, that I was turning the whole thing over to the Lord for judgment and that Ray should do as he thinks best. He had represented to me at a previous meeting that he was the managing partner in the operation and that he had the power to make decisions, and that Yanke himself had assured him that he would write the check. (Remember here dear readers, some people no matter what degree of interest they share, they perceive of themselves as owning and originated the project. Beware of such people.)

This had the effect of binding us together. He asked that he might be allowed to participate in the Everest Project. I explained to him what the EP required in terms of research, mathematics and diligent pursuit and discipline. I agreed that I would have him as an investor on the Everest Project.

A miracle is happening. The idea of the EP is so farfetched that I almost never share it with anybody, yet here is a man excited about it, and probably believes in it more than I really do deep down within me. I know it can be done, but like climbing the real Mount Everest it will require such an excess of energy, discipline, courage, and toughness that is really beyond human expectations. That is why I call it EP.

The miracle is Ray and I together praying, sharing, and crying with many tears. We should be bitter enemies as he has moved in and is now occupying, managing, and stewarding what once was my Ranch, which the Lord took away from me. Of course my inadequacies probably had a lot to do with it.

Ultimately we had the same vision. I shared that my vision for the Ranch of a full time Christian center. He said he had the same vision. What, how can this be? He then waxed prophetically and said after Yanke and his friends visit the place a few times and they will ask him for some proposals on what they should do with it. What will happen is that he will give them several options, one of which is to give it away and take a tax write-off. Is it possible that the Lord will do this? Who knows? I am not a prophet. You dear reader and posterity who read this will indeed know, maybe after I am long gone.

By the way Gus Carlson died today. He went to the end screaming as if the demons were after him - very, very sad indeed. He had rejected God all his life. You dear children must understand that the purpose of life is to come to know God. If in your lifetime you do not come to know God, the creator of the universe, the one who designed you in great detail, and continually cares and provides for you, if you do not know him, your life is a failure. It would have been better if you had never even been born.

You great grandchildren, and great, great, grandchildren of Gus who read this, if by the grace of God you have come to know God, rejoice and worship and give thanks for the grace God has given you.

A week or so after the meetings with Ray Hamill, I politely declined his offer of $20,000. My thinking was that to accept such a ridiculous offer would compromise my position. By accepting such an offer I would be saying to the world and to God, "I am satisfied." Instead my conscience told me I had to place the whole matter before God and He would judge between me, Hamill, the Cooks, Yanke, and MacAlvain.

My perception is that Hamill became very angry. Why? That is somewhat a mystery to me, but I suspect Hamill might have expected some cut out of the pie. Otherwise, I just do not understand his anger.

This is not the end of the story. In the fall my hunting buddy, Dale, and I made a plan to get to our hunting camp by going through the Voss property east of the Ranch. We unloaded our horses near the next beach upriver above the ranch and proceeded up the hill on an old jeep trail. When we got to the Voss property, I saw Hamill approaching me on the road that goes to the Voss Place from Elkhorn Creek on foot about 300 feet ahead of two other people near a parked vehicle. He was armed with a pistol on his hip. My 45 auto was concealed within my jacket and he did not know I was armed. I was leading my horse and I was about 100 to 200 feet in front of my friends. Hamill immediately launched into an intimidating posture saying I had no business being there and was trespassing. I had every right to be there having the permission of the landowner to cross his property. Hamill thought to intimidate me and my friends.

I became angry at Hamill's threatening manner as I just knew he was going to intimidate my friends. I thought to myself that I had better be prepared for anything, so I drew my 45 auto pistol from its holster, worked the bolt to put a shell into the chamber, and replaced it back in my holster all in one motion. The 45 auto has a triple safety mechanism so carrying a loaded 45 normally is no problem safety wise, but I normally feel it is safer to carry it without a shell in the chamber. I then told Hamill that if he wanted a fair fight, I was ready.

Hamill then saw that I was armed, and better armed than he was, and angry at his impertinence. Being the chicken shit coward that he is, he carefully and slowly removed his pistol from its holster and placed the pistol on the ground and turned his back to me. By that time my friends had arrived. I did not want this scene to get out of control, so I then kicked Hamill's pistol into the brush off the road down into a gully.

My hunting buddy, Dale, has a real stupid mule that just keeps on going. That mule continued down the road while its owner started talking to Hamill. Since I did not want to spend the rest of the day chasing that stupid mule, I went after the mule. Hamill then had the chance to tell a bunch of lies about what had happened. When I returned with the mule, my friends had decided to return down the hill and give up our hunting expedition.

Hamill then took me aside and said to me, and I quote,

> "As far as I am concerned this whole action is over and done with and that he had no animosity."

Hamill lied as he often does, and he and his friends then filed legal charges against me. After a mess that would be rather tedious and involved in the telling, I was charged with a misdemeanor, "Rude display of a weapon". The court system eventually dismissed the charge against me.

INTERACTION WITH BROTHER

I really don't remember clearly my motivation but I apparently had wanted to have a normal friendly relationship with Hamill. Somehow in a conversation with my brother Orneal, I had suggested that he talk to Ray Hamill. That in hindsight was a terrible mistake as it eventually destroyed my very close relationship with my brother.

Hamill must have told Orneal a whole package of lies and Orneal believed them. Orneal then wrote me a letter and accused me of all kinds of crimes and told me I was destined for hell if I did not do a 180 degree turn. I responded with the following letter.

Dear Neal

I have received your letter.

I understand the hyperbole of your parables and your intent but I do not think your enemies will. Therefore, I suggest you destroy your copies of that letter or at least never let it be seen by any of them.

Gordon made the comment to me that Neal loves you enough to take the time to write you a letter. I appreciated that. I understand your intent to write me a letter out of your love for me. My intention in this response is to assure you of my love for you and also to make some suggestions to you which come out of my experience and my love for you.

First let me assure you that the Lord Jesus loves me. He takes very, very good care of me. I walk with him and I learn new things about him every day. I love him very much.

397

You should also understand that I have enemies. The Lord gives me enemies so that I will learn from them and grow in grace and love and patience. Enemies serve a very useful purpose.

You have been a student of the scriptures. Proverbs 14:5 says, "From a liar comes forth lies". I have known Mr. Hamill a long time. I have had numerous business dealings with him, almost all of which were disasters. I know him reasonably well. Most of the time I do not believe he is a child of God. To characterize him, he is a Judas type, a fake Christian. The standard of scripture is Matthew 7:20, which says, "By their fruits you shall know them." He has a very lovely Christian lady as a wife, whom I believe is a child of God.

Ray Hamill has made numerous enemies in this area with his lies, half-truths, and deceitful practices. I suggest you talk to my daughter Cindy. She could give you a list of other people to talk to if you wish to establish Mr. Hamill's truthfulness. Even the deputy sheriff when he interviewed me made a similar statement.

Ray Hamill is right now stealing my telephone line by using it without paying for it. This telephone line has a replacement cost of about $150,000. I send him letters but he laughs about it. Shall I sue him? I have not and probably will continue to let him use it without any consequence.

The disturbing thing to me is that you apparently believed Mr. Hamill. This calls into question in my thinking your ability to discern the truth. That is very disturbing. You have been in the Lords work a long time. You manage people and hire and dismiss people. I would think an essential part of managing people is to be able to clearly discern the truth in any matter so that you can make correct and righteous decisions.

I know Mr. Hamill's methods. They are evil. The dispute on the mountain was not about land but about the right of the people in my party to proceed peacefully up the trail which they were fully in their rights to do. Ray knew that I would just ignore his intimidation and threats and just proceed up the trail. But he also knew that the people in my party would not, given his threats and intimidation. Ray was fully armed and acting in a very threatening manner.

Neal I hate evil. Evil makes me very angry. You are right. I lost my cool on the mountain and became very angry. He threatened me and I challenged him to a fair fight. If Ray had not proved to be such a coward and drawn his gun, and the Lord God had not intervened, I would have probably have drawn my gun and filled him full of holes. I did not know it at the time but I was much better armed than he was so in all likelihood, in the act of self-defense, I would have continued shooting until he stopped shooting which would have been disastrous for both of us.

Probably Ray laid his gun on the ground because he saw I was well armed which he did not expect. He used to think of me as a wimp which he could push around at will. After all Jerry is a namby-pamby Christian type. He probably turned his back because he would, if he had the opportunity, shoot his enemies in the back. I have told you that Ray is a highly intelligent quick thinking person. I am sure he measured all of this and then calculated to determine his response. He knows that I am not going to shoot him in the back, so he takes no risk.

Neal, you should understand that I was purposely set up. Ray and his boss knew I was coming up the trail. I did not know I would encounter Ray or that he would attempt to intimidate the people in my party. I once had the sheriff called out on Ray's boss for trespassing, so his boss had plenty of motivation to conduct a setup.

Ray and his witnesses (Ray's boss and his boss' son) perjured themselves. His witnesses by their own statements were 300 feet away yet they heard and saw everything. The people in my party (there were four of us, seven horses, and one mule) were 200 feet behind me and approaching me as rapidly as they could and saw and heard nothing. Rather interesting, don't you think? The public defender and the prosecutor must have integrated all this into what they believe to have happened as they came up with a, "Rude display of a weapon", as a misdemeanor charge.

Sure, if I had followed my own inclinations, I could have gone to a jury trial and established my complete innocence. Geneva and certainly you by your telephone conversation to me were to my understanding very concerned about the potential risks in that so I eventually bowed to Geneva's advice (and yours by inference) and made a plea bargain which without Geneva, and you, and others I would not have done.

Neal, I write this all to you because I am concerned about your practical theology. I know that I am a sinner and fully depraved and incapable of doing any good as the Westminster Catechism teaches. (This comes from the TULIP expression of the reformed faith, in this case Total Depravity which is based on Romans 3:23.) Yet I have been saved by the grace of God. Any good work that I attempt to do is always contaminated by my sinful nature. This is solid reformed theology and what the Bible teaches.

You too, Neal, need to understand that you too are depraved. If one ever entertains even a thought that one is better than the next human being, i.e. stuck-up as we used to say in junior high, this attitude is evil in God's sight. This attitude is probably the most despicable one can possess. Harshly judging a Christian brother and pointing out his sins comes from that sort of attitude. I would think the approach you used in accusing me of sin would apply when some Christian brother is living in some habitual sin or has a sin habit which he is ignoring or that he seems unaware of that needs correcting. In my case I very seldom become angry. In that I am like my father who very seldom became angry, but when he did he could become quite angry, as you probably well remember.

Let me suggest Neal, that you too as well as anyone else, are fully capable of shooting someone full of holes. All you need is the right situation, the right provocation, and the right opportunity. Anyone who even has thought of such a thing is fully as guilty as if he had done it as Jesus said in Matthew 5:21-23.

You seemed to have, in your zeal for the law, have come up with the practice of pointing out to people their sins. You should remember that that is the devils work, which is to accuse the brethren. (Rev 12:10) Our Christian friends from PBC and our real Christian friends from around here empathize with us in our problems and trials and pray for us. You seem to have gotten into the mode of accusing and pointing the finger. Remember that Jesus said, "By the standard you judge you will be judged" (Matthew 7:1-2). You seem to have reached the place in your understanding where you are saying the same things to me as Job's three friends were saying to Job,

"Confess now what you have done that is causing you all these problems."

Remember God thoroughly condemned the theology of Job's three friends.

Neal, you say make the 180 degree turn. Turn to what? I walk with the Lord continually. He loves me. He takes care of me. He has appointed a place for me in eternity. What else am I to do but to accept his love? If my enemies steal my property, if my enemies set me up to embarrass me and humiliate me, so what? I fully expect the Lord to take care of them either in this world or the next.

You seem to have forgotten that the great Christian heroes of the past usually were beheaded, burned at the stake, imprisoned, beaten, and what not else. Did these people not make the 180 degree turn you seem so concerned about?

Of course, there are consequences to the past decisions I have made. I fully understood those decisions and the business risks that I took. In hindsight, if I had made a few simple decisions differently today I would probably be a multimillionaire and an owner of vast ranch land. Would that be better for me and Geneva and my family? I doubt that very much. God loves a humble and contrite spirit. I doubt that I would even be capable of such a spirit if I were a multimillionaire land owner.

Those decisions taught me great things about God and myself. Would I have learned any of those things if I had not the opportunity to make those decisions and see the consequences of those decisions? That's what life is all about. As Dave Roper says,

> "The purpose of life is to come to know God. If you have lived your life and did not come to know God, your life has been wasted."

How true. That is why Neal it is so wrong to judge other people and their motives. First you just do not know another person's real motives - they are hidden from everyone except God. And secondly, you do not know what is God's plan for that person's life. As Ray Stedman has said, God uses even the sin in your life to complete to perfection his purposes in your life.

Remember that, ultimately, we all are to be judged by God and God judges our motives. I can assure you my motives are pure. I love God and I love God's people. I even love my enemies.

Your brother Gerald

Dear reader I want to pass on to you a little practical wisdom to be learned from the above account. Know who your enemies are. Never be alone with an enemy. Enemies can make up lies, get some friends to repeat the lies and take you to court and have you falsely accused and prosecuted. Being falsely accused of a crime and unable to prove your innocence is very, very, devastating thing to have happen to you. It can destroy you.

Let me reflect a bit on Ray Hamel. My thinking is that Ray is a Judas type. He took up an offense against me and chose to become my enemy for a reason I cannot understand and is unknown to me. Ray is a very personable, charismatic type and loved to tell stories which I enjoyed, so I exchanged stories with him and considered him a friend.

I am reminded by the scripture passages Jesus used in reference to Judas. Paraphrasing the scriptures, He was my friend and ate with me and walked with me and fellowshipped with me, and yet he betrayed me for 30 pieces of silver. Just think about it! 30 pieces of silver (about $1000 in 2012 dollars) buys one almost nothing, except in Judas's case, a junk piece of land nobody wanted, where human corpse, cast off bodies of people nobody wanted to mourn, could be disposed of. Can you imagine Judas betraying Jesus for that? Betraying the Lord of the Universe for 30 pieces of silver? Absolutely astounding!

Can you imagine why Ray Hamill would betray me? I can't. What a tragedy.

CORRESPONDENCE WITH BROTHER

The following is a letter I wrote to my brother, Orneal Kooyers, in May of 2009. The letter states a very, very important truth that personal righteousness comes from love and devotion to Jesus and not from following the law. That dear reader may seem to be splitting hairs, but it is not. Love and devotion to Jesus is the most important principal you will ever understand.

Dear Brother Neal,   May 9, 2009

I really appreciate the time and effort you put into writing such a long letter to me. It proves you love me and are concerned about my salvation and that I should have a correct theological understanding of everything. Thank You.

I have attached two messages of mine from the past that I preached in the Little Salmon River Bible Church or the local Pentecostal group started by some ladies. They should give you a better understanding of what I believe, rather than you should put me into the category of Neo-evangelicals.

I accept from you your concession that the game is over, and that you have conceded, and that I won with the score of 1 to 0.

I am very concerned that you may have fallen into the error of the Post Millennialists and the Re-constructionists. They somehow believe that one of the main goals of our lives as Christians on the earth is to improve society, eliminate wrong doing, and bring the Kingdom of God to the earth. On the contrary, Jesus said to, "Go and make disciples of all nations, immersing them into the name of the Father, the Son, and the Holy Spirit, and teaching them to obey everything I have commanded you". He did not say anything about making the earth safe for the Kingdom on earth, in fact He said you will be persecuted, abused, and even put to death.

I always thought you went to Papua New Guinea to make disciples, not establish some moral society over there. Of course, when there are large numbers of believing Christians in a society, the society tends to become much more morally sound. That is a byproduct of the success of the Gospel, not the goal.

Oliver Cromwell, that great Puritan leader eventually became essentially the dictator of all of England in the 1650's. The puritan movement turned more than half of all the English people into being very devout highly committed people for the Kingdom of God - practically the establishment of the Kingdom of God on earth. What happened to all this huge success? Cromwell died of pneumonia and the country fell into chaos and the monarchy came back in three years. Was it all for naught? Why did God permit this? It does not seem to be God's plan to establish an earthly Kingdom of God on the earth.

Your insight about Greek prepositions does not change the thrust of my argument. I accept that the preposition means up to this point and something more is coming. That certainly is what happened. Jesus did not repeal the Law, but He fulfilled it, and then added to it. My point is that love and devotion to Jesus, which comes through faith is counted for me as righteousness, just as faith did for Abraham the spiritual father of all believers, not following the law, which was given later through angels to Moses. Never throw out the concepts of the written law, but when God's law is written on my heart, I hate sin and any form of corruption from the depth of my being. Sin is ugly, awful, and terrible in anybody and I am absolutely appalled by it. But following rules does not make me any more righteous, but on the contrary, love and devotion to Jesus makes me a whole complete person as both God and I want. Neal, do you understand that? You said that in the pursuit of holiness the Christian sets out the law and follows it. No Neal, that is wrong, my pursuit of holiness is love and devotion to Jesus, not following rules. Jesus through the workings of the Holy Spirit works on me from the inside out.

Think about it Neal, as you watch the TV or a movie or walk down the street, and some babe shows up, just the thought in your mind for a millisecond that that babe would be fun in bed, will condemn you to Hell if following rules makes you righteous, because you have violated the Law as defined by Jesus Himself. That tiny passing thought lost it for you. I have no righteousness in myself except for the fact Jesus, by dying on the cross, paid the debt of my sin, and He has made me righteous. As a result I have love and devotion to Jesus. (Christ in me the hope of glory Col: 1:27)

You threw out the Jewish ceremonial law, but not the civil law so you believe the civil law is still in effect. Why then do you not redistribute all your property to your neighbors every 50 years as the Jews were commanded to do? The jubilee is a civil law not a ceremonial law. So if you have thrown out that civil law how many other civil laws have you thrown out? Do you want to make a list for me?

God's goal is a people for fellowship for eternity. Jesus said we are to eat Him, really to absorb Him. Then as we set our goal to absorb Him and practice that absorption, He promised us that He will raise us up on the LAST DAY. This life on earth is full of trials and tribulations. They are meant to bring us to Jesus. (John 6:26-71)

God runs the world. God runs everything. Your concept of the reality of time and space has very much confused you. The universe is not deterministic as the followers of Newton would have you believe. Our cultural and educational system is absolutely saturated with Neutonianism, so I am not surprised at your false beliefs. Your concept of a changing value of the constant c, which also happens to be the speed of light in a vacuum as measured from the earth is nonsense and has confused you and entered into your theology.

The reality of the universe boils down to two concepts men have created. First is Quantum Mechanics. The second is called Relativity, a poor term. Reality is, that with Quantum Mechanics everything is statistical and fluctuation, an absolutely random soup so to speak. Relativity says the measurement of time and space is a function of the state of the observer. For example, if you could observe the time on a clock located on a photon left over from the beginning of creation arriving from outer space, its clock would read zero. As far as that photon is concerned the universe was just created an extremely small part of a second ago.

Reality is that the integration of all the vast statistical soup in the universe is the determined council of God Himself. God integrates over the grand canonical ensemble of statistical soup and makes the sun get up in the morning as well as everything else that happens. The sun getting up is not the result of some deterministic law of Neutonianism. Instead God gets it up. Without God determining the whole integration of the statistical soup, the universe would not exist. The universe is not as simple as your little treatise on the speed of light would have you believe.

Neal, I write all this and take the time to do this because I am very concerned about your salvation. Others in the family are concerned about your salvation so it is not just my observation. I know it seems like a very small difference. It is not! One's concept of Jesus and how one thinks of Jesus are essential for eternal life. We are to absorb Jesus' life into our life. That's why He gave us Communion to celebrate. We are to be reminded at each time we celebrate Communion that we are to eat and drink Jesus, otherwise why would Jesus give us the ceremony? Yes our sins are washed away by the shedding of His blood and his body was broken for our sins, but the essential concept in the ceremony is to remind us to absorb Jesus. As Paul says, we are not under the Law. We practice what the law teaches because we love Jesus and we know that the Law reflects God's character and we want our own character to be like God's character.

I am motivated to write all this because I recently read the book of Ezekiel. Chapter 33 lays out the principle that if you as a watchman observe a brother in sin and you do not warn him, he will die in his wickedness, but his blood will be on you. If you do warn him and if the brother still sins you are blameless, but if the brother repents you have gained life.

Neal, in the most solemn terms I ask you to examine what you are doing in this business of promoting the dedication to following the Law and examine your own life very carefully. Among those of your relatives I have discussed this with, they are almost unanimous in their concerns of you being on the wrong track, and are very concerned about your salvation itself. As your kid brother, I understand that it will be very difficult to accept it from me. But I don't think anybody else will challenge you on it. I love you and highly respect you, especially for the mentoring you gave me when I was young. And it saddens me very greatly that it has come to this. But you must repent!

You have treated some people with a great deal of unkindness, especially in my memory of Board members you asked to leave the Board. The Christian man of God just does not treat people that way. My children and grandchildren were offended by your behavior at Lost Lake. I as your blood brother did not personally take up an offense. Nevertheless, you came across to them and Geneva as a very poor representative of God's missionary, and they did not see you acting as a man of God would. Geneva saw you as being angry recently in Santa Cruz when you told me to shut up.

Muslims and Mormons are examples of those whose religion is to follow rules and laws. Eventually they add to the rules and laws to make themselves even more righteous. Then they define their own rules so that righteous acts includes multiple wives, making slaves of women, stealing from non-Mormons and non-Muslims, and even murder of unbelievers because, as the Koran teaches, they have made a new law that murder and stealing from gentiles is a righteous act! Neal, once you get into rule making there is no end of new rules. And then they can define their rules so that love, joy peace, kindness, goodness, and such are thrown out when contesting with a gentile. Wow, what corruption, and it is the result of making rules to follow as part of a collective concept of a group. That corruption can suck you in. Religion based on rule following has power to be a terrible corruption and a very wicked evil. Neal, flee from such and put it out of your life before it is too late.

Neal, this is extremely important. You do not become righteous by following the Law. You just do not. Righteousness comes through faith, with love and devotion to Jesus, and it is the gift from God. The pursuit of holiness is not following rules but absorbing the life of Jesus.
Love in Jesus,
Your brother
Gerald

Over the years Neal and I have had discussions about the methodology that God used to create the universe. One idea that Neal seemed to propagate was that the universal constant c, which is also the speed of light in a dielectric free medium has varied since creation so has to change the apparent time since the universe was created. He put it into a publication of his printed thing called Tidbits and Musings #56. I responded as follows:

I respond to your #56
Consider the first five verses of Geneses:

> [1]In the beginning God created the heavens and the earth. [2]The earth was formless and void, and darkness was over the surface of the deep, and the Spirit of God was moving over the surface of the waters. [3]Then God said, "Let there be light"; and there was light. [4]God saw that the light was good; and God separated the light from the darkness. [5]God called the light day, and the darkness He called night. And there was evening and there was morning, one day.

As I read these verses, God is providing us a clear point of reference. Clearly the progression is from creation of the Universe to the surface of the waters on the surface of the Earth. God's Spirit was hovering or moving over the surface. Then God said, "Let there be light". It seems to me you are taking huge liberties with the text. God did not say He created light but said let there be light on the surface of the Earth. This is a huge difference.

You put an unwarranted emphasis on the electromagnetic spectrum. There are four basic forces in the creation, that of the weak nuclear force, the strong nuclear force, the electromagnetic force, and the gravitational force. In the creation of the heavens and the earth all four forces must be present to have a creation of the heavens; otherwise you have no creation of the heavens (or the universe) as we know it. These four forces are what constitute the universe. They are what define the universe. Matter and energy are produced and exist because of these four forces.

c, which just happens to be the speed of light in a dielectric free medium, is a fundamental constant which is involved in determining the magnitude of the four forces in their relationships to one another. c also shows up in defining quantum mechanical effects at extremely small dimensions. A slightly different c than the one we have makes for a very different universe, probably one that cannot exist, and certainly not one for human habitation.

Let me suggest that the idea of electromagnetism being created after the heavens and earth were created is absurd.

Brother, Gerald

GRIEF AND DAUGHTER CRYSTAL

In the beginning of 2012 Geneva and I went through a period of great grief when it became publicly known that, John Cook, the husband of our precious daughter Crystal was conducting an adulterous affair. What a terrible horrible grief. I had written John a letter about a year before because most of my family was concerned about his apparent relationship with a lady Crystal and John had brought into their family, calling her their adopted daughter. A copy is as follows:

John,   February 1, 2011

Out of love and concern for you and your family I write you.

It appears to believers and unbelievers watching that you are involved in an affair or are conducting an appearance of an affair. (I Thess. 5:22 "Abstain from all appearance of evil". KJV)

A Christian leader and the preacher of righteousness must be above reproach. (I Timothy 3:7, "He must have a good report of them that are without lest he fall into the condemnation of the devil." KJV) Thus this appearance of an affair is in-congruent with Christianity.

This needs to be terminated through a decision by you. The continuation of this relationship damages Christ's Church. You have become a laughingstock to unbelievers. The cause of Christ is being damaged. God will not be mocked. God will deal with it as God in His sovereign will determines, but as your father-in-law and a believer in Jesus Christ I am warning you that this is sin and you need to repent and put an end to it.

None of us are without sin so please understand that I humbly bring this to your attention. I have a very grave concern that if this relationship continues it will have a devastating effect on you and your family. I truly love you all! You have a very fine wife and lovely children. They need to be nurtured and cared for. They are your first responsibility after your service to God, but before your service to the Church.

You may feel that you may be stuck to a "Tar Baby". In that case I urge you most sincerely to seek wise counsel of Christian leaders and the most wise counsel of your wife as to how to extricate yourself from the "Tar."

I have wanted to discuss this matter with you for a while. There has not been an appropriate time to discuss alone with you. As you go through this decision process I will continue to pray for you and your family, and make myself available to discuss and pray with you. John, I am here to help. May the Lord Jesus richly bless you.
In the Love of Christ,
Gerald P. Kooyers

At that time John gave me a brief non statement on anything in response.

About a year later when the affair was publicly revealed, I wrote the following letter to my precious daughter Crystal, after the adulterous affair my son in law John Cook was conducting with a woman whose name was Jana became public knowledge. This adultery was identified as polygamy by Jana's father, who took Jana's sister's letter, which claimed a polygamist relationship, to John's School Board, and the whole thing was picked up by the Associated Press and broadcast by the internet to the whole world. John then resigned as Superintendent of the Horse Shoe Bend Unified School District.

My dearest daughter Crystal,   January 20, 2012

My grief over the media reports of you, John, and Jana, seem to overwhelm me with sadness and has put my spirit in depression.

I clearly remember the day when you came to me and asked me if you should marry John or not, and you said you would do as I would direct in the question of whether you should marry John or not. I confess I did not do my homework on John, and I, therefore, deeply repent of my laziness and lack of action, and very humbly ask for your forgiveness. Crystal please forgive me. I deeply regret not responding to your need when I clearly was your spiritual leader, and responsible, and should have given you solid measured advice. I repent.

This recollection is now wrapped in sadness and despair as these news reports and these public talk show host discussions about polygamy in Horseshoe Bend indicate something has gone awfully wrong in your marriage.

I am perplexed about where to begin this discussion. Russ Atkins called me the other evening and told me your church has put you under church discipline for polygamy. That discipline, Crystal, is intended to heal and restore you to fellowship with the Christian community. Please listen to the church people and church leaders as you promised when you became a church member and follow their leadership to restore you to fellowship. These leaders of your church hold the keys to the Kingdom of God. Church discipline has the power to destine you for hell and then put you into hell. The Church into which you were baptized puts power into the hands of the Elders of the Church to turn you over to Satan himself for discipline. You may not necessarily believe this but that is of no account as your mother and I publicly declared before God and His people that you, our baby daughter, would be raised up in the truth of the Kingdom of the Lord Jesus. You were taught this, the truth, and I know you have believed this truth, and you understand this truth. And if the Elders discipline you and turn you over to Satan for his discipline that will indeed happen and the consequences of that is an awful horror to even think about.

Crystal, there are many, many people who deeply love you, including me, your mother, and your brother and sisters. We are all available to help you, and will be available to you for anything, at any time. Talk to us.

Since I have had very little discussion with you about spiritual matters over the years since you left home and got married, I wish now to give you some fatherly instruction. Please follow my arguments carefully and pray about them.

We humans are destined for eternity. This life here on the earth is only a beginning. The wonders of eternity we can only slightly imagine. Think carefully about what I tell you, it is a matter of life and death.

We are spiritual beings. God breathed your spirit into your single cell beginning with coded information from me and your mother that gave you life in a body of flesh. You grew and developed into a very fine, very intelligent, very capable lady with zero defects, except for the fallen state within your genetic code you inherited from our forefather Adam. We humans function in four realms, that of spirit, body, soul, and heart. Your heart resides deep within your spirit, and when you came to believe in God, and put your trust in God, by faith you were given a new cleansed heart. From out of the heart comes either righteousness or wickedness.

In some spiritual complex way we do not understand with our minds, because it is spiritual, humans are given a taste of worship through the sexual act between a man and a woman. This was demonstrated in ancient god temples when men came to worship the god, they engaged the temple prostitutes. Before Christianity came into being and began to dominate culture, widespread sexual corruption and perversion existed in Greek, Roman, Jewish, and other cultures. Even today in the higher levels of Hindu, Buddhist, Muslim sages and gurus, sexual corruption and perversion prevails and dominates and is a dominate part of the higher inner leadership.

Let me give you a quote from one of our modern prominent female historians in her book about the history of fornication, an unbeliever in Jesus at that, who dislikes, and maybe even hates, Christianity:

> "The apostle Paul's Christian writings in the Bible, the ideas of sexual morality and the resulting social change, were revolutionary in their formulation as even those of the old Greeks, that of Plato, the Pythagoreans, and the early Stoics. In the first century as Christianity was starting to grow and went out to conquer the world, there was absolutely no reason to think that driving the universal lifestyle of fornication from the world would take hold with any greater success than Plato's socialist ideals of civic moderation and justice, or the Pythagoreans' aims to improve moral character through pro-creationism, or the early Stoics' plan to train citizens to achieve right reason and action through mutually friendly and communal sexual ideas. But Christianity conquered all! Fornication was banished to houses of whoredom and removed from cultured polite Christian society, and since Christianity dominated, polite secular society also conformed to the Christian standards.

The apostle Paul in his missionary activities issued a universal and Christ-centered Biblical imperative against the fornicating lifestyles of the Greeks, Canaanites, and rebellious Israelites. Christian human sexual and reproductive concepts must be devoted strictly to the biblical God through virginity, or paired marriage in the body of Christ. This pattern of sexual devotion provides for the only permissible basis of social order, for all of humanity, and as such must serve The Almighty God alone. The Apostle Paul, the Christian Gospel, absolutely insists that all those who come to be Christians must cease from dedicating any aspect of their minds or sexual bodies to their former pagan gods. Christians must vilify unbeliever pagan sexual heritage as wicked, and this heritage is even a deadly fornication against God Himself. Thus, a new order, a new order of virginity, celibacy, or marriage in the Lord, is the sole path to salvation and immortality. This, of course, was how God intended it from the beginning - one man and one woman, each woman to have her one only husband, and each man to have his one only wife."

That historian clearly understood Christianity, even though she did not like it and opposed it. Thus it must be absolutely clear from the history of Christianity and the New Testament Bible that polygamy is not Christian. It never has been and it never will be. For 2000 years the Church of Jesus Christ has rejected polygamy and all forms of fornication and adultery. That unbeliever historian clearly sees Christianity for what it is and polygamy is not part of Christianity. Polygamy exists only in cults that might call themselves Christian, but are not Christian, or in the Muslim religion, or some other pagan thing.

So how is it that you and John and Jana have embraced polygamy? I have come to understand, and let me suggest it to you, that when humans perform the sexual act there is a spiritual interaction where the woman's spirit is added to the man's spirit and the man's spirit is added to the woman's spirit. The apostle Paul says our spirits are like a cup meant to hold God's spirit. But our spirit cups can also hold evil spirits or demons. As sundry sexual contact is encountered evil spirits or demons are added into the spiritual mix. So every prostitute, or high school or college immoral woman, that John ever encountered, added her spirit to John's spirit, and so then demons

413

have had access to John's spirit, and now all these evil spirits have been added to your spirit. Demons are out to possess you. Their weapons are deceit and lies. Satan himself is the father of lies. Once you accept the lies put into your heart (through your spirit) from demons, you believe the lies. Ultimately the evil spirit's goals within your spirit are to lead you into insanity and death. Satan's and his cohort's goal is death, here and now, and into eternity.

You do not know how many demons Jana may have absorbed into her spirit cup in her lifetime. These demons have now been added to your spirit cup through John. It is now no wonder that you cannot even now think correctly or clearly, and have believed the lie that polygamy is a correct lifestyle. What a lie!

Crystal I grieve for you. If you continue in polygamy you will not have a ministry among Christians. Your work among the pro-life movement will end when they find out you are engaged in polygamy. You will not be asked to sing or play your harp in churches, weddings and other Christian events when they understand you are a polygamist. Do you really want your ministry and service to the Lord Jesus Himself destroyed?

It is now clear to those (me and other real Christ loving Christians) who have watched John operate and in close contact with John, that John has been corrupted. He grew up in a family with a Mormon father and a war bride mother new to Mormonism, and is a son of the military culture with its widespread permissiveness and perversion; so permissiveness and perversion must seem normal to John. Crystal, I deeply grieve for you.

Let me review with you the experiences I have had with John. I appointed him manager of Salmon River Challenge. He falsified boatmen training report cards, and by that act committed perjury. The State of Idaho through the Idaho Outfitters and Guides Board had the evidence which was provided by the Turnipseeds. I was faced with the choice of terminating John or facing the criminal prosecution of Salmon River Challenge, and the termination of the outfitting license of Salmon River Challenge. Being the kind man that I am, I quietly fired John and told nobody but the State of Idaho Guides Board about it. In hindsight, that was stupid, and only protected John from prosecution for perjury.

John once thought the ranch needed cleaning up and dumped some of my equipment and valuables into the town dumpster. What presumption. I ordered him to get the stuff back. He reluctantly did it.

In the words of an office lady who worked for me at Salmon River Challenge thirty years ago and this is a direct quote,

"John lies and John believes his own lies."

You remember when John thought to accuse me and mom of some imagined evil doing so that mom was not to see her grandchild that you gave birth too. You must remember the daylong meeting at the ranch where Russ Atkins, Jackson Cramer, and one of Jackson's elders from Moscow, Idaho, spent a whole day with us in a meeting to resolve any issues between us. Those Christian men gave the Christian council and opinion that there was nothing to any of John's allegations, and told John so, and John said he would think about it. Then John did nothing to prevent your mom from enjoying the fellowship of your children, much to your mother's relief.

After I was forced by economic forces to file for a second bankruptcy, which then effected John's grandmother, June Cook, John became very angry and very vociferously turned the pastor of the Community Church, Fred Emery, against me so that Fred attempted Church discipline against me because I had not paid my real estate taxes, an absurd allegation since the County of Idaho will always get it's tax money no matter what I do. Fortunately, the other elders of the Community Church did not buy into it, but John's actions eventually resulted in destroying my ministry at the Community Church.

John reported to everybody that he could that I had caught and kept an illegal fish, a steelhead. Your mom and her brother who fished with me that day were witnesses to the fact that it was a legal fish. John lied.

The book of proverbs says that a liar hates those he lies about. So John hates me. Why I do not know except for the fact I asked you to wait a year before marrying John. In my mind I thought this daughter of mine, this highly intelligent, very competent, Crystal, will figure this guy out herself during the course of a year. So I did not do my homework and I let you, dear Crystal, down. Again, please forgive me. You married a liar and now you have believed his lies and you are willing to accept John's lust for polygamy. Crystal, I am so very, very, sorry.

The book of Proverbs says from a liar comes forth lies. John can no longer be believed in anything. Your mother and I understood this some time ago. We just concluded to take John with a grain of salt. Crystal, you just cannot believe anything he says. Crystal you cannot believe anything he tells you. John seeks to alienate and keep you away from anyone who might minister to you. He has done this over the years to your mother and me. Trust your sister Susanne and others like her who have understood your situation for some time, and, consequently, love you very deeply, and want very much to help you.

To be involved in continued public sin results in great shame. With your public sin of polygamy you will not be able to look people in the eye. Shame will overwhelm you. You will be embarrassed. How will you ever be able to converse and interact with the people you have ministered to in the past? All those people you ministered to over the years, and greatly benefited from your nurturing and ministry, will even be embarrassed to talk to you and will avoid you. The real Christians among them will cry out to God asking why oh why? What happened to Crystal? Has she become a captive of Satan? They will indeed grieve and mourn over Crystal as I will, indeed.

Crystal, I give you true testimony, the most effective prayer I ever made was when I asked God to remove all and any evil spirits from within my spirit. It worked. From that day on I had a clear vision of what I was to do even though I might not like what I was to do or what was going to happen to me. The Holy Spirit of Jesus moved into my spirit in a new way. Confusion disappeared. Jesus' love covered me. I now wake up in the morning praising Jesus and telling Him I love him, and even when I am wandering around in the mountains by myself, I find myself praising Jesus.

Crystal, pray that same prayer. Ask God to remove any and all evil spirits from the cup of your spirit. Ask God to cast those evil spirits into the deepest pit of Abaddon, into hell itself. I assure you; God will hear that prayer and act on it.

Crystal, as you well know there is forgiveness in Jesus. Spend time in deep prayer, confessing and worshiping Jesus. Ask Jesus for wisdom so you will know what to do.

As your father I now want to give you deep thoughtful measured advice. You must get out of your present situation with John. The path of a lustful adulterous pervert leads only to complete oblivion and destruction and eventually to hell itself. You will be dragged down with it. You must flee now. Do not wait. Once out of the John situation you must repent. Cry out to Jesus and lay your soul bare before Him and repent, repent, repent!

You have a loving heavenly Father who is ready and waiting to embrace you with his open arms - all you have to do is flee Satan and turn toward your Father God.

God hates divorce. I hate divorce. You have Biblical ground for divorce from the words of Jesus Himself. Do it quick. You are in danger of being sucked into hell.

You yet have the responsibility of your youngest daughter and a teen age son. They need nurturing and loving care from their mother. They are your God given responsibility, and you must get them out of the John situation, and give them the loving care they need to mature into a Christian man and a Christian woman. Crystal, do it; do not wait.

Remember, all of us, I, your mother, your brother, your sisters, your Pastor, your Church, and many others are ready to help. Call on us.

With much tender loving care,
Your father,
Gerald

As I write this in the spring of 2012 we, of course, do not know the final outcome of this whole matter. Geneva and I pray often that Crystal and John will come to repentance. Life has its terrible complexities. Sin, grief, and repentance are part of life. They all seem to be part of the process of how and when we come to know and deeply love God, or the process where we come to hate God and then deceive ourselves into believing that He does not exist in order to protect our little egos. Oh, what grief.

This brought into my memory letters Geneva and I had written to Crystal years before this in 1986. At that time John had decided I was a sinner, and he told Geneva and me we would no longer be permitted to see their children, which, of course, are our grandchildren. That greatly grieved Geneva; so we responded by writing letters. They are as follows:

My Dearest Daughter Crystal   March 24, 1986

It was with considerable grief that I read your letter of March 15, 1986. Nevertheless, I thank you for it and appreciate the time you spent to prepare it. I have examined myself as a result of your letter and deeply appreciate your love and concern for me.

I am not sure where to begin, but first let's examine the concept of truth in love as described in Ephesians 4. I suggest you read and study that passage, especially verse 15, "Instead speaking the truth in love", and verse 25, "Put off falsehood and speak truthfully to his neighbor". This means that we all are to speak truthfully to each other in the context of love. We are not to speak things so as to intentionally hurt one another.

It is my conviction that one of the greatest functions of a wife as the helpmate God has given us husbands is the speaking of truth. Two together are much stronger than two, each by themselves. Men, in seeking their aspirations and dreams, are tempted to cut corners and do things which perhaps are of a gray nature rather than a clean black and white in the ethical realm. A wife's function can be to point out these areas and remind her husband of the truth. A wife, and this I have observed in many very sad divorce cases, can be docile and obedient, and in that obedience she assumes she is to be quiet and not speak up and let her husband do as he wills. The husband then becomes very willful doing as he pleases, mistreating his wife, and because he has very little restraint and believes that in everything he does he is right, makes stupendous mistakes which ultimately ruin him and those around him.

An example of this is my own brother Howard. Carole never spoke up about anything and Howard became like a loose cargo in a ship, knocking off people here and there as he rolled through life, eventually discarding Carole with her six babies.

Now in your situation Crystal, you are one of my loveliest daughters. You have a quiet spirit, and you honor and respect your husband. You are very beautiful in the Lord with qualities of peace and joy. One of your most important duties must now and continually be to speak to John the truth and the truth in every situation you and he face together in life - in doing that you will be a great helpmate. And then John will be successful, which is one of the things I perceive he wants most in life. One cannot be successful if he acts on the basis of false information or premises. One must love the truth in order to be really successful.

Now, let's get to the hard part. Let me quote Connie from last summer, "John lies to all of us, but John believes his own lies". Crystal, I understand this hurts, but I am trying to speak the truth in love so that the relationship between you and John, Geneva and I can be healed. John has lied to all of us - Geneva, Susanne, Ronda, Connie, the boatmen and me. If I accept Connie's words, then in John's own image of himself, he is not lying. Thus, the problem is very difficult. Let me review a few things. John lied about his license, told Rhonda a different versions of stories than he told Susanne, gave instructions to send such and such boatmen, then changed it, and then said he didn't, and told one person a boatman will work for no pay and another person that the boatman should be paid. John also forged my name, Ross Bagley's name, and Dale Turnipseed's name on training cards. The examples are many, and seem to indicate a lifestyle. As John's wife, you will continually need to point out the truth to John in a quiet respectful way. God will certainly help you in this if you ask in prayer.

Let's now examine the charges you laid on me. You lived with me for 18 years. You know me. Your mother and I supported you through college. We provided well for you and your brother and sisters. We have supported missionaries, churches, church projects, and at times friends in need. In all of these years, have you known me to commit fraud or swindle anyone? One who deceives and commits fraud and swindles, keeps things for himself and attempts to gain for himself, and does not give to others as your mother and I have all our lives together. Your charge of swindling is just plain false. SRC ended the season with about $20,000 in bills to pay. I had no other money. It was impossible to pay anybody until assets were sold. Your charge of swindling is simply not true.

Let me clear up your understanding of idolatry. Idols serve men to help them. Men seek gain or favor with the gods; consequently, they pay homage or serve these idols so that they may gain wealth, power, women, position, etc. An idolater invokes the imaged power of his idol so as to help him gain. Your mother and I have been blessed with a measure of money. This has come about by hard work, perseverance, and providence. Money has little real meaning to us, and if it were completely to disappear from our lives, our lives and relationship would be little different. Your mother and I serve the Lord Jesus Christ. We will continue to do so the rest of our lives and in eternity.

Crystal, we don't worship our possessions. We have plenty of stuff and are stewards over that stuff. Please don't misunderstand that.

As far as reviling is concerned, I think you confuse direct speech about a situation with what you call reviling. Your mother and I have a direct responsibility from God to govern our children. We must admonish, reprove, and otherwise rebuke our children. That is our job. I have never reviled anybody in town. That is a lie. Bring anybody to my face who will say I "reviled" him. You will find nobody. I hold everybody in respect because they are God's children. Have you ever heard me tell a joke with a racial slur? Have you heard me put anybody down just to make myself look good? Crystal, be honest. To accuse me of being a reviler is a lie.

Crystal, please look at the lawsuits. Lawsuits are not a prima facie case for doing wrong. Clancy is greedy and wants more money. Reinhard did not deliver as he promised. Arty Johnson died because of unthinking and evil people. The savings and Loan Company did not pay as they promised and damaged us and committed fraud. We could not pay the banks because the savings and loan did not pay us. Others came about because we could not pay our bills; there is nothing intrinsically wrong in this. My mistake was one of presumption. I assumed my income stream would continue like it did in the past. That's an easy error for anyone to make.

You falsely accuse us about our possessions. We are stewards over what God has provided. Out here on a ranch, many of our possessions are tools or machines which are required to sustain life out here. When anyone borrows or steals them, they put our ability to maintain the place in jeopardy. Therefore, we cannot let anyone borrow, use, steal, keep, etc. these tools and machines without risk of big problems. Lots of stuff around here does not belong to me, but to a partnership for which I am responsible. These assets need to be protected or sold, that is my responsibility to my partners. I think you confuse worship of possessions with respect for other people's property. It is wrong for you or John to appropriate for your own use, property which belongs to Geneva and me. It is wrong to take our property and give it away to somebody else. This is a simple extension of the commandment, "thou shall not steal". John has a weakness in this area. For example, he borrowed Steve Cook's pickup the other day and took it to Grangeville without telling Steve. Kim indicated Steve was quite upset. This is simple disregard for other people's property.

Susanne is well taken care of and you need not worry about her. If you really are interested in Susanne, remember our stipulations when we helped you and John through college, that when you are out of college and can afford it, you would repay the sum we advanced by helping your sisters. You can start, if you like, by sending Susanne $500.00 per month, or any amount you think appropriate.

Let's look at SRC for a moment. I hired John and gave him a tremendous opportunity. I put him fully in charge to sink or swim, expecting him to tell me what he was doing so that I could guide and advise him and avoid repeating past mistakes. Remember, we had a meeting together before John was hired, stating he needed to communicate to me all that was happening. I put him in charge of a company with little debt and great potential. He then almost never talked to me. He gave people raises without discussing it with me. He built equipment at great cost which we could have done without. He neglected marketing and sent somebody who knew less than he did out to sell trips. He mistreated guests so that in all likelihood, they will not come back for another trip. The whole thing was a disaster. John sunk. John and I are equally the blame for the failure. Me because I should have put many more constraints on John and forced him to meet with me every day and forced him to do the right job every day, and John, because he presumptuously took off thinking he knew everything there was to know about river outfitting and needed to talk to nobody. John gave raises to people whose salaries should have been cut. He hired the wrong people; he fired the wrong people and did not watch his costs. SRC under John was a disaster.

Now you and John come along and seem to blame me for SRC problems. I spent very little time on SRC and since John did not come to me, but figured he knew how to do everything, I just gave him lots of rope and he hung himself. If you and John blame me for all of SRC's problems, you do not face the truth.

Please understand that I am not saying that I am not a sinner. I have Adam's sinful nature and yes, I sin. Remember too the scriptures clearly teach we are to love one another and to forgive one another. I have forgiven and after this is over, will forget everything that's happened. I hold nothing against John and you, and freely forgive John of anything he might have done against me. You know I forgive you.

Crystal, false accusations of the brethren is the work of Satan. See Rev 12:10, 2 Peter 2:11 and Jude 9. Be very careful before you accuse anybody. As Jude says, even Gabriel the archangel, did not accuse Satan in the dispute over Moses' body.

The context of I Corinthians 5:9-13 is that the message therein is directed to the church or the body of believers related to the one who is within their midst, and yet calls himself a Christian and yet lives in immorality. The church, through the elders and pastors, are to exert this authority. You err if you think you can apply this to just anybody to fit some dishonorable scheme such as putting people out of your life whom God has placed there. A higher rule exists, that is, "Honor your father and mother". The procedure to follow is Matthew 18. You and John have not done that. If you think a meeting last summer in the context of SRC business or your brief time with me was Matthew 18, you are mistaken. Get all of the wrongs I have committed against you and John together. Make a list and come, as directed to Matthew 18, "If your brother sin against you" and lay them before me.

When you speak to me, you need to consider my answer and then answer back to me. Don't think I am unresponsive. I am an engineer and a scientist. You need to logically present me with your facts, hear my answer and answer back again and examine my response. I am searching for the truth and will not just accept what you say without skepticism so as to not examine the facts. You have not confronted me in any way. John just shuts up and says nothing. Neither of you have executed Matthew 18.

Crystal, your mother and I love you very much. We want the best for you and John and your family. To accuse us falsely and to then use that to break fellowship would be a great sin. Please do not do that. We would be grieved very much. Don't let John use false accusations as a cover to satisfy some imagined revenge of his. He has already said in another context that your mother and I will not see our grandchildren. This is wrong. We love you. You are part of us. Please do not grieve us.

Let's have a meeting together with the four of us and if you like, a third party reference and proceed along the lines of Matthew 18. Let's heal this up and enjoy sweet fellowship together.

Love,
Your father, Gerald

I have provided this above letter in this thing to give you dear reader understanding and wisdom. The roots of John Cook's behavior and the terrible adulterous decent into the lie of polygamy are indicated in his behavior in 1986. If one had all the wisdom in the world what would one have done about it in 1986? I did not do my homework on John when Crystal asked me if she should marry John or not in 1981. The fact that she asked me the question indicated she had doubts about it. I deeply repent of the wrong I did to Crystal by not doing my homework on John and giving Crystal a clear answer of no, Crystal,

"Do not marry John".

LEADERSHIP AND COMMUNITY CHURCH

While looking for lost documents I came across two letters to Dave Roper, past pastor of the Cole Community Church in Boise. Geneva and I knew him from our days at the Peninsula Bible Church in Palo Alto, California when Dave was a pastor there for many years. I wrote these letters when I was in the process of being removed from the leadership of the Salmon River Community Church in Riggins. This also pertains to the Cooks and in this case also to John Cook and also involved Fred Emery, the pastor of the Community Church in Riggins.

Dear Dave,   March 19, 1993

I purposely waited several weeks until the first of February and now have waited again before writing you this letter so as to reflect on it correctly.

You and your ministry have had a very deep, profoundly beneficial effect on my life, that of my wife, Geneva, and my children. For that we thank God most earnestly. We appreciate very much the dedication and diligence you put into proclaiming the word of God in a most correct, concise, easy to understand, and spiritually uplifting manner. This happened, of course, over the years while you served at PBC, and continued here in Idaho as we have received consistently your teachings through tapes and written sermons. We have thanked God again and again for the benefits we have received through your ministry of teaching.

Your ministry has benefited thousands which perhaps no man can count. My father was a pastor in the Presbyterian Church, but a conservative one in a liberal denomination, since he had graduated from Calvin College and Seminary in Grand Rapids, Michigan, and also took a Masters Divinity Degree from Westminster Theological Seminary in Philadelphia in 1930. I lived, grew up, and was enveloped by dinner table talk into church problems and controversies. I have since wandered through many churches and several denominations so it is not without the background of some very educated experiences that I make the very positive and heartfelt observations about your ministry.

It is my expectation that you will receive a very great reward for your services before the judgment seat of the Lord Jesus Christ.

424

It has, therefore, then struck me as quite inconsistent with the above observations that your Institute of Biblical Studies has produced a man like Fred Emery, and sent him out to preach and teach the gospel of the Lord Jesus Christ.

I asked Fred one day if he had ever read Ray Stedman's book, "Authentic Christianity". He said no, he had never heard of it. Dave, how is that possible? If your Institute of Biblical Studies is to have a positive effect in the Kingdom of The Lord Jesus Christ, then your trainees must of all things understand the new covenant and certainly go forth from their preparation committed to proclaiming the new covenant gospel and all its ramifications. To not have this as one of your main goals would mean that your institute is just one more wart on the whole body of institutions which pass themselves off as seminaries or would be seminaries. Stedman's book must certainly be required reading for deep study for all students which pass through your system.

I have made the assumption that any institution with which you are associated would proclaim the new covenant gospel of the Lord Jesus. If I am in error in this assumption, then I stand corrected and would appreciate your statement to that effect.

Fred's teaching and ministry, in the practice thereof, is a ministry of legalism and perfectionism which may properly be called Phariseeism for in practice it is just like that of the Pharisees. The Pharisees put burdens on people. Fred in his counseling of couples in trouble, and other counseling tells people to shape up. He gives them rules to follow. He places before them a standard of performance which they must perform to in order to be accepted and loved by their fellow Christians. People who are not "faithful" according to his measure of performance are put down and rejected from his sphere of important people in the body. He looks at outward appearances; people that look good impress him. He does not look at the heart of a man or woman whether he or she loves the Lord Jesus and is committed to serving Him. Rather Fred looks for attendance at meetings and is impressed by puffed up speech. Fred seems to have no discernment about who loves the Lord deeply and who loves the Lord little.

Dave just so you understand the effect of this let me describe the church situation in Riggins. There are two main evangelical churches, the Assembly of God Church and the Salmon River Community Church, and two sort of peripheral small groups, the Catholics and the Mormons. Last fall some people organized a potluck at the High School on a Sunday afternoon of all the "Christians in Riggins". The Assembly was calling a new pastor so none of them showed up. Maybe three of us and our families from the Salmon River Community Church showed up. There were over 50 people there who called themselves Christians and did not attend any church. Many of them are my friends. Since then a new church has been started, led by two women, one from New Zealand. Their roots are in YWAM (Youth with a mission). This group has gathered all the misfits in town. The prostitutes, bar keeps, and establishment church rejects, are flocking to its services in a room behind the main town bar. Dave, these people soon came to know that Fred's Pharisee gospel has no power for them and they have rejected it. These are hurting troubled people in many cases, yet they know that the Lord Jesus has the answer and they love Him.

Dave, I really appreciate your efforts to work out reconciliation in the meeting we had together. The real issue, however, never was addressed. Please accept my sincere thanks to you for taking time out from your very busy schedule to spend time with an old faithful friend to help in what was probably an impossible situation.

The real issue is the New Covenant Gospel. Fred's gospel is a Pharisee version of some legalistic system which I don't even want to understand. Needless to say, my efforts to kindly persuade him in this area eventually got convoluted in the ramifications of my financial affairs, so that so much dust got thrown into the air that the main issue is completely lost, and seemingly, I am no longer in a position to even suggest to Fred that the OTHER GOSPEL he is preaching is not that of the Lord Jesus Christ, and not that which the Apostle Paul preached.

Dave, I feel sure that you too saw through the trumped up meaningless charges which Fred used to remove me from my ministry. You concluded it rather well saying that I, Jerry Kooyers, had or have a bad attitude about real estate taxes. Dave, you probably well suspect that I have lots of bad attitudes. They come and go as Satan himself makes his attacks on me. You can be assured that my mind logically judges attitudes of all types and properly condemns the bad ones and puts them in their place through the Holy Spirit within me.

Dave, since I have been effectively removed from my responsibilities as a ruling Elder which include that of watching over the purity of the word and the supervision of its proclamation, and that you and George confirmed that removal through your presence and advice given that I should resign, it is now your responsibility before the Lord Jesus Himself to supervise Fred and watch over the preaching and purity of the word proclaimed in the Salmon River Community Church. It is not as if you have been formally given this responsibility, it is yours by default.

As I awake almost every morning, first giving thanks to the Lord for life and His presence, and praise him for a few minutes, then often indignation swells up within me, and I cry out before the Lord, "How long will you permit the terrible devastating effects of Fred's Pharisee gospel on the little flock in Riggins". Dave, anguish comes over me when I reflect what a poor job you and George did on investigating the real roots of what seemingly might be construed as a simple case of a poor attitude about taxes. It is as if you and George don't care about that little flock. You seem to care not that they be fed rocks and not bread. Deep within me Dave this matter will not rest. I love that little flock. My grandchildren need a little fellowship where they can grow and be nurtured. That little flock has very precious people within it and now their love grows cold. Dave that Pharisee gospel simply must go!

It is my prayer before the Lord, and I ask you also to join me to pray that Fred be removed by the Lord Jesus Himself from being pastor of the Salmon River Community Church.

Dave, be assured of my continued deep love and respect for you and your ministry. You have been a great influence on my life, and any confidence I have in the Lord has been through the Holy Spirit using many of your sermons and teachings to work in my life.

The Lord did not promise us that serving Him would be easy. I am sure your ministry is not easy, and I grieve that perhaps I have contributed to its pain. If so, please forgive me.

With deep love and respect,
Gerald P. Kooyers

Here is the second letter about a year later.

Dear Dave,   April 16, 1994

The thought keeps coming to me again and again that I need to write you a letter. Our financial situation keeps going on according to some script. The Lord God takes very good care of Geneva and me so we really have no concerns except to learn all that the Lord Jesus intends for us to learn.

My spirit does not rest about the situation in the Salmon River Community Church. If you will remember, last year about this time I gave over to you the responsibility before the Lord to supervise Fred Emery and watch over the preaching and purity of the Word proclaimed in the Salmon River Community Church. This came about as you will remember because of the counsel given and the involvement of George Peltier directly into the situation between Fred and me. Fred has told me he directly relied upon George Peltier and his counsel for Fred's actions against me and my removal from leadership. Fred represented to me that George completely concurred in the action that Fred would take. You should understand that that action was wrong and evil, and without foundation in any church polity of the reformed persuasion which is my experience. Subsequently, Geneva, George, Fred, you and I met in McCall, so I assume you are apprised of the facts.

At that meeting in McCall Fred made the statement that he would not make John Cook, who is my son in law, an Elder in the Salmon River Community Church. Now I know my son in law, and an important issue between Fred and me continually, was that I consistently maintained that John Cook was not qualified to be an Elder, while Fred over several years wanted to make him an Elder. Because of our local church policy that the Elders do things unanimously, John did not become an Elder. After my removal, sometime about June of last year John Cook became an Elder in the Salmon River Community Church.

Now I know my son in law a little. He comes out of Mormonism. His only training in the scriptures is what he received in the Mormon Church. I encouraged Fred many times to disciple John but it is my belief that nothing was accomplished. You should understand that John Cook makes a very good first impression and that he is a close friend of Fred.

In the fall, Bill Wicks, resigned his position of Elder and moved to Lewiston. On Labor Day Elder Dwaine Clemons was killed in a plane crash. Now the only Elders are Fred Emery and John Cook.

The situation in the little flock of believers in the Salmon River Community Church just continues to deteriorate. Attendance is low; a few new people in town attend there. Fred's reputation among unbelievers in the town of Riggins also continues to deteriorate. Fred's ministry seems to be completely rejected by God fearing Christians in Riggins who until just recently have had no other place to fellowship as the Assembly of God Church in Riggins has had its problems too.

Fred has John teaching and preaching quite a bit. Fred seems to not understand its Mormon character. Perhaps that is because Fred's Phariseeism is maybe not much different than Mormonism.

Dave, I am terrible grieved by this situation. It consumes me every day. It is a major subject in my prayers. I am very impatient with God's delay in dealing with the situation. I struggle and cry every day about how long that little flock of believers will be given stones instead of bread. It hurts terribly. I feel responsible. I am responsible. You will remember that I called you for suggestions for pulpit supply when that little church was without a pastor. You sent me George, Fred, and Tom Manning. Subsequently, Fred became the Pastor upon my recommendation.

My conscience greatly troubles me because I was the major person and the leader who changed the church government. Consequently, now there is no way the congregation by itself can remove Fred.

The ministry now in the Salmon River Community Church, the terrible hypocrisy, the wicked false teaching, the rejection of everything good and what would be encouraging to hurting believers, is astounding to me. My dear friends who still attend there are subject to all this. Some will not leave because it is, "Their Church", even though they know what's going on is wrong.

My approach so far has been to just be quiet. I say very little and do not talk to people of the flock except for greetings and pleasantries. Some of my dear Christian friends now do not attend church.

Dave, what am I to do? Can you do anything? Are you concerned? Did you accept my challenge of responsibility when you effectively ratified my removal from leadership of that little flock?

Yours, in His service,
Gerald P. Kooyers

Here also is a letter I wrote to Fred Emery, at that time the pastor of the Salmon River Community Church.

Dear Fred,   March 13, 1993

Your recent letter expressed a prayer for reconciliation between us.

It seemed best that I put down in words what exactly is the issue between us and then you can determine if you are interested in reconciliation.

First I want you to understand that my complete devotion is to the Lord Jesus Christ as my Lord and Savior and my primary interest is the spiritual welfare of the saints of the Lord Jesus that make the Salmon River Community Church their church home.

Given that premise, the primary duties of the pastor and elders of the Salmon River Community Church is to proclaim the Gospel of the Lord Jesus in a clear, forthright, truthful manner, and to love and protect the flock from the attacks within and without from Satan and false teachers motivated by greed and base interests.

One of the greatest attacks of the false teachers against the Church through the ages and again at the present time is the doctrine of what can be properly called Phariseeism. For the purpose of this statement let that term include legalism and perfectionism. Essentially this false doctrine is that our salvation depends on Christian believers attaining some level of performance in their lives in order to be saved and enjoy the fellowship of The Spirit of The Lord Jesus. Now there are many who would deny that they are teaching such a doctrine yet continually act and conduct their affairs as if they believed and hold to such teaching.

Now Fred, you are holding to such teaching in the practice and conduct of your ministry. Over the years I have known you I have on many occasions spoke to you of these things in a very smooth perhaps obtuse way so as to cause you to think about and consider the scriptures so as to come to understand the correct Gospel of the Lord Jesus. You seem unteachable. I now come to you bluntly and forthrightly.

In your practice, in your attempts to counsel couples and others who come to you for help, from many reports I understand you tell them to shape up and do this and that. You lay rules and burdens on them. You tell people, "It will not turn out as you think". "You should do this and this". You preach to them rules. If I were to make a study, I could come up with hundreds of examples from people in this community who have been offended or otherwise reported to me and others of the statements of your ministry. In my own case you have accused me of sin because I cannot pay my real estate taxes. In my own case I finally saw the utter devastating effects of your false teaching, because it came at me directly rather than at others.

A most important activity of any pastor has got to be the love and care of his flock. He must love them, empathize with them, grieve with them, rejoice with them, celebrate with them, very simply identify with them, their needs, hurts, and trials. On the contrary, you, Fred, remind me of the Grand Inquisitor appointed by Pope Alexander VI. The inquisitor went around searching for alleged sinners. If he found any they were punished, perhaps by burning at the stake or banishment.

You had it right Fred when you quoted Galatians about Paul's statements of about those who teach another gospel. Fred, you practice, "another gospel". Fred I urge you in the most strident terms to study Galatians very intently.

431

Study the background and understand just exactly what Paul is teaching and what the Gospel of the Lord Jesus is. It will not do any good for me to tell you because you have not believed me and will not believe me, and as far as I am concerned you are unteachable.

Fred, consider the terrible devastating effects of the practice of your false teaching. People are left cold and trapped in a joyless exercise in an impossible task of obtaining perfection by performance. We humans are hopelessly morally flawed creatures that can never hope in this life to attain any level of perfection or proper performance. Jesus said any man who looks at a woman with lust, or anyone who covets another's property has sinned. That means that if you entertain for even one microsecond a lustful thought or desire of someone's property you have sinned and come short of the Glory of God! Fred, don't you understand this?

Yet you accuse me of sin and Dave Roper reduced it simply to, "A bad attitude about taxes", and because of that you say I am unqualified to be a leader and teacher among the Body of the Lord Jesus. You hypocrite! Jesus said, "Watch out for the leaven of the Pharisees, for it is hypocrisy". You yourself told me in the beginning of your ministry in Riggins about lustful thoughts you had toward certain women of the Body. Have you forgotten that, and now you no longer have lustful thoughts? I don't believe it! Don't your lustful thoughts make you more unqualified to be a leader than my alleged bad attitudes?

Fred, my prayer now before the throne of God is that the Lord Jesus Himself will remove you from being the pastor of the Salmon River Community Church. You simply are not qualified. For a week in December when you were contemplating the actions you conceived against me, I attempted to communicate with you. I called your house every day and in my search for you got a brief itinerary from your wife of your daily activities. One day you sheet rocked, one day you drove bus, one day you went to Boise, one day to Moscow. I did not detect any one day that week that you spent any time ministering to the flock of the Lord Jesus in the Salmon River Community Church. Does this happen every week? What are your priorities? Do you enjoy ministering to the flock? Fred, think about it, you will do yourself a favor by resigning now and finding a way to support your family properly. After all, that is your first priority before God.

Fred, if you don't do your job you don't deserve your pay. And more importantly, it is immoral to accept your pay when you have not earned it.

Fred you seem to ask about reconciliation. The only way you can be reconciled to me is to confess to me and to the Lord Jesus the evil conceptions and intent of your actions to remove me falsely from my leadership position, and to ask for my forgiveness.

Secondly, I suggest you take a leave of absence and go work under a man of the Lord Jesus who will teach you the true Gospel of the Lord Jesus so that you understand it, believe it, and are committed to it, and more importantly, practice it.

About the corporate minutes - the Board of Directors must elect a new Secretary. That person cannot be the President of the same non-profit corporation. That person must come to me and I will assign him certain tasks which must be accomplished, since for the last year I have been very busy in a new profession and have neglected them. When the records are perfect then I will give them to the new Secretary.
Gerald P. Kooyers
cc: Elder Bill Wicks
       Elder Dwaine Clemens

Here are a couple more letters about reconciliation with Fred.

Dear Fred: August 19, 1994

It's been about two years and three months since I first came to you and said I had a problem with the Cooks. Given all that's happened it seems time for a review. My spirit does not seem to rest about the matter, so, this letter to you.

My mind keeps reviewing the facts and your part in them. My conclusions are not good and I hereby submit them to you.

First of all understand that the Cooks goal is to rob me of my property. It is no small sum and that makes the issue difficult. Understand that I have had professional appraisers study the property and have dealt with a number of potential buyers so I understand the approximate value of the property. If the Cooks were to obtain the property they stand to gain almost one million dollars. Unfortunately, my children's inheritance through a corporation they control and my retirement plan all have essentially all of their assets in this property, so that if I were to just let myself be robbed and give it to the Cooks, it would not be fair to my wife and children. I would, of course, then be neglecting my responsibility to them. Perhaps if it were mine alone, I might indeed just turn the other cheek and let the Cooks rob me.

Fred you are intricately messed up in this. You are a party to the Cooks robbery. Otherwise, if that were not so you would have acted quite differently. Let's review your accusations before the Elders which were your basis for church discipline against me. 1) I am not in subjection to government, (did not pay my real estate taxes). 2) I pursued legal action against a fellow believer, (June Cook). 3) I do not have a good reputation with those outside the church. Fred, if you have any capacity for thought at all you must see that these indictments are either not true, plain nonsense, or lies! Yet you actually put them in a statement to me informing me of my church discipline and attempting to remove me from my position as Elder!

Fred, may the Lord Jesus himself rebuke you.

It's not too late to repent! I say again and again, REPENT! REPENT! REPENT!

Can one play with red hot coals and not be burnt? Can one let himself be willingly used in a satanic plot and not be scorched? Fred, turn from your evil ways. REPENT! REPENT! REPENT!

It's not too late yet.

Remember, Dwaine went to his reward. Your time may come anytime. It still is not too late to repent; it is very good for the soul.

I empathize with you. The burden you carry must be tough. Unrepented sin gnaws at you and eats up your insides. It makes you restless; it makes you wander around like Cain. It makes you ineffective in your ministry.

Fred, if you are not going to repent and make restitution, then at least hit the road. Why extend your condemnation by being a hypocrite leader of a body of believers. The judgment of the Lord Jesus is very hard on false teachers and hypocrites. Remember, Jesus spoke his strongest words against the hypocrite Pharisees. (YOU NEST OF SNAKES!)

Fred, I speak (and write) with the authority of your Elder. I was the Church Leader Deacon, along with others, who was responsible for calling you to be the Pastor of the Salmon River Community Church. None of your machinations have removed me from being before God delegated the spiritual position of supervision of your ministry.

Fred, in the Name of the Lord Jesus Christ, I command you, repent, or leave.

Gerald P. Kooyers

Dear Fred: August 26, 1994

Thank you for your quick response to my letter of August 19, 1994. I will answer your letter point by point.

These letters are not intended to be venomous, but to be restorative in character.

1.   Fred, this is Matthew 18. You have sinned against me and I am coming to you directly. This is the stage of "one on one". I write it down so things can be clear and that I have a record and make no mistakes. I am willing to talk to you any time, and I certainly have a track record with you of courteousness at all times.

2.   My letters do follow the principles of (a) purity in Christian relationships, (b) truth spoken in love, (c) impartation of grace. That's what this is all about. Do not delude yourself and make up rational excuses in your mind so you don't have to consider and reflect on what I am saying to you.

3.   Fred, do not misunderstand. I have never suggested the Elders did anything inappropriate. In fact, they never did anything. I voluntarily took a leave of absence. When I come to you and say you have sinned against me with wicked malice, I say it is your motivation that is evil. You plotted evil against me and presented falsehoods, lies, and nonsense to your, "other respected leaders in the church body at large". What kind of advice do you think they can give you when you tell them lies?

4.   Fred, you misunderstand if you think I have a "position of self-exaltation". I have waited a year and a half to start this process. It is the Lord himself that is motivating me and nothing else. This business is painful for me and I would not do it unless God himself was prompting me. The Lord commands you to repent or leave; this is not my voluntary concoction.

5.   Your appeal for me to submit to church leadership is meaningless. The church leadership has never asked me to do anything, except to come and attend the church services in the letter of May 26, 1993. They have given me no guidance whatsoever. You also planted this idea in Russ Adkins. He also suggested to me to go to the Elders and submit. Submit to what? Submit to being robbed of my property? Fred you ought to be glad nothing of that sort ever happen or it would have only compounded your duplicity. Attempt at reconciliation is what this process is all about.

Fred, think about the whole tenor of your letter. You have again created straw points to deflect yourself from the real issue so you don't have to think about the real issue. The real issue is your evil wicked heart that plots evil schemes. You never even denied in your letter that you are "intricately messed up in the Cooks scheme to rob me of my property" as I said you were in my letter. You have convicted yourself by not even dealing with or denying my accusation. This is the issue that is separating us.

Fred, it is you who has exalted himself with pride. You have decided that you yourself are the only source of truth for governing the church body. You have decided that anybody who does not submit to your will must be defamed and run off. Your commitment to collective church leadership which you made when you became pastor of the Salmon River community Church is a sham and a lie.

I suggested that what you teach is another gospel. Your response was not to examine what you teach and study what you teach and deal with it before the Lord, but to blast off and defame anybody who might even suggest such a thing. It is you that has overweening pride in your own conceptions and imaginations.

Apply your own accusations to yourself. Examine yourself. Repent. Repent. Repent. It is still not to late.

Fred, in the Name of the Lord Jesus Christ, I command you, repent, or leave.

Gerald P. Kooyers

Here is a letter written a few years before the ones above to Fred that may have started his campaign against me.

Dear Fred,   December 11, 1991

Enclosed is an article for you that is probably the best laymen discussion of the theory of relativity I have ever come across. I thought you might enjoy it.

It got me to thinking so I thought I would write you something about the subject of the six day creation and the things we discussed the other night.

You made the comment after some of my arguments that I was probably a product of my education and the ideas I expressed came from some part of the past history of my education and not from the Bible. Please let me suggest that, of course, we are all a product of our education. As I listen to your arguments and your sermons let me suggest that underlining a lot of the ideas you express is the notion that time has always been and will go on forever, i.e. that a continuous universe exists where beyond the stars is still more space and that space and time go on forever and ever. These ideas are only a few hundred years old and were developed by Immanuel Kant and others to refute the idea that God made the universe. Isaac Newton developed the equations of motion based on experiments. Newton was in all probably a Christian and developed his ideas on the basis of science and did not express theological ideas even though at the time he was severely criticized by the human church powers that existed since his ideas implied that the earth was not the center of the universe. It remained for Kant and others to extrapolate the concepts of Newton to a continuous infinite extent universe existing in a steady state to show that modern thinking man did not need God.

These ideas of Kant are saturated throughout our textbooks and the conventional wisdom of our society and I suspect you also believe them at least unconsciously. The fundamentalists of the early 20th century developed their ideas of six 24 hour day creation to refute these Kant ideas which suggested that God was not needed, which, of course, the fundamentalists, and you and I believe to be false. However, in that process the fundamentalists still accepted the idea that the universe and time are infinite in extent and go on forever in every direction. As a sidelight comment, the concepts of soul sleep and other weird ideas were created again to handle the problem of a concept of time that is believed to be absolute and extends infinitely forward and backward.

Now in the last 10 to 15 years physicists have established beyond any reasonable scientific doubt that the universe is finite, and that time began at some event in the past, and that time and space are intricately tied to gather so that time is just and another dimension like the three space dimensions, and that at some event in the future, time and space will come to an end. This has very profound implications and proves Kant and his ilk to be wrong. More importantly, a beginning and an end imply a causative agent which to any honest thinking man must be God. The only questions the philosophers and theologians have left to discuss are not the existence of God but what kind of God is He. Of course, the Bible has the answer, but many will continue not to believe it.

As your friend and fellow believer in the Lordship of Jesus Christ I urge you to exorcise all the false concepts of Kant and his ilk out of your thinking. Understand that time is a variable like space. Time is relative and its amount depends upon where you are measuring it. God does not have a clock and is not bound to a place in time and space like we are. That space is defined by the amount of matter within it, so for instance the earth does not revolve around the sun, but the earth travels in a straight line in a space that is curved by the presence of the sun. For example, consider the 24 hours that the earth needs to rotate. On the earth it takes 24 hours. Measured from anywhere else it is something different than 24 hours. On an imaginary spaceship speeding by the solar system it might be 1 hour or even 5 minutes. To someone sitting on the surface of the sun it's also different than 24 hours. Now what clock did God use? Since there were no men around with clocks to measure how long God took for a day I suggest that to make a big thing of a 24 hour creation day is ridiculous.

As I read and study the Bible I have come to understand that God is gentle with his creation and the men who inhabit it. I just do not read anywhere in the Bible that toads are turned into princes or pumpkins into coaches. God fashioned his creation. He made it. He said it was good and was satisfied with it. To think that God would create something with the appearance of age just to fool me I find repugnant. God has always dealt with me honestly, lovingly, justly, and has always seemed concerned with my welfare. To think that God caused the earth to appear from a formless glob like a toad from a prince, I also find repugnant. The Bible says that God made the earth like a skillful craftsman, like a pottery maker making pottery. He fashioned it. He formed it. Peter says God made the earth out of water and by water. In other words He used means to make and fashion it. All of that takes time from the standpoint of an earth observer. God does not have a clock, so it did not take God any time at all!!!

Time does not exist in God's presence. Just like space does not exist in God's presence. God exists in something which might be called eternity. The coming of Jesus was an event in both time and eternity. This is how God is continuously present with us. Time and space mean nothing to Him. Peter confirms this as he says that to God a day is like a thousand years and a thousand years like a day.

Well, I thought I would write you these things. I believe it's important that we as church leaders should present to the world truth and sincerity. It does not do the Kingdom of God much good for us to lose ourselves on tangents or promulgate weird ideas, or to make God seem ridiculous. It's important that we not rob God of his glory. We should be very careful not to say to the world more than what God wants us to say and yet to say all that God wants us to say. We must present to our flock the whole counsel of God and where God has not clearly defined things we must say we do not understand everything or should remain silent.

Your Christian Brother,
Gerald

Well this concludes my rendering of the saga of the interaction with the Cooks and Fred Emory, and the extension of it into the Salmon River Community Church. You can understand that the whole thing was rather complex and involved lots of people. Such is life. You learn from it. Things are not always as they seem. Learn from it. God wants us to practice good and not evil. Study the Bible carefully, especially Jesus's words to establish in your mind what is good and loving and practice it. You practice it because you love Jesus.

As a historical note, John Cook left Riggins a year or so later. The congregation of the Community Church eventually changed the bylaws. I, myself, had written the bylaws and filed with the State of Idaho, the Articles of Incorporation. I had created the Church Bylaws giving what was called elder rule in 1991. So it was very difficult for the congregation alone to remove the pastor. Fred somehow had decided to leave Riggins and went to a Church in Kamiah for a few years, and then to a pastorate in Missoula, Montana. A few years later Fred was killed by a drunken woman's car when he was riding on a motorcycle.

God is very, very patient with us; however, eventually He calls each one of us home to eternity.

A word of wisdom here – one can create a perfect Church government structure, but the structure is worthless when wicked men, who do not fear God, occupy the Church government positions.

Eventually, the leadership of the Salmon River Community Church through my daughter, Cindy, received a recommendation from Dave Roper to obtain Jim Thibodeaux as pastor. He is a most excellent Christ loving pastor and the Church in 2014 is flourishing. Praise the Lord Jesus!

INVESTMENT ADVICE

The following ideas come from a letter I wrote to a gentleman by the name of George Friesen. I met him at Sky Valley Park in Southern California, and we got into a discussion about investments. He asked me for advice on an investment he was considering. I wrote him a letter dated March 28, 2000. It is as follows:

> Even though I have known you only a few days, I feel it is appropriate to put my thoughts down in writing in response to your statement to open yourself up and be vulnerable. Understand too that I also am opening myself up and being vulnerable. Also, I write this more for my benefit than for yours as your request to me to consider the Mayo Venture stimulated me to put my thoughts in writing.

> I perceive you love the Lord Jesus and seek to promote His Kingdom. In is in that spirit that I respond to your statements. I perceive we both have the same goals. Understand that the Lord has lead me through Job like trials and it is from the depth of that experience that I have come to the conclusions that I pass on to you.

> First let me give you a little of my background so that you can understand my perspective. My father was a pastor, and I grew up in a pastor's home with very loving parents who taught me to love the Lord Jesus from my earliest memories. I do not remember a day that I did not love the Lord Jesus.

> My father's view of money which I learned from watching him as

441

opposed to direct instruction from him was that money was to be avoided and an intrinsic evil. He would never accumulate money. In his later years he even spent his social security money on educating his grandchildren. During his life he received very little for his hard labors and never complained about it at all, and we lived in poverty continually. My mother made do and we actually lived quite well with plenty of food, often just given to us. Every once in a while some well to do person in the congregation would give my dad an automobile, usually a new one, so we rode around in good style, appropriate for a preacher.

My father was way over educated having spent twelve years in preparation for the ministry, including eleven years of Latin and eight years of Greek and Hebrew. He always recommended to me an education so I went off to college and became over educated also. I stopped working on a PhD in Electrical Engineering at Stanford University when the financial pressures of my growing family became too much to handle.

At some point in my early professional career, I threw out of my belief system, which came from my father's belief system, the intrinsic evil of money. When I found employment after college, I took the job that paid the most money. I became a bright young research engineer, conceived some useful far out ideas and received stock options for my efforts that became worth a small fortune. This was in the early 60's when few people had heard of this. I decided I wanted to control my own destiny and that I liked making money so I left my employer and started my own software business. Eventually, I created a computer based commodity trading system that just coined money in the futures trading business. I became a Commodity Trading Advisor registered with the Commodity Futures Trading Commission. My company was a CTA for 16 years. Brokers with the national stock firms raised money for my firm to manage.

I tell you this information to give you the understanding that I was in the position like that of your Eddie Mayo, of managing money for investors like yourself.

Some friends and I spent about a million dollars (in 1979 dollars) on a gold mining venture. I raised the money for a mine operator who turned out to be a thief. I had built into the agreements loopholes so that when 1 concluded he was a thief, in order to save the investment; I forced him out and took over the management of the mine myself. This, of course, caused lots of problems and lawsuits. Eventually, the mine came to nothing with the United States Bureau of Land Management and the United States Court legal system confronting us at every turn. Then three men managed to get themselves killed in the mine. That finally did it and was enough for me. I pulled the plug on that mine with complete loss of our investment, and was left with lawsuits, which dragged on for years.

Given the sum of all this experience I submit to you the following rules for making investments. These rules are based on all of my experience and what I understand the scriptures to teach.

The scriptures teach me that we are not to trust in riches. Money is, therefore, a tool and not a security. Money can be very corrupting. In fact I am convinced that churches and para-church organizations become corrupted and compromised by their continual search for money. The gathering of money becomes a thing in itself. The sin of Balaam is just that - using ones place in the Kingdom of God to gather money to satisfy one's own greed. The deeds of the Nicolaitans, which the Apostle John says Jesus hates, seem also to be the same thing. That is, using God to promote one's own greed. That is very widespread in the visible kingdom of God.

I was once a deacon in a denominational church. I saw the poor corrupted by the handouts they received from us deacons. What's going on? I still do not understand it. We are given the mandate by God to help the poor and needy and yet in our efforts to help them we corrupt them compounding their sin. In my father's case, he was not corrupted by the handouts. Perhaps that is the key. Spiritual men are not corrupted by handouts and gifts of money, but the unspiritual are, and it makes no difference whether they are poor people or executives in a para-church organization.

The scriptures teach that gathering money a little bit at a time over time promotes stability, and that speculation or the search for quick money leads to poverty. In my experience the search for quick money or speculation involves taking risk. It is the risk that is the problem. Risk taking is addictive and eventually the successful risk taker takes on even greater risks that eventually do not work and he loses everything. The pages of the Wall Street Journal are full of horror stories of excessive risk taking causing spectacular failures. A few years ago a very, very large British Bank which had been in business for over 200 hundred years was brought to failure and destroyed by an obscure unsupervised employee trading in Singapore in the Japanese NICKI index.

Presumption on the future is another cause of catastrophes. One assumes that one's income will continue so he risks all of it. The scriptures teach we do not know what will happen tomorrow and, therefore, we are told to not presume on the future.

Probably the most important principal of investing is to invest in things you know something about so you understand what is going on. When I was in the corporate world, I was working for the company that gave me stock options. I knew the company I was working for and could understand what was happening, therefore, I had reasonable expectations of what would happen in the normal course of events. Therefore, that was a good investment. I knew nothing about mining when I went into the mining business. Therefore, in hindsight, investing in a mining venture was stupid and bound to fail.

When I got into the money management business for futures trading, I had been trading futures for 10 years. I had thoroughly tested my trading system against extensive scientific and statistical principles. It became a great success.

To summarize, here would be my rules for investing:

Money is a tool to be used for the Kingdom of Jesus Christ

> Be in ventures with steady incremental return
> Avoid presumption on the future
> Have firsthand knowledge of the venture
> Avoid the addiction of risk taking, or in other words pursue
> ventures that are near sure things.

In applying these rules to your proposed investment, I see trouble in two areas. The first is lack of first-hand knowledge of the oil and gas business, and the second is that borrowing against your home presumes on the future.

The positive areas are first; the oil and gas business will be around for a while, and second, if the venture is successful, a steady stream of revenue might be expected if the venture has been represented truthfully.

I would like to comment on your interpretation of the parable of the talents. Your interpretation has been generally accepted by many scholars so you are not alone in your understanding.

It seems to me Jesus cannot be talking here about money. The context is the subject of the kingdom of heaven. The kingdom of heaven is comparable to a man about to go on a journey. The talent was a unit of money, a large sum. (Editor's note - about 700 ounces of gold, or in 2010 US dollars about 1.2 million dollars.) The man in the parable in trusting his possessions to others is obviously Christ himself. Does Christ have in His possessions money? Think in bigger terms. Christ gives us of his possessions, the currency of the Kingdom of Heaven, and that is righteousness. We are each given a gift of righteousness; we are entrusted with the righteousness of Christ, some more, some less. The question is what do we do with it? Do we multiply righteousness by loving and caring for those around us or do we bury what Christ has given us in the ground and hide it? Those who bury the gift Christ has given them, are sent off to be with the hypocrites, to the place of weeping and gnashing of teeth.

That is the end of the letter to this friend that I have not seen since. Did he borrow against his house and invest in that oil and gas venture? I would have liked to know. So let us now conclude investing principles and go on to additional subjects.

JOSHUA VIST TO THE GOLD MINE

Here is a reflection on the gold mine where my partners and I spent about a million ($1,000,000) in 1980 dollars in the period from 1979 to 1982. I write this about 25 years after the mine came to disaster where three men died, probably murdered.

My grandson Joshua Lawler as a result of a previous conversation called me up and started the process for a visit to the mine on Saturday October 27, 2007.

Joshua is here visiting and working for my daughter Cindy and husband Guy Carlson as a gofer doing anything, i.e. logging, painting, chasing down parts or anything else. He is enjoying Idaho. It seems in California he bought a very expensive high powered motorcycle and his mother, my daughter Brenda, thought he should move out or sell his motorcycle. He left the comforts of home, kissed his mother goodbye, and came here to Idaho, I think, to finish growing up.

Anyway, he stirred me up to go visit the mine. It is a long way in there, not in miles but in time. I got started about 9:30AM, picked Joshua up at Cindy's, went up river, took the French Creek grade, went over Marshall Mountain, and down to the mine. We got there about 2:30. The snow had mostly melted on top, and since the road has been heavily used, the road was good and seemed very easy compared to the old days.

Joshua had spent a day working for Guy's dad, Mick Carlson, moving sheep off of Marshall Mountain about four weeks before, so we had a running account from Josh about his sheep moving experience. That day it was snowing with lots of snow so he could not see much except for the sheep. Instead the view today was spectacular as we could see hundreds of miles from the top. The snow had almost all melted when we went over the top.

446

I showed Joshua the way to get to the top trout fishing lake, in my opinion, in all of Idaho. He made careful note of it.

We descended and arrived down at our old Gerber mine property and nobody seemed about. A gentleman from the East is building a wonder on the Gerber property. It is difficult to describe. They say it is to be a family residence, a cabin. They have been working on it for five years and expect to work on it for another five years.

After I had reconnoitered about to find the road down to the Warrior mine on the old Schmidt property, I returned to the main construction. There I meet the owner, Bill Riddle, and the General Contractor, Chris Olson, who is from McCall, along with another man. Riddle was a gentleman with fine manners. I introduced myself and told him I had lots of mine assays available for his mines. We discussed mining a little. I asked him for permission to visit the Warrior Mine down Bear Creek below the Gerber property and look around his construction. He said that was fine.

The construction about was not really understandable. There was a temporary bunk house with cooking facilities and several trailer houses for living. The main building under construction has very thick concrete walls supporting huge steel beams and very high ceilings. It has at least three stories. There is another huge building behind the first. My guess is that they are spending two million a year out there so by the time they are finished they may have 20 million dollars into a family residence. Others have said they plan to spend 30 million out there. That does not seem at all prudent to most Idahoans. I loved it. It's great. It is going to be quite a cabin.

Remember that Idaho County has no building code and no building permits are required so every man can do what is right in his own eyes with no interference from the government. Riddle is building what he thinks best, and the main interference from the government standpoint, federal only, is the Bureau of Land Management, aka, BLM. They harass him about the road to the place. The cost of the whole thing is awesome.

Geneva, Joshua, and I put on our hard hats, gathered up our pack sacks with our lunch and flashlights and went down the road maybe 3/8 mile to the

Warrior mine. We got to the cook shack site and everything was burned up. A forest fire must have come through sometime during the last 10 years. The Cook Shack was gone. The mine office trailer was gone. The ore tramway was gone. The tool shed was gone, and Schmidt's old honeymoon cabin was gone. Everything all gone! Even the old log cabin in the bottom of the draw below the lower audit was gone. How sad. It filled me with grief.

In some places the trees were also all burned up, but near the bottom of the draws and along Bear Creek the timber was still green and standing but with burnt signs along the bottoms. It made me very sad to see everything gone. Most people would not have recognized the place. And, of course, with everything gone, even people's memories of what was there, representing a large investment, will be all forgotten, and no one will know or remember what was once there.

From the cook shack site we went up the road to the lower portal. Lots of fallen trees blocked our path. The timbers around the portal were all burnt up and large rocks had fallen over the portal. There was room to crawl into the tunnel however, much to Geneva's distress. She stayed at the portal while Josh and I went back to the Y where the tunnel forked about 500 feet in. The air did not seem too good to me, perhaps because of the small hole at the portal opening so I did not encourage Joshua to go past the Y even though he was very curious. He did not seem to be spooked by the mine tunnel at all. I related to him most of the details of the mine accident where three men died in that very tunnel, and Dan Cook and I rescuing the fourth, Rocky Wilson. I am barely able to tell the story now without tears coming to my eyes.

When I tell the story now I still am not able to tell people those men were murdered, even though both Dan Cook and I have come to that same conclusion independently. It just seems unthinkable. Three men murdered in my mine! Those words can hardly be written. The evil, pain, and injustice of it all seem overwhelming. Dan Cook has concluded he was the target of the plot. Dan was not at the mine that day because my daughter Cindy had ran away into the wilderness the day before that day and he was trying to come up with some way to find her before something bad happened to her. So in hindsight Cindy's running away probably saved Dan

Cooks life.

Dan also suggested and thinks that somehow Arty Johnson, the third man who died in the tunnel had a hand in that murderous plot. If so, it is God's retributive justice at work. The unexplained explosion happened after the long Labor Day holiday weekend. No caretaker was at the mine that weekend. So if it was a murderous plot, Arty would know who booby trapped the day box and he knew well the suspected murderers.

Rocky, the man we rescued had met Arty on the road going into the mine and had asked for Arty's help because he thought there might have been an accident. Arty went with Rocky to the tunnel, but then instead of leaving after they found Glen's body, obviously dead of carbon monoxide poison, as Rocky wanted to, Arty insisted on going to the end of the tunnel to inspect the day box where the explosion took place.

As I think about it now, a murderous plot starts to make sense. How did Arty know the day box was at the end of the tunnel to the right of the Y? Why did he want to inspect the day box against Rocky's advice? Was he a criminal wanting to return to the scene of the crime? If so, he paid for it with his life, as both Arty and Rocky collapsed from carbon monoxide poisoning themselves about 100 feet from the portal opening. Arty fell into about a half inch of water at the bottom of the tunnel, and the autopsy showed his lungs contained water and sand, and he had swallowed his tongue, which I had a very difficult time getting out of his throat when I gave him mouth to mouth resuscitation. Rocky fell unconscious without falling into the water, so Dan and I rescued him about one hour later and he lived. Arty did not. The above statement of the facts comes from Rocky's testimony at the civil trial for negligence and my personal observation.

This visit to the mine started the process for reliving a lot of very painful memories.

We hiked back up the trail to the Gerber Property where the construction is going on, put our stuff in the truck, and started home. We decided the road down the French Creek grade was a little too miserable so we went on the paved Warren Wagon Road to McCall.

In our discussions about the construction project, Geneva observed that

449

Olsen was a Bruce'ee Shoe'ee, meaning he was in way over his head. I agreed. That project is vast, the waste unbelievable, and the scope unimaginable. Geneva and I have been there, and down that road before. We know the symptoms and the results. I felt sorry for Riddle, mainly because of the huge waste and costs associated with building something like that so far from civilization, and employing people with an Idaho zero sum mentality. As far as that goes, I feel sorry for Olsen too. It is tough being in a project like that which is over your head.

The thought came to mind, to both Geneva and I, that if something happens to Riddle during this undertaking, another huge white elephant relic (in addition to the one I built) will be left in Idaho County for posterity to shake their heads about.

We stopped for a hamburger at My Fathers Place in McCall and got home about 8:30.

While reading this memoir for perhaps the last time and again being grieved by the memory of the mine disaster, I now recall that on the night of the disaster a man took me aside and told me directly that the mine safety inspecting official that day most likely had told the miners to do something to change their procedures that caused the explosion. I was terribly numbed by the event at the time and was surrounded by a large number of people, so I did not even think any more about what he had said until now 35 years later in 2016.

Now as I perhaps proof read this thing for the last time I started to think. If the mine had been sabotaged as both Dan Cook and I fifteen years after the event concluded back in 1996, and the deed was instigated by Al Osborn, wow, what evil. Al is the only person I know who could have been sufficiently motivated to do the evil deed. Al had left the mine employment saying he was going to have a very miserable winter and everybody around him was going to be miserable. Then months later by a clever ruse, Dan Cook had retrieved the compressor Al had sent men to get from the mine. They had gotten it all the way to McCall where Dan convinced the would be thieves to give it to him. Al claimed he owned control of the compressor as he had a relationship with the owner, but I was then leasing it, so I had told Dan to go get it.

The conflict between us began when Al was working for MSHA (Mine Safety and Health Administration). He and I had had a meeting and I said his son had to go as the mine manager. Subsequent to this meeting Al quit his job at MSHA and came and managed the mine himself. He was an even a worse manager than his son. They both just accomplished nothing, so I had then told Al he was terminated.

Now after 35 years the thought has come to me that the mine safety official may very well have been involved or did the deed. Al may have had information on him or somehow otherwise motivated that official to have a hand in the deed. As I think about it why did that informant person who I had never seen before and have never seen since, make a special attempt to approach me to tell me the MSHA inspector was involved? That inspector had stayed in McCall that evening after the afternoon inspection at the mine, and almost immediately after the explosion became known, came back to the mine, and ordered it officially shut down. How did he find out about the explosion so quick and why did he act so quickly?

Dear reader this book is written to give you wisdom and understanding. I am examining myself as to why I put completely out my mind for 15 years, the possibility of those miners being murdered, and then for another 20 years I put out of my mind the possibility that the MSHA official maybe was involved. It is just too ugly and too terrible and so shocking a thought; I just put it out of my mind.

There is a psychological factor here that is very difficult to understand. The human soul has the capability to go into denial and just put the just too terrible ugly facts out of the consciousness. So dear reader when faced with terrible, terrible possibilities, watch yourself so as to not go into denial, and so then not to act with truth and righteousness and face your responsibilities.

Those murdered young men, Glen's wife, and their friends, are entitled to justice. By going into denial I let them down. Then the county legal system, the MSHA bureaucracy, the State of Idaho, all of us, let them down.

Glen's wife's life was, subsequently, ruined. Other lives were very damaged and consumed with great grief. Morgan's mother was in terrible grief. The precious lives of two very young men were terminated. Parents and others were put into deep grief. All of this is ugly beyond comprehension. Sin indeed has terrible consequences.

Yet we must understand. God rules and God's justice will prevail. In eternity all will be made right. The wicked are punished and those washed clean and forgiven of their sins by the power of the death and blood of the Lord Jesus Christ, are to be ushered into eternal life. Jesus has taken all the crimes of believers on to Himself. He paid the price of God's judgement.

Denial, I have concluded, is a psychological thing the soul performs to protect itself from perhaps going into insanity. Nevertheless, your thinking self must be in control, and you must at all times face your responsibilities. Denial is a destructive thing. Watch yourself and be aware of it.

Let's think about the disaster and examine the facts. Dynamite does not go off by itself. It must have a cap in it. Electric caps do not go off without electricity. The day was clear and a lightning strike is extremely unlikely. It would have had to come from the sky and hit down into a canyon near the mine portal and go 700 feet up a mine rail. That is very, very unlikely. Maybe Morgan rubbed the wires of a dynamite cap in some dynamite against his rain-suit to see if it would go off while a cap was in dynamite? No, never. Morgan was a very well-adjusted young man with lots of friends. He had been one of my river boatmen.

So one must conclude somebody who knew what he was doing created a hidden bobby trap so when Morgan opened the dynamite box or the cap box to replace unused dynamite or caps back into the boxes, a trigger was set off which set off a firing mechanism which caused everything in the day box area to explode. There were several boxes of dynamite and several sacks of prel (ammonium nitrate soaked in diesel fuel now called ANFO) in the day box location at the end of an otherwise unused tunnel. Morgan's shadow silhouette could be seen on top of the tunnel above where the day box had been so Morgan was bending over the day box when it went off. We only found a small piece of Morgan's foot bone, maybe the size of a silver dollar.

Otherwise, he had been vaporized. The residue scum of his body on the walls of the tunnel eventually formed a gray mold.

Who is clever enough and skilled enough to create such a bobby trap bomb? He or she must have made a little battery operated trigger mechanism attached to a cap in a stick of dynamite inserted somewhere so that when the box is opened it is fired. That is not a simple thing to do and very dangerous to make. Did Al Osborn or his son Russ have the skill to do this? They did not seem to be that competent.

The event happened after a long Labor Day weekend. I did not have a watchman at the mine that weekend. It did not seem that any passersby ever came to the mine, as when I did have a watchman, he or she reported no visitors. A four wheel drive vehicle was required to climb back out of there. Arty, the third man killed, had a supposed mine on a mining claim (It had a short tunnel Arty messed with once in a while.) just past my mine, maybe a half mile or so up on a bench east of Bear Creek. He and his wife on the old mining claim had an old cabin there in a delightful location above a lake with a nice view of the lake and the Salmon River Mountains. The place usually had a nice summer garden with its nice irrigation system. The pile of beer cans outside the cabin window made a huge impression. Arty was a friend of the Osborns, and if the Osborns were there that weekend then he certainly knew about it and probably was involved. If that is the case it is a marvel of God's retributive justice that Arty did not survive the trip into the mine with Rocky to see what had had happened.

So who did it? Someone certainly had time to set it up over the Labor Day weekend. Or perhaps the mine inspector had a little device he placed near the day box when he inspected it so any movement set it off. If somebody had set it up over the weekend why did it not go off when the mine inspector inspected the day box? The miners where probably drilling the face, or starting to wire the face, that was to be blasted, when the inspector showed up. Glen or Morgan probably got the dynamite and caps earlier in the day from the day box in order to have the dynamite and caps for the face operation unless, they had resupplied the day box from the main supply in camp. Why did it not go off then if somebody had set it up over the week end?

Why did MSHA not make a big issue of three men killed in a mine accident? It was national news. I was even interviewed for TV at the mine. The TV people came by helicopter. Even though I was prepared by the interviewer, I could not control myself when we went live and I started to cry right in front of the TV cameras. So then they made a grief story of it.

MSHA went through the motions of an official investigation, but only a little protest on my part caused them to give it up. They threatened a small fine for negligence but had no follow through after a brief letter of reply on my part. At the time I was relieved they were not going to harass me. Now as I think about it, what is the purpose of MSHA if they are not going to seriously investigate a serious mine accident that killed three men!?

Yes, who did it and why? Al Osborn was a wicked, angry, man, and certainly was one who had the motivation, but the doing of it required a person of skill and knowledge, who also had access to the day box at the right time.

Al had worked for MSHA and probably had friends at MSHA or more likely had information quite damaging to some person at MSHA who he then blackmailed into performing the deed or ordering it done. One can readily understand that under such circumstances as those why MSHA quickly swept it under the rug and convinced their superiors that it was a freak accident that required no investigation, and there was no negligence on the part of the mine owners. After all did not their inspector conduct an inspection of the mine that very day not two hours before the explosion?

Well dear reader, ponder all this for a spell. Murder, MSHA, denial, wonderful young men, all encompassed in the terrible event at my mine that I ran for me and my limited partners, and so was, therefore, in the overall, responsible. After 35 years I am still terribly grieved. May God have mercy on those murderous, wicked, evil, perpetrators.

Dear reader here is some sage advice. **Never trust the government!** Wow, what a statement. This is contrary to all I ever was taught in all the schools I ever went to. My parents and family, all my relatives, even distant ones never said such a thing. I very seldom have read that anywhere else, but here dear reader I write it down for you. **Never trust the government!**

My experience covered direct very time consuming relationships with the bureaucracies of United States military, the Commodity Futures Trading Commission, the Bureau of Land Management, the Forest Service, The Mine Safety and Health Administration, the Internal Revenue Service, the Idaho Outfitters and Guides Board, the California Superior Courts, the Idaho Courts, the Federal District Courts, and the United States Bankruptcy Court. Take it directly from me; never trust any of them. They are your enemy. If there were to be any exception to this rule it would be the military. With them my relationships and dealing was always very professional, but yet there too were some very corrupt people. Another exception might be the Idaho Outfitter and Guides Board, as that agency was run by the outfitters themselves. That might explain it. Yet, you must not trust any of them.

The IRS is the most incompetent. Yet in my experience if you just shake off their continual very wicked, mean, intimidation, and ignore it, and keep probing, eventually you might find in their bureaucracy some kind lady who will empathize with you and tell you what you need to do. It is all really very unbelievable.

ON THE MENDOCINO PRESBYTERIAN CHURCH

I once wrote a letter to a man by the name of Stephen R. Warner who did a PhD thesis on the Mendocino Presbyterian Church where my father had been Pastor from June 1947 to June 1952. I mailed the letter and also emailed it and received a very nice letter in response. I include it here to give you an understanding of my father's ministry in Mendocino.

The letter is as follows:

Dear Prof. Warner;

My sister found a copy of your book, "New Wine in Old Wineskins", back in 2004, discarded in an old second hand store, bought it for $.50, and promptly found another copy for me, and sent it to me.

I enjoyed your excellent well written scholarly book immensely. I now just read it again with much pleasure and thought I would write you a letter. My father, Jacob Mulder Kooyers, who signed his name J. M. Kooyers, called Jake by my mother and spoke to as Reverend Kooyers by everybody else, was Pastor of the Mendocino Presbyterian Church from June of 1947 to June of 1952. In your book you dismissed his ministry service as unsuccessful, and I wish to comment on that and provide you with additional information. I am not sure of your informant's bias who provided you with the "unsuccessful" opinion information, or the criterion used to decide that the ministry was unsuccessful

Let me give you my observations and then provide historical details. The overall effect of my father's ministry was to lay a foundation of solid believers which are difficult to obliterate by a subsequent liberal ministry, especially those who love and respect the Presbyterian Church and its magnificent theological statements. The pastor who followed my father, whom you gave the name of Althorpe (As I remember, I believe his real name was Idsaith) was a very outgoing pleasant person, and as you noted in your book, was well received and popular. In comparison with such a popular individual I can understand why some would attach unsuccessful to the previous ministry. I know nothing of Idsaith's theology but assume it was benign liberal, which I expect did not undo the solid core of orthodox Christian belief in the church, which was there when my father left. Let me suggest that the foundation of solid reformed, Presbyterian belief left by my father, laid a solid foundation which 20 years later contributed to all the remarkable transformations that occurred in the Mendocino Presbyterian Church.

Let me first provide you with my father's biographical information. He was born in Muskegon, Michigan on August 30, 1896. At about 13 years of age he went to work as an office boy at the Hastings Piston Ring Company, which eventually, I believe, became part of General Motors. He became a bookkeeper at the company and at about 21 years of age was teaching Sunday School in his local Christian Reformed Church. The Elders of the church approached him and suggested that he go to Theological Seminary and prepare for the ministry and committed themselves to partially supporting his studies.

He then spent four years at prep school, four years at college, and three years at seminary, graduating from Calvin College and Seminary in Grand Rapids, Michigan in June of 1928. The Christian Reformed denomination which supported the seminary had few openings and after waiting for a call for a year, he went to Westminster Theological Seminary in Philadelphia, Pennsylvania, for a year and received a Masters Degree of Theology in June of 1930. Westminster had just been founded by people who had left Princeton Theological Seminary because of its perceived liberalism.

My father then served in the Presbyterian Church, USA, and predecessor to the United Presbyterian Church in small congregations in Wisconsin. He served at Athens from 1930 to 1936, Oxford from 1936 to 1939, Hixton from 1939 to 1943, and South Range from 1943 to 1946. He usually served two or three congregations in the immediate area preaching three times or so on Sunday. We moved to California in 1946 after the war, and my father accepted the call to Mendocino in the spring of 1947, waiting until we children had completed school to move from San Jose to Mendocino in June of 1947.

My father married my mother, Alice Margaret in July of 1922. Children were Howard in 1923, Orneal in 1926, Gordon in 1930, myself, Gerald in 1935 and my sister Marcia in 1936. Note that he started his family while still in college, unusual for those days.

My father was what we would now call a conservative in a liberal denomination. Much intensive discussion was held around the family dinner table about theological issues. My parents declared that we were "Reformed" and "Presbyterian" and not "liberal" or "fundamentalists" or "fundys" as we called them. Liberals were those who generally did not believe in Jesus divine ministry and were those that who seemed to dominate the Presbyterian Church, USA, especially the leadership. Fundys were those who took the Bible very literally and were usually disparaged as misguided, whereas the liberals were despised as unbelievers, essentially because liberals generally made solemn promises to adhere to the constitution of the Presbyterian Church including the Shorter Catechism, the Longer Catechism, and Confession of Faith, but in reality, hypocritically dismissed it as nonsense and archaic.

My father's ministry in Oxford, Wisconsin began with a split (much to his surprise when he arrived there) in the Presbyterian Church wherein the Fundys had pulled out and formed their own church. The last time I visited Oxford in about 1998, the Independent Fundamental Church of America congregation was flourishing and the Presbyterian Church was all but dead.

The ministry in Mendocino seemed to be quite enjoyable by my parents. The other main church in town was the Catholic and they seemed quite benign and friendly compared to those in Wisconsin. A handful of Baptists started a church of a Fundamental nature sometime during my father's ministry in Mendocino but they also were of a pleasant nature. As you noted the pay was very small, as I remember maybe $100 a month. I never remember my parents complaining about the pay, but after the Johnnie Belinda bonanza was spent, (Every one of us was on the Warner Brothers payroll at unbelievably high wages; I earned $15 a day or about $300 a month when yet only 12 years old; the money saved from that adventure made me into a confirmed capitalist) my mother became a teller at the Bank of America in Mendocino. Dr. Preston was very generous, providing us with our needs whenever extraordinary expenses occurred.

My father was extremely well educated in the classics and languages. He told me he has studied Latin for 8 years, Greek for 6 years, and Hebrew for 4 years. Unfortunately, his sermons are written in shorthand and I cannot now read them. He may have been too much for Mendocino. He was a quiet man, very studious, and not outgoing, and did not have a forceful speaking manner. His sermons were intellectual and generally topical as opposed to verse by verse exposition. His sermons had powerful content and dealt with the exposition of the whole Bible. The young people learned the Westminster Shorter Catechism and the Westminster Confession of faith; Presbyterian documents ignored and sneered at by the liberals.

His conservatism and sound theology got him into trouble at Presbytery meetings. The Presbytery to which the Mendocino Church belonged included the very liberal San Anselmo Theological Seminary. Periodically, seminary students would come up for examination by the Presbytery and my father would get his turn to ask questions. He was soon dismissed as a, "Dutch Calvinist", by the liberal professors who dominated the institution.

This background may have been long and lengthy but now I would like to comment on his ministry. My father was good at one on one situations and brought many to a saving knowledge of Jesus Christ as Lord of their lives, especially older and middle aged people as compared to the young who normally are the mainstay of new church members. Mendocino in those days was almost a ghost town. The war had caused much neglect of everything; even the local State Parks were overgrown and seemingly abandoned. Mrs. McCollum, a very generous Lumber Baron Widow was still alive, and Dr. Preston the retired town medical doctor was the mainstay of the Church. The elders as I recall were usually Dr. Preston, and Alma Mendoza, wife of one of the owners of Mendoza Brothers General store, and the proprietor of the other grocery store in town, Chet Bishop. The town being almost dead did not present many opportunities for church growth, yet as your statistics show church members were added during his ministry.

My father gave me the job of counting the church attendance every Sunday morning, which I did as surreptitiously as possible. When we first arrived in 1947 only a handful of people were attending Sunday morning services. I do not remember the actual numbers but it had to be in the 20's to 30's. Near the end of his ministry in Mendocino, the Church was almost half full, maybe 50 to 60 in attendance. My father did not have an emphasis on increasing the number of church members.

The Johnie Belinda bonanza enabled much improvement to the church edifice. A new roof was put on, including the steeple. That was done with a huge scaffold which I surreptitiously climbed a few times to enjoy the spectacular view from the top of the steeple. Wow, was that exciting for a kid.

I thank you again for writing such a fine scholarly thoughtful book. I am an Old Blue myself, BS in 1957, MA in 1959.

Cordially,
Gerald P. Kooyers

I received the following letter in response to my letter:

September 15, 2010
Dear Mr. Kooyers

Many thanks for your informative and very gracious letter. I regret that the only characterization of your father's pastorate in my book consisted of that one word, "unsuccessful" (p. 89). Of course I did not mention his name, but I know that anyone with access to the PCUSA's annual reports could look up the Mendocino church and the date of 1952 and identify him. More to the point: that judgment, based on a remark of one informant and the fact that church membership in the 1940s lagged behind population growth (see pp. 184-185), was really beside the point of my main topic, how the church fared in the 1960s and '70s. In fact, it was a gratuitous remark, and I wish I hadn't said it. Especially in that light, you own remarks about the book are extremely kind. Thank you again.

Your recollections of your father and of your own sojourn in Mendocino are very absorbing. Your father's origins in the CRC, his college and seminary education at Calvin (which I know well) and his Master's work at Westminster (which I know of) certainly would have made him an outlier in the mostly liberal Presbytery of the Redwoods as I knew it in the 1970s. And it is possible that his scholarly sermons might have been over the heads of many of the church members. But it is also the fact that, as I say on pp. 88-89, for a whole host of reasons Mendocino Presbyterian was fortunate in its leadership, and it entered the period of my interest in comparatively good shape.

As you state, at least two reasons for the church's relatively strong financial position in the period of your father's pastorate were the windfall provided by the filming of Johnny Belinda and the support provided by Dr. Preston (who, of course, later gave the money that was used to build the educational wing, now known as "Preston Hall"). It was quite fascinating to hear of how well you were paid by Warner Brothers (as an extra?) in 1947–$300/month!–which I think was a good deal more than the church paid your father. (When I graduated from high school, twelve years later, I got a very good job, as a forest firefighter, for about the same rate of pay.

But Dr. Preston, to my knowledge, never joined the church. He may have been a member of the Board of Trustees, which I believe was considered a secular arm of the church before the 1960s. My informants told me that he never could bring himself to make the required profession of faith.

Yes, the man I call "Althorpe" was in fact Martin Eidsath, who served the church as pastor for two discontinuous terms (1931-35 and 1952-57) as well as serving as interim in 1966-67. He loved the church very deeply, and the love was returned. I was able to interview him for my research, and, as a man mature enough to be moderate of passion; he did not offer many strong opinions. But he made it clear that he was disappointed by the pastorate of the man who succeeded him (whom I call "Ward Higginson") and was very proud of the search committee when they had the courage to call David Ng to be Higginson's successor as pastor in 1962. It took guts for them to do so, but Eidsath assured them that they had made the right choice. (I tell this story on pp. 92-94).

I do not think that Eidsath fits very easily on the liberal-evangelical continuum I set forth in my book. Ronn Garton called him a "plain Christian", perhaps in the sense of C. S. Lewis's "mere Christianity". Nor, to judge from your letter, would your father fit on that continuum. From what you say, Rev. Kooyers would have been a "confessional", not an "evangelical", Christian. Theologically conservative, yes, and with a high view of scripture, but more a scion of the Calvinist roots of the Presbyterian Church than of the revivalism that inspired Fuller Theological Seminary, where both Ronn Garton and "Larry Redford" were trained.

When I began my research on the church in 1975, I was very much on the lookout for the kind of "solid, reformed Presbyterian belief" that you refer to. (As I relate in the book, I was a member of the PCUSA Church in Los Gatos in 1957-59 was myself steeped in Barthian theology.) But I found very little evidence of such a theological commitment among the congregants in Mendocino. Evangelicalism, whether radical, as in Larry Redford, or moderate, as in Ron Garton, had seemed to carry the theological day.

But what was there was a core of strong leaders, many of whom had joined the church under Eidsath's two pastorates, and, by 1975, many had joined under Garton's then two-and-a-half year old pastorate. (One of the remarkable things about rapid church growth is that it tends to dilute institutional memory.) Men and women like them kept the church going through thick and thin, and, among other things, served on the search committees that brought Ng. Tritenbach, and Garton, for all the theological differences among them. Yes, one of those leaders was Alma Mendosa (who was also the school principal for many years). She was very helpful to me during my research. Her sister-in-law Mamie Mendosa was also a pillar of the church. I believe that Chet Bishop had died before I came to Mendocino.

Although the book is mainly a story, it does have a thesis, a rather "unreformed" one. Theological and other movements are the motive force that bring human energies into the church. But they come and go. In the end, "the church abides" (pp. xii). Maybe this is why I am now a Lutheran!

Have you checked out the Mendocino church recently? They celebrated their 150th anniversary last year. Ten years ago, they dedicated a work of art, a bell rope that recounts in history of the congregation in colorful strands. It's called the "Reep rope" in memory of long-time head usher Harold Reep (1910-1992–I call him "Dwight Perkins"), who kept the attendance records after you left and rang the bell to call people to worship. The church also has a spiffy web site, which includes a very attractive photo of your father (under history/pastors). I am sure the current leadership would be very interested in your recollections.

Thank you again for your very kind letter.

Sincerely,
Steve Warner

ON THE CHRISTIAN REFORMED CHURCH

To provide background and understanding of my relationship with the Palo Alto Christian Reformed Church (PACRC) and my thinking at that time about the Church and the denomination, consider the following letter written in August of 1974. A year later in 1975 after a new pastor had come, Geneva and I slowly started to consider a change and move our church attendance to the Peninsula Bible Church. That move turned out to greatly benefit Geneva, me, and our family. The PACRC had extended a call to Rev VanderBerg and he had sent a letter to the elders with a long list of questions. My answer is as follows:

Dear Rev. VanderBerg   August 1, 1974

It seemed best that several of the elders write you answers to your questions. This would alleviate our problems of communicating to one another here for the purpose of agreeing to answers and provide you with different respective elder perspectives.

First, so you understand my viewpoint, I am 38 years old, have six children, and am a research scientist in essentially a self-employed status. I am more and more involved in problems requiring complex analysis for decision making in economics and military planning. I never remember a day I did not love Jesus Christ.

I will try to be very frank in answering your questions. It probably will be evident that I have very serious reservations about the Christian Reformed Church being able to carry out the Lord's mandates. It seems to me that the Christian Reformed Church is now going in the wrong direction. Nevertheless, the Lord's Will certainly will be done, and I wait for His direction.

First the answers to your questions:

I sent you a directory listing the occupations of the most of our members. We range in age from early 20s to 50s with a few now older people. Income I guess averages $15,000 to $20,000. Almost all come from Christian Reformed background or from the Netherlands. By CRC standards they are generally spiritually mature; many have graduated from Calvin College. Many are able to teach Sunday School, lead Bible Studies, etc. Their commitment to the Palo Alto Challenge in my opinion is poor. This comes from basically two reasons. 1) Most are rather in the age where they are building families and careers and don't have time, and 2) the preaching in Palo Alto has not used God's Word to clearly set forth what duties God requires of mankind and, therefore, most in Palo Alto are ignorant of what needs to be done. One might ask, what are the elders doing? My answer to that is that the Christian Reformed Church is absolutely dominated by the clergy. Ministers in the CRC are tremendously respected and, therefore, one pastor over a period of a few years can make people feel so complacent, self-satisfied, and immune to God's Word that they are immobile. It goes so far that one of our members who takes the great commission seriously, who invites, "new culture", people to his home, works with them and brings them to church, is viewed with benign tolerance by most and considered mentally unstable by some. This is not a Palo Alto problem. The churches in our Classis I am familiar with are in a worst state then us.

We have about 50 active families. Attendance is about 200 in the AM and 125 in the PM. Giving increased consistently until about December of last year and is now declining. The cause of this is most likely the present economic conditions, the worst of which is inflation.

Palo Alto is a lovely city of excellent moderate climate. The cost of homes is so high that only the relatively rich can now move into the area. The geographical center of our congregation is constantly moving south towards San Jose where homes can still be purchased for a moderately high price. To a great extent the cause of this is the fact that huge amounts of land adjacent to Palo Alto is either in large undeveloped parks or owned by Stanford University. Stanford has chosen to put some of its land out to long term lease to modern light industry. Thus very large numbers of people commute into Palo Alto to work from considerable distances. This puts pressure on land prices so that the average working man cannot afford to live in Palo Alto. The exception to this is an area between the major freeway servicing the area and the San Francisco Bay which is now totally populated by black people.

Our outreach programs go in fits and starts. We have no effective programs. We participated in Key 73 but the follow up programs to that died in a very quiet way. Our members are very capable of leading societies, Sunday Schools, etc. In fact the talent is outstanding. I believe they would be willing, but are now not motivated.

An excellent spirit of love seems to exist in the Palo Alto congregation. I have difficulty distinguishing a genuine spirit of love from that of blissful tolerance. On the other hand, if we had some poor or others obviously in need, a genuine spirit of love most likely would be observed.

We have very active women's societies. They are led by their own members. We have no men's societies. We have had a Saturday men's bible study and prayer breakfast. Our pastor led this but it slowly died out. I believe that this breakfast would succeed if the pastor's expectations were not too high, was organized, and ended on time, so members could go on with their normal Saturday activities. Some of our members now attend the men's prayer breakfast at the Peninsula Bible Church in Palo Alto.

In the past our Sunday School was very well attended by our congregational children and consisted of half community children. For years our percentage of neighborhood children attending Sunday School was the highest in this Classis. Over the past few years the Sunday School attendance has declined to where now only a handful of neighborhood children attend. This is partly due to the declining birth rate and the older age of families in our community. The girls club (grades 5-8) has had a very good community impact in that more than half the girls are from the neighborhood and we have had talented women from our congregation leading this group and teaching crafts. A great challenge now exists in the high school age group. We have large numbers of teen agers in the congregation and in the neighborhood and a very effective program needs to be developed.

Attendance by congregational children in Sunday School and Catechism is near 100%

The work of the consistory has been organized by the pastor. While we are vacant I do it. Our past pastors wife was highly organized and she typed the bulletin. Now one of our member's wives does it. The office bearers have usually done a very good job. Sometimes we are slow to start discipline proceedings. The deacons have only a few poor.

In the past it has seemed that the elder's duties to supervise the pastor and the preaching were not exercised at all. The pastors we have had either possessed extensive experience and needed no counseling or otherwise were so recently out of Calvin Theological Seminary and so highly opinionated and indoctrinated in Seminary ideas they would not listen to counseling. To state it fairly, no opportunities were provided in my recollection to reflect on the Church programs, type and style of preaching, effectiveness of the preaching, needs of the congregation being met in the preaching, etc. in the consistory meetings. Instead our meetings are taken up by the mundane matters, denominational correspondence, building programs, and discipline questions. Only seldom for instance and only then when a new Sunday School Superintendent was to be appointed, was a review of the Sunday School problems, programs, and goals conducted. I view this as a lack of leadership. It is very difficult in my experience, for elders to provide the leadership when a pastor is present. It is my prayer that if the Lord inclines your heart to accept our call, you would view the consistory members as counselors and so organize the meetings that goals, plans, and programs are clearly thought out in the light of scriptural principles, sincerely prayed about, and carefully implemented.

On the subject of additional training – we have had no programs in this area. A church in our area, the Peninsula Bible Church, pastored by Ray Steadman, whom you may have heard about, (Body Life Services), conducts extensive classes and training for its members in personnel counseling. The Lords work in our area has greatly benefited from these programs, and I for one, hope and eagerly pray for some such program in the Palo Alto Christian Reformed Church.

The expectations of the congregation in Palo Alto regarding the sermon and their needs are quite different. Most expect and want a nice soft sermon which tells them how good they are, to sit back relax and enjoy the Lord's blessings and hear they have been saved no matter what they do or how they conduct their affairs. They in fact need preaching based on sound biblical principles on what duties God requires of them, how the Lord expects their affairs to be conducted, what relationships God expects between husbands and wives, parents and children, believers and unbelievers, etc. and what people are to believe concerning God. For years none have heard preaching or even remember the words of Matthew 25: 34-46. The preaching has deteriorated to such an extent in this CRC and most others I have attended as well, that the youth have great difficulty in recognizing the truth. It is not that the sermons are incorrect or contain heresy, in fact they are very correct, but that the sermons are not effective, achieve little in the way of motivation of the believers, and do not generate much lasting spiritual benefit.

The challenges for the ministry from my perspective in Palo Alto listed here in order of importance are:

Biblically sound, well thought out, reformed preaching
Organization and direction of small group meetings with the following type of subjects;
Spiritual growth
Discipline of children
Relationships, parent-child, man-wife, church-individual, from God's perspective, i.e. what is Christian culture
Living the Christian life
The total Christian witness
Youth and youth programs.
Community witness
Well run and organized Sunday School
Well run and organized classes for inquirers using biblically sound Christian principles, with the goal of making disciples for Jesus Christ.
Organization and promotion of fellowship activities.

The obstacles to an effective ministry in Palo Alto from my perspective, ranked in order of difficulty are:
General basic member apathy. I believe this can be overcome by a correct biblical appeal to their conscience.
Career goals demanding most of the male member's time,
child raising demanding most of that of the women.
Lack of faith in the power of God to change people's lives.
Materialistic orientated member's goals.

Members lack of confidence in CRC power structures, i.e. Classis, Synod, Calvin College and Seminary, Banner, Board of Publications, etc. An agonizing realization that these power structures are self-serving, demand huge amounts of local funds, and exist mostly to provide jobs. These power structures tend to follow conventional wisdom and promote the, "let's get along syndrome", rather than advocate God's truth. This realization saps the member's motivation and strength and leaves them in an agonized state of bewilderment.

From my perspective the long range hopes for the life of the PACRC are:

A reformed biblically based Christian witness in Palo Alto organized and prayerfully led.

20% member growth rate per year (including perhaps a 5-8% growth from other CRCs.

Radio ministry

Extensive counseling ministry (many more people besides the pastor involved, perhaps the pastor just coordinate it)

Extensive program of adult education in Christian living and witness.

I would predict the following church life if present trends continue and we remain a typical CRC:

Normal CRC preaching as such as now comes out of Calvin Theological Seminary.

5% per year member growth rate (all of the new people from CRC backgrounds)

Mediocre mutual admiration society with most church programs in the doldrums.

Our present church building has been recently been remodeled. It is nice looking and meets our present needs. The parsonage is being remodeled. It now has four bedrooms, two baths, and a small but very modern kitchen.

Pastor responsibilities and expectations in order of importance to me are as follows:

	% of time	hours/week
Preaching and sermon preparation and study	60%	30
Planning and long range thinking	20%	10
Training classes for teachers, counselors, etc. including prep	12%	5

Visiting sick	12%	5

Coordinating elder, deacon, councilor, and other visits of sick, poor, those needing spiritual advice, financial advice, and community contacts

	2%	1
Catechism teaching (High School age only)	2%	1
Family visiting	2%	1

Note: That this is a 50 hour week. Depending on your strength more or less time could be used.

From what I have been able to discern, you are a serious, hardworking, goal orientated individual. Some have said you are very perceptive and can identify with those who have needs. Others have said you are very progressive (in left field?). Other than that I know little about you. If you are of a sober mind, believe in the power of prayer, can visualize God's goals in Palo Alto, and have a mind to develop programs and implement them God's way to achieve God's goals then all of the other characteristics are of little account, and you are desperately needed in Palo Alto.

The Palo Alto CRC is very pliable and would accept most any kind of change and few care to do things as they always have been done. Unfortunately, most changes are made without any adequate thought of the long range consequences or whether these changes are in tune with God's way of doing things, and, consequently, have a long range detrimental effect which the planners never even considered. A tremendous responsibility rests on the shoulders of one who goes around changing things. Often the reasons for doing things a certain way have long been forgotten and these are rediscovered in an ensuing disaster. Things must be done God's way. The Bible provides that direction. I will accept any program or change that is done God's way.

We in Palo Alto have made no provision for continuing the education of the pastor.

Your wife is expected to be a serious minded person exhibiting the Christian virtues. She, of course, is an example for the younger women to follow and should conduct herself with decorum. There would be little objection to her working. If the purpose of her working is to supplement the family income,

469

then you would be well advised to ask the consistory for a raise. There is plenty of work to do in this church for wives.

I think the others have answered this question of schools.

The cost of living in the San Francisco Bay Area is the third highest in the United States, after Honolulu and New York City. If you come and find you need more salary, ask for it. If Christ's Gospel is presented in Palo Alto God's way, so much money will flow into the treasury we will not know what to do with it. I have six children and spend about $125/week for food.

As you can tell from the tone of my letter I am very concerned about the future of Christ's Church in Palo Alto and the Christian Reformed Church. We need the right kind of leadership very badly. We must have a spiritual man who waits on the Lord and acts in faith knowing the Lord will bless his work. We need new programs with insight and innovation. The potential is there. There are churches in our area that have increased their membership by 20-30% per year for many years and now number thousands of members. They have now started Christian Schools, something the Christian Reformed Church has done for years, and yet we in Palo Alto have none of our own, nor do we really participate in theirs.

God will accomplish His works, but he uses men to do it. If you come to Palo Alto with the intention of glorifying Jesus Christ and the commitment to do everything within your power to promote His Kingdom, then you will receive all the support I can give you. We desperately need a man who can visualize God's goals for Palo Alto.

Yours in His Service,
Gerald P. Kooyers
Vice President
Palo Alto Christian Reformed Church

As I edit this thing in 2011 and reflect on the history of the CRC, I observe that the Christian Reformed Church continued on in the doldrums and eventually split from the more conservative types who formed a group called the United Reformed Church. My view of the CRC Church has not changed. It still continues on with a continued slow drift to the left and into unbelief.

Church leadership, I conclude after a lifetime of observation, is extremely difficult. In the end of the matter God will accomplish His goals in spite of the inadequacy and sin of church leaders and other men and women members and non-members of churches. In my experience God can save people even when they somehow fall into a cult.

My idealism, as expressed in this letter to Rev. VanderBerg, eventually was pulled into reality. I have found that I often had in hindsight very good and correct ideas, but very few people except for my wife followed me, and she because she loved me and respected me, put up with my mistakes, and always it seemed had high hopes for me. Geneva is simply a very marvelous, very sound, very understanding, God loving woman, possessing that very unique feminine beauty, that of a meek and quiet spirit.

LETTER TO DAUGHTER KIMBERLY

Dearest Kim   August 21, 1994

Today as I was traveling home from church (AOG) I listened to the Irish music you provided me and I thought to myself, my, my, I do love that daughter Kim.

I not only have that normal love for you that a father has for his daughter that comes naturally by some genetic process, but in addition to that there is something very special for you which I think I will attempt to explain. First, please forgive me for typing this letter rather than longhand. It is so much easier this way and the computer can correct my spelling.

Thank you very much for the music. I enjoy it.

Love is a very complex thing which I suppose is hard to explain. The quality that you seem to be generating that is especially appealing to me is the capacity of being able to make good decisions! In a report or market letter I received a story was told of a very young man of 29 becoming a President of a large bank. The young man went to an old very experienced banker and asked him what it takes to be a good banker. The old banker said, "Make good decisions". The young man said yes, but how do I learn to make good decisions? The old banker said, "Make bad decisions". Life is a lot more complex than that. Sure we learn from our bad decisions. However, most of us and that includes me make so many bad decisions that we are forever wounded and scarred so that many, many doors of service are closed to us.

My prayer is that you will be spared from the scars, wounds, and debilitation caused from making too many wrong decisions. You have made a great start. Very, very great potential lies before you. It's yours to take or blow away.

How does one avoid making too many bad decisions? First, walk closely with the Lord Jesus. Of course, you might say, that's what I have been doing most of my life. That's true. Now I could suggest some disciplines to perform which somebody like Fred Emory would tell you to do, but that would be disastrous. Disastrous because the emphasis would soon be on the form and performance of these disciplines and not the substance of what you want accomplished. Getting up at 5 AM to read and study your Bible might be one of these disciplines. If the purpose of this was somehow through this to obtain the approval of the Lord Jesus, you would be making a terrible mistake. You would start down the path of prideful self. God hates pride. In His children God eventually brings them very low through sin, trials, and troubles to utterly reduce them of pride.

No, you want to walk with the Lord Jesus. If that means getting up at 5 AM to read and study your Bible, then do it. Any other time is just as good. The goal is to seek the Lord Jesus. You must believe that the Lord rewards those who seek Him. Get to know the Lord. How? You get to know the Lord by reading about Him and how He has dealt with His servants in the past. You get to know the Lord through prayer and petitions. Some prayers He answers yes, and some He answers no, and to some His answer is to wait. This way you get to know God's character. Therefore, pray, ask petitions, and give thanks continually. This way you develop a dialogue with God

Himself, none other than the creator of the universe! Wow. Why wouldn't everybody seek this? A very good question.

Ray Stedman in his study of Ecclesiastes suggested that a man or woman of the Lord, who has a right relationship with God, could put his or her hand to work to achieve anything, whatever her soul might dream of doing. Yes, I agree. Yes, what an aspiring concept. Instead of obligations, forms, rituals, and other pagan type stuff, superstitions, taboos, etc. etc. you have an astounding freedom to set out to do anything your heart desires! Wow, wow, Selah! Just think of that!

Now avoid sin. Don't even think sin. That's where the battle of life is -- in the mind. Take captive all your thoughts as the apostle Paul tells us. Why? Because sin entraps you, makes you a slave, ruins your life, and takes away your freedom. Soon you can't even make simple right decisions because you are hooked and trapped. Sin leads to death. Death is boredom, sloth, sniveling, envy, slander, etc., etc... I don't need to list them all.

On the other hand, remember you are forgiven. No matter what happens, no matter what you do, you are forgiven. Do not let the devil, or anyone else for that matter, accuse you of anything. You are forgiven and washed clean from anything past, present, or future. Go on with confidence doing all that you set out to do. Of course, I am not talking here about willful presumptuous sin. Anyone who sins presumptuously, planning what she knows is evil, is simply not a Christian; she is just fooling herself, and the Spirit of God is not within her.

So! Set out on your life's quest. Walk humbly before your God. Seek Him with all your might. Love Him with all your strength, soul, spirt, and heart. Enjoy God. Celebrate! Let your heart sing and be merry. God loves you. And so do I, immensely,

Your Father,

Jerry

As I reflect on the above in 2016, Kimberly somewhere sometime, probably about the time I sent that letter, made some bad decisions and now seemingly does not walk with the Lord. I suspect the resulting consequences of these bad decisions cause her to doubt the loving care of the Lord Jesus. She says she believes in God but not the way I do. She does not teach her children about Jesus or attend any Christian fellowship. That makes me very sad as Kimberly is a loving, caring, generous woman. She really should belong to Jesus. My prayer is that she may repent and come to Jesus.

You dear reader, must understand that decisions have consequences. Letting lust, greed, or stupidity of one kind or another lead you to a bad decision can destroy you now and on into eternity.

Dear reader let me make a comment here on the complexities of becoming a real solid eternal citizen of the Universal Church of Jesus Christ. Becoming a true believer in Jesus Christ is a complex thing. Decisions must constantly be made. These decisions either lead you up a path to Christ washed righteousness or the path down to fiery hell and eternal oblivion.

When I was young, sometime in the early junior high, some boys about my age in Mendocino decided we wanted to form a club, really a sort of gang. We built a three story clubhouse from miscellaneous boards gathered from sundry places next to the Protestant cemetery. Some other boys across a draw did the same and a rivalry got started. A whole book could be written about all those adventures and fun childhood times in Mendocino but that is not the purpose here.

During the course of our gang conflicts, I stole a block and tackle from the other gang. After a time with some ugly gang fights with dirt clods and apples, the gangs broke up and quit. Later a kid from that other gang and I decided to build a tree house halfway up a set of redwood trees about a hundred feet off the ground out in the redwood forest behind the place where he lived. Another redwood tree had fallen against a main group of redwoods so we could climb up the tree that had fallen at a 45 degree angle against the others, and so gain a not easy access to the tall trees where the limbs begin, and then to climb limb by limb to the tops of the redwood trees which were about 200 feet high. I tell you the view even to the ocean from the top of that redwood tree swaying back and forth with the breeze about

200 feet above the ground was extremely invigorating, very spectacular, and sent huge streams of adrenaline through my veins.

Well we gathered up lots of beams, boards, and such to build this treehouse and got started. We decided we needed a block and tackle to lift the stuff up into the trees so I went home and got mine. Joe Gots, the other kid, recognized it as his and called me a thief. That ended that treehouse project as he took up a great offence at me.

I understand now that God in His sovereignty was ending that tree house project. That project was very dangerous and given my normal character flaw of trying to complete a project once it got started even if it was impossible, we may very well of killed ourselves.

God used my gang mentality so I could justify within me the stealing of a block and tackle because I thought it was the spoils of war between our gangs. God used the discovery by Joe of his lost block and tackle as the event to end our friendship and terminate the project.

I confess that God has done that many, many times during my whole life. God used the stupid things I did, some of them rather wicked, to form me, discipline me, shape me and my attitudes, and make me into the person both God and I want me to be.

So what is going on? In my life God used my sin and depravity to bring me close to my Lord and Savior Jesus and to cause me to love Jesus intensely. In other people's lives, such as my precious daughter Kimberly, her decisions lead her down a path away from the loving arms of Jesus. What a great mystery! In the end of this matter, I conclude we can only pray for each other.

Jesus said that in the final judgement humanity will be judged and then divided. Let me quote from Matthew 25:31:

> But when the Son of Man comes in His glory, and all the angels with Him, He will sit on His glorious throne. All the nations will be gathered before Him; and He will separate them from one another as the shepherd separates the sheep from the goats; and He will put the sheep on His right, and the goats on the left.

Then the King will say to those on His right, "Come you who are blessed of my father, inherit the kingdom prepared for you from the foundation of the world. "For I was hungry and you gave me to eat; I was thirsty, and you gave Me drink; I was a stranger, and you invited me in; naked, and you clothed Me; I was sick and you visited Me; I was in prison and you came to Me." Then the righteous will answer Him, "Lord when did we see you hungry, and feed you, or thirsty, and give you drink? "And when did we see you a stranger and invite you in. or naked, and clothe you? "And when did we see you sick, or in prison, and come to you?" The king will answer and say to them, "Truly I say to you, to the extent that you did it to one of these brothers of Mine, the least of them, you did it to Me."

Then He will also say to those on His left. "Depart from Me, accursed ones, into the eternal fire which has been prepared for the devil and his angels; for I was hungry and you gave nothing to eat; I was thirsty and you gave me nothing to drink; I was a stranger, and you did not invite Me in; naked and you did not clothe Me; sick, and in prison, and you did not visit Me." Then they themselves also will answer, "Lord, when did we see you hungry, or thirsty, or a stranger, or naked, or sick, or in prison, and did not take care of you?" Then He will answer them, "Truly I say to you, to the extent that you did not do it to one of the least of these, you did not do it to Me." "These will go away into eternal punishment, but the righteous into eternal life."

No complex theology here. The criterion for final judgment deciding eternal punishment or eternal life for you is that, to the extent you care for the brothers and sisters of Jesus, you did it to Jesus Himself.

Yes, love for Jesus manifested through Christian brothers and sisters in the faith is the ultimate criterion for eternal salvation. Of course, we do not truly know who are the real brothers of Jesus, so we loving Christians care for everybody we can.

FOURTEEN

REFLECTIONS ON LIFE

In this chapter I will try to put a summary on my whole life and discuss miscellaneous happenings that left sharp memories. That is, I will try to give meaning to it all in the context of my whole life.

A well-known professional football coach once said, "Nice guys finish last". That philosophy of life is contrary to my Christian understanding of life.

Growing up as a Christian, I was taught and so have believed that my life was one to be lived to serve God. God demands that I love those people God brings into my life, even my enemies.

Thus the living of life creates great conflict as to how to implement the imperative to love fellow man. When living out one's life, one encounters wickedness, evil men, and evil women. How is one to deal with such? How should I have dealt with the Cooks?

Does loving man mean that you must trust them? No, it does not. The Westminster confession has it right when it says all men are depraved and come short of the glory of God.

At the time of this being written in 2015, the political process of choosing the next President of the United States is taking place. Republican political candidates who were nice guys in the last decade lost. Their opponents were not nice. Now a businessman of a few billion of wealth says he is running for president of the United States of America. In a book he has written, "In business dealings nice guys lose". So he applies this principle of not being nice to his political opponents. He verbally attacks them and fights them in aggressive terms, calling them lots of very bad names.

The last republican president was nice to his adversaries and held his peace. In so doing his opponents destroyed the effectiveness of his presidency, took over the country, and now are doing their most to destroy the country, its moral standards, and its culture.

What a dilemma. Nice guys lose, and in the political process the country that elected the not nice guys lost, and is continuing to lose, losing big time. So what are those people who love God to do?

Of course, Christians go to the Bible. The Psalms of David deal with this dilemma. During the course of my life, even though I read the Bible once in a while, I have been very slow to understand words written by King David in the psalms. One must study them. David was a superb outstanding prophet of God. Many of his words actually became words Jesus our Lord, as the Messiah of God, used as His own expressions 1000 years later. David brings down the wrath of God on his enemies. In David's thinking his enemies are God's enemies. Yet God says vengeance is mine, I will repay. Thus we Christians must leave our enemies in the hands of God.

The Cooks chose to be my enemies rather than my friends. In my inner heart of hearts, I did not really believe that to be possible; so I lost big time. So here is my advice. All of man are depraved; so they all are your enemies. Trust none of them.

One must thoroughly examine each person that God brings into your life. Are they trustworthy or not? Someone has said each man or woman has his or her own price. True. Do not put your life and welfare in the hands of anyone who has the potential to destroy your life.

Now, of course, the greatest application of this principle is in choosing a life partner. Choosing a life partner is very difficult as feelings and emotions and one's internal concept of beauty and handsomeness get in the way. King Solomon in his book of Ecclesiastes said he has discovered only one man among a thousand trustworthy, and none among women. The scriptures say lands and wealth are inherited from parents, but a good wife comes from the Lord. So your life partner, if you are looking for a good one, comes from the Lord; so the selection of a wife or husband must be a matter of deep fervent prayer, and involves wresting with God about the choice.

Some of the most awful, ugly trajectories of life I have ever observed, are beautiful young Christian ladies, well educated, well endowed, with quiet and gentle spirits, very, very lovely in every sense - choosing for husbands the worst kind of men - depraved, drunkards, abusive, full of lies, deceitful. It makes one stop and think Christian culture is wrong in letting young Christian women choose their own husbands.

Perhaps parents' choosing the spouse for their children is the best way after all. But then as even happened to me in my life, when my precious daughter, Crystal, came to me and asked my advice about a potential husband, I did not do my homework, and thoroughly check out the prospect. I repent! I confess my guilt! Wisdom comes slowly. As the old cliché says - "Too soon old, too late smart".

In the case of the Cooks, I could have crammed them down in the first bankruptcy process. I did not. I did not even consider it. Yet, in hindsight I would have benefited greatly from cramming down the debt owed them and extending the time period for payment as it was my legal right to do. My attorneys only mildly suggested it in passing on the subject. Incompetence? Yes.

Assume all attorneys are incompetent. They make money by running the clock. They do not care about your welfare or your success. If they are diligent and win for you, their benefit is they may attract additional clients. Their money clock runs when they appear in court for you or work on your file awhile. They do not have a direct benefit by winning your case. Understand that.

Supervise your attorneys. Make them work and clearly explain what they plan to do and how they are going to do it. They may not like your approach, but why spend money on attorneys who lose? You not only lose what you pay them, but you also lose what you maybe have to pay your adversary.

If you lose and face money a judgment, do not sweat it. Hardly any judgments are paid in full and most are paid off with little money and some none. Protect yourself ahead of time and stick assets somewhere where they are hard to find. Most attorneys are lazy and could care less if assets are not found to seize, as long as the attorney himself is paid his fees, and even then the attorney may neglect it as he may have other more profitable work to do.

Sometimes the judge will make you put up a bond or pay money into a trust fund. Be careful, and normally do not do it! Once the court gets control of your money it will invariably be paid to the attorneys and others of their friends and consultants. Remember, attorneys are friends of the judge, and it is all a game to them, with you paying the tab.

Do not fear bankruptcy. Bankruptcy has a very bad connotation, but in practice it works very well for the bankrupt business or person. Everything gets quite delayed a long time, and it stops the IRS in its tracks. Chose a bankruptcy court somewhere out in Timbuktu. This raises the costs to your adversaries, as after driving a few times to Timbuktu or flying in an expensive rinkie-dink airplane to get there, they will consider your low ball money suggestions more favorably.

In a legal contest it is very important to run up the costs of your adversaries and minimize your own costs. Adversaries tire quickly if they are writing their attorneys an awful, ugly check every month. After a time of doing this their attitude changes a lot and they start to wonder if all this leaching attorney business is really worth it, and maybe messing up your life, and getting imagined damages out of you, is not really worth it.

This legal mess you are in probably was caused by your adversary thinking you have some money he or she might use much better than you. Therefore, showing off your wealth or giving the impression you are rich just invites adversaries to come after you and make lawsuits against you. Business is a somewhat complex operation and sometimes you will make a mistake or inadvertently misrepresent a matter. Of course, being completely honest and having high integrity is the best policy to follow. But sometimes when one is very busy or lacks understanding of the matter, mistakes are made and you create a mess, and business associates, competitors, or suppliers can get quite upset with you. As Jesus says, make peace with your adversary before he hauls you into court. That is the best policy. Admit your mistake and try to heal up the scene, and do it quickly.

OF FAITH AND ITS CONSEQUENCES

My life consisted of great success and what in my own personal belief was great failure. As I wrote a friend, success breeds failure, and failure breeds success. So how does one put it all together so as to avoid the huge pits and huge highs? Of course, one answer is to set out to lead a simple humdrum life and do not set out to do great things or to conqueror the world. Some would say this is the Biblical view, which is to keep your life simple and work the earth or the marketplace in a gentle way, or just get a job so as to generate a slow steady income and avoid stress and sorrow and the needless tribulations of business life.

One turning point in my life with a great deal of clarity occurred in about 1976 when I was sitting under the spiritual guidance of Pastor Ray Stedman at the Peninsula Bible Church in Palo Alto, California. Ray was preaching on the book of Ecclesiastes and came to a chapter of instruction which indicated,

"Put all there is to your life and set out to accomplish anything under the sun."

At least that is how I interpreted his preaching on the instructions from the Ecclesiastes Preacher. Perhaps that instruction gave to me the theoretical basis to an operating life system, so that I then set no limit to what I might hope to accomplish. This occurred, as I recall sometime in the summer of 1976, when I was actually at that time in dire financial straits as the business of Universal Computer Applications, a partnership I was in, was coming apart. Thus within my mind, filtering Stedman's proclamations, I set no limit within myself of what I might try to accomplish.

Up until then I was a well-educated research scientist, and then a contract computer programmer and analyst, working out a career, living well, doing very interesting computer applications to scientific and engineering things in collaboration with others, yet financially highly rewarded, but nothing individually really super extraordinary or super outstanding.

Then, of course, as a result of my new business structure in 1977, and with the commodity trading system I created, I started to make lots of money as has been recounted in this thing. So I went off into the stratosphere of personal achievement in some uncontrolled not well thought out blast.

That, in hindsight was a great error. One must always keep ones wits about him, plan, and analyze where one wishes to go. Of course, one does not often completely understand the opportunities that come along but, nevertheless, one wishes to take advantage of them. But, out there in the real world, are nests of thieves, pits, sinkholes, and what not, just waiting for the unschooled to be sucked into.

 The naive and simple do indeed fall into sundry traps. Thus, if off on a great quest, every possible opportunity must be studied with great care and analyzed rationally to avoid the sinkholes. This is not easy.

Anyway, back to this account. I had very carefully thought out, using the scientific statistical principals I had learned in my university education at Stanford and Cal, and then applied to the military analysis projects I had done, and then to the commodity trading scheme.

I then rigorously tested this commodity trading scheme. I knew it would statistically work before I managed any money, like the house in a gaming casino. It then, subsequently, actually worked with real money, much too some peoples surprise. I then generated lots of income, and money flowed in in huge amounts.

I structured the business following the pattern of people already in the business. That was a very wise thing to do. In this case I was not the pioneer. Being a pioneer in anything is very difficult. One then has to learn everything the hard way from scratch. That is very costly and usually most pioneers eventually fail. Being able to observe the pioneers and then pattern the business structure after them with my own improvements and wrinkles to their structure, was again a very wise thing to do.

Why did I not do the same thing when I got into the other businesses? - Just stupid pride and presumption. Since I was once quite successful, deep down within me the fallacy developed that everything I would set my hand to do would be successful. How stupid. There is an old Roman proverb; I paraphrase a bit as it is in Latin:

"Presumption - the insanity of men whom the gods destine to destroy."

Yes, that's it! Presumption on the future! Indeed a great folly. Only God knows the future, and to presume on it is a great error, and leads to consequences one never anticipates. There is no substitute for careful rational analysis and evaluation of risk.

I hired more people to do the expanding back office work at my company, UCA Systems, Inc., and then programmers to automate the whole thing. That was fine and added to the wonderful professionalism of the operation.

But then I hired my old friend and mentor, Paul Chaikin. In hindsight I did not think that through. I must have imagined some huge financial conglomeration where Paul would provide input. I thought I needed help to see clearly the visions of the future; Paul seemed to be very good at that. In practice Paul spent an inordinate amount of time concentrating on his own trading.

Then I also imagined the scientific research part of the operation would also be a big thing, so I hired Paul's brother so as to get into the combustion research business. What presumptuousness. I knew nothing about combustion processes, its engineering, and research. In hindsight that was a huge presumption which I now think was rather stupid.

And then I got into the mining business! I knew even less about mining than I did about combustion. In the process of getting started in the mining business, I got into the river outfitting business. Outfitting was lots of fun but it lost money like the other businesses. Why did I do all that?

That is a hard question to answer. Caution is a very valuable characteristic. Yet excessive caution will prevent one from getting into an otherwise great opportunity. One can read books about the experiences of sundry people to generate knowledge that one might apply to new situations. Unfortunately, books are usually written to sell books rather than to impart knowledge to subsequent generations, so one has to read carefully and sort out the useless and wrong information. That is not easy.

When one gets going good on doing something, the internalized assumption is that the good thing will go on forever. False! It is very important to run scared, meaning to watch ones back trail, and not make gross assumptions about the future. For some of you who might not understand that idiom, deer and other game animals constantly watch their back trail; that is where they have been, in case a predator, such as a lion or man, is about, and finds its trail.

Thieves, crooks, and do-gooders are a real danger and can destroy one's life completely. How does one spot these disasters before they happen? That is probably the most important thing to watch out for in your life. In my case I made the internal assumption that big banks and savings and loan operations are honest. After all, are they not regulated by the government of the United States? False! I did not even consider that the largest savings and loan institution in the world at that time might be a criminal enterprise. The thought would not even have approached my mind let alone be thought through.

Here is a great lesson for you dear reader. Carefully weigh in the balance of truth the idea that you might be dealing with criminals in any important transaction you might consider which could cause you great damage and terrible grief. Watch for very strange behavior. I thought the Savings and Loan was acting against its own self-interest. Yes, very strange, but unknown to me was they indeed had criminal intent! When you encounter such unfathomable lack of self-interest or other weird phenomena, get them out of your life quick!

To a certain extent if you fall into the hands of thieves it is your own fault. Maybe you placed yourself in a position where you should not be. For example, showing off a roll of $100 bills around in a bar, and then walking out into a dark street. Thieves, lawyers, crooks, and criminal institutions do very similar things. They wait for a target who is trying to do something far out and yet does not have the experience to detect their criminal intent. In my case I was trying to finance a big white elephant house in an area without comparables so most normal banks would not consider a construction loan for such a thing. So I was in fact looking for a marginal banking institution, while not fully realizing it, or even thinking about the possible dangers.

Of course, eventually, I found a bank, one suggested by the wife of an ex business partner who was in the real estate business, who, she said, gave loans to everybody. Unfortunately, that was true, and that bank turned out to be a criminal enterprise; that bank destroyed my financial life. I never recovered. The worst part of such an involvement is all the leaching attorneys, accountants, judges, do-gooders, advice givers, you name it that moved into my life and caused the terminal end of normal carefree, happy, confident, fun living.

Just for the record, to give you another example, consider my own blood brother, Orneal; that he fell into a similar trap. He was trying to manage his retirement funds. He spent a good part of his life as a missionary to Papua New Guinea and spent a good part of that in the horrible, hot, steamy, Sepik swamps with hordes of mosquitoes, translating the Bible and bringing the gospel to the native people. His mission board of directors provided him with a fine lot of retirement funds year by year, but then made the mistake of letting Orneal manage the retirement funds himself. I was on Neal's non-profit corporate mission board.

Everything goes fine for 20 years until Neal can no longer be in New Guinea because of health issues. Back in the good old USA, Neal develops plans for the investment of these retirement funds for increased performance. He has dreams of helping sundry people, grand kids, great grand kids, Christian Missions, and lots of other Kingdom projects. That motive is all very normal and very, very good.

But then, perhaps motivated by a desire for a high return on his retirement money, he starts to read about certain kinds of trusts and gets hooked up with some, "real honest", Mormon types who convince him to put his money with an offshore trust in the Bahamas, who invest in, "car", loans and pay high returns.

The nice righteous good Mormon people even charge him a $10,000 fee to set up these trusts which he gladly pays. Then the trusts invest his money, and he receives beautiful reports of nice fat profits like that crook, Madoff, was sending to his clients in the 2000's. Of course, it is all fictitious and one day Neal comes to the terrible observation that his retirement funds have all evaporated - gone with the wind.

But then, and this is how all the world found out about all this, the Internal Revenue Service wants the tax due from these fictitious profits! The IRS does not care if the profits are fictitious. Profits are profits and must be taxed! So Orneal then defends himself without an attorney in tax court against the IRS. Astoundingly, Orneal wins! But then all the dirty linen is displayed to the world by the tax court records put out on the internet. Reading the account it looks like the crooks went off with maybe a half million dollars. The perpetrators of that fraud eventually went to federal prison but that does not get Orneal's retirement money back. You too can be caught and trapped by a fraud, so watch out!

In my case the law never caught up with the American Savings crooks. After the United States government sized American Savings, the prime instigators of the fraud went on to Wall Street and ripped off some Wall Street types with their loan fraud schemes. Eventually, they tried to do it again a third time in real estate operations in Arizona, but made the mistake of involving some politicians. That got them discovered and sent to prison. It seems strange, and a huge failure of the United States legal system, that it took three major loan fraud schemes for the United States legal system to finally send these big time perpetrators of loan fraud off to jail.

Dear reader, remember, the legal system of the United States is fundamentally a massive fraud itself; it exists to feed the attorneys, judges, prosecutors, and others with a nice comfortable life at the expense of taxpayers and victims, and has little to do with the application of real justice.

But, alas, my financial resources are gone and my financial life is ruined. Do not expect the legal system of the United States to give you justice. It is nothing but a crock barrel of decayed male bovine scat, from which attorneys and judges make a fine stinking living.

Now it is important to remember that neither Orneal nor I are completely innocent in this. We tried to do something which was not really reasonable for a prudent man to expect. So we took an imprudent risk and then lost big time. So dear reader, your goal must be to develop prudence, so that you understand the risk, and understand that thieves and crooks are waiting by the side of the road for the imprudent to wander into their bailiwick where the imprudent can be fleeced. You only need to be fleeced once by such crooks and all your life savings or assets are gone. It is extremely difficult to start over so financial destruction is a paradigm event in your life.

As another example, the bank that ripped me off also ripped off a chiropractor in Los Altos, California. My family knew his family a little as we both lived in the same town of the reasonably rich, Los Altos Hills. He had a nice successful practice, was about my age, and has a beautiful wife and beautiful family of five daughters and one son just like Geneva and me. His wife played the piano and organ for the First Baptist Church in Los Altos. He wanted to build an office building for his practice and rent out the lower floors to little boutique stores such as abound in Los Altos. Just like me he got a construction loan from American Savings. The rest is history.

His wife once told me her husband was never the same again. I found out about this by doing a little research on American Savings and discovering a lawsuit filed against American Savings by the chiropractor. His two story building stood as a half-finished eyesore on a prominent street corner in Los Altos for maybe two years or so, much to the disgust of the residents and city fathers. But in the end, like me, he lost it all. The criminals were never prosecuted or even called to public account - normal standard operating procedure in the United States of America.

So how do you, dear reader, avoid such disasters? Seek lots of advice. The scriptures say there is much wisdom in many councilors. Keep your wits about you and study prudence, especially in financial matters. Never get yourself into a position where anybody or anything can control your destiny. When you plan to build something, count the cost and have the money set aside and in your hand. Never let a third party be in a position where they can at will stop the flow of expected funds when that flow of funds is crucial to your project, which is crucial to your life as a whole.

ABOUT THE MINE DISASTER

As I reflect on my life it still seems impossibly incredible that two very young promising men were murdered in my mine. I am left with profound sadness about those young men. They were men of great potential. Their lives were terminated in my mine. The legal authorities of the State of Idaho and the United States of American never even looked into the disaster.

The federal Mine Safety and Health Administration did their thing, and it was a joke. They started the process to levy a fine on me for who knows what, but gave it up. Was their inspector who inspected the mine that very day of the killing, three hours before, involved, and had responsibility?

Yet my belief is those young men were murdered. May God's curse of hell be upon those murderers, and yet, yes, may God have mercy on their souls.

SPIRITUAL THINGS

The conclusion of the whole matter of this book is about spiritual things, walking with the Lord Jesus. Please consider the following very carefully.

I am going to conclude this book with the imperative to you to read my booklet published in 2014, "Christ Rules in Four Realms", by Gerald Paul Kooyers, available on Amazon. My sister, Marcia, is the force behind this mini book publication. It is a parallel to the understanding of the Eigen theory I have presented. She thinks it is quite profound and reflects the understanding that the Tabernacle of Moses is a picture of Jesus Christ in the Old Testament.

My Eigen understanding of the Tabernacle came to me one night when I was sleeping with my wife Geneva at my daughter Brenda's house while she was away on a business trip. I had been praying for understanding of the tabernacle from the Lord. I woke up in the middle of the night, and it was all clear to me. I got up, went downstairs to my computer, and wrote it up. Is that the spirit of God connecting to me through my spirit? Sinners like me will never know for sure.

Since then my understanding has expanded and expanded, and then my sister provided the understanding of Jesus Himself being represented in the Old Testament Tabernacle, as a pre-incarnation Jesus dwelling among the Hebrews.

The Bible says we humans are made in the image of God. So yes, the Tabernacle is a divine representation of the perfect man Jesus. But then we humans, too, just as Jesus is fully human, are human man, and have, therefore, a representation, and are four-realm persons, pictured by the Tabernacle also.

I wrote another book in 2015, "Hearts of Understanding and the Demise of American Culture", By Gerald Paul Kooyers. It builds on this understanding of the tabernacle, and presents man as composed of body, soul, spirit, and heart. I believe it to be a significant contribution to the universe, that of understanding mankind. It is a must read.

FINAL THOUGHTS

Growing and developing the Christian life is a very profound subject. The Lord did not give very specific instructions as to how we should grow as we come to know Him. So as a final, final thought, consider now what The Lord Jesus said in the parable of the sower when He quoted the words of Jeremiah the prophet:

"You will keep on hearing but will not understand;

You will keep on seeing but will not perceive;
For the heart of this people has become dull,
With their ears they scarcely hear,
And they have closed their eyes,
Otherwise they would see with their eyes,
Hear with their ears,
And understand with their heart,
And return,
And I would heal them."

Eyes are a symbol for the spirit. So here again we have a Four Eigen, Four Realm operation. We process with our minds, which are part of our souls, hear with our ears of the flesh in the real world, and see and perceive with our spirits in the spirit realm; we understand and believe with our fourth Eigen heart deep within our spirit. Then Jesus heals us and puts us in His Eternal Kingdom. Oh! Yes! Thank you Jesus!

So all of this life on the Earth is about hearing and seeing and understanding. We believers have been given the scriptures to instruct us, given faith in our spirits in the Lord Jesus so to love Him, and have received the power of the His blood to cleanse us from sin, and have been given the Holy Spirit to witness within us and to guide us. How this all unfolds in our state of sin and misery is a very profound thing, and the process is different for each one of us. We live our lives out in the world, in our flesh, being tempted by the world, the flesh, and the devil. If we belong to Jesus, it all works out for our salvation, despite our inadequacy, degradation, and depravity. If we do not belong to Jesus, it all works out for our damnation into hell. Given our free wills we have choices to constantly make. These choices direct our development and growth in our path to eternal life, or direct our path to oblivion. As the scriptures say,

"Work out your salvation with fear and trembling."

So dear reader, work out your own salvation. God is good. Trust Jesus in everything. God loves you.

End